India Studies in Business and Economics

The Indian economy is considered to be one of the fastest growing economies of the world with India amongst the most important G-20 economies. Ever since the Indian economy made its presence felt on the global platform, the research community is now even more interested in studying and analyzing what India has to offer. This series aims to bring forth the latest studies and research about India from the areas of economics, business, and management science. The titles featured in this series will present rigorous empirical research, often accompanied by policy recommendations, evoke and evaluate various aspects of the economy and the business and management landscape in India, with a special focus on India's relationship with the world in terms of business and trade.

More information about this series at http://www.springer.com/series/11234

Madhusudan Bhattarai · P.K. Viswanathan
Rudra N. Mishra · Cynthia Bantilan
Editors

Employment Guarantee Programme and Dynamics of Rural Transformation in India

Challenges and Opportunities

Springer

Editors
Madhusudan Bhattarai
Jalsrot Vikas Sanstha (JVS)
Kathmandu
Nepal

and

ICRISAT
Hyderabad
India

Rudra N. Mishra
Gujarat Institute of Development Research
Ahmedabad, Gujarat
India

Cynthia Bantilan
Research Program on Markets, Institutions and Policy
ICRISAT
Hyderabad
India

P.K. Viswanathan
Amrita School of Business, Amrita Vishwa Vidyapeetham (Deemed to be University)
Kochi, Kerala
India

ISSN 2198-0012 ISSN 2198-0020 (electronic)
India Studies in Business and Economics
ISBN 978-981-10-6261-2 ISBN 978-981-10-6262-9 (eBook)
https://doi.org/10.1007/978-981-10-6262-9

Library of Congress Control Number: 2017951145

Printed on acid-free paper

This Springer imprint is published by the registered company Springer Nature Singapore Pte Ltd.
part of Springer Nature
The registered company address is: 152 Beach Road, #21-01/04 Gateway East, Singapore 189721, Singapore

Foreword

The Mahatma Gandhi National Rural Employment Guarantee Act (MGNREGA) is the world's largest and most ambitious rural development programme, providing wage employment in unskilled manual work to over 50 million rural households in India. Ten years on, the support to this programme continues unabated, laying to rest initial scepticism of its viability. The budgetary allocation for the programme over a decade had increased approximately threefold, from 113 billion rupees in 2006–07 to 380 billion rupees (or 6 billion USD) in 2016–17. That said, it is only timely that we now attempt to comprehensively look at the empirical evidence to assess the impact that MGNREGA has had on livelihoods and rural development.

Over the years, a number of empirical studies have attempted to analyse specific dimensions of the programme, especially with respect to its implementation, performances and outcomes. As with many other social and welfare-based programmes implemented in India, the MGNREGA has shown to have high regional variations in performance because the responsibility of implementation lies with the states. A limitation of previous studies has been that they were confined to a few states, restricting the generalizability of their results.

This volume attempts to provide a deeper understanding of the performance of the MGNREGA by bringing together a range of empirical studies exploring the multiple implications of the programme across 12 states. It successfully highlights distinct development and governance issues, socio-economic conditions and nature of institutions across various states that have influenced the implementation and performance of the programme. This compendium of empirically grounded research papers by over 25 researchers, who have conducted research on the MGNREGA since its inception, provides insights into state-level variations of the programme, its implication on rural transformation process in India and its envisioned future.

From this work, we draw new information and insights into the multidimensional impacts, including economic and social impacts, of MGNREGA across spatial settings—from Kerala to Tripura, contributing to the otherwise scant literature on the programme's impact across geographic locations. The findings from these works provide insights into the major limitations of the programme and justify some of the restructuring processes currently being carried out by various government agencies to further improve the effectiveness of the programme.

The chapters in the book are analytically rigorous in exploring the multidimensional impacts of MGNREGA across states. The empirically rich case studies tackle important issues of this welfare programme through the lens of the right to work campaigns, rural development, ecology, human development, food security and livelihoods of the rural population. I congratulate the authors and co-authors of each chapter for their commendable work in providing unique insights into the functioning of the MGNREGA in various contexts. Likewise, I also commend the editors of this volume for giving this book its vision and for bringing together such crucial and varied topics that have been impacted by the MGNREGA. I would also like to extend my appreciation to the Springer Publishers' team for bringing out this volume targeted at a diverse audience.

This volume will be a useful read and reference to government officials and policymakers concerned with rural development and welfare. It is also a valuable source of references for graduate students and researchers engaged in fields of agricultural and rural development, regional planning, labour economics, development studies, development economics and related fields of study.

Prabhu Pingali
Director, Tata-Cornell Institute for
Agriculture and Nutrition
Cornell University

Preface

The dynamism cast by the implementation of the Mahatma Gandhi National Rural Employment Guarantee Act 2005 (MGNREGA) in India since early 2006 has been quite fascinating as evident from the growing volume of empirical literature over the years on different dimensions related to the performance and outcomes of the programme. Over the last 10 years, the MGNREGS has also evolved significantly and is now providing subsistence level of employment and social safety net benefits to over 50 million of poor households annually in rural India. It has evolved as one of the largest welfare programme in the world. After Public Food Distribution Systems, probably, MGNREGA scheme also stands as the second largest in terms of coverage of the rural poor by a Social Protection Programme in India.

Incidentally, in terms of public policy discourse, since its inception in 2006, the MGNREGA has become a fascinating rural development policy agenda in India, with diverse perspectives across key stakeholders and diverse implementation modes, performances, and varied outcomes across the states/regions of India. Over the years, international development agencies and rural development professionals around the world have also shown keen interest in assessing the programme impacts, its implementation outcomes to rural poor, as reflected by the growing empirical literature on MGNREGA from academic institutions, civil society organizations as well as international agencies across the world. Recently, one of the World Bank studies has also pointed out that the experiment of MGNREGA is one of the success stories of poverty alleviation initiatives in the developing world. Besides, the MGNREGS has also immensely contributed towards rural transformation process in India over the years with far fetching implications for livelihoods of agricultural labour force and its targeted beneficiaries.

Despite the initial lukewarm response of the government after coming to power in May 2014, the Government of India has in fact increased annual allocations to the MGNREGA activities substantially. The Government of India spent INR 463.83 billion (USD 6.8 billion) for MGNREGA work activities during 2016/2017, which was about 25% increase in the expenditure than that of the fund spent for the programme in the previous year. However, evidences suggest that several performance indicators of the programme have either stagnated or declined in recent years, with notable variations across states, regions and beneficiaries.

Likewise, the programme also faces several criticisms from the academia and policy circles in particular, in view of the overall ineffectiveness in achieving the prime targeted goal of 100 person days per beneficiary household per annum. The latest interventions in terms of redesigning and widening the scope of the MGNREGA through the convergence approach, are currently being spearheaded by the national government and implemented by some state governments with varying choice of development programmes and implementation activities. In many respects, the implementation of MGNREGA schemes in rural India can also be compared with the proposed Sustainable Development Goals (SDGs) and the objectives of reducing inequality in India. For instance, several recent studies have attempted to link MGNREGA-related schemes with meeting SDGs in India, with positive impacts on economic, social, institutional and governance structure and environmental services in rural India.

In this respect, the present volume is an important and timely addition to the existing literature on MGNREGA and its impacts, as many of the chapters contained in this volume provide more empirical evidences as to how a holistic assessment of a programme can be done by integrating its multi-level economic, social, institutional and environmental impacts. These issues are in fact critically linked with achieving SDGs related targets and indicators in India by 2030.

More specifically, the present volume takes a critical look at the status of implementation and performance of the MGNREGA across states since its implementation. It assesses the emerging dynamics, especially, its interface with the rural labour market, and changes in social and institutional settings, and local participation. The studies presented in the volume are unique in terms of the use of empirical analysis across states using appropriate interdisciplinary research methods relying on both quantitative and qualitative techniques. The content and coverage of each of chapter in the volume are unique in terms of the presentation of empirical case studies using interdisciplinary research perspectives, with rigorous analytical and methodological approaches. To the best of our knowledge, there has been hardly any attempt to provide a consolidated and critical review of the status of implementation and the impacts of the MGNREGA across many states, based on both macro- and micro-scales of analysis. The uniqueness of the volume lies also in the fact that authors of each chapter have been engaged in research on various aspects of MGNREGA implementation ever since its launch in 2006. Thus, this volume is expected to fill the gap in literature on several counts.

Actually, motivation for this volume originated from the National Workshop on 'MGNREGA and the Emerging Rural Context: Learning from Selected States', held at the Gujarat Institute of Development Research (GIDR), Ahmedabad, during 10–11 December 2013, jointly organized by the GIDR and the International Crop Research Institute for Semi-Arid Regions and Tropics (ICRISAT), Hyderabad. During the workshop discussions and brain storming sessions, it was felt that a huge knowledge gap exists regarding MGNREGA and its performance and outcome across states. It was felt that there was a need for literature that used both micro- and macro-analytical methods, looked at the stakeholders' perspectives on the outcome of the programme, and catered to its institutional and governance related aspects.

Besides the papers presented at this workshop, few chapters were also solicited later to provide a holistic perspective on the programme implementation and its outcomes across states to get a wider national flavour about the same. Thus, the present volume is an outcome of the constant and determined efforts we made over 3 years. The volume provides a holistic perspective on the MGNREGA programme activities and their impacts with detailed studies in 12 states of India, from Kerala in the South to Tripura in the Northeast of India. A wider coverage of geographic areas, implementation-related issues and policy and institutional dimensions makes this volume unique among the other studies on MGNREGA.

The consolidation of the volume in its present form is an outcome of the persistent efforts and cooperation extended by all the authors of its chapters, and by many personalities, who deserve our special appreciation and gratitude. With research rigor and application of advance tools and techniques of analyses across the disciplines, we expect that this book will be useful to the academia, as well as rural development practitioners and policy makers.

It is also our sincere hope and wish that this volume would generate policy discussion and further research on several unexplored issues of MGNREGA activities such as economy wide effects, social and institutional outcomes, environmental management and sustainable development related dimensions of the programme. We also expect that it will bring out the need for appropriate changes in policy, institutional and governance systems related to the MGNREGA to transform the programme into a robust, dynamic and more sustainable model in the future. It is our hope that with the growing interest of public policy discourses to meet the Sustainable Development Goals (SDGs) and its various targets on poverty alleviation by 2030, the MGNREGA programme activities, may also be integrated with the Government of India's priority actions for meeting the globally committed SDGs agendas and the milestones in the near future.

Kathmandu, Nepal — Madhusudan Bhattarai
Kochi, India — P.K. Viswanathan
Ahmedabad, India — Rudra N. Mishra
Hyderabad, India — Cynthia Bantilan
May 2018

Acknowledgements

This book bears the testimony of collective efforts made by many organizations and scholars who together have contributed developing the 13 chapters included in this volume. While working on this volume, we have been immensely benefited from several organizations and individuals, besides the respective chapter authors. Here, we acknowledge contribution of all those personalities and organizations, who have wholeheartedly provided critical supports to us, directly or indirectly, in shaping this volume to this form and to this quality.

We would like to express our gratitude and special thanks to the International Crops Research Institute for Semi-Arid Tropics (ICRISAT), Hyderabad, India, for providing support for undertaking a study on the 'impact assessment of MGNREGA-related activities in six states of India from 2012–15', which formed the base for development of this volume. In this regard, the funding to the editors to undertake field research and for the activities in relation to preparation of this volume was provided by the ICRISAT implemented project on Village level Studies in South Asia (VDSA), and partly by the CGIAR Research Programme on Policies, Institutions and Markets (CRP-PIM), led by the International Food Policy Research Institute (IFPRI), USA. We express our sincere gratitude to the organizations that we had previously worked and the current organizations—in particular, the ICRISAT (Markets Institution and Policies Research Programme), Hyderabad, the Gujarat Institute of Development Research, Ahmedabad, the International Food Policy Research Institute, New Delhi and the Amrita School of Business, Kochi, Kerala.

We also would like to express our deepest sense of gratitude to Prof. D.N. Reddy, Hyderabad, for his invaluable guidance and encouragement in the whole process of planning of manuscripts to publishing of this book. We sincerely thank all authors for their unwavering support and kind cooperation throughout the process of publication of this volume. The volume would not have seen the light of the day, without their pain staking efforts in preparation of the chapters, and untiring support in revisions and updating the manuscripts. We are also grateful to Dr. G. Ravi Kumar and Ms. Hema Iyengar (formerly at GIDR Ahmedabad) who have provided the excellent research support to this work. Likewise, a special word of thanks to all the workshop participants on MGNREGA-related subjects that we organized at different places, civil society organizations, local key informants, including leaders; government officials; members of NGO and various funding agencies; professional experts, all those who have provided support to each of the chapter contributors of this volume at different stages of their work.

We thank Dr. Prabhu Pingali, a renowned expert on International Agricultural Development and Professor and Director at Tata-Cornell Agriculture and Nutrition Initiative, Cornell University, for kindly agreeing to write the Foreword for the volume. Thanks are also due to Ms. Nupoor Singh, Mr. Praveen Kumar, Ms. Krati Shrivastav and the Editorial team at Springer, for their untiring efforts, in transforming the manuscript into the present volume.

Needless to say that we, the editors, are solely responsible for all the errors and omissions that may still remain in this volume.

Madhusudan Bhattarai
P.K. Viswanathan
Rudra N. Mishra
Cynthia Bantilan

Indian Measurement Unit and Conversions to Metric System

One Lakh = 100,000 (One hundred thousands)
10 Lakhs = One Million
One Crore = 10 Millions
100 Crore = 1 Billion
1000 Crore = 10 Billions
One lakh Crore = 1000 billion (or 1 Trillion)
₹ = Notation for Indian Rupees. (conversion: 1 USD = About Indian Rs. 65.0 (in 2016)

Contents

Editors and Contributors

About the Editors

Madhusudan Bhattarai is a former principal scientist (economist) for the Markets, Institutions and Policies Research Programme at the International Crops Research Institute for the Semi-Arid Tropics (ICRISAT), a CGIAR centre, where he coordinated the semi-arid tropic (SAT) India component of the ICRISAT village studies project. He has a Ph.D. in Applied Economics from Clemson University, SC, USA, with specialization in natural resources economics and public policy analysis. After his Ph.D., he worked for over 15 years at three CGIAR centres and other international development agencies in India, Sri Lanka, Thailand, Taiwan, and other countries in Asia. His expertise relates to public policy analysis, the economics of agricultural and rural development programmes, natural resources management, rural labour markets, institutional economics, transactional cost analysis, governance analysis, village studies and social protection programmes.

P.K. Viswanathan is a professor (economics) at the Amrita School of Business, Amrita University, Kochi, India. He has a Ph.D. in Economics from the Institute for Social and Economic Change, Bangalore, India. His research and teaching interests relate to the economics of natural resources management; agrarian transformation and rural livelihoods; aspects of technology, institutions, policies and governance; climate change impacts on natural resources, environment and agriculture; conservation of biodiversity and ecosystems; sustainable energy policy; globalization and its impacts on agriculture and trade; and welfare impacts of trade certifications in India's plantation sector.

Rudra N. Mishra is an assistant professor at the Gujarat Institute of Development Research (GIDR), Ahmedabad, India since 2007. He obtained his Ph.D. from the Centre for Development Studies (CDS), Thiruvananthapuram, India. His research and teaching interests relate to poverty analysis, economic analysis of health and nutrition, rural livelihoods, gender analysis, rural labour markets and time allocation and issues related to tribes. He also teaches topics related to statistics and econometrics, sample surveys and research methodology at GIDR and other academic institutions.

Cynthia Bantilan is a former research programme director for the Markets, Institutions Policy Research Programme at the International Crops Research Institute for the Semi-Arid Tropics (ICRISAT), in Hyderabad, India. She has been involved in agricultural and rural development strategy and policy research in India for over 25 years. She also directed the Impact Assessment Programme at ICRISAT for the semi-arid tropics globally. She spearheaded innovations implementing key research programmes on agricultural markets, institutions and policy using macro- and micro/village level studies for sub-Saharan Africa and Asia. She specializes in agricultural research evaluation and impact assessment, strategic analysis, econometrics and agricultural statistics, monitoring and evaluation, analysis of livelihood strategies and development pathways, poverty and income distribution, and applications for decision support and science policy. She has guided the research work of over 100 graduate students.

Before joining ICRISAT, she was an associate professor of economics and statistics at the University of the Philippines at Los Banos. Then, she also served the Philippine government in various capacities: national policy adviser for poverty and income distribution at the National Economic and Development Authority (NEDA), national adviser on Agricultural Statistics for the Department of Agriculture; and principal adviser at the National Statistics Office for 5 years.

List of Contributors

Vinoj Abraham Centre for Development Studies (CDS), Trivandrum, Kerala, India

Ravindra Adusumilli Watershed Support Services and Activities Network (WASSAN), Hyderabad, India

A. Amarender Reddy Center for Sustainable Agriculture, Monitoring and Evaluation, National Institute of Agricultural Extension Management (MANAGE), Hyderabad, Telangana, India

Cynthia Bantilan Research Program on Markets, Institutions and Policy, ICRISAT, Hyderabad, India

Madhusudan Bhattarai Jalsrot Vikas Sanstha (JVS), Kathmandu, Nepal; ICRISAT, Hyderabad, India

Indraneel Bhowmik Department of Economics, Tripura University, Agartala, Tripura, India

Pritam Bose Department of Economics, Tripura University, Agartala, Tripura, India

M.G. Chandrakanth Institute for Social and Economic Change (ISEC), Bengaluru, Karnataka, India

Ashima Chaudhary Watershed Support Services and Activities Network (WASSAN), Hyderabad, India

Pradip Chouhan Department of Economics, Tripura University, Agartala, Tripura, India

Samrat Goswami Department of Rural Studies, Tripura University, Agartala, Tripura, India

Nicky Johnson Centre for Management in Agriculture (CMA), Indian Institute of Management, Ahmedabad, Gujarat, India

Jayanti Kajale Gokhale Institute of Politics and Economics, Pune, Maharashtra, India

Parmod Kumar Agricultural Development and Rural Transformation Centre (ADRTC), Institute for Social and Economic Change (ISEC), Bengaluru, Karnataka, India

Aasha Kapur Mehta Department of Economics, Indian Institute of Public Administration, New Delhi, India

Pulak Mishra Department of Humanities and Social Sciences, Indian Institute of Technology, Kharagpur, India

Saswat Kishore Mishra Department of Humanities and Social Sciences, Indian Institute of Technology, Kharagpur, India

N. Nagaraj GPS Institute of Agricultural Management, Bengaluru, Karnataka, India

D. Narasimha Reddy University of Hyderabad, Hyderabad, India; Institute of Human Development, New Delhi, India

A. Narayanamoorthy Department of Economics and Rural Development, Alagappa University, Karaikudi, Tamil Nadu, India

Namrata Singha Roy Department of Economics, School of Economics and Commerce, Adamas University, Kolkata, West Bengal, India

Amita Shah Gujarat Institute of Development Research, Ahmedabad, Gujarat, India

Tushaar Shah International Water Management Institute (IWMI), Anand, Gujarat, India

Sangeeta Shroff Gokhale Institute of Politics and Economics, Pune, Maharashtra, India

P.S. Srikantha Murthy Department of Agricultural Economics, University of Agricultural Sciences, GKVK, Bengaluru, Karnataka, India

R. Suresh Department of Economics and Rural Development, Alagappa University, Karaikudi, Tamil Nadu, India

Gourav Kumar Vani College of Agriculture, Powarkheda, Madhya Pradesh, India

Shilp Verma IWMI—Tata Water Policy Program, International Water Management Institute (IWMI), Anand, Gujarat, India

P.K. Viswanathan Amrita School of Business, Amrita Vishwa Vidyapeetham (Deemed to be University), Kochi, Kerala, India

Acronyms

AIADMK	All India Anna Dravida Munnetra Kazhagam
BAU	Business As Usual
BJP	Bharatiya Janata Party
BPL	Below Poverty Line
CACP	Commission for Agricultural Costs and Prices
CAD&WM	Command Area Development & Water Management
CAG	Comptroller and Auditor General
CBOs	Community Based Organizations
CDS	Current Daily Status
CITI	Confederation of Indian Textile Industry
CPWD/PWD	Central Public Works Department/Public Works Department
DBT	Direct Benefit Transfer
DMK	Dravida Munnetra Kazhagam
DP	Dalit Panthers
FGD	Focus Group Discussions
GDP	Gross Domestic Product
GoAP	Government of Andhra Pradesh
GP	Gram Panchayat
GPS	Global Positioning System
HAHP	High Area with High Productivity
HALP	High Area with Low Productivity
IAY	Indira Awas Yojana
ICRISAT	Centre for Research in Semi-Arid Tropics
IIA	Indian Industries Association
IWMI	International Water Management Institute
IWMP	Integrated watershed Management Programme
KNMK	Kongu Nadu Munnetra Kazhagam
LPG	Liberalization, Privatization and Globalization
MDG	Millennium Development Goal
MEGS	Maharashtra Employment Guarantee Scheme

MGNREGA	Mahatma Gandhi National Rural Employment Guarantee Act
MIS	Management Information Systems
MoRD	Ministry of Rural Development
NFFWP	National Food for Work Programme
NSSO	National Sample Survey Organisation
OBC	Other Backward Communities
PDS	Public Distribution System
PMK	Pattali Makkal Katchi
PMKSY	Pradhan Mantri Krishi Sinchai Yojana
PRI	Panchayat Raj Institutions
PT	Puthiya Tamizhagam
RRR	Repair, Renovation & Restoration of water Bodies
RTWB	Restoration of Traditional Water Bodies
SAM	Social Accounting Matrix
SCs	Scheduled Castes
SGRY	Sampoorna Gramin RozgarYojana
SSR	Standard Schedule of Rates
SSS	Shramik Shakti Sangams
STs	Scheduled Tribes
TDP	Telugu Desam Party
UID	Unique Identification
UPS	Usual Principal Status
VDSA	Village Dynamics in South Asia
WTO	World Trade Organization

List of Figures

List of Tables

Chapter 1
Introduction

Madhusudan Bhattarai and P.K. Viswanathan

> *The Mahatma Gandhi National Rural Employment Guarantee Act (MGNREGA) is the single most innovative programme from India and a lesson to the whole world*
>
> Joseph Stiglitz (Nobel Laureate), July 2016

1.1 Introduction

The initiation of National Rural Employment Guarantee Act of 2005 (NREGA in short), later renamed as the Mahatma Gandhi National Rural Employment Guarantee Act (MGNREGA) in 2009, is indeed a landmark rural development programme in the history of Independent India. This is both in terms of the process and spread of activities carried out, and level of participation by rural poor in the development activities. In fact, the popularity and importance of India's signature social welfare programme—NREGA—is also being discussed worldwide, especially in the developing countries, for its adaptability and replication. No doubt, after initiation of this programme in February 2006, it has also brought about several structural and functional changes in implementing rural development programme in India.

M. Bhattarai (✉)
Jalsrot Vikas Sanstha (JVS), 20694, Kathmandu, Nepal
e-mail: madhu.bhattarai2010@gmail.com

M. Bhattarai
ICRISAT, Hyderabad, India

P.K. Viswanathan
Amrita School of Business, Amrita Vishwa Vidyapeetham (Deemed to be University), Kochi, Kerala, India
e-mail: pkviswam@gmail.com

M. Bhattarai et al. (eds.), *Employment Guarantee Programme and Dynamics of Rural Transformation in India*, India Studies in Business and Economics,
https://doi.org/10.1007/978-981-10-6262-9_1

Unlike other Rural Development programmes so far implemented in India, NREGA[1] is a right based employment guarantee programme, which has given a right to all rural poor and vulnerable households to demand for minimum of 100 days of employment per annum. Given the nature of monsoon dependent agriculture and erratic rainfall pattern of monsoon, the 100 days of employment during the slack period of farm operation is a very critical livelihood support to millions of rural poor and vulnerable population living below poverty line in the country.

In fact, India has a long history of 'public spending for rural development and poverty reduction programmes ever since its Independence and MGNREGA may be considered as the largest and the widely appreciated flagship programme in view of its outreach and impacts on the rural economy and society. In what follows, we provide a brief account of the historical evolution of MGNREGA in India.

1.2 Poverty Reduction Through Employment Generation in India: A Historical Perspective

Provision of social safety net (SSN) to the poor and vulnerable sections of population through public work programmes has a long history in the Indian sub-continent. Even in Kautilya's Artha Sasthra (an economic programme of states and duties of government to its citizen written about 2400 years ago by famous ancient eastern philosopher Chanakya), emphasis was given to the provision of adequate social safety net measures to the poor and vulnerable sections of population in a country to ensure happiness to king and kingdom. For instance, as Chanakya then writes in the Kautilya Artha Sasthra "*In the happiness of his subjects lies his happiness; in their welfare his welfare; whatever pleases himself he shall not consider as good, but whatever pleases his subjects he shall consider as good.*" (Chanakya quotes, 350–283 BCE).

Subsequently in medieval times, the kings and temple institutions in Indian sub-continent have built several public works—water ponds, irrigation canals, road, temples, and related community level work programmes to provide employment and welfare to the needed section of population, when other forms of employment were not available in the society. In colonial period, public workfares were organised in India by the government largely to distribute food and other relief measures at the famine struck communities.

Since independence in 1947, various welfare oriented rural development programmes have been initiated by the central and state governments of India to provide employment security and livelihood benefits to the poor and vulnerable

---

[1]In this study, Mahatma Gandhi National Rural Employment Guarantee Act (MGNREGA), or the term "Mahatma Gandhi National Rural Employment Guarantee Scheme" (MGNREGS) has been used interchangeably. Before, 2009, the same MGNREGA programme was called as NREGA (or NREGS) in India. The same programme was renamed from NREGA to MGNREGA by the Government of India in 20.

sections. These schemes were grouped under rural development programme, or rural employment creation and/or poverty alleviation programmes. Considering the scale of population living in rural India now, and the magnitude of poverty and vulnerability situations, it may not be feasible to provide full employment to all the needy, but the various schemes implemented from time to time, have provided some relief to the poor. In terms of its scale and coverage across various parts of India, MGNREGS is one of the prominent welfare enhancement and social safety net programmes in rural India in recent times.

Evolution of various employment generated related social welfare programmes, or schemes that are linked with employment generation purposes (or EGS related areas) and implemented at various periods of time are summarized in Table 1.1. At present, not all of these schemes are in operation with the exception of a few. Over time, many of the programmes with narrow scope have been either abandoned or merged with other schemes and implemented at large areas/regions of the country. The Community Development Programme that was initiated in 1952 was the first large scale social welfare programme with employment support and asset creation in the rural areas.

Table 1.1 Evolution of employment generation related programmes in India

Year/Period	Employment generation related programmes	Major purpose and highlights of the programmes
1952	Community Development Programme (CDP)	Overall development of rural areas and people's participation
1960–61	Rural Manpower Programme	A comprehensive work programme for better utilization of the unemployed and under-employed work force in rural areas
1966–67	High yielding variety programme (HYVP)	To increase the productivity of food grains by adopting latest varieties of inputs of crops involving farm employment generation
1971–72	Crash Scheme for Rural employment	Employment generation in the country targeted at the rate of 25 million man-days per year in each district through the execution of labour intensive projects and creation of durable assets in consonance with local development plans
1972	Maharashtra Employment Guarantee programme (EGS)	The Maharashtra Employment Guarantee Scheme (EGS), the first right based employment programme in India, ensured a guaranteed and productive employment at a wage with minimum level of subsistence to reduce rural poverty. By reducing risks faced by poor households, and by constructing productive assets and infrastructure, the scheme also aimed to

(continued)

Table 1.1 (continued)

Year/Period	Employment generation related programmes	Major purpose and highlights of the programmes
		have a longer-term developmental role. This is considered as a precursor of MGNREGA
1971–72	Rural work Programme (Drought Prone Area Programme)	Protection from drought by achieving environmental balance and by developing ground water
1972	Employment Guarantee Scheme of Maharashtra	To assist the economically weaker sections of the rural society
1972	Crash Scheme for Rural Employment (CSRE)	For rural employment
1977	Wage Employment Programme or Food for Work Programme	This programme was further strengthened in the 1980s
1979	Training Rural Youth for Self-Employment (TRYSEM)	Programme for Training rural youth for self-employment
1980	Integrated Rural Development Programme (IRDP)	All-round development of the rural poor through a programme of asset endowment for self-employment
1980	National Rural Employment Programme (NREP)	To provide profitable employment opportunities to the rural poor
1983	Rural Landless Employment Guarantee Programme (RLEGP)	For providing employment to landless farmers and laborers
1983	Self-employment to the Educated Unemployed Youth (SEEUY)	To provide financial and technical assistance for self-employment
1986	Self-Employment programme for Urban Poor (SEPUP)	To provide self-employment to urban poor through provision of subsidy and bank credit
1989	Jawahar Rozgar Yojana	For providing employment to rural unemployed
1990	Scheme of Urban Wage Employment (SUWE)	To provide wages employment after arranging the basic facilities for poor people in the urban areas where population is less than one lakh
1993	Employment Assurance Scheme (EAS)	To provide employment of at least 100 days in a year in village
1997	Swarna Jayanti Shahari Rozgar Yojana (SJSRY)	To provide gainful employment to urban unemployed and under employed poor through self-employment or wage employment
1999	Swarna Jayanti Gram Swarozgar Yojana (SYGSY)	For eliminating rural poverty and unemployment and promoting self-employment
2001	Sampoorna Grameen Rozgar Yojana	To provide wage employment and food security in rural areas and also to create durable economic and social assets

(continued)

Table 1.1 (continued)

Year/Period	Employment generation related programmes	Major purpose and highlights of the programmes
2004	National Food for Work Programme	To give food through wage employment in the drought affected areas in eight states. Wages are paid by state government partly in cash and partly in food grains
2002–03	Jai Prakash Narayan Rojgar Guarantee Yojana (JPNRGY)	Employment guarantee in most poor districts
2005	Mahatma Gandhi National Rural Employment Guarantee Act (MGNREGA)	To create a right based framework for wage employment programmes and make the government legally bound to provide employment to those who seek it
2008	Prime Minister's Employment Generation Programme (PMEGP)	To generate employment opportunities in rural as well as urban areas through setting up of new self-employment ventures/projects/micro enterprises

Source Authors' compilation from various sources, and individual studies on the topics

"Food for the work programme" initiated in India in 1960s were earlier form of employment guarantee scheme. Under this, food and basic support for survival needs were provided to the famine or food insured communities through targeting the population who were willing to participate in the unskilled manual work of the public works programme. The need to participate for manual work programme is a critical factor for low cost targeting the population that are vulnerable and urgently in need of the social safety net supports from rest of the population. At many times, they are also source of confusion and controversial debates on the subject matter as well.

After a series of severe drought and famine like situations, the Maharashtra state government introduced a drought relief programme in 1972 with the objective of providing employment to rural poor, called as Maharashtra Employment Guarantee Scheme (MEGS). There were several changes in the programme, but in 1977 this became an act, and institutionalized in the state of Maharashtra by taking the fund from payroll tax, and passing an act in the Maharashtra state assembly in 1977. The 1977 MEGS Act stated as "An Act to make effective provision for security of right to work by guaranteeing employment to all adult persons who volunteered to do unskilled manual work in rural areas in the state of Maharashtra." The MEGS act was conceptually the same as that of the unemployment insurance scheme widely practiced in some of the developed countries, financing it from payroll tax systems. In 1970s and 1980s, this MEGS was very popular Rural Development scheme, and provided short run benefits and relief to the vulnerable communities as well as the farming communities through asset creation and building basic rural infrastructure, or improvement of agricultural productivity.

In reality, MEGS has become a model (basis for) scheme for the employment programmes in India. In view of increasing unemployment and labour force in the country, learning from success (and shortcoming) of MEGS, National Rural Employment Guarantee Act (NREGA) was notified by the Government of India on

7th September 2005 and passed by the parliament. The MGNREGA guarantees 100 days of employment to every rural household during a financial year, whose adult members volunteer to do unskilled manual work. The act came into force on 02 February 2006 and it was implemented in a phased manner. It was notified in 200 most backward districts in its first phase of implementation. In Financial Year 2007–08, it was extended to cover another 130 districts in phase two. The remaining districts were notified under NREGA with effect from 1st April 2008. As a result, since early 2008, NREGA has covered the entire country with the exception of districts that have a hundred percent urban population. The NREGA was renamed as the Mahatma Gandhi National Rural Employment Guarantee Act (MGNREGA) by the then Prime Minister Man Mohan Singh, while addressing a meeting held to celebrate the golden jubilee of the Panchayat raj institutions in India on 02 October 2009.

1.3 MGNREGA and Its Salient Features

Since 2009, not only the name and contents of the programme have been changed, but also the funding for the programme was almost doubled, and it turned an integral part of the rural development and social safety net measures in rural India covering nearly 50 million households annually, who voluntarily participate in the programme by providing un-skilled manual labor. In 2012/13, with USD 8 billion per annum of government expenditure for the MGNREGS related activities, this is also one of the largest employment generation related social safety net measures in the world.

The total budgetary expenditure for MGNREGA[2] indeed also varies year to year. In monetary terms it has increased in the recent past, though in real terms, it gives a different picture altogether. The total expenditure for MGNREGA accounted for 0.36% of annual GDP of India in 2013, which got reduced to 0.26% of GDP in 2016/17 (details are in Chap. 2 and in subsequent chapters). In the recent years, larger chunk of the rural people are directly engaged in any of the MGNREGS related activities for about 50 days of manual work activities provided by the local governments (see Appendix Table 1.2 for a detailed overview of physical and financial performance of MGNREGA since its inception).

In due course, the scope of the MGNREGA activities has been widened with active participation from most of the states, though with differences in the intensity of implementation. Given the federal structure of the Indian constitution with

[2]MGNREGA is the act that was passed by the parliament in 2005. For the ease of reading, in this volume, we have used the term MGNREGS, MGNREGA, or NREGS interchangeably.

Table 1.2 Physical and financial performance of MGNREGA since its implementation

Coverage: employment, expenditure and social groups	Phase I	Phase II	Phase III							
	2006–07	2007–08	2008–09	2009–10	2010–11	2011–12	2012–13	2013–14	2014–15	2015–16[a]
1. Number of districts under NREGA	200	330	615	615	615	615	632	632	632	659
2. Number of households covered by the programme										
(2.1) Households with job cards (million)	38	65	100	113	119	123	130.1	128.1	128.0	128.4
(2.2) Households provided employment (million)	2.1	3.4	4.5	5.3	54	50	49.9	47.9	41.4	34.0
(2.3) Total households (million)	900	1,440	2,160	2,840	2,570	2,110	2,302.9	2,202.8	1,662.3	1,202.9
(2.4) Average no of days employed per household	43	42	48	54	47	42	46.15	45.99	40.15	35.37
3. Share of marginalised groups in NREGA employment (%)										
(3.1) Women	40	42	49	49	48	48	47.04	47.97	50.23	52.72
(3.2) Scheduled Tribes (ST)	36	29	25	21	21	18	17.93	17.88	18.44	18.09
(3.3) Scheduled Caste (SC)	26	27	29	30	31	22	22.79	22.93	22.23	23.36
4. Expenditure on NREGA										
(4.1) Total expenditure (Rs. million)	8,813	120,570	272,510	379,050	397,720	376,370	397,782.70	385,526.20	360,245.60	266,485.10
(4.2) Average expenditure per district (Rs. million)	44	48	44	62	640	610				

(continued)

Table 1.2 (continued)

Coverage: employment, expenditure and social groups	Phase I	Phase II	Phase III							
	2006–07	2007–08	2008–09	2009–10	2010–11	2011–12	2012–13	2013–14	2014–15	2015–16[a]
(4.3) Average expenditure per person day (Rs.)	98	110	126	134	153	178	172.73	175.02	216.72	221.54
(4.4) Average wage per person day (Rs.)	65	75	84	90	100	117	117.91	120.26	145.56	159.89
(4.5) Share of wages in total expenditure (%)	66	68	67	68	68	70	68.26	68.71	67.17	72.18

Note[a]Performance until 8th December 2015

agriculture and rural development issues being the subjects of interest to both the centre and states, different states have implemented the programme with localizing it and with appropriate changes. This is also one of the reasons for variation in performance and effectiveness of the programme across states and regions in India.

MGNREG programme has been designed to meet dual purpose of social needs of poor section of rural population as well as needs of overall sections of the society. That is, while providing social safety net to the poor and vulnerable rural households, utmost care was also given to linking the activities and interventions with the process of growth and asset creation activities. This 'dual purpose' feature of the programme is also one of the reasons for controversies in its implementation and not being able to satisfy the programme objectives across states on a uniform basis.

The MGNREGA also has some of the unique features like bottom-up planning and implementation, demand-driven structure for work activities, and in-built framework of social audits and empowerment in lowest tier of panchayat and at hamlet level settlements.

Salient Features of the MGNREGA are summarized below:

- The scheme and targeted population are self-selecting. That is, those who are interested to do manual unskilled work, have to demand for work at their Gram Panchayat. Each household is entitled to 100 days of employment in each fiscal year. Forest Right Act (FRA) beneficiaries are entitled to 150 days of employment. In states like Rajasthan, communities like the *Sahriyas* have been given an entitlement of 200 days.
- After the compilation of the work demanded, Panchayat has to provide employment within the 15 days. If employment is not provided within the 15 days, there is a provision of paying unemployment allowances to the job seekers.
- Public work under MGNRGA should be provided within the 5 km radius of the village, beyond the 5 km, 10% of extra wages to be payable to meet the transportation and living expense of workers.
- The wages under the scheme has to be paid weekly, and not beyond a fortnight.
- After 2009, wage rate has been paid in piece-rate basis in most cases, after measurement of work done by a group of labor force. This has provided flexibility of timing of work as per the local agro-climatic condition, and agricultural seasonality of work demand.
- Panchayat Raj Institutions should organize Gram Sabhas to plan and take decision about the nature and choice of works to be undertaken in each of the financial year.
- Every district has to prepare a shelf of projects to be undertaken under MGNREGA, the exact type of work to be done vary by states and several factors. Some of the major categories of permissible works are as follows:
  - Renovation of traditional water bodies including desilting of tanks.
  - Development of lands of the SC/ST/BPL/IAY and land reform beneficiaries.

  - Rural connectivity.
  - Drought proofing.
  - Central government notified work in consultation with state governments.

- The wage and material expenditure should be in 60:40 ratio at block level of work distribution.
- Social Audit has to be conducted at least once in every six months.
- The minimum facilities should be provided at worksite such as creche, drinking water, and shade (For further details on work procedures and guidelines of MGNREGA, see MoRD 2012).

Within a village, the Panchayat office needs to plan for detailed implementation of modalities and integrity of MGNREGA work in the village.

(a) **Implementation Status of the programme**

The NREGS scheme was introduced across states in India in a phased manner as discussed above. In April 2008, the NREGS was expanded to entire rural area of the country covering 34 States and Union Territories, 614 Districts, 6,096 Blocks and 2.65 lakhs Gram Panchayat. By the end of 2015/16, the scheme was functioning in 648 Districts of India, which includes ongoing work in 6,849 Blocks and 250,441 Gram Panchayats in India (NREGA website).

(b) **Major activities covered under MGNREGA**

Majority of the MGNREG activities are related to agricultural and allied activities, water conservation, irrigation ditch cleaning, rural road connectivity, etc. Permissible activities are clearly stipulated in Paragraph 1 of Schedule-I of Mahatma Gandhi NREGA, under Ministry of Rural Development. The variety of activities permitted and allowed to be undertaken by MGNREGA are discussed in Reddy (2014), MoRD (2012), Desai et al. (2015). Recently, the works have also been selected to facilitate rural sanitation projects in a major way. Overall, the works funded by MGNREGA have been divided into 10 broad categories; they include: Watershed, Irrigation and Flood management works, Agricultural and Livestock related works, Fisheries and works in coastal areas and the Rural Drinking water and Sanitation related works. The actual nature and types of work done in a year greatly vary by states.

In the MGNREGA 2.0 (after the second generation reforms for the rural job scheme), the priority of the works are decided by the Gram Panchayat in the meetings of the Gram Sabhas and the Ward Sabhas. The second-generation programme of MGNREGS has added 30 new works in the Schedule 1 and now it also supports rural sanitation projects such as toilet building, soak pits construction, and solid and liquid waste management. Though the overall 60:40 ratio of labour and material component are maintained at the Block level (Thaluka/Mandal), some flexibilities are there in maintaining this ratio even at district level for certain works based on the local context (MoRD 2013).

In fact, recently, Construction of Angan Wadi Centre (AWC) building has also been included as an approved activity under the MGNREG Act. This created direct linkage with nutrition and health sectors in the rural economy, and provide child-care support to the labor force, especially women family members. A 'Guidelines for construction of Anganwadi Centres' under MGNREGS, have been issued jointly by the Secretary, Women and Child Development (WCD) and Secretary, Ministry of Rural Development, on 13th August, 2015. Under MGNREGS, expenditure up to Rs. 5 lakh (Rs. 0.5 million) per AWC building for construction will be allowed. Expenditure beyond Rs. 5 lakh per AWC including finishing, flooring, painting, plumbing, electrification, wood work, etc. will be met from the related component of ICDS funds. The construction of toilet and Anganwadi Centers under MGNREGA programme not only provide a direct support to the efficient running of ICDS and Anganwadi Center across the parts of rural India, but it may also enable several million of rural women to participate in paid employment and income generation activities in their village. These activities include both farming as well as non-farm sector activities. Thus, strengthening rural sanitation and ICDS programme through MGNREGA activities will help the EGS programme to directly contribute in improving the nutrition, education, and sanitation status in rural India, with short run as well as long run public goods benefits.

1.4 Performance of NREGA

Performance of MGNREGA is often one of the most debated issues in public policy and news media in India. Any discussion on "performance of MGNREGA" is also one of the politically charged policy issues in recent times. The public opinion as well as the academia working on the subject seems to be divided into different camps. A Report of Government of India (MoRD 2015) suggest that, despite maximum of 100 days of employment cap for an individual in a fiscal year, the average person days employment generated per household in 2015–16 was only 49 days, which was the highest level of employment provided by the programme in the last eight years.

There is still huge demand for works under MGNREGA, specially in slack season of agriculture, however, number of days of employment provided by MGNREGA has not been improved due to several loopholes in the administrative and financial management systems that exist. Recently, the central government has emphasized more on improvement in timely payment of wages to laborers, linking the programme with livelihood programmes and other sanitation (national sanitation complain, ICDF, etc.) so that more numbers of working days are added, and timely payment of wages ensured with the use of ICT and other relevant technologies.

A recent report from the MoRD[3] suggest that total of about 2.35 billion person days' of work were generated in 2015/2016. Then, about 55% of the total beneficiaries were women, a large number of whom belonging to scheduled caste, scheduled tribes and other vulnerable sections. On an average, about 49 days of work was created in the 2015/16, which was the highest in the past 8–10 years. In 2015/16, the MGNREGA budget was set as Rs. 37,000 corer (Rs. 370,000 million), while the actual expenditure incurred was at Rs. 43,000 crore, by providing additional Rs. 6,000 crore in the year than actually planned earlier. In fact, the MGNREGA had created 2.35 billion person days of employment in the fiscal year 2014–15, which was itself a five-years' record in its performance. This suggests still a growing demand for the MGNREGA across India, despite the rise in agricultural labor wage rate in the local markets.

The performance of MGNREGA in terms of its implementation greatly varies across states of India, as also reported by various studies on the topic. State level local institutions have greater role in setting up the implementation institutions, laying out administrative and financial outlays, planning and designing of the programme, and selection of expenditure modalities. Depending upon the institutional capability of the state level local institutions and government machinery, the programme performance is also expected to vary across states. Viewed from this angle, it may be observed that three northeastern states (Tripura, Mizoram and Sikkim) were relatively on top in providing number of jobs per person than rest of the country. For example, in Tripura, under MGNREGA, an astounding 94.5 person days per household jobs were created during 2015–16, against the national average of 48.5 days in the same year. Mizoram and Sikkim states held second and third places respectively, by providing 69 and 67 days of jobs per person during the same period. Whereas, in terms of total expenditure incurred, Tamil Nadu, Andhra Pradesh, West Bengal, and Rajasthan were much ahead than rest of the states. This was due to the large numbers of labor force participated in the programme in these states. Since the total number of work days provided was lower in these states, it reflected on the lower number of average workdays per household compared to the three NE states.

The MGNREGA implementation performance report published by the central government for the year 2015/16 revealed that over 257,847 grama panchayats spread over 6,858 blocks and 661 districts across the country have been served by the programme. However, as per the report, about 40,000 panchayats (about 16%) did not provide any job to any worker during the period. Most of these 40,000 panchayats fall in the states of Chhattisgarh, Gujarat, Haryana, Maharashtra, Punjab, Utharakhand and Uttar Pradesh. The average days of employment provided per household in 2014–15 were only 40.17, significantly lower than 46 days as reported in 2013–14. Thus, with an average of 40.17 days of employment, 2014–15

[3]These updated recent data on MGNREGA are data are taken from MoRD publication on 'Performance, Initiatives and Strategies FY 2015–16 and FY 2016–17'.

was the worst performance year in the last 10 years, whereas 2009–10 was the best performance year with an average of 54 days of employment provision in a year (http://www.financialexpress.com).

1.5 MGNREGA Achievements, Relevance, and Growing Concerns

Several empirical studies have demonstrated that the MGNREGA have helped greatly in providing supplementary household income to rural poor of about 10% of the annual income, and this programme has contributed largely in checking distress migration of entire household/family from rural to urban, while women workers obtained employment from this scheme locally as well. However, some members who can earn more still move out of village to urban centers seeking better work and income opportunities, whereas, other members continue to stay back and work under MGNREGA or take up other available works in the village itself (Desai et al. 2015).

MGNREGA schemes have also indirectly helped in reducing dropouts and increasing the retention of children in schools. This is because, school going childrens' mothers have now stayed back in the village for the sake of their children's education rather than migrating out with their spouse in search of better wage and longer employment (authors field observations in ICRISAT rural villages in SAT regions in 2013–14). Likewise, a study using difference—in difference method of impact assessment in a dry region of India has shown that debt burden of participant households declined sharply over non-participants after the implementation of MGNREGA in their villages (Bhattarai et al. 2014). Similarly, the recent UNDP Global Human Development Report refers to the MGNREGA as one of the milestones in social protection measures in the world, in comparison to schemes in other countries, such as: (a) the Rural Employment for Public Assets in Bangladesh; (b) Jefes De Hogar in Argentina; and (c) the Karnali employment programme in Nepal. However, the programmes in Bangladesh and Nepal are limited in scope in terms of their inclusion criteria of beneficiaries (Chakraborty 2016).

As reported in many studies, the MGNREGA scheme have helped the poor and vulnerable sections of the population in rural India. The fact that workers belonging to marginalized and vulnerable social groups have benefited from the MGNREGS at the national level makes it a unique programme. Almost half of the workforce comprised of women and the proportion of scheduled caste workers was around 22% and scheduled tribe around 18%. This suggests that the scheme has been able to influence the lives of rural poor especially the marginalized and vulnerable social categories and groups. A study by IFPRI (Liu and Barrett 2013) has reported that the MGNREGA might have contributed for a decline in underweight children (less than five years) and for improving their status. For instance, there were only about 30% underweight children in 2014 vis-à-vis 43.7% in 2005. Likewise, Desai et al. (2015) reported that the MGNREGA provided benefits to both poor and non-poor households, of which, the poor are more likely to be attracted by the programme, and hence, it is a good self-targeting social safety net programme.

Using a rigorous impact assessment procedure based on difference-in-difference evaluation method, Desai et al. (2015) also reported that MGNREGA participation across India has been dominated by poor and socially vulnerable (agricultural wage laborers, schedule tribes (adivasi), and schedule caste (dalits) and other backward classes, and landless, marginal and small farmers); and MGNREGA was instrumental in reducing poverty among these groups. The NCEAR study reports that MGNREGA reduced poverty overall by up to 32% and prevented 154 million people from falling into poverty; and it made greater impact in less developed area and among the socially vulnerable groups (Desai et al. 2015).

However, over last few years, there was also a marked decline in the delivery, budget expenditure in real terms, and implementation of the total schemes faced a setback in many places, though the trend varies from state to state. Though the nominal figures on total allocation of funds for the MGNREGA activities have increased over the years, its value in real terms had declined. For example, the share of total fiscal expenditure for MGNREGA works in 2008/09 was close to 1% of the national GDP, which declined to 0.36% of in 2012/13, and 0.26% in 2016/17. Over the last two years, there were also concerns as regards the changing labor to material ratio of the programme expenditure from 60:40 to 51:49.

On the other hand, some amount of disillusionment and disappointment against the programme has also set in the minds of the labor force in recent years. This is largely due to administrative delays in the disbursement of wages to workers for more than 2–3 months, and uncertainty of work availability in the next season so that the labor force can decide whether to migrate out of the village or remain locally for seasonal jobs Basu and Sen (2015). Recently, questions have been also raised on MGNREGA implementation, its planning process at local level, poor awareness and capacity building among the local panchayat level workers, introduction of complex ICT and new software without adequate training to local staffs working in rural areas, and growing level of corruption and mishandling of financial resources allocated for MGNREGA work.

Even after a decade of implementation of NREGA, the rural workers are facing acute shortage of work, long-delays in receiving wage payments, lack of transparency in work allocation, wage payment, and uncertainty in continuation of work next season or next year. This situation has been primarily due to the result of various moves by successive governments to undermine NREGA across the country. For example, the budgetary allocations for the programme were drastically reduced from almost 1% of the GDP in 2008–09 to about 0.3% in 2013–14. Likewise, in 2011, NREGA wages were delinked from minimum wage rate; as a result, the MGNREGA wage rates have stagnated in real terms for the past several years.

In addition, changes are being done in the working procedures of MGNREGS, year after year, which has also exerted additional pressures on villages and local level institutions to cope up with the MGNREGA work activities. At many places, local administrations are unable to cope with the constant changes in the work schedules and guidelines of MGNREGA by the Ministry of Rural Development, and the excessive reliance on technology for the implementation of the programme (Agrawal 2017), but without proper training to the local staff in using the technology.

Of late, discussions were also taking place at the policy and governance circles as regards restricting the scope of MGNREGA to the 200 backward districts where the programme was originally launched in 2006. The logic for this argument is that a broad-based employment guarantee programme is not required in other parts of the country where market wage rate is already higher than the minimum wage rate prescribed in MGNREGA. However, this change of rolling back the policy, may severely twist the spirit of the right based employment guarantee principle of the MGNREGA Act. This would also potentially impact labor market in rest of the country greatly, altering the employment security and bargaining power of unskilled labor in large parts of India.

The fact remains that the poor and vulnerable section of households are not restricted to only those 200 districts where the programme was launched in 2006, but instead, are scattered all over. Even in the states of Kerala, and Punjab, where the wage rates are already nearly double than the NREGA wage rates, the poor households and labor in these two states are still demanding for MGNREGA wage work during the slack season of farming, when adequate employment are not available. On the other hand, implementing MGNREGA to all over India has financial implications, as non-targeted households are also getting benefits.

Over the 10 years period of its implementation, the MoRD and the implementing agencies have also learnt from the country-wide experiences leading to several reforms in implementing the scheme. Over the last five years, nearly 2/3rd of total expenditure was made in agriculture and allied activities, and 57% of all workers were women, well above the statutory requirement of 33%, and nearly 20–23% of the total workers belonged to scheduled caste and scheduled tribe categories. During the fiscal year 2015–16, actual expenditure under MGNREGA was INR 413 billion (USD 6.35 billion in 2015 exchange rate), which was the highest expenditure in nominal terms since its inception. Out of this, about 73% was for wage payment, with women accounting for 55 and 95% of the payments made through electronic fund management system (NREGA web site at www.nrega.org.in).

Thus, the MoRD has also introduced an electronic fund management system, and coordinated with banks and post offices, besides monitoring of dues clearance time and process. This was intended to ensure the timely release of funds to states and the block and panchayat level agencies to provide work on demand. The government has also increased number of work to up to 150 days in drought-affected districts. Likewise, the Central government was also planning to issue a Master Circular, which will consolidate all key instructions from the government on the implementation of the MGNREGA across the states and regions. Similarly, the MoRD has also planned to train and place 10,000 barefoot technicians from worker households to efficiently managing the process at local sites.

Besides, the Ministry of Rural Development has been trying to bring about major reforms in implementation of the MGNREGA programme and to meet the demand for work in drought affected areas, as well as to create durable and income generating assets mostly linked to augmentation of irrigation potential and thus addressing the agrarian distress permanently. In the year 2015–16, MoRD allowed state governments to provide employment under MGNREGA wherever needed, particularly more in drought-affected areas, through earmarking additional resources available from the central government. The central government has expanded the job entitlement from 100 to 150 days of MGNREGA work in a year to additional 2.05 million households in 2015/16 in drought-affected regions of ten states. All of these efforts benefited 4.4 million of households at all India level who have completed 100 days of employment under MGNREGA scheme in that year.

Of late, the government of India has started several new programmes on sanitation, nutrition, and health sectors in the rural areas as convergence schemes. The government ministries were planning to construct 3.3 million of Individual House Hold Latrines (IHHL) in rural India, as part of Swachh Bharat Mission, and 63,000 Anganwadi centers were constructed to strengthen rural infrastructure (MoRD 2016). The central governmental agencies were trying to establish a close linkage between MGNREGA work and labor use on these new schemes initiated, such as Sanitation campaign, Pradhan Mantri Krishi Sinchai Yojana (PMKSY), ICDF, and other related programmes. It is expected that, convergence of these programmes in rural areas will address both short-run as well as long run needs of the society. More importantly, a proper convergence of MGNREGA work with these national level programmes will provide continuity of the employment guarantee programme in the long run with sustained funding from state and central governments.

More recently, the Ministry of Rural Development (MoRD) was also planning to link MGNREGS job cards with AADHAR numbers and bank account numbers at the household level. Use of electronic Fund Management System has also ensured timely payment of the labor wage. The quality of implementation of the scheme greatly varies across the states. In many states, it has been reported that people usually do not come forward for MGNREGA works in their village, because there are other works with higher payments available in the village itself. This is also perfectly all right, as MGNREGA is a last resort for employment, as a social safety net to the society, when the alternate jobs and livelihood opportunities are not available in the local areas.

1.6 Impacts of MGNREGA: Burgeoning Empirical Literature

Ever since its inception, the MGNREGA has evinced lot of interest among scholars who have undertaken research on various aspects of the programme in terms of its effectiveness, performance in meeting the targets, usefulness in serving livelihood needs, providing services to rural poor and its effect in creating assets and infrastructure in the rural communities. However, there is paucity of empirical studies addressing several unexplored issues, such as: (a) whether MGNREGA has led to an increase in rural wage rate in India? and (b) whether, MGNREGA has enabled reducing the debt burden and food insecurity and vulnerability of poor and low-income rural households. After 10 years of experience of its implementation and the impacts on different sectors of the rural and urban economies, it is felt by many that the MGNREGA programme should be analyzed within a broader perspective of rural development and its effectiveness in serving the immediate needs and requirements of the rural poor and vulnerable sections of the communities.

Contradicting several studies on the performances of MGNREGA, one study by NCEAR, using panel household analysis across large geographical setting, has reported very positive impact of the MGNREGA programme on reduction of poverty, food insecurity, and debt burden among the rural poor and vulnerable households (Desai et al. 2015). The findings of this study are quite revealing with respect to the performance and evaluation of the programme as also reported by government agencies and several other empirical investigations on the performance of the programme (see, MoRD 2012).

Due to large number of people involved in the programme and getting benefited out of it, the successive national and local governments have been compelled not to change the major course of the programme implementation. In 2014 and 2015, the national government also floated an idea to have a major change on the course of action and priority of the MGNREGA programme and its implementation strategies. However, due to changing governments in several states of India, the actual implementation of the new reforms in the programme has not been much effective. Instead, the national and state governments have slightly increased the budgetary provisions for the MGNREGS during the fiscal years of 2014/15 and 2015/16 than the provisions made in the preceding years.

Whether and why NREGA activities are needed in India now when the economy is growing at almost two-digit level for the last one and half decades? This is one of the hotly debated policy issues in India now. In fact, there are other issues like changing dynamics of public policy related to MGNREGA and other flagship programmes, especially after mid 2014, following a change in the government at the centre. The question on the rationale of MGNREGA programme has also been widely contested in academic and policy circles since its implementation in 2006. On the one hand, one section argues that while the universal access and right based approach of the programme must be continued in the present format covering the entire country, the implementation part needs to be fine-tuned to make it relevant for the current context.

On the other hand, another section of scholars are of the view that the programme must be downsized and implemented only in those areas of less developed and marginal communities, where it is needed the most. They also argued that the nature of work undertaken in MGNREGA should include more non-farm activities keeping in view the growing size of the rural non-farm sector. No doubt, each of the two alternate strategies discussed in the literature here signify different implications of the MGNREGA on the rural poor.

More recently, several of the rural development sector think tanks and public policy experts in the central and state governments have been greatly concerned with 'whether to implement the MGNREGA programme as it has been implemented so far, or to adapt and transform it to new ways to address the short-run as well as long-run problems of employment creation and livelihood improvement in rural India'. Within the Ministry of Rural Development, there was a debate as to 'whether to merge MGNREGS work activities with the farm operations, as in the case of EGS implementation in Maharashtra—which has been in operation in Maharashtra state since 1972, or to make the MGNREGS programme and its implementation agencies stand alone and separated from the other rural development agencies (Aruna 2013).

To sum up, the overall performance of the programme has been satisfactory. Of course, there are also several issues and challenges and the entire dynamics of the programme and its implementation across states and regions within need a deeper understanding in terms of reflections of the realities from the grassroots level.

1.7 About the Present Volume and Its Relevance

In this regard, the present volume takes a critical look at the status and implementation of the MGNREGA across states in India and the emerging dynamics in the rural context, especially, its interface with the rural labour market. The volume is an effort to consolidate some of the illustrative state level experiences of successes and failures in the implementation of MGNREGA by taking cases across over 15 states of India, and by different authors. It also attempts to explore some of the future courses of action that may help evolve a sustainable strategy for implementation of MGNREGA and for achieving inclusive growth with secured employment in India. The studies presented in the volume are unique in terms of the use of empirical analysis across states using inter-disciplinary research methods, and relying on both quantitative and qualitative techniques.

The idea of this volume came up at a workshop jointly organized by the Gujarat Institute of Development Research (GIDR) and International Crops Research Institute for the Semi-Arid Tropics (ICRISAT) held at GIDR Ahmadabad, during 10–11 December 2013. The workshop was attended by over 25 eminent scholars and partners who have been working on MGNREGA across the states. At the workshop, a multi-disciplinary team of policy analysts and scholars had presented papers on various aspects of MGNREGA implementation across states: the performance, and the future direction of the programme. After the workshop, it was thought to develop a volume by compiling the selected papers on various topics of implementation of MGNREGS, covering several themes and contemporary issues of the programme with a pan India coverage, i.e., from Tripura in northeast to Kerala in South India. Later on, a few papers were solicited from other scholars working on MGNREGS. Again, in view of the change in the government at the national level in May 2014, it was felt to specifically look at the changes in the policy discourses on MGNREGA. Hence, a few more papers were invited covering the most contemporary scenarios of implementation of the programme. Thus, we have a carefully scrutinised collection of empirical papers from eminent scholars in India and abroad who have been engaged in research on MGNREGA and its implications on the ground across states.

The volume covers issues that are expected to throw light on redesigning and reframing MGNREGS activities so that the programme create significant impacts on inclusive growth in rural areas. The scope and coverage of most of the literature and books available on MGNREGS at present is somewhat limited, as it largely focuses on a particular state, or at the most, one or few states. Likewise, there are several studies which rely heavily on the standard macro level data on MGNREGA while examining the performance of the programme across the states, such as number of Labor days of employment provided, and wage payment per day, etc. Such analyses are limited by the fact that they do not provide a critical view of the impacts of the programme at the micro contexts. The present volume addresses this limitation by providing more focused analysis in the empirical contexts of a district or a village or even a particular case study context.

Many of the chapters in this volume have been prepared with series of consultation with the programme beneficiaries, by undertaking proper statistical sampling and analytical procedures. These chapters have compiled the stakeholders' perceptions towards the programme implementation in their villages, and the extent of participation, engagement in the same and the benefits out of the programme.

The volume of employment generated since the inception of the programme (from 2006–07 up to 2015–16) of MGNREGA has been around 19 billion person days that averages around 2 billion person days every year. Set in this background, the main objective of the Chap. 2 by Parmod Kumar is to analyse the impact of MGNREGA on the rural livelihoods through generation of additional employment especially among the deprived sections of the society including the Scheduled Castes (SC), Scheduled Tribes (ST), Other Backward Communities (OBC) and women. The Chapter throws some light on the issue of migration of labour from rural to urban areas due to lack of employment opportunities in the villages and examines how MGNREGA has been able to make any dent on labour migration.

D. Narasimha Reddy et al. in Chap. 3 examines the interesting aspect of the impact of MGNREGA on rural wages as well as the dynamic interface between MGNREGA and the rural labour markets. The Chapter presents a comprehensive view of the changes happening in the rural labour markets in the context of the wider uptake of the MGNREGA works in the villages. Based on evidences as emerge from several studies, the Chapter engages with some of the important concerns arising from the wide-scale implementation of MGNREGA, such as: the burgeoning labour shortage, increasing farm wages and rising farming costs, farm mechanization, peak-season labour adjustments, labour migration, etc.

The paper observes that the eventuality of farm labour shortage may not be strictly ascribed to increased rural worker participation in MGNREGA. The fact remains that labor scarcity has emerged as one of the major constraints to increase agricultural production in India. The study suggests for some policy interventions based on macro and micro levels analysis of the trends in implementation of MGNREGA, which mainly include: (a) development of labor saving technologies and machines to overcome labor scarcity; (b) an inclusive farm mechanization programme for women and youth, strengthening rural-urban connectivity; (c) social protection for migrant labor and capacity building programmes for skill augmentation; and (d) development of MGNREGA calendar depicting the schedule of time-period representing the lean-season during which the work will be implemented.

While a large number of studies have looked into the nature and progress of employment creation under the scheme, there have been very few studies looking into the equally important issue of asset creation under the same. In this regard, Chap. 4 by Verma and Shah reviews and synthesizes the evidences of asset creation under the MGNREGA based on field case studies of more than 140 best-performing MGNREGA water assets. In retrospect, when it was launched, the MGNREGA was expected to create useful, productive and durable assets, both public and private. To understand the impacts of MGNREGA on creation of durable assets, the IWMI had undertaken surveys in 2009–10 and 2010–11. The surveys indicated that where implemented well, the MGNREGA made significant and positive income effects through rural asset creation. The programme witnessed a significant turnaround in respect of water security programmes, investing some US$3 billion annually, by way of construction, repair and renovation of rural water assets.

The reviews of case studies of best-performing MGNREGA water assets indicated that, on average, the best-performing assets are able to generate gross returns equal to their investment in a little over a year. The chapter offers eight practical suggestions for maximizing MGNREGA's net positive impact. Broadly, the propositions reflect four principles: *prioritization*, *capacities*, *incentives* and *exit* (by '*exit*' it implies a gradual decline in demand for work under MGNREGA).

The Chapter argues that focusing on non-wage benefits of MGNREGA can elevate its performance; and, in the process, build stakes for rural communities. Doing this will require significant capacity-building investments in local institutions (PRIs, block and district administration) and creative, context-specific arrangements for ensuring sustainability of assets. There is also an urgent need to build capacities and enhance opportunities in the non-farm sector. MGNREGA work should not and cannot be a permanent occupation for poor households. Over years, the dependence of poor households on MGNREGA and the willingness of people to work at government-prescribed minimum wages must decline. This would be a robust indicator of MGNREGA's success. This can be done by building high-performing assets that help uplift the village economy to a level of prosperity which crowds out the need for minimum-wage work.

Chapter 5 by Narayanamoorthy et al. explores the argument that 'whether the NREGS had increased the farm wage rate substantially resulting in a sharp reduction in farm profitability'? It uses the cost of cultivation survey data published by the Commission for Agricultural Costs and Prices. Based on data for the period 2000–01 to 2010–11 from few states, viz., Andhra Pradesh, Odisha, Punjab, Karnataka, Maharashtra, Madhya Pradesh and Rajasthan, the study examined five different foodgrain crops, namely, paddy, wheat, jowar, gram (channa) and tur (red gram) for the analysis. The study refutes the argument that the profitability of foodgrain crops had declined after the introduction of MGNREGS. This is not only true with high area with high productivity (HAHP) states but also with high area with low productivity (HALP) states.

However, it also shows that the real cost of human labour input had increased considerably in all five crops in both HAHP and HALP states following the implementation of NREGS (2006–07 to 2010–11). The profitability calculated in relation to all paid out costs (C2) had either increased or the losses incurred reduced in all five crops in both the HAHP and HALP states. The number of years of profit realized by the farmers has also increased in most crops during the post-NREGS period as compared to pre-NREGS period (2000–01 to 2005–06). Increased productivity in most crops seems to have helped to increase the profitability by negating the increase in human labour cost. The analysis also indicates that the labour scarcity accentuated due to NREGS may have increased the cost of human labour at a faster pace. Hence, arrangements may be made to link up NREGS with agricultural operations to reduce the labour scarcity and also to improve the profitability in crops cultivation.

Maharashtra was the pioneer state to provide guarantee of employment to rural poor during the drought years of early 1970s. After the implementation of MGNREGS in 2006, both the schemes were being implemented in Maharashtra simultaneously. In this context, the Chap. 6 by Kajale and Shroff examines the employment profile and the assets created under the state run EGS and centrally sponsored MGNREGS in Maharashtra.

It analyses phase wise performance of the MGNREGS, extent of employment generated, assets created and expenditure incurred on the works carried out during 2008–09 and 2012–13. Various factors responsible for the poor performance of the scheme till 2010–11 were also examined. The chapter also discusses limitations and potentials of the scheme as well as policy implications. The analysis shows that EGS as well as MGNREGS have been successful as employment guarantee programmes as they have provided employment whenever and wherever the need arose. However, it is felt that this has not led to creation of durable and good quality assets that would enhance overall productivity of the agricultural sector.

The Chap. 7 by Mishra and Mishra assumes relevance in the context of the announcement of new guidelines/framework towards planning for MGNREGA works in convergence with other government programmes. Accordingly, the new guidelines have made it mandatory for the states to ensure that at least 60% of works undertaken in a district in terms of costs is spent for creation of productive assets that are directly linked to agriculture and allied activities. This is very important considering that creation of productive assets is necessary not only for making ecological regeneration but also for ensuring sustainable growth of agriculture sector and creation of livelihood opportunities in a village economy.

The Chapter also discusses the experience of initiatives towards convergence of the MGNREGA with other developmental schemes in the states of Odisha and West Bengal. It is expected that such convergence initiatives would lead to not only optimum utilization of public investments in conservation and management of natural resources, but also in creating assets that would help in mitigating adverse effects of climate change and create conditions for sustainable development of the rural economy.

The Chapter also discusses some pertinent issues: What are the different types of convergence models that have been initiated in Odisha and West Bengal? How have the joint efforts of various line departments contributed to conservation and management of natural resources? Are assets created under convergence initiatives sustainable in the long-run? How have these assets contributed to agriculture sector, particularly to enhance production and yield, changes in cropping pattern, crop diversification, and multiple cropping? Can the existing institutions contribute to management and utilization of the assets created under convergence? If not, what institutional supports are necessary in this regard?

The Chap. 8 by Vinoj Abraham is an attempt to understand the process of asset creation under the MGNREGS covering four south Indian states, viz., Kerala, erstwhile Andhra Pradesh, Tamilnadu and Karnataka. The Chapter presents an interesting analysis of how the different states have behaved in respect of setting the local governance institutions for the effective implementation of the state sponsored flagship programmes, especially, the MGNREGS. The interface between the MGNREGS and the local settings has been presented as highly varying across the states. The Chapter endeavor to argue the case that the type of asset creation, methods of asset creation and maintenance, and benefits accrued by the local people across the four states is largely influenced by the local polity, local governance structure and democratic practices at the local level.

The flagship programme MGNREGA is in practice in all the states since the last 10 years, with dual objectives of creation of jobs and productive assets in rural India. The small north eastern state of Tripura has successfully implemented the programme and marked notable success. In this regard, the Chap. 9 by Bhowmik et al. is an effort to look into the impacts of the scheme on the participating households in the Dhalai district. The study reveals that MGNREGS has impacted on livelihood of the participating households, though most of the households survive on daily wages. Increase in asset base also portray that income assurance has been evident. The study also finds more job opportunities for the unreserved categories in the scheme as it witnessed a decreasing trend in allotment ratios for the STs in the study area.

However, with the recent changes in the operational framework, the participants became apprehensive about the future of the scheme.

Chapter 10 by Vani and Srikantha Murthy explores the multiplier effects of NREGS employment in a village economy context using the Social Accounting Matrix (SAM) framework. A good number of research studies have been conducted on efficacy of the scheme in achieving targets set under the Act. However, most of the studies had considered only direct employment creation through this programme and there were only a few studies undertaken to assess the impact of MGNREGS on the village economy as a whole. One such research was conducted by Indira Hirway, M.R. Saluja and Bhupesh Yadav in Nana Kotda village in Gujarat in January 2008. The Chapter suggests that making the programme more demand driven, taking more labor intensive work activities under MGNREGA would also ensure more circulation of MGNREGA expenditures within the local economy, which would produce more employment and income locally due to increased feedback and inter-sectoral linkage (or multiplier) effects.

Nagaraj et al. (Chap. 11) make an assessment of the impacts of MGNREGA, on some of the indicators, such as households' labor market participation, income, employment and productive assets creation based on macro level studies of six states, viz, Karnataka, Rajasthan, undivided Andhra Pradesh, Gujarat, Madhya Pradesh, Maharashtra and micro level insights from Karnataka villages. It also analyzed other critical issues such as whether MGNREGA programme has been successful in providing 100 days of employment per annum to rural families demanding employment and to what extent the MGNREGA has offered social protection to the rural poor?

The study indicate that at macro level the performance of MGNREGA is not even across states even after a decade of its implementation. Only 7–12% of the households could receive 100 days of employment from MGNREGA in the study states. The trend of absorbing higher proportion of youth population under MGNREGA work pose serious implications in terms of labor scarcity in farming.

It was observed that the benefits obtained are largely at community level through asset creation that included desiltation of irrigation tanks and construction of check dams benefiting bore wells through groundwater recharge, and assured source of drinking water for livestock even during summer months. Likewise, the other sets of infrastructural benefits were improvement in rural connectivity due to road works, construction of school buildings and thus helping village children by reducing the drudgery of travelling to far away schools and so on.

However, though MGNREGA works were able to assure sustainable development through improved Natural Resource Management in some regions, it fails in providing social protection where the leadership of implementing agencies is weak and leaders lack dynamism. Stringent rules and regulations resulted in inordinate delays in executing works and late payment to workers.

Chapter 12 by Ravindra and Chaudhary makes a strong case for enhancing the scope of Employment Guarantee scheme for inclusive and resilient growth in rainfed areas under the new 'inter-sectoral convergence' guidelines set by the Ministry of Rural Development in the implementation of flagship programmes. It notes that unfortunately, the perception of 'durable assets' in MGNREGS is limited to physically measurable constructions (digging, filling of earth and brick and mortar). The same analogy can be extended to other qualitative aspects of public goods that can potentially provide environmental services in rainfed areas. In fact, the *Agro-ecological restoration* needs to be considered as a 'durable asset' creation under MGNREGS, even if it does not involve brick, mortar or earth work.

With the fast spread of Non-Pesticidal Management (NPM) and organic agriculture, the scope for local inputs to substitute for external chemical inputs which are often subsidised, has increased; such demand is also universal across the rainfed areas. Conversion of this potential demand into local enterprises needs considerable skilling, innovations and effective demand generation. MGNREGS can be an effective platform in incubating such local labour intensive enterprises. Provision of labour subsidy for such enterprises for a defined incubation period can be an effective instrument for their promotion.

The Chapter then argues that MGNREGS is uniquely positioned to make a substantial contribution to drive sustainability, resilience and growth in rainfed agriculture, livestock and fish production systems. Its strength lies in its universal presence, focus on labor, well laid out systems of payments, social audit and intensive coverage of rainfed geography. All that is needed is providing interpretative flexibility on the concept of 'creation of durable assets' in natural resources development and drought proofing. The Chapter also lays out some boundary conditions for not compromising the constitutional mandate of MGNREGA. Such expansion of scope of the Scheme without compromising its own objectives can potentially have multiplier effects of its investments in achieving resilience and growth of rainfed agriculture.

Chapter 13 by Shah et al. provides a narrative of the journey of MGNREGA by highlighting the important challenges along with the changing approaches in its implementation in the recent years. It observes that though MGNREGA in its present form had significantly contributed towards improving the status of the rural households, continuity of the programme in future will be beset with many challenges. While the very nature and content of the programme had undergone significant modifications and adaptations over the past one decade of its existence, its future scope and potential appears to be rather bleak in view of the changing facets of the rural economies as well as the socio-economic and demographic characteristics of the households. The Chapter observes that from a future perspective, employment guarantee programme, ideally, should take into consideration of the multifunctional nature of the impact that the assets, related mainly to natural resources, are expected to generate, especially, if initiated through a developmental mode. The various facets of the impact may thus, include not only income and employment, but also larger developmental objectives such as environmental sustainability, intra-village equity, and building of institutional capacities through democratic decentralization.

1.8 MGNREGS: A Future Perspective

With increasing efforts at the national level to implement the MGNREGS in convergence with several of the other flagship programmes supported by the national and state governments, it seems that the programme would continue to stay benefiting the rural households in most parts of the country. The concept of '*convergence planning*' of MGNREGA is being undertaken by MoRD since 2009, with the line state and local government agencies working in tandem to implement various rural development programmes at the panchayats. The main logic behind this innovative convergence planning is to have inter-sectoral convergence of development programmes to realize optimum utilization of public funds, as also to obtain maximum returns out of the public investments in terms of more number of employment and wages earnings out of limited public funding [For details, see in this volume: Mishra and Mishra (Chap. 7, this volume), and Adusumilli and Chaudhary (Chap. 12, this volume)]. Given the potential of spreading the multiplier impacts of the programme in convergence with other state support programmes, it is quite likely that the programme would still continue to influence the public policy making and governance in India in the years to come. More importantly, in a vibrant democratic system, as in India, the nature and scale of the existing social safety net programmes (including MGNREGS) can also create its own check and balance on the democratic governance process, as a large segment of the rural population has already become a major stakeholder and beneficiary of the programme. This signifies that a democratically elected political party (or political leader), which has to face election in each four to five years of time, would less likely to scrap out the MGNREGA from India now, unless other forms of alternate livelihoods with significant impacts and welfare outcomes are created in the rural economy.

One of the positive impacts of the MGNREGS has been the rise in rural wages in many states of India after introduction of MGNREGS (see also Chap. 5 by Narayanamoorthy et al., this volume), especially, in Kerala, Punjab, Andhra Pradesh, Haryana, Karnataka, Bihar, Rajasthan, West Bengal, Jharkhand and Uttarakhand. However, it is important to consider that the MGNREGA notified wages in these states are still lower than the mandated minimum wages set for unskilled agricultural laborers. In many of these states, adult population often prefer migrating out from the villages to urban areas in search of higher wage rates, and MGNREGA is not yet an attractive option for these rural youth. Besides, the profiles of the existing work activities assigned under MGREGS are such that they neither warrant using technical skills nor provide avenues for learning new skills or technical expertise. Thus, it is a real challenge before the policy makers to reinvent the programme with more and more work programmes that provide greater scope for skill development and thereby a progressive shift in the profile of the rural labour force. This makes a serious case for giving a facelift for the rural workforce by way of skilling and training in new employment opportunities with immense potential for increased wage levels and earnings in tandem with the rising costs and living standards.

In fact, MGNREGA interventions assume greater significance in the heightened context of the distress induced by persistent drought in rural areas. This raises an important issue as to 'whether MGNREGA should also continue as a drought-relief measure in the drought hit areas'. By virtue of the notification by the Ministry of Rural Development (MoRD), the drought-hit areas are entitled to get 50 additional days of employment per year from the existing 100-day per year mark. But, increasing number of days of work in these villages from MGNREGA is a real challenge, as currently only 4% of the employed households are able to get 100 days of employment (during 2014–15). This is due to either rationing of work or lack of availability of work. Even when the programme was at its peak of success in 2008–09, only 14% of the rural households participated in the programme had 100 days of employment in a year, which had declined to 10% and remained at that level until 2013–14. This calls for revisiting the programme and the implementation strategies to make them much more sensitive to the drought affected regions as a measure of livelihood security and distress mitigation. These are also serious challenges, since the vibrancy and sustainability of the programme invariably depends on the financial strength of the implementing agencies (national and state governments).

Focusing on the links between right-to-work (MGNREGA), ecology, and health, it appears that these three aspects of overall human development, especially amongst the poor, have to get integrated in the next phase of development of MGNREGS. The specific question that needs immediate understanding is to know the macro-micro level interactions in rural India in relation to MGNREGS interventions. In the absence of this, it may lead to 'double-discrimination' of the rural poor who are still waiting to become an important part of the development process. Furthermore, in the absence of alternative employment growth paths, the MGNREGS activities may be continued in the future, though with minimal economic gain in the short run.

From a future perspective, employment guarantee programme, ideally, may also need to take into consideration of the multifunctional nature of the impacts that the assets, related mainly to natural resources, are expected to generate further employment, especially, if initiated with a broader developmental perspective in mind. The various facets of the impact may thus, include not only income and employment, but also larger developmental objectives such as environmental sustainability, intra-village equity, and building of institutional capacities through democratic decentralization.

Appendix

(See Table 1.2).

References

Agrawal, Ankita. 2017. Ten Ways MGNREGS Workers Do Not Get Paid. *Economic and Political Weekly* 52 (6).

Aruna, S. 2013. *Mainstreaming of Resource Convergence in Policy Making, Programme Design and Execution.* UNDP India.

Basu, Parantap and Kunal Sen. 2015. *Welfare Implications of India's Employment Guarantee Programme with a Wage Payment Delay.* IZA Discussion Paper 9454. Accessed January, 2016.

Bhattarai, M., Padmaja, P., and Bantilan, C. 2014. Impact of MGNREGA on Rural Credit Structure in Andhra Pradesh state of India: Household Level Panel Data Analysis from 2006–2012, Socioeconomics Discussion Paper Series 28. [Socioeconomics Discussion Paper Series]. Available at: http://oar.icrisat.org/8407/1/ISEDPS_28_2014.pdf

Chakraborty, Sujit. 2016. *Rural Job Scheme: Three Northeastern States on Top, to at Bottom.* (http://www.business-standard.com/article/news-ians/rural-jobs-scheme-three-northeastern-states-on-top-two-at-bottom-116042700556_1.html).

Desai, Sonalde, Vashishtha, Prem, and Joshi, Omkar. 2015. *Mahatma Gandhi National Rural Employment Guarantee Act: A Catalyst for Rural Transformation.* New Delhi: National Council of Applied Economic Research.

Government of India. 2016. *Performance, Initiatives and Strategies FY 2015–16 and FY 2016–17.* http://timesofindia.indiatimes.com/ity/delhi/Govt/articleshow/52957362.cms.

Jaitely, Arun. 2016. Delivers a Key Note Address at MGNREGA SAMMELAN-2016.

Khera, Reetika. 2010. Wages of Delay. *Frontline* 27 (10), May 2010 http://www.frontline.in/+static/html/fl2710/stories/20100521271010500.htm. Accessed November 30, 2016.

Liu, Y., and Barrett, CB. 2013. *Heterogeneous pro-poor targeting in India's Mahatma Gandhi National Rural Employment Guarantee Scheme.* Discussion Papers No. 1218, Washington, DC: International Food Policy Research Institute (IFPRI).

Ministry of Rural Development. 2008. *MGNREG Act 2005, Operational Guidelines 2008.* New Delhi: Government of India.

Ministry of Rural Development. 2012. Mahatma Gandhi National Rural Employment Guarantee Act, 2005—Report to the People, Ministry of Rural Development, New Delhi: Government of India.

Ministry of Rural Development. 2013. *MGNREGA Operational Guidelines 2013.* 4th ed. New Delhi: Government of India.

Ministry of Rural Development (Government of India). 2013. Comptroller and Auditor General of India (2013). Report of the Comptroller and Auditor General of India on Performance Audit of Mahatma Gandhi National Rural Employment Guarantee Scheme. Report No-6 of 2013-Union Government (Ministry of Rural Development).

Ministry of Rural Development. 2015. *MGNREGA Report to the People 2015.*

Ministry of Rural Development. 2016. State-wise Details of Average Days of Employment Provided per Household under Mahatma Gandhi National Rural Employment Guarantee Act (MGNREGA) from 2013–14 to 2015–16.

Press Information Bureau. 2016. *Centre Releases its Share of Funds for MGNREGS.* Ministry of Rural Development.

Rahul, Amit. 2015a. *Relevance of MGNREGA Today.* Thumb Print—A Magazine from the East.

Rahul, Amit. 2015b. Thumb Print—A Magazine from the East. May 12, 2015.

Rajya Sabha Session—239 Starred Question No. 97 (https://community.data.gov.in/average-days-of-employment-provided-per-household-under-mgnrega-from-2014-15-to-2015-16/).

Reddy, D.N. 2014. *Impact of Mahatma Gandhi National Rural Employment Guarantee Scheme on Rural Labour Markets.* Working Paper No.58, ICRISAT, Hyderabad.

Sujatha. 2015. *MGNREGA: Progress Made by Modi Government in One Year*. http://www.mapsofindia.com/my-india/government/mnrega-progress-made-by-modi-government-in-one-year.
Telangana, Andhra Pradesh Reap MGNREGA Awards (2016), http://www.thehansindia.com.
United Nations Development Programme. 2015. MGNREGA Sameeksha—II: An Anthology of Research Studies (2012–14). http://www.financialexpress.com/economy/mgnrega-scheme-3-n-e-states-on-top-two-at-bottom/244193/.

Part I
MGNREGA: Macro Perspectives and Analysis

Chapter 2
Employment Generation Under MGNREGA: Spatial and Temporal Performance Across States

Parmod Kumar

2.1 Introduction

The Mahatama Gandhi National Rural Employment Guarantee Act (MGNREGA) is being implemented by Government of India since 2006. Annual budget expenditure for the programme has been fluctuating year to year, with budget allocation of ₹ 38,500 crore (or USD 10.5 billion) in the fiscal year of 2016–17. With an accumulated budgetary expenditure for the programme of about ₹ 3065 billion (i.e. over 46 billion USD) during the last 10 years (till mid of 2015), the programme has been acclaimed as one of the largest employment generation programme in the world. In-built with various transparency and accountability measures and provisions for social audits, this Act, for the first time brings the role of the state as a provider of employment and livelihood in India. The Act was initially launched in the selected 200 poorer districts of India in February 2006, and was broadened up to encompass all the districts in the country from 1 April 2008.

The objective of the Act is to enhance livelihood security in rural areas by providing at least 100 days of guaranteed wage employment in a financial year to every household whose adult members volunteer to do unskilled manual work which is primarily for natural resource management offering gender-neutral wages. The major goals of MGNREGA are:

This chapter has been extracted from a mimeograph by the author, titled 'Impact of MGNREGA on Wage Rate, Food Security and Rural Urban Migration: A Consolidated Report submitted at Institute for Social and Economic Change', which was completed and uploaded on the Institute for Social and Economic Change (ISEC) website in 2013. This chapter is a revised and updated version of this mimeography.

P. Kumar (✉)
Agricultural Development and Rural Transformation Centre (ADRTC), Institute for Social and Economic Change (ISEC), Nagarabhavi, Bengaluru P.O. 560072, Karnataka, India
e-mail: pkumar@isec.ac.in

M. Bhattarai et al. (eds.), *Employment Guarantee Programme and Dynamics of Rural Transformation in India*, India Studies in Business and Economics,
https://doi.org/10.1007/978-981-10-6262-9_2

(a) To provide a strong social safety net for the vulnerable groups by providing a fall-back employment source, when other employment alternatives are scarce or inadequate; and
(b) To act as a growth engine for sustainable development of an agricultural economy in addition to the empowerment of the rural poor. The Act mandates 33% participation for women as compulsory (details about MGNREGA and its activities are available at <http://nrega.nic.in/netnrega/home.aspx>).

In this context, the main objective of this Chapter is to analyze the impact of MGNREGA on the rural livelihoods through the generation of additional employment especially among the deprived sections of the society including the Scheduled Castes (SC), Scheduled Tribes (ST), Other Backward Communities (OBC) and women. The Chapter throws some light on the issue of migration of labour from rural to urban areas due to lack of employment opportunities in the villages and examines how MGNREGA has been able to make any dent on such incidents. Household perceptions on the functioning of MGNREGA are also analyzed based on review of earlier studies as well as using macro and micro level data.

This study uses both primary and secondary data. Secondary data were collected primarily from the MGNREGA website (http://nrega.nic.in/netnrega/home.aspx) maintained by the Ministry of Rural Development, Government of India. Primary data was collected from the selected villages and households in seven states across the country. The data was collected through structured questionnaires. The primary data pertain to the reference period, January–December 2009. In addition to the household questionnaire, a village schedule was also used in each village to gather information based on 'Group Discussion' with the *Panchayat* Members, Officials, educated and other well-informed people available in the surveyed villages.

This chapter is divided into five sections. The next section presents a review of studies on the various aspects of functioning of the MGNREGA Scheme. Section 3 analyzes total employment generation under the scheme and its various socio-economic characteristics, numbers and nature of projects taken up and amount spent under the scheme and various qualitative indicators of the working of the scheme. Section 4 brings out observations on employment generated; wage rate obtained across gender, migration issues and food security aspects at the household level. Section 5 concludes the chapter and puts forth policy suggestions on how to improve the functioning of MGNREGA.

2.2 Functioning and Outcomes of MGNREGA: A Review

The literature on various aspects of MGNREGA functioning has been expanding as the programme encompasses the whole of rural India and a huge budget compared to any other social welfare programme. Compared to the preceding programmes, like the National Food for Work Programme (NFFWP), the MGNREGA has generated roughly three to four times the number of work days. The Programme has therefore succeeded in providing the much needed wage employment to the rural masses. Among the many studies focusing on the implementation and operational details of MGNREGA, the important ones are Aiyar and Samji (2006), Bhatia and Dreze (2006), Chakraborty (2007), Comptroller and Auditor General (2008), Ambasta et al. (2008), Jha et al. (2009, 2011), Gopal (2009), Khera and Nayak (2009), Adhikari and Bhatia (2010), Shankar et al. (2011), Dutta et al. (2012), Liu and Barrett (2013), Anderson et al. (2013) and so on.

Aiyar and Samji (2006) explored the case of strengthening of social audit in order to improve the effectiveness of MGNREGA Programme. They argue that the earlier wage employment programmes failed due to the common problems of ineffective targeting, leakages and poor quality asset creation, etc. They argued for a clear separation of functions across tiers of government. The Gram Panchayat (GP) along with Zila Panchayat should be responsible for all operational activities whilst the state government should take overall monitoring and regulation of the process. In such a system the regular flow of information would be crucial as well as the enhanced ability of citizens to exercise enforceability through tools such as social audits and community score cards will have to play a major role.

After reviewing MGNREGA scheme all over the country, The Comptroller and Auditor General (CAG) report in 2008 flagged out many loopholes in the implementation of MGNREGA across the states (CAG 2008). In 26 states, 558 village panchayats were surveyed by the CAG report spread over 68 districts and 141 blocks. The study observed that, as many as 70% of villages checked, no proper records were maintained on the number of households who demanded jobs, and actual number of people who benefited from the job guarantee scheme. This study reported that in 340 villages spread over 24 states, no meetings were conducted for identifying the households to be registered under MGNREGA. No door-to-door survey was conducted in these villages to identify persons for MGNREGA card. Some households were not registered despite submitting applications on the ground that their names did not feature in the BPL survey list.

After analyzing the budgetary appraisal of MGNREGA, Chakraborty (2007) reported that existing institutional arrangements in poorer states were not good enough to implement the programme in an effective manner. Only half of the total available funds were utilized and the utilization ratio was particularly low in poorer states. There was an urgent need for both vertical and horizontal coordination across levels of governments within the states. The paper suggests that the devolution of responsibilities and strict accountability norms would accelerate capacity building at the level of the panchayat and the scheme could effectively function as a demand-driven one.

Based on their evaluation study in Chhattisgarh, Dreze et al. (2008) reported that MGNREGA was functioning in Chhattisgarh far better than the other employment programmes. They observed that there was virtually no check on the embezzlement of NFFWP funds in Surguja district of Chhattisgarh. The situation was so bad that it was constrained to describe NFFWP as '*Loot for Work Programme*'. In the same district, it was interesting to hear from a wide range of sources that the enactment of MGNREGA had led to a steep decline in the incidence of corruption. This was borne out by the muster roll verification exercises. In a random sample of nine works implemented by *Gram Panchayat*, it was found that 95% of the wages that had been paid according to the muster rolls had actually reached the labourers concerned. A similar exercise conducted in Koriya, the neighbouring district, led to similar estimates of 'leakages' in the labour component of MGNREGA by only 5% or so. In Jharkhand, detailed muster roll verification of MGNREGA works in five randomly selected *Gram Panchayats* of Ranchi District estimated leakages of around 33%. Another study by Bhatia and Dreze (2006) highlights the weaknesses in the implementation of the project in Jharkhand.

Similarly, Afridi (2008) discussed the nature and characteristics of monitoring the MGNREGA's implementation with a focus on the community control mechanisms existing in the two pioneering states of Rajasthan and Andhra Pradesh. Based on a closer look at the social audit process held, he pointed out that conduct of audits in villages without the support of NGOs and members of civil society is wishful thinking. Jacob (2008) suggested that the MGNREGA programme has immense potential to improve the gap between urban and rural India and lead to rural development in terms of basic infrastructure like roads, and enhancing agricultural productivity from irrigation works.

A study (ISWSD 2008) reported that in many parts of Kerala and Karnataka, large number of workers had demanded for increasing the work days under MGNREGA at least to 200 days per year per household. However, in both the states, there were few complaints regarding non-payment of minimum wages. In gross violation of the Act, workers at many MGNREGA worksites (e.g. in Uttar Pradesh and Jharkhand) were earning less than the minimum wages. Ambasta et al. (2008) while evaluating the performance of MGNREGA in its first two years highlights major issues confronting its implementation. It found that issues such as the lack of trained professionals for time-bound implementation, understaffing and delay in administration, lack of people's planning, poor quality of works and assets created, inappropriate schedules of rates, unnecessary bureaucratic interventions and mockery of social audits were hindering the implementation process.

Khera (2008) reported that the role of farmer's organization was very effective in making MGNREGA perform better. Aiyar and Samji (2009) documented the Andhra Pradesh experience of institutionalizing social audits into the implementation of the MGNREGA and used it to analyze the social audit process. The paper draws on empirical work aimed at measuring the effectiveness of social audits conducted in Andhra Pradesh between March and December 2007. The paper offers some interesting insights into the effectiveness of regular, sustained social audits. Emerging empirical evidence on the social audits suggests that social audits, in fact, have a significant and lasting effect on citizen's awareness levels.

Khera and Nayak (2009) studied on perceptions of women workers on MGNREGA across a vast coverage of samples from Araria and Kaimur (Bihar); Surguja (Chhattisgarh); Palamau and Koderma (Jharkhand); Badwani and Sidhi (Madhya Pradesh); Dungarpur and Sirohi (Rajasthan); Sitapur (Uttar Pradesh).

They found that the participation of women workers varied largely across the states. The overall women participation rate across sample states was 32%, whereas the same in Rajasthan was 71%. In other states, the women participation rate varied from the highest at 44% in Madhya Pradesh, followed by Chhattisgarh 25%, Jharkhand 18% to the lowest at 13% in Bihar and mere 5% in Uttar Pradesh. Thus, in all states, except in Rajasthan and Madhya Pradesh, the women participation rate was far lower than the 33 as stipulated the MGNREGA guideline. Of the total sample, more than two-third of the sample workers stated that the MGNREGA had helped them avoid hunger, while 57% reported that they could avoid migration. A majority 79% of women workers were found to collect and keep their own wages. The study reported major barriers to women's participation as inflexible social norms, illegal presence of contractors, lack of childcare facilities, and delayed payment of wages.

Jha et al. (2009) covering 900 households examined the extent of elite capture in MGNREGA in Andhra Pradesh and Rajasthan. They observed that area of land owned is a negative predictor of MGNREGA participation in Rajasthan, but the situation is reversed in Andhra Pradesh indicating poor targeting due to the possibility of elite capture in that state. In another study, Jha et al. (2011) analyze the nutritional impact of MGNREGA wage, non-MGNREGA income and Public Distribution System (PDS) participation. It found that MGNREGA affects the nutritional status of households with respect to two macro-nutrients, namely calories and protein as well as various micronutrients. Assessing the link between information, access and delivery of MGNREGA in Andhra Pradesh, Maharashtra and Rajasthan, Shankar et al. (2011) observed that information increases the propensity of access by those who are not MGNREGA's primary target, whereas, lack of information unambiguously disadvantages the poor.

According to the NCAER-PIF study (Sharma et al. 2009), there were two possible outcomes of MGNREGA, *viz*., (i) slightly improved share of ST households in employment; and (ii) that the Act outshined the earlier programmes in terms of increased women participation. The range of wages realized by workers under MGNREGA varied from state to state, but in a large majority of states, the average wages were little higher compared to the statutory minimum wages.

Gaiha et al. (2009) constructed an intuitive measure of the performance of the MGNREGA and analyzed whether excess demand under MGNREGA responds to poverty and whether recent hikes in MGNREGA wages were inflationary. The analysis confirms responsiveness of excess demand to poverty. It was noted that the apprehensions expressed about the inflationary potential of hikes in MGNREGA wages were confirmed. The higher MGNREGA wages were likely to undermine self-selection of the poor in the programme. The study suggested the need for a policy imperative in order to realize the poverty-reducing potential of MGNREGA. Such a policy might ensure a speedier matching of demand and supply in districts that were highly poverty prone, as also to avoid the trade-offs between poverty reduction and inflation.

Kareemulla et al. (2010) evaluated MGNREGA in four states (*viz*. Rajasthan, Andhra Pradesh, Karnataka and Maharashtra) with a specific focus on desirability, quality and durability of assets created and its effects on the livelihoods of beneficiaries. They found that a wide variety of works were taken up under the scheme, including works on soil and water conservation structures and rural roads, which matched the requirements of the people. However, it was noted that the quality and maintenance of assets need more attention in the coming years so that investment made would not go futile. They concluded that scheme was achieving its primary objective of employment generation but the assets created were generally seen as a by-product in the study areas.

Adhikari and Bhatia (2010) reported that the direct transfer of wages into worker's bank accounts was a substantial protection against embezzlement and control of corruption. Respondents had a fairly positive attitude towards bank payments and showed their interest in learning how to use the banking system. However, poor record-keeping, inability to cope with mass payment of MGNREGA wages, large distance to the nearest bank or post office caused hardship to the workers. While the wage payment through banks was reported a positive feature, the study exposed the limited capacity of the banking and post office systems in fighting corruption.

Dey (2010) studied the performance of the MGNREGA from three perspectives. It examined the targeting aspect of the programme; the efficiency of the implementing PRI bodies; and the impact of the programme on various outcomes at the household level. The study, covering 500 randomly selected households, 2249 individuals and 70 schemes located in 13 Gram Panchayats in Birbhum District of West Bengal, observed that the programme was likely to be accessed by poorer households with lower land holding status, low monthly per-capita income and other household related characteristics.

Harish et al. (2011) evaluate the impact of MGNREGA on income generation and labour supply in agriculture in one of the districts in the central dry zone of Karnataka. The study showed that with the implementation of MGNREGA, the number of days worked in a year had increased significantly to 201 days, reflecting 16% increase. It was observed that MGNREGA contributed to an increase in consumption expenditure while reducing the debt burden of the beneficiaries. A regression analysis of the determinants of participation revealed that gender, education and family size of the workers were significant factors influencing the worker's employment under the Programme. The increase in income was to the tune of 9% due to additional employment generated from MGNERGA. Further, the study revealed that implementation of MGNERGA works has led to labour scarcity to the tune of 53 and 30% for agriculture operations like weeding and sowing, respectively. There was a decline in area for labour-intensive crops like tomato and ragi to the extent of 30% due to MGNERGA.

Basu (2011) examines labour and output market responses to MGNREGA and determine the optimal compensation to public work employees consistent with the objectives of productive efficiency in agriculture and welfare maximization of the labourers. By accounting for the seasonality in agricultural production and the institution of permanent labour contracts, it shows that technological change and productivity increases in MGNREGA programmes tend to make labourers better off as compared to a direct increase in the wage paid at the relief programme. Further, an optimal wage that maximizes expected agricultural output may be in conflict with the one that maximizes the expected lifetime utility of labourers indicating trade-offs between different policy objectives. Further, in the event of high elasticity of MGNREGA with respect to permanent labourers, a specific subsidy targeted towards the hiring of permanent labourers would best serve the twin objectives of increased expected agricultural productivity and increased welfare for the labourers. The paper concludes that MGNREGA by introducing contestability in the agricultural labour market can yield a host of interesting implications for the wage and employment patterns of the rural poor.

Mukherjee and Sinha (2011) using a theoretical model analyzed the impact of MGNREGA scheme on rural labour market; income of the poor households; and overall agricultural production. It finds that the income from MGNREGA alone can be a substantial part of the target income of the poor. The poor may exhibit a backward bending supply curve of labour which may lead to an aggregate reduction in agricultural output. This adverse production effect could happen even when the MGNREGA activities lead to a moderate improvement in agricultural productivity.

Berg et al. (2012) test the impact of the MGNREGA on agricultural wages using monthly wage data for the period 2000–11 for a panel of 249 districts across 19 states. They observed that on average MGNREGA boosts the real daily agricultural wage rates by 5.3%. It takes 6–11 months for an MGNREGA intensity shock to feed into higher wages. The wage effect appears to be gender-neutral and biased towards unskilled labour. They found it was positive across different implementation stages and months and remained significant even after controlling for rainfall, district and time fixed effects, and phase-wise linear, quadratic, and cubic time trends.

Dutta et al. (2012) used National Sample Survey (NSS) data for 2009–10 to verify the guarantee of employment at the stipulated wage rates to the households seeking employment under the Act. They observed considerable unmet demand for work under MGNREGA in all states and confirmed that poorer families tend to have more demand for work expectations on the scheme and that despite the unmet demand; the self-targeting mechanism allows it to reach relatively poor families and backward castes. The extent of the unmet demand is greater in the poorest states, ironically where the scheme is needed the most. Labour-market responses to the scheme are likely to be weak.

Imbert and Papp (2012) estimated the impact of MGNREGA on wages and employment using NSS employment and unemployment cross-sectional data. They used quinquennial surveys as well as thin round surveys starting from 60 rounds up to 66th round. They found that MGNREGA increases public works employment by 0.3 person days per month, further, the casual wage income of the workers increased by 4.5%.

Liu and Barrett (2013) using 2009–10 NSS data, analyzed patterns of job-seeking, rationing and participation in the MGNREGA. At the national level, they found that the self-targeting design of MGNREGA leads to greater rates of self-selection into the programme by poorer and Scheduled Tribe or Scheduled

Caste households. They argued that households near the poverty line were more likely to receive the jobs they sought than were the poorer households, although those in the upper per-capita expenditure classes were least likely to secure MGNREGA jobs. They further observed that MGNREGA fares less well in reaching poor female-headed households, due both to self-selection and rationing effects. Male headed households were more likely to seek and receive MGNREGA jobs across most of the per-capita expenditure classes. They suggest that there was room for improvement and perhaps much to be learned from an in-depth comparative analysis of MGNREGA programme implementation across states that had demonstrated greater or lesser success in targeting the poor with job opportunities.

Anderson et al. (2013) examine the role of Unique Identification (UID) in the functioning of MGNREGA and how this new system can bring efficiency in its functioning. They use control group methodology for testing the efficiency of UID system in improving MGNREGA. The new UID system will enable payments to go through the banking system, as bank accounts for MGNREGA workers will be linked to the UID. As a result, the actual transfer of payments will immediately reach the hands of who it is intended for. This should drastically reduce the inherent corruption in the current system as reported by several studies and increase the amounts and reliability of payments to the workers.

Thus the studies covered almost all aspects of working of the MGNREGA scheme, viz., issuance of job cards and employment generated; monitoring, regulation and social audit of the scheme; fund utilization under MGNREGA; payment of minimum wages and provision of stipulated 100 days of employment; issues of elite capture and participation of Scheduled Caste, Scheduled Tribe and women in the programme; impact of the Scheme on rural migration, poverty and nutrition; assets creation under the Scheme and their usefulness; role of PRIs and decentralization in decision-making; and impact of MGNREGA on agricultural wage rate and so on. In summary, the MGNREGA Scheme has high expectations in terms of employment generation, alleviation of poverty, food security, halting migration and overall rural development. In the next section, we look at various aspects of the functioning of the MGNREGA Scheme based on the secondary data portrayed on MoRD website, followed by a section based on primary survey findings in 7 states. The last section presents the final conclusion and policy implications.

2.3 The Work Mechanism of MGNREGA

The thrust of MGNREGA is to build a model of governance based on the principles of transparency and grassroots democracy. As per the Act, the village and district panchayats will be principal authorities for planning and implementation of the scheme. The district programme coordinator at district level and the programme officer at the Block level (BDO or equivalent officer) coordinate the implementation of MGNREGA. The Local administration is legally bound to provide work on demand to any worker or group of workers who apply for work, within 15 days of receipt of a work application for public works under the MGNREGA. If the local administration fails to provide work, an unemployment allowance is to be paid to the workers. While 90% of the cost is borne by the Union government, payment of unemployment allowances is borne by the State Governments. Under MGNREGA, the emphasis is placed on labour-intensive works, thus prohibiting the use of contractors and machinery.

As per the provision of the Act, Gram Sabha (Village Committee) is supposed to assist in the identification of households, and recommend developmental works and conduct social audit of the programme. Based on the Gram Sabha's recommendation, the village panchayat will identify a shelf of projects to be taken up in its area and will forward to the programme officer for scrutiny. The district coordinator is supposed to finalize and approve block-wise shelf of projects to be taken up for implementation. Although the list of permissible works under MGNREGA is somewhat restricted, there is ample scope for undertaking projects that provide economically useful assets. There are several provisions which are of special interest to women workers. First, the act mandates that at least one-third of the workers should be women. Second, the wage earned is equal for both men and women. Besides this, the MGNREGA also provides for childcare facilities at the worksite. Further, in order to monitor wage payments under MGNREGA, the Government of India has shifted from direct cash payment of wages to transfer through bank accounts. Thus, MGNREGA includes a range of transparency measures to maximize vigilance of public funds by workers themselves.

2.3.1 Total Employment Generated and Their Socio-economic Characteristics

The overall performance of MGNREGA in terms of numbers of days of employment created and the number of projects completed in all states during the year 2013–14 (up to the end of October 2013) are provided in Table 2.1. A total number of 2.3 crore households were provided employment during the financial year 2013–14 till the latest estimates were available, and a total number of 63 crore man-days of employment were generated through MGNREGA during this period. Looking at the socio-economic structure of beneficiaries, around 23 and 15% was the share of Scheduled Caste and Scheduled Tribes, respectively, in the total man-days generated while women had above 55% share in the total employment generated. Around 44 lakh works were taken up out of which, around 10% works were completed and the rest 90% were ongoing at the terminal point of the study.

The MGNREGA programme has already completed more than a decade. We have compiled data up to October 2013 as discussed above. In order to provide a snapshot of MGNREGA work since its inception, we used the information available on the MGNREGA website which covers seven full financial years starting from 2006–07 up to 2012–13 and data for the financial year up to October 2013.

Table 2.1 MGNREGA statistics for the financial year 2013–14 (As on 6 December 2013)

Description	Latest estimates
Employment provided to households (crore)	2.31
Total person days generated (crore)	62.57
Person days generated for SCs (crore)	14.45 (23.1)
Person days generated for STs (crore)	9.59 (15.33)
Person days generated for Women (crore)	34.91 (55.78)
Person days generated for Others (crore)	38.53 (61.57)
Total works taken up (lakh)	44.18
Work completed (lakh)	4.22 (9.56)
Works in progress (lakhs)	39.96 (90.44)

Note Figures in parentheses are respective percentages of total
Source http://nrega.nic.in

Table 2.2 provides statewise statistics on number of days of employment created, their socio-economic characteristics and the number of projects completed and ongoing. Overall, 81 crore households were issued job cards during the period from 2006–07 to 2013–14 (up to October). Out of which, around 35% demanded employment and around 97.5% were provided employment. Around 34 crore households were provided employment during the period 2006–07 to 2013–14 averaging around 4.5 crore households working in MGNREGA per annum that constitutes roughly around 30% of the rural households in the country as a whole.

The states that employed more than 3 crore households during the implementation of this programme (2006–07 to 2013–14 up to October) were Andhra Pradesh, Uttar Pradesh, Rajasthan, Tamil Nadu, West Bengal and Madhya Pradesh. The states that provided employment between 1 and 3 crore households included Bihar, Chhattisgarh, Jharkhand, Assam, Odisha and Karnataka (Fig. 2.1). All other states provided employment to less than one crore households. However, the more pertinent question is how many person days of employment were generated by different states under this programme. Figure 2.2 presents the aggregate statistics of total person days of employment generated under MGNREGA during the period of 2006–07 to 2013–14 (up to October). A total number of 1.5 thousand crore man-days of employment was generated under MGNREGA during the period. Out of the total person days generated, the share of Scheduled Castes and Scheduled Tribes was 27 and 22%, respectively, while the share of women in total employment was 48% (Fig. 2.2 and Table 2.1).

Table 2.2 Employment generated through MGNREGA and its socio-economic characteristics (2006–07 to 2013–14)

Name of the States	Cumulative No. of HH issued job cards (in crores)	No. of HH who have demanded employment (in crores)	No. of HH provided employment (in crores)	Percentage of HH provided employment	No. of days of Employment provided (per HH)	Person days in crores					Works ongoing (in crores)	Works completed (in crores)	Total works (in crores)	Works completed (%)	No. of HH availed 100 days of Employment	Percentage of HH completed 100 days of employment
						Total	SCs (%)	STs (%)	Women (%)	Others (%)						
Andhra Pradesh	8.57	4.08	4.08	100.00	50.82	207.37	25.31	14.91	57.82	59.78	1.13	0.22	1.35	16.40	490,5592	12.02
Arunachal Pradesh	0.09	0.07	0.05	74.40	28.32	1.38	0.45	87.40	27.94	12.15	0.00	0.00	0.00	23.12	17,985	3.70
Assam	2.54	1.19	1.14	96.34	33.47	38.26	9.22	32.44	27.93	58.34	0.02	0.01	0.03	30.22	380,266	3.33
Bihar	8.51	2.39	2.32	97.40	30.92	71.85	40.95	2.29	28.42	56.77	0.12	0.04	0.16	25.15	1,003,496	4.32
Chhattisgarh	2.85	1.80	1.76	97.53	47.89	84.09	12.96	39.29	45.98	47.75	0.06	0.05	0.11	46.92	1,093,631	6.23
Goa	0.01	0.00	0.00	99.53	24.79	0.10	3.93	23.97	70.40	72.20	0.00	0.00	0.00	29.89	678	1.74
Gujarat	2.34	0.61	0.59	97.36	37.00	21.86	11.77	42.67	45.40	45.55	0.03	0.05	0.08	59.56	321,998	5.45
Haryana	0.39	0.15	0.15	95.70	39.22	5.73	51.47	0.00	36.49	48.52	0.00	0.00	0.01	53.05	63,756	4.36
Himachal Pradesh	0.68	0.33	0.31	95.10	47.95	14.90	31.35	8.11	49.98	60.54	0.03	0.02	0.05	45.33	202,038	6.50
Jammu And Kashmir	0.53	0.27	0.25	92.28	43.17	10.78	6.84	20.02	13.63	73.14	0.03	0.01	0.04	32.62	147,968	5.92
Jharkhand	2.82	1.23	1.22	99.20	42.19	51.33	16.46	40.81	32.10	42.74	0.10	0.04	0.14	30.90	523,126	4.30
Karnataka	3.26	1.20	1.13	93.85	47.22	53.22	18.26	9.93	43.17	71.81	0.17	0.05	0.21	21.83	772,301	6.85
Kerala	1.52	0.78	0.73	93.19	39.79	28.97	15.93	3.72	90.98	80.36	0.03	0.06	0.09	66.12	592,212	8.13
Madhya Pradesh	8.03	3.04	3.01	98.97	52.46	157.85	18.35	42.73	43.11	38.93	0.30	0.14	0.44	32.59	2515,984	8.36
Maharashtra	4.30	0.67	0.66	98.06	46.65	30.80	12.53	25.27	43.99	62.21	0.10	0.01	0.11	13.26	511,089	7.74
Manipur	0.28	0.25	0.25	98.47	59.45	14.73	6.96	65.14	39.59	27.90	0.00	0.00	0.01	48.10	358,487	14.47
Meghalaya	0.27	0.21	0.20	95.90	46.02	9.13	0.53	93.29	46.58	6.18	0.01	0.00	0.01	31.83	125,782	6.34
Mizoram	0.13	0.12	0.12	99.11	71.71	8.43	0.03	99.79	31.03	0.18	0.00	0.00	0.00	35.58	299,150	25.44
Nagaland	0.23	0.22	0.22	99.87	63.68	14.04	0.34	97.51	33.27	2.14	0.00	0.00	0.01	38.76	369,167	16.75
Odisha	4.26	1.18	1.13	95.67	39.96	45.13	19.77	39.20	36.91	41.03	0.10	0.03	0.13	23.55	483,165	4.28
Punjab	0.49	0.15	0.15	95.95	27.37	4.06	77.65	0.02	36.46	22.33	0.01	0.00	0.01	36.76	25,521	1.72
Rajasthan	6.05	3.48	3.37	96.69	60.57	204.10	23.70	27.49	67.81	48.81	0.13	0.05	0.18	26.50	5,464,900	16.22

(continued)

Table 2.2 (continued)

Name of the States	Cumulative No. of HH issued job cards (in crores)	No. of HH who have demanded employment (in crores)	No. of HH provided employment (in crores)	Percentage of HH provided employment	No. of days of Employ-ment provided (per HH)	Person days in crores					Works ongoing (in crores)	Works completed (in crores)	Total works (in crores)	Works com-pleted (%)	No. of HH availed 100 days of Employment	Percentage of HH completed 100 days of employment
						Total	SCs (%)	STs (%)	Women (%)	Others (%)						
Sikkim	0.05	0.04	0.03	95.75	62.76	2.11	7.46	40.73	45.04	51.81	0.00	0.00	0.00	34.68	59,476	17.69
Tamil Nadu	4.94	3.38	3.37	99.65	49.37	166.27	42.26	1.71	78.98	56.03	0.04	0.02	0.06	37.25	4,532,597	13.46
Tripura	0.42	0.39	0.39	99.51	67.60	26.47	18.65	43.44	42.96	37.91	0.02	0.04	0.06	61.14	792,636	20.24
Uttar Pradesh	9.11	4.07	3.92	96.47	42.21	165.62	47.84	1.68	19.43	50.48	0.27	0.21	0.48	43.70	2,443,749	6.23
Uttrakhand	0.64	0.28	0.28	99.24	38.79	10.72	23.21	3.62	41.69	73.17	0.02	0.01	0.03	39.62	93,252	3.37
West Bengal	7.83	3.38	3.27	96.58	28.36	92.64	35.34	12.56	30.33	52.09	0.10	0.09	0.19	48.39	543,778	1.66
Grand Total	81.15	34.96	34.09	97.51	45.24	1541.94	26.87	21.95	48.04	51.18	2.81	1.18	3.99	29.59	28,643,780	8.40

Source Data from NREGA website: http://nrega.nic.in

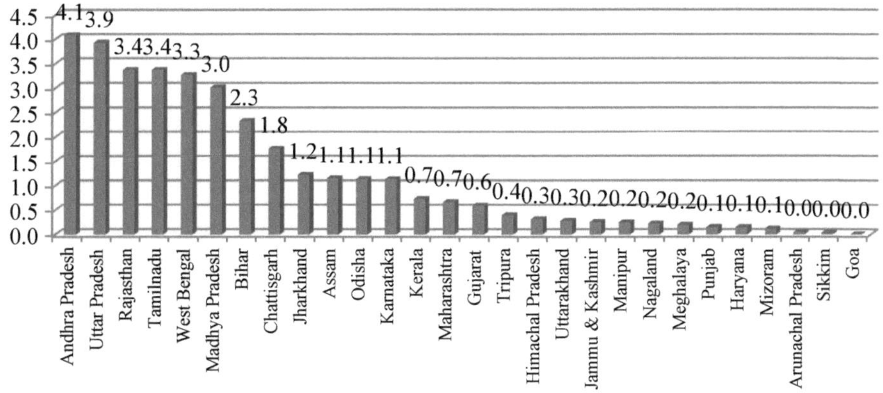

Fig. 2.1 Cumulative number of HH provided employment during 2006–07 to 2013–14 (numbers in crore)

Fig. 2.2 Total person days generated under MGNREGA during 2006–07 to 2013–14 (days in crore)

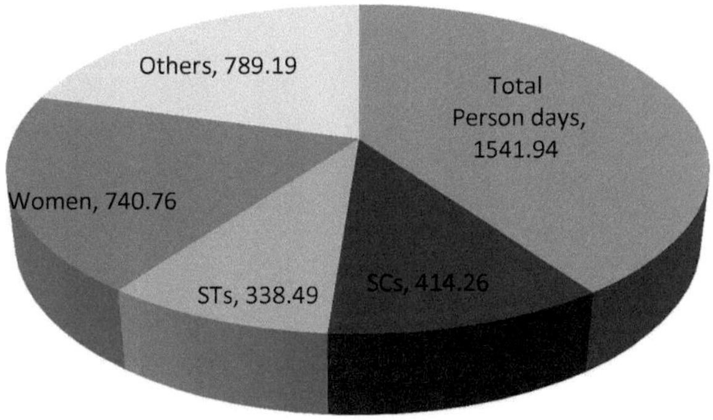

The undivided Andhra Pradesh topped in the generation of total person days (207 crore), followed by Rajasthan (204 crore), Uttar Pradesh (166 crore), Tamil Nadu (166 crore), Madhya Pradesh (158 crore) and West Bengal (93 crore) during the reference period. On the other hand, richer states like Haryana and Punjab generated less than 6 crore person days during the same time period. However, the participation of economically weaker community, *viz.*, Scheduled Castes in percentage of person days worked in MGNREGA was highest in the richer state like Punjab (77%), Haryana (52%), Uttar Pradesh (48%) and Tamil Nadu (42%) while Scheduled Tribes topped in north-eastern states like Mizoram (100%), Nagaland (98%), Meghalaya (93%), Arunachal Pradesh (87%) and Manipur (65%). The percentage of women share in MGNREGA work was highest in Kerala (91%), Tamil Nadu (79%), Goa (70%), Rajasthan (68%) and Andhra Pradesh (58%). Women share in the work was lowest in Jammu & Kashmir (only 14%), Uttar Pradesh (19%) and Bihar, Arunachal Pradesh and Assam (28%, each).

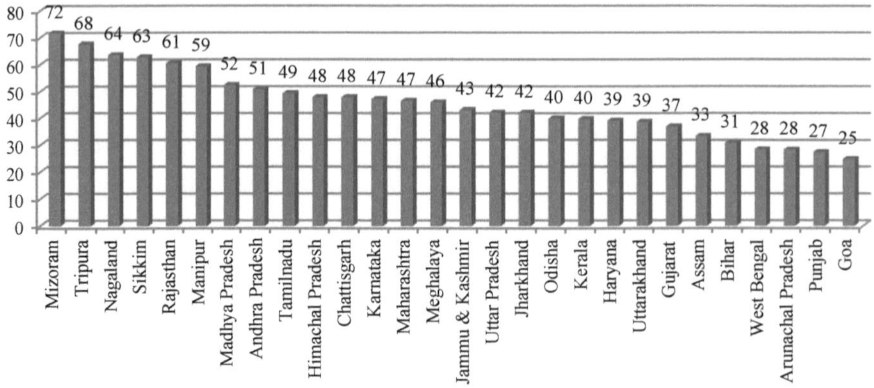

Fig. 2.3 Numbers of days per household employment generated under MGNREGA during 2006–07 to 2013–14

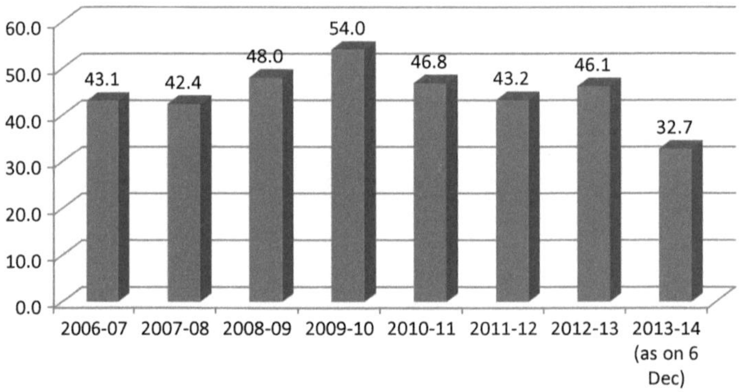

Fig. 2.4 Employment generation under MGNREGA—All India (number of days per household)

Statewise employment performance of MGNREGA is summarized in Fig. 2.3 for the period 2006–07 to 2013–14 (up to September). It depicts the number of days of employment provided per household every year under MGNREGA since the inception of the programme. A total number of 45 person days of employment has been provided under MGNREGA at the aggregate level over the period, whereas the target set is 100 days of employment per household. In other words, not even half of the set target has been achieved by MGNREGA in terms of providing employment. Only in the year 2009–10, 54 days of employment, that is slightly above 50% of the target was achieved (Fig. 2.4). In the initial years of 2006–07 and 2007–08, a total number of 43 and 42 days of employment was generated. The number of days had increased to 48 days in 2008–09, which went up to the maximum of 54 days in 2009–10, but again came down to 47 days in 2010–11, further slid down to 43 days in 2011–12, followed by a slight increase to 46 days in

2012–13. In the last financial year, only 33 days of employment was generated up to the month of October 2013 which is not expected to surpass the last two years range of above 43–46 days.

Looking at the distribution of different states (Table 2.2 and Fig. 2.3) the highest number of days of employment (60–70 days) was reported by the north-eastern states of Mizoram, Nagaland, Tripura, Sikkim and Manipur. Among the mainland states, Rajasthan, Madhya Pradesh and Andhra Pradesh provided between 50 and 60 days of employment. The states that lie in the middle providing 40–50 days of employment included, Chhattisgarh, Himachal Pradesh, Tamil Nadu, Karnataka, Maharashtra, Uttar Pradesh, Jharkhand and Odisha. The states, namely, Haryana, Jammu & Kashmir, Uttrakhand, Gujarat, Kerala and Assam may be considered as low performing as they provided only 30–40 days of employment per household per annum. The states that lie at the bottom included Bihar (31 days), Arunachal Pradesh, West Bengal and Punjab (28 days each) and Goa (25 days) of employment.

We now turn to the question, 'how successful the MGNREGA programme has been in providing 100 days of employment to those who demanded work?' While the per household average employment provided in all the states was far less than 100 days at the aggregate level, there were some households who completed 100 days of work in MGNREGA. Table 2.2 provides statistics on the number of households who availed 100 days of employment in each state during the whole period of analysis. Out of the total 34 crore households working in MGNREGA during the reference period, only 2.9 crore households (ie. 7.65%) completed 100 days of employment. Among the states, Rajasthan provided 100 days employment to 55 lakh households, followed by Andhra Pradesh (49 lakh households), Tamil Nadu (45 lakh households) and Madhya Pradesh and Uttar Pradesh (25 lakh households each). On the other side, the richer states like Haryana provided only 64 thousand households and Punjab only 25 thousand households hundred days of employment under MGNREGA since its inception.

It is interesting to note that while bigger states, like Rajasthan, Andhra Pradesh and Tamil Nadu had topped in the completion of hundred days of employment, it was the north-eastern states that topped in the percentage of households who completed hundred days out of the total households working in MGNREGA. Around 25% of the beneficiary households completed 100 days in Mizoram, 20% in Tripura, 18% in Sikkim and Nagaland each, 16% in Rajasthan and 14% in Manipur. Tamil Nadu and Andhra Pradesh were the other states where around 10–13% households completed hundred days of employment. Goa, Punjab and West Bengal were at the bottom where only less than 2% households completed hundred days of employment (Fig. 2.5). At the national level, only 8.4% households completed hundred days of employment during the entire period of MGNREGA implementation till October 2013. This indicates the ineffectiveness of the programme in providing hundred days work to all household who opted for working in the MGNREGA programme.

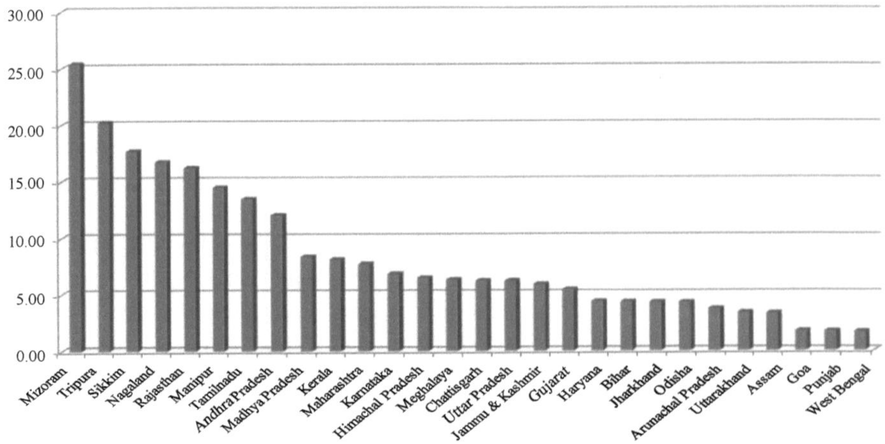

Fig. 2.5 Percentage of HH completed hundred days of employment during 2006–07 to 2013–14

2.3.2 Number of Projects Completed and Total Amount Spent

There are around nine broad categories of works in which MGNREGA wage earners are employed. They are: (a) rural connectivity; (b) flood control and protection; (c) water conservation and water harvesting; (d) drought proofing; (e) microirrigation works; (f) provision of irrigation facility to land owned by SCs, STs and others; (g) renovation of traditional water bodies; (h) land development; and (i) other activities approved by Ministry of Rural Development (MoRD), Government of India.

The percentage distribution of works completed or ongoing during the entire period of MGNREGA implementation up to October 2013 is shown in Fig. 2.7. Among the different activities undertaken, water conservation was the leading activity which occupied around 24% projects (completed or under progress). This was followed by Rural connectivity projects (17%), Provision of irrigation (14%), Drought proofing (13%), Land development (10%), Renovation of traditional water bodies and Microirrigation (6% each) and Flood control (3%). Other works, including Rajiv Gandhi Seva Kendra occupied around 7% among the total works completed or undergoing during the reference period (Fig. 2.6).

Statewise details of works completed/under progress are given in Table 2.3, while Table 2.4 presents the details of the total amount spent on each programme under MGNREGA up to December 2012. It reveals that a total number of 1 crore projects were completed and around 2.9 crore were ongoing during the reporting period. Out of total 4 crore projects taken up, around 30% were completed and rest 70% was in progress. Total amount spent on the above projects aggregated to ₹ 103,204 crores (44%) on the completed projects and ₹ 131,880 crores (56%) on the ongoing projects during the period. Thus, a total of ₹ 235,084 crore was spent

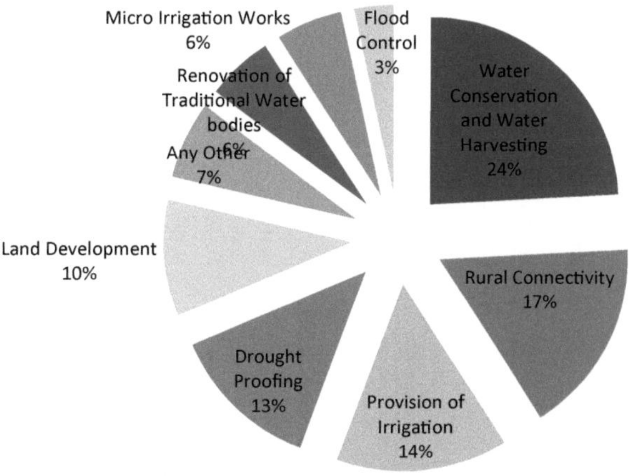

Fig. 2.6 Share of different activities in MGNREGA work during 2006–07 to 2013–14

on the MGNREGA during the period spanning seven and a half years since its launching, with an average of slightly less than ₹ 30 thousand crore every year.

While presenting the national budget for the financial year 2013–14, the then Finance Minister allocated a sum of ₹ 33 thousand crore for MGNREGA work during the financial year 2013–14. Working out the total expenditure incurred per project for the completed projects, it turned out to be around ₹ 87 thousand per project (completed) while it was ₹ 47 thousand per project (ongoing works) giving a combined average of ₹ 59 thousand cost per project for all MGNREGA works undertaken so far at the aggregate level.

Figure 2.7 presents the status of works completed or ongoing for each of the above nine categories of activities during the reporting period. Out of the total 4 crore projects undertaken, around 96 lakh projects (24%) were taken for water conservation, 67 lakh (17%) for rural connectivity, 58 lakh (15%) for provision of irrigation, 52 lakh (13%) for drought proofing, 40 lakh (10%) for land development and 23 lakh for renovation of traditional water bodies and microirrigation, each and around 13 lakh (6%) for the flood control and protection. The total amount spent on completed and ongoing projects during the reporting period is given in Table 2.4, which show that a sum total of ₹ 2.35 lakh crore were spent on MGNREGA works during the reference period.

Out of this, an amount of ₹ 75 thousand crore (32%) was spent on rural connectivity, ₹ 45 thousand crore (19%) on water conservation, ₹ 27 (11.5%) and 25 (10.6%) thousand crore on renovation of traditional water bodies and drought proofing, respectively, ₹ 17 thousand crore (7.2%) on provision of irrigation, ₹ 16 thousand crore (6.8%) on land development, ₹ 12 thousand crore (5.1%) on microirrigation, ₹ 11 thousand crore (4.7%) on flood control and around ₹ 6 thousand crore (2.6%) on other activities including Bharat Nirman Works (Table 2.4).

Looking at the statewise numbers of works completed or ongoing under MGNREGA, Andhra Pradesh topped the list with a sum of 135 lakhs works

Table 2.3 Statewise works completed/progress under MGNREGA: 2006–07 to 2013–14 (number of projects)

Name of the States	Rural connectivity		Flood control and protection		Water conservation and water harvesting		Drought proofing		Micro irrigation works	
	Completed	Ongoing	Completed	Ongoing	Completed	Ongoing	Completed	Ongoing	Completed	Ongoing
Andhra Pradesh	96,072	332,649	21,065	123,352	740,931	4,166,080	143,666	2,133,419	376,592	79,8429
Arunachal Pradesh	1358	4135	478	1313	181	532	300	1007	410	1589
Assam	40,333	101,689	7232	12,810	4606	12,129	12,819	34,698	3245	7242
Bihar	171,453	368,650	22,021	30,746	52,580	88,956	49,496	483,797	33,588	68,356
Chhattisgarh	91,054	163,096	3134	5461	42,829	67,189	25,962	36,512	9358	18,293
Goa	384	602	308	816	26	77	0	0	13	47
Gujarat	34,055	50,061	21,610	33,457	274,251	55,316	33,699	44,872	2152	4120
Haryana	17,607	16,049	1480	1368	6929	6657	2052	706	8300	4634
Himachal Pradesh	62,887	76,446	24,101	28,775	36,386	45,728	4433	5527	17,514	21,865
Jammu and Kashmir	48,709	113,499	36,935	67,761	12,582	21,969	1397	2426	15,401	32,092
Jharkhand	87,228	170,077	1380	2503	182,157	400,014	6350	22,832	4289	10,354
Karnataka	53,274	195,123	43,371	143,692	81,071	282,463	60,952	233,728	24,480	107,565
Kerala	15,139	8803	144,198	65,111	85,059	51,230	16,704	8042	51,489	26,332
Madhya Pradesh	159,245	485,482	6886	13,849	286,594	610,645	141,083	444,608	16,291	27,902
Maharashtra	8071	97,378	794	3035	73,094	281,498	26,814	290,489	1053	7399
Manipur	11,157	15,694	8632	4532	3770	4139	5524	5008	2418	3961
Meghalaya	15,284	34,309	1236	2333	5653	11,489	3115	6545	1132	2098
Mizoram	9680	19,943	451	1431	669	978	1247	1146	45	132
Nagaland	10,230	31,182	2116	1492	5195	4250	2422	1933	2326	3235
Odisha	100,955	300,250	1703	5474	59,131	203,444	18,819	73,121	2362	13,072
Punjab	12,141	15,197	1022	1451	737	972	3592	7425	2483	2725
Rajasthan	96,038	329,594	4403	15,908	77,562	209,918	15,922	65,295	18,707	51,608
Sikkim	1265	3263	683	1481	714	906	1875	1307	404	844
Tamil Nadu	49,546	76,873	1270	1429	34,490	54,179	20	698	28,543	45,246
Tripura	77,346	51,055	6145	2901	55,988	41,135	21,244	22,493	34,691	19,940
Uttar Pradesh	768,128	1,078,544	95,639	130,862	187,423	300,482	106,272	148,556	93,070	132,081
Uttrakhand	10,449	17,765	30,578	49,775	33,419	38,916	10,406	15,631	11,216	16,009
West Bengal	249,932	264,990	50,444	44,475	168,582	169,640	161,177	213,229	43,854	41,273
Grand Total	2,299,020	4,422,398	539,315	797,593	2,512,609	7,130,931	877,362	4,305,050	805,426	1,468,443

(continued)

Table 2.3 (continued)

Name of the States	Provision of irrigation facility to land owned by		Renovation of traditional water bodies		Land development		Other activity approved by MRD		Total	
	Completed	Ongoing	Completed	Ongoing	Completed	Ongoing	Completed	Ongoing	Completed	Ongoing
Andhra Pradesh	178,432	1,445,415	169,653	240,612	480,878	441,458	5292	1,596,704	2,212,581	11,278,118
Arunachal Pradesh	3	47	44	100	139	1290	214	386	3127	10,399
Assam	8934	11,325	2205	4363	8256	23,621	6631	9764	94,261	217,641
Bihar	6196	17,549	31,225	49,156	20,130	60,066	15,082	28,623	401,771	1,195,899
Chhattisgarh	149,507	99,959	42,582	50,645	146,154	130,673	3780	10,009	514,360	581,837
Goa	0	22	112	286	362	975	2	6	1207	2831
Gujarat	34,166	73,672	15,508	15,201	17,328	14,409	24,774	19,514	457,543	310,622
Haryana	221	557	2925	3114	7080	5645	1072	3447	47,666	42,177
Himachal Pradesh	18,436	25,661	10,616	9188	30,266	34,032	4210	4694	208,849	251,916
Jammu and Kashmir	1824	1475	5082	8660	16,765	34,168	2403	9454	141,098	291,504
Jharkhand	82,383	245,775	22,708	38,241	44,653	67,748	10,031	29,178	441,179	986,722
Karnataka	71,740	217,398	23,588	109,093	84,405	278,475	20,258	90,995	463,139	1,658,532
Kerala	29,605	17,765	76,302	36,574	168,587	86,313	2923	2187	590,006	302,357
Madhya Pradesh	498,100	892,407	32,280	66,484	287,962	396,537	12,998	43,320	1,441,439	2,981,234
Maharashtra	17,747	205,425	10,130	43,678	8834	27,899	3223	23,162	149,760	979,963
Manipur	121	139	1099	618	3847	4723	1191	1920	37,759	40,734
Meghalaya	60	115	2119	3164	2261	5019	547	2181	31,407	67,253
Mizoram	17	30	46	58	2288	3349	1334	1497	15,777	28,564
Nagaland	121	64	658	216	6014	2584	777	2229	29,859	47,185
Odisha	47,063	135,351	44,764	166,316	23,558	50,193	18,362	81,140	316,717	1,028,361
Punjab	5	16	6378	17,049	3761	7936	2274	2947	32,393	55,718
Rajasthan	172,731	376,559	44,095	122,296	25,862	77,916	17,756	63,047	473,076	1,312,141
Sikkim	5	16	69	105	1630	4579	265	513	6910	13,014
Tamil Nadu	2347	6579	94,071	164,219	858	6403	166	398	211,311	356,024
Tripura	6814	1340	18,781	19,106	93,243	53,383	60,708	26,940	374,960	238,293
Uttar Pradesh	346,603	293,826	115,361	123,932	236,892	254,645	139,757	228,512	2,089,145	2,691,440
Uttrakhand	1808	2025	5206	9346	9270	20,014	1053	3314	113,405	172,795
West Bengal	44,048	57,322	104,647	94,581	85,787	80,329	5850	9190	914,321	975,029
Grand Total	1,719,037	4,127,834	882,254	1,396,401	1,817,070	2,174,382	362,933	2,295,271	11,815,026	28,118,303

Source Data from NREGA website: http://nrega.nic.in

Table 2.4 Statewise works completed/progress under MGNREGA: 2006–07 to 2013–14 (amount spent in Rs. 100,000)

Name of the States	Rural connectivity		Flood control and protection		Water conservation and water harvesting		Drought proofing		Micro irrigation works	
	Completed	Ongoing	Completed	Ongoing	Completed	Ongoing	Completed	Ongoing	Completed	Ongoing
Andhra Pradesh	132,725	266,257	17,308	18,954	282,201	328,702	58,889	79,896	122,307	80,349
Arunachal Pradesh	1383	3237	741	1048	153	275	219	424	282	892
Assam	108,688	188,426	38,185	55,059	10,766	63,607	7783	16,989	8278	13,955
Bihar	414,436	265,008	29,648	28,787	70,108	67,018	24,017	146,007	35,634	40,763
Chhattisgarh	189,845	266,619	7144	11,864	80,890	95,590	31,874	443,472	25,463	49,101
Goa	384	178	290	230	24	17	0	0	18	7
Gujarat	44,619	38,911	17,889	20,588	45,145	27,900	10,049	14,140	1869	1712
Haryana	28,805	23,321	2057	2014	13,752	11,771	2169	769	9819	4868
Himachal Pradesh	43,124	53,692	19,489	19,885	22,703	19,937	2933	2551	14,389	14,935
Jammu & Kashmir	39,209	40,364	28,128	21,422	7055	5477	914	875	10,383	10,858
Jharkhand	92,222	135,953	2036	2832	122,054	180,601	4063	18,906	5187	7947
Karnataka	72,874	111,914	70,909	96,820	79,803	110,186	31,858	63,520	27,821	52,467
Kerala	7193	2764	55,282	17,589	53,313	19,692	8909	2461	23,383	7705
Madhya Pradesh	329,666	526,028	14,158	11,208	232,843	363,973	44,279	115,125	15,435	26,266
Maharashtra	23,480	135,098	1471	5013	105,266	372,686	561,301	403,847	356	1979
Manipur	52,343	51,823	14,394	7630	10,172	8995	9178	8011	12,551	16,832
Meghalaya	35,180	39,596	3372	3721	6649	7094	4198	4048	1996	1701
Mizoram	43,902	50,391	832	504	2040	1428	3223	785	152	129
Nagaland	83,294	78,581	7887	2669	6703	3401	5347	3542	9094	3642
Odisha	90,800	229,009	1571	4121	27,037	117,620	4340	29,316	2797	9215
Punjab	11,910	14,523	1709	2434	713	882	1489	2176	1563	2155
Rajasthan	220,979	693,470	9844	33,745	154,238	391,973	18,943	90,645	30,671	83,176
Sikkim	1938	4903	1219	2592	213	1096	598	938	658	1073
Tamil Nadu	126,183	152,188	3794	4171	105,413	130,905	49	219	82,856	98,477
Tripura	105,375	40,610	8903	1777	44,592	10,334	21,975	10,685	23,755	8739
Uttar Pradesh	636,707	587,497	71,143	67,109	187,913	180,279	52,125	53,527	43,800	52,641
Uttrakhand	6524	7532	27,466	29,465	20,189	15,053	7482	6635	10,329	9955
West Bengal	333,576	242,484	69,105	58,808	183,097	102,444	42,802	37,740	54,901	32,219
Grand Total	3,277,363	4,250,378	525,972	532,059	1,875,045	2,638,938	961,004	1,557,250	575,747	633,759

Table 2.4 (continued)

Name of the States	Provision of irrigation facility to land owned by		Renovation of traditional water bodies		Land development		Any other activity approved by MRD		Total	
	Completed	Ongoing	Completed	Ongoing	Completed	Ongoing	Completed	Ongoing	Completed	Ongoing
Andhra Pradesh	120,024	214,876	240,826	167,178	149,580	97,842	3896	38,956	1,127,756	1,293,011
Arunachal Pradesh	3	0	62	54	79	716	46	78	2969	6724
Assam	1603	2048	6026	9393	16,037	33,950	6407	9531	203,773	392,958
Bihar	7007	8901	32,091	35,311	21,683	29,415	11,923	20,743	646,546	641,953
Chhattisgarh	38,601	27,644	88,391	92,205	48,461	41,113	1379	8085	512,048	1,035,693
Goa	0	5	73	69	413	259	2	0	1203	765
Gujarat	11,617	21,810	15,241	7399	4383	4396	4480	19,471	155,292	156,326
Haryana	247	279	4756	5118	10,580	8523	2897	7980	75,082	64,644
Himachal Pradesh	9951	6714	5651	4797	16,804	12,986	2194	2098	137,238	137,596
Jammu & Kashmir	1166	453	2657	2331	14,603	11,981	2322	6100	106,438	99,862
Jharkhand	58,311	91,997	15,621	20,100	15,845	21,476	3566	18,536	318,906	498,349
Karnataka	21,115	28,382	26,350	45,423	50,561	73,015	15,859	41,760	397,151	623,488
Kerala	21,615	8298	35,249	12,172	123,831	36,485	1643	757	330,418	107,924
Madhya Pradesh	251,448	281,179	34,364	44,473	65,988	99,762	2918	5302	991,099	1,473,316
Maharashtra	15,463	65,294	48,930	47,750	6711	8404	1315	8234	764,294	1,048,306
Manipur	146	450	3909	1000	15,029	11,385	5298	4079	123,020	110,205
Meghalaya	62	88	1750	1748	4595	5419	2149	5292	59,952	68,707
Mizoram	328	433	71	71	5603	3087	4370	1817	60,519	58,646
Nagaland	447	12	755	204	8457	3884	5237	5263	127,221	101,200
Odisha	7342	13,821	22,210	72,317	3636	7425	21,411	66,590	181,143	549,434
Punjab	4	2	8070	18,119	4193	6224	2067	4876	31,718	51,392
Rajasthan	73,072	127,180	89,451	256,152	25,410	64,214	30,560	61,335	653,169	1,801,890
Sikkim	7	10	23	105	1338	2443	69	178	6062	13,339
Tamil Nadu	1503	2729	301,011	432,977	933	3639	585	366	622,328	825,671
Tripura	4496	518	10,315	2200	62,512	13,467	29,255	20,769	311,177	109,099
Uttar Pradesh	61,344	45,349	164,895	98,327	100,240	82,516	44,239	55,867	1,362,405	1,223,110
Uttrakhand	733	581	3347	2563	9547	10,685	588	1813	86,204	84,282
West Bengal	30,332	14,402	138,552	73,727	69,451	42,493	3438	5833	925,255	610,149
Grand Total	737,989	963,455	1,300,648	1,453,281	856,503	737,205	210,115	421,713	10,320,386	13,188,037

Source Data from NREGA website: http://nrega.nic.in

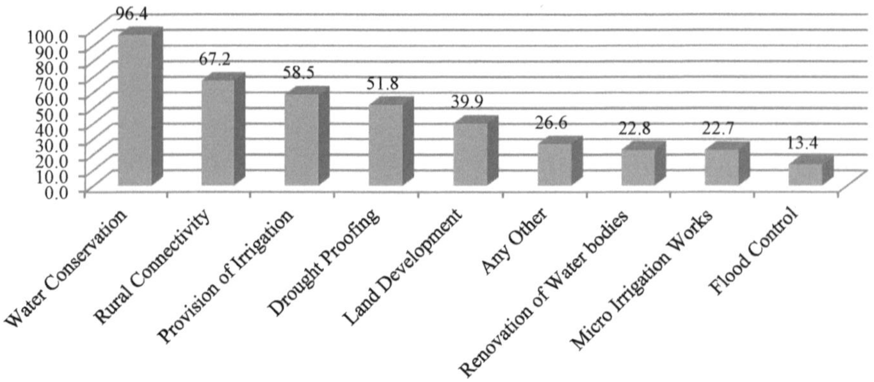

Fig. 2.7 Numbers of works undertaken under MGNREGA during 2006–07 to 2013–14 (lakh)

undertaken during the entire period. Uttar Pradesh was second with 48 lakh works followed by Madhya Pradesh (44 lakh works). Karnataka, Rajasthan, West Bengal, Bihar, Jharkhand and Odisha fall in the middle order with a number of projects ranging between 20 and 10 lakh. The states that lie in the lower stratum included Meghalaya, Nagaland, Punjab, Haryana and Manipur with numbers of projects between 50 and 100 thousand, while Mizoram, Sikkim, Arunachal Pradesh and Goa had less than 50 thousand projects.

Glancing through the total budget spent on the completed and ongoing projects by different states as presented in Table 2.4, it may be noted that Uttar Pradesh topped the list with a total budget of ₹ 26 thousand crore, closely followed by Madhya Pradesh, Rajasthan and Andhra Pradesh with almost similar amount spent on all projects at the aggregate. Maharashtra, Chhattisgarh, West Bengal, Tamil Nadu and Bihar spent slightly less each varying between ₹ 13 thousand and 18 thousand crore. Nagaland, Manipur, Uttarakhand, Jammu & Kashmir, Meghalaya, Haryana and Mizoram spent only around or less than two thousand crore each, while Punjab, Sikkim, Arunachal Pradesh and Goa lie at the bottom with less than one thousand crore spent on MGNREGA during the period.

The expenditure incurred on the completed and ongoing projects was not exactly similar to that of allocation of projects in different states indicating cost differences across the projects as well as per project cost across states. While an average amount of around ₹ 59 thousand was spent per project at the aggregate level, the highest amount per project was spent on the renovation of traditional water bodies, ie. ₹ 121 thousand. It was followed by ₹ 112 thousand per project on rural connectivity. Flood control was in the third place with an expenditure of ₹ 79 thousand per project. Micro irrigation had a spending of ₹ 53 thousand per project followed by drought proofing ₹ 49 thousand per project, water conservation ₹ 47 thousand per project, land development ₹ 40 thousand per project and provision of irrigation ₹ 29 thousand per project (Fig. 2.8).

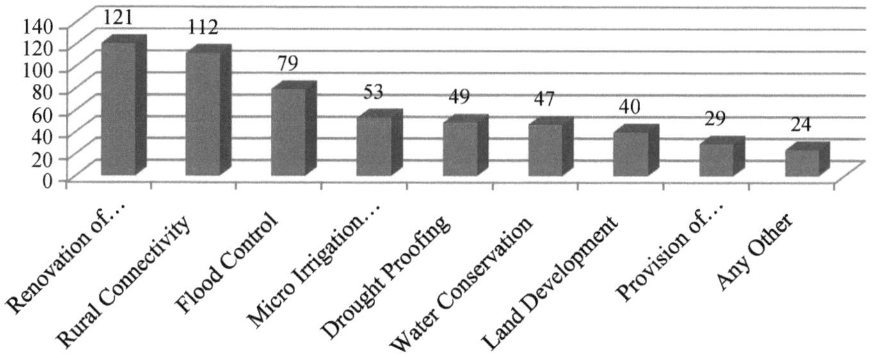

Fig. 2.8 Amount spent under MGNREGA (₹1000 per project) during 2006–07 to 2013–14 (₹1000 per project)

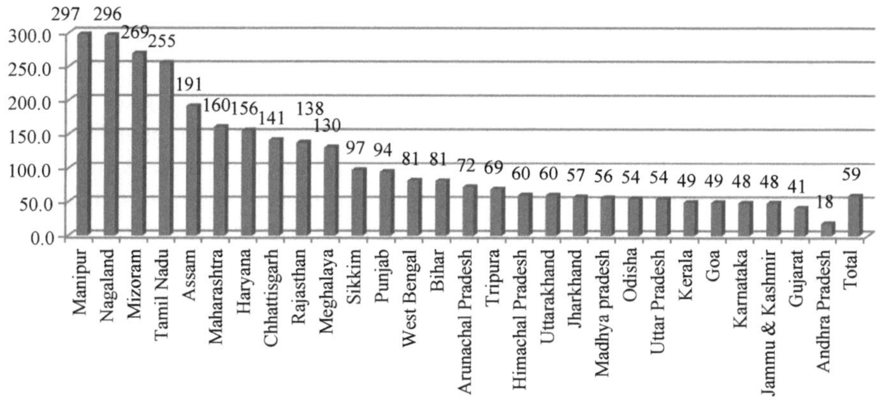

Fig. 2.9 Statewise amount spent under MGNREGA during 2006–07 to 2013–14

Thus, while water conservation topped in the total numbers of projects undertaken, the spending on per project was much less on water conservation compared to rural connectivity that topped among all projects not only in the total amount spent but also amount spent per project. Statewise total expenditure per project (aggregate of all categories) is presented in Fig. 2.9. Highest amount per project was spent in Manipur (₹ 297 thousand), followed by Nagaland (₹ 245 thousand), Mizoram (₹ 269 thousand), Tamil Nadu (₹ 255 thousand), Assam (₹ 191 thousand) and Maharashtra (₹ 160 thousand). The states that were at the bottom in spending per project were Andhra Pradesh (₹ 18 thousand), Gujarat (₹ 41 thousand), Karnataka and Goa (₹ 48 thousand), Kerala (₹ 49 thousand) and Uttar Pradesh (₹ 54 thousand) only.

2.3.3 *Performance of MGNREGA—Some Qualitative Indicators*

Table 2.5 provides details of social auditing and inspection carried out for MGNREGA work in different states in India. The Gram Panchayats open muster rolls to carry out registration of workers demanding employment under MGNREGA. These muster rolls are verified under social auditing. During 2008–09 to 2013–14 (up to October), a total number of 10.52 crore muster rolls were opened at the aggregate (all states) out of which around 85% were verified by the authorities who carried out the auditing work. The verification process was more than 70% in all the states except West Bengal, where it was only 59%. Social auditing of MGNREGA work of the Gram Panchayats (GP) was held in around 87% of the GPs during 2008–09 to 2013–14. The social audit was held in above 90% GPs in Tamil Nadu, Madhya Pradesh, Kerala and Nagaland, whereas, it was held in less than 60% GPs in Arunachal Pradesh, around 60–65% GPs in Jammu & Kashmir and Karnataka.

As regards the inspection of the MGNREGA works taken up by GPs, it is mandated that regular inspections are conducted both at the district and block levels. In this regard, the percentage of works inspected at the district level was very low, ie. only 12%, whereas the works inspected at the block level were as high as 81% during the period. Almost half of the works were inspected at the district level in Arunachal Pradesh while the proportion of inspected works was half to one-third in Assam, Sikkim, Nagaland and Kerala. In rest of the states, less than one-third works were being inspected at the district level. On the other hand, West Bengal, Uttar Pradesh and Maharashtra had less than half of the works inspected at the block level. In Rajasthan, Chhattisgarh and Tamil Nadu almost all the works taken were being inspected at the block level, while in rest of the states, more than half to three-fourth works taken up were inspected at the block level.

Complaint redressed system was adopted under MGNREGA and a total number of 215,542 complaints were registered in all the states during the period of analysis, out of which, around 84% were redressed. Complaint redressed was 100% in Goa, Arunachal Pradesh and Mizoram. It was less than 80% in Madhya Pradesh, Maharashtra, Odisha, West Bengal and Gujarat while in rest of the states; over 80% complaints were redressed. MGNREGA not only provides employment to the households but also brings awareness among the households.

The efforts are being made to bring more transparency in the payment system. The Gram Panchayats are encouraged to make payments to the workers through banks or post office. The number of active bank accounts exceeded 20 crore on individual accounts and 3 crore on joint accounts during the period. Similarly, the active post office accounts during the same years exceeded 15 crore on individual accounts and around 1.8 crore on joint accounts. Thus, a total number of 41 crore individual and joint accounts in post offices and banks were operative through which payments were made for MGNREGA works (Table 2.6).

Table 2.5 Social auditing and inspection of MGNREGA work (2008–09 to 2013–14)

Name of the State	Must roll verified		Social audit		Inspections conducted			Gram Sabha held			Complaints	
	No. of muster rolls used	% of muster rolls verified	Total Gram Panchayats	% of GP where social audit held	Total works taken up	%of Works inspected at district level	% of Works inspected at block level	Total Gram Panchayats	No. of Gram Sabhas held	No. of VMC meetings held	No. of complaints received	%of Complaints disposed
Andhra Pradesh	15,256,472	91.33	22,025	84.92	2,961,546	9.14	91.27	22,025	21,232	7112	9486	96.38
Arunachal Pradesh	19,312	99.41	313	58.93	2437	45.38	90.07	313	189	124	5	100.00
Assam	2,215,732	82.28	1886	88.13	111,733	35.71	101.51	1904	5742	3121	1687	90.16
Bihar	6,848,974	84.91	5307	91.83	548,555	9.00	60.85	5137	16,948	16,902	13,720	61.81
Chhattisgarh	7,364,510	82.78	8089	92.44	684,369	19.20	87.53	9544	12,046	5110	11,625	85.28
Goa	7370	94.67	142	73.54	1806	8.75	89.04	172	411	22	4	100.00
Gujarat	2,264,472	97.37	13,777	93.28	612,509	9.86	95.13	14,744	20,008	17,301	4708	79.25
Haryana	446,733	98.66	5979	60.27	80,898	9.21	73.07	5535	6683	3299	661	88.05
Himachal Pradesh	950,859	86.54	4430	80.45	301,485	13.38	85.44	2903	7576	13,166	2633	85.83
Jammu and Kashmir	607,317	85.80	2548	65.55	170,958	17.08	76.87	2563	3087	2834	1893	96.20
Jharkhand	6,210,689	92.21	4445	122.64	899,744	16.14	71.40	5073	23,270	19,340	6447	90.65
Karnataka	1,429,346	88.71	4041	60.02	822,657	11.89	76.04	4094	4398	1897	3264	87.38
Kerala	2,470,199	88.82	2242	77.26	331,141	31.07	90.47	2583	16,105	19,947	1536	91.02
Madhya Pradesh	8,694,851	87.32	21,544	91.39	2,834,452	13.11	93.46	20,784	52,174	34,859	28,621	73.58
Maharashtra	925,445	88.05	18,179	79.97	194,925	11.17	52.03	18,752	23,614	9713	468	73.93
Manipur	808,504	88.05	2029	94.68	27,634	27.46	74.17	2402	3590	3006	1184	89.95
Meghalaya	763,359	86.82	1602	71.28	43,016	14.33	83.83	1681	3392	3160	1050	86.00
Mizoram	230,216	103.95	585	71.26	12,817	30.77	99.42	570	600	990	138	98.55

(continued)

Table 2.5 (continued)

Name of the State	Must roll verified		Social audit		Inspections conducted			Gram Sabha held			Complaints	
	No. of muster rolls used	% of muster rolls verified	Total Gram Panchayats	% of GP where social audit held	Total works taken up	%of Works inspected at district level	% of Works inspected at block level	Total Gram Panchayats	No. of Gram Sabhas held	No. of VMC meetings held	No. of complaints received	%of Complaints disposed
Nagaland	100,110	93.63	1109	99.44	37,598	33.88	82.44	1160	1776	1661	48	68.75
Odisha	5,445,318	86.54	7373	95.68	1,050,512	15.03	74.17	6178	8104	13,201	8646	79.26
Punjab	295,491	91.33	9439	95.71	54,264	20.11	83.85	9591	11,209	5024	630	81.43
Rajasthan	14,962,913	97.64	7337	90.11	841,546	19.90	148.12	7083	7435	9531	45,460	85.44
Sikkim	38,747	97.90	161	69.16	9046	33.00	96.29	164	431	34	5	80.00
Tamil Nadu	2,287,101	100.01	13,293	107.47	267,117	14.36	99.70	14,272	29,826	2513	2332	97.73
Tripura	2,008,475	88.54	1039	89.15	254,039	11.56	49.87	1039	1019	3538	190	86.32
Uttar Pradesh	13,824,894	71.40	45,966	82.56	2,325,857	10.46	53.90	38,098	36,637	33,994	61,460	90.21
Uttrakhand	1,250,775	73.07	5869	88.17	157,424	11.42	64.96	5869	5767	6418	1540	87.34
West Bengal	7,454,365	59.25	6322	71.73	803,781	3.59	37.17	3276	4908	2852	6101	78.45
Total	105,182,549	85.46	204,191	87.06	16,443,866	12.75	81.06	194,419	312,577	231,023	215,542	84.13

Source Data from NREGA website: http://nrega.nic.in

Table 2.6 The MGNREGA payment processed through banks/post office (2008–09 to 2012–13)

State	No. of active bank account during the financial year 2008–12		Amount of wages disbursed through bank accounts (in lakhs.)	No. of active post office account for financial year 2008–12		Amount of wages disbursed through post office accounts (in lakhs.)	Total no. of accounts use during the financial year 2008–12 (No).			Total amount disbursed (in lakhs.)
	Individual	Joint		Individual	Joint		Individual	Joint	Total	
Andhra Pradesh	22,125,456	0	394,046.94	42,043,964	0	808,835.74	64,169,420	0	64,169,420	1,202,882.7
Arunachal Pradesh	21,494	24,469	677.54	11,695	8630	299.45	33,189	33,099	66,288	977
Assam	5,703,034	197,343	95,646.95	5,010,532	119,764	62,480.54	10,713,566	317,107	11,030,673	158,127
Bihar	6,479,061	333,180	45,795.39	23,157,465	660,261	280,992.25	29,636,526	993,441	30,629,967	326,788
Chhattisgarh	11,407,540	73,186	187,901.99	16,491,178	211,570	201,899.95	27,898,718	284,756	28,183,474	389,802
Goa	34,475	77	1165.9	0	0	0	34,475	77	34,552	1166
Gujarat	1,932,740	2,610,942	59,221.44	4,940,075	4,575,279	114,429.75	6,872,815	7,186,221	14,059,036	173,651
Haryana	857,602	732,424	61,864.24	62,872	58,554	3581.33	920,474	790,978	1,711,452	65,446
Himachal Pradesh	3,439,016	194,048	122,274.09	285,601	15,419	9980.15	3,724,617	209,467	3,934,084	132,254
J& K	1,584,941	59,762	61,997.69	11,646	3466	533.01	1,596,587	63,228	1,659,815	62,531
Jharkhand	4,098,462	626,363	81,722.79	9,735,868	1,321,331	243,991.71	13,834,330	1,947,694	15,782,024	325,715
Karnataka	11,897,536	3,528,235	442,482.38	2,031,841	3,030,668	73,287.31	13,929,377	6,558,903	20,488,280	515,770
Kerala	5,218,247	1894	176,256.46	290,630	382	7471.65	5,508,877	2276	5,511,153	183,728
Madhya Pradesh	22,075,781	8,598,461	747,073.59	3,368,858	1,416,761	125,028.63	25,444,639	10,015,222	35,459,861	872,102
Maharashtra	3,083,926	217,317	64,163.93	4,246,868	139,114	106,456.36	7,330,794	356,431	7,687,225	170,620
Manipur	359,537	5909	37,000.36	574,904	0	19,801.65	934,441	5909	940,350	56,802
Meghalaya	151,475	37,389	32,651.95	188,854	18,465	5044.47	340,329	55,854	396,183	37,696
Mizoram	82,809	62,108	14,139.42	138,069	159,825	18,904.43	220,878	221,933	442,811	33,044
Nagaland	0	4591	110,752.64	0	0	0	0	4591	4591	110,753
Odisha	7,748,786	706,114	124,108.73	4,112,687	1,291,956	93,912.53	11,861,473	1,998,070	13,859,543	218,021

(continued)

Table 2.6 (continued)

State	No. of active bank account during the financial year 2008–12		Amount of wages disbursed through bank accounts (in lakhs.)	No. of active post office account for financial year 2008–12		Amount of wages disbursed through post office accounts (in lakhs.)	Total no. of accounts use during the financial year 2008–12 (No).			Total amount disbursed (in lakhs.)
	Individual	Joint		Individual	Joint		Individual	Joint	Total	
Punjab	1,408,591	283,549	25,740.76	418,789	47,440	7120.67	1,827,380	330,989	2,158,369	32,861
Rajasthan	16,310,043	3,749,423	622,331.03	22,460,108	1,292,003	493,892.13	38,770,151	5,041,426	43,811,577	1,116,223
Sikkim	156,091	18,419	11,459.04	100,201	11,881	5284.05	256,292	30,300	286,592	16,743
Tamil Nadu	35,021,217	523,462	11,566.79	8875	2408	0	35,030,092	525,870	35,555,962	11,567
Tripura	271,203	1,212,990	59,151.96	202,405	372,610	20,073.81	473,608	1,585,600	2,059,208	79,226
Uttar Pradesh	33,039,242	2,780,426	1,221,270.1	761,804	48,979	28,893.86	33,801,046	2,829,405	36,630,451	1,250,164
Uttrakhand	3,060,330	325,669	63,417.57	654,146	57,462	18,522.96	3,714,476	383,131	4,097,607	81,941
West Bengal	11,527,289	3,879,158	247,013.49	14,573,671	3,148,637	258,281.34	26,100,960	7,027,795	33,128,755	505,295
Total	209,095,924	30,786,908	5,122,895.1	155,883,606	18,012,865	3,008,999.7	364,979,530	48,799,773	413,779,303	8,131,895

Source Data NREGA website: http://nrega.nic.in; Unit = Rs. One lakh = Rs. 100,000

Looking at the statewise performance, the highest number of bank and post office accounts were operative in Andhra Pradesh (6.4 crore), Rajasthan (4.4 crore), Uttar Pradesh (3.7 crore), Tamil Nadu (3.6 crore) and Madhya Pradesh (3.5 crore) during the reporting period. The north-eastern states, namely Manipur, Meghalaya, Mizoram, Nagaland, Sikkim and Arunachal Pradesh were at the bottom having less than 10 lakh accounts in operation for MGNREGA.

The more important issue is how much amount was being paid through these accounts under MGNREGA. Table 2.6 also presents the amount disbursed through bank/post office for making MGNREGA payments to the households employed. A total sum of ₹ 81 thousand crore were disbursed through banks and post offices during the period, out of which, ₹ 51 thousand crore (63%) were through banks and ₹ 30 thousand crore (37%) through the post offices. Statewise, the highest amount was disbursed by Uttar Pradesh (₹ 12.5 thousand crore), followed by Andhra Pradesh (around ₹ 12 thousand crore), Rajasthan (₹ 11 thousand crore), Madhya Pradesh (₹ 9 thousand crore) and Karnataka (around ₹ 5 thousand crore). Arunachal Pradesh in North East was at the bottom in disbursal of total amount through banks and post offices.

It is interesting to note that out of the total amount paid through banks and post offices in MGNREGA, the average amount paid through bank/post office per account was ₹ 1.97 lakh. Statewise, the highest amount paid per account was in Nagaland (₹ 24 lakh), Meghalaya (₹ 9.5 lakh), Mizoram (₹ 6 lakh), Sikkim (₹ 5.8 lakh) and Tripura (₹ 3.8 lakh). The lowest amount was paid in Tamil Nadu (only ₹ three thousand), Bihar (₹ 1 lakh) and Gujarat (₹ 1.2 lakh).

Table 2.7 shows the unemployment allowance paid to the households in lieu of not being able to provide employment to them after having registered a household's name for MGNREGA work. According to the legislation on MGNREGA, if a member of a household has not been provided employment after issuing him/her a job card after a lapse of 15 days, the GPs are supposed to provide unemployment allowance and such amount would be borne by the concerned state government. Following this rule, during the period 2007–08 to 2013–14 (up to October) unemployment allowance was due for 4.83 crore person days for which employment was not provided to the job card holders.

However, there was hardly any unemployment allowance paid to the job card holders as only in West Bengal, Nagaland, Karnataka, Tamil Nadu, Uttar Pradesh and few other unemployment allowances were paid for few days. Even in the states where some unemployment allowance was paid, the amount paid per day was much less than the stipulated minimum wages set by the states, except the case of Tamil Nadu. However, it is interesting to note that the allowance paid even in those states was only a small fraction of the total number of days for which unemployment allowance was due. At the aggregate, out of 4.83 crore days for which unemployment allowance was due only 2478 days of allowance was paid that makes only 0.01% days of unemployment allowance paid and it was not more than 0.04% in any state.

Table 2.7 Unemployment allowances paid in lieu of not providing employment (2007–08 to 2013–14)

Sl. No.	State	Unemployment allowance due	Unemployment allowance paid		Amount paid Rs. per day	% Days for which unemployment allowance paid
		No. of days	No. of days	Amount (in Rs.)		
1	Andhra Pradesh	0	0	0	0	0.00
2	Arunachal Pradesh	1,547,352	0	0	0	0.00
3	Assam	37,064	0	0	0	0.00
4	Bihar	1,270,148	0	0	0	0.00
5	Chhattisgarh	1,111,264	0	0	0	0.00
6	Goa	83,088	19	1438.5	76	0.02
7	Gujarat	692,117	19	1820	96	0.00
8	Haryana	18,930	0	0	0	0.00
9	Himachal Pradesh	621,270	12	1320	110	0.00
10	Jammu & Kashmir	4,889,440	33	1146	35	0.00
11	Jharkhand	129,936	0	0	0	0.00
12	Karnataka	745,276	322	10,836	34	0.04
13	Kerala	775,611	31	1038	33	0.00
14	Madhya Pradesh	627,763	21	1214	58	0.00
15	Maharashtra	413,621	0	0	0	0.00
16	Manipur	1,238,993	0	0	0	0.00
17	Meghalaya	276,807	0	0	0	0.00
18	Mizoram	1,342,045	0	0	0	0.00
19	Nagaland	2,080,547	663	11,620	18	0.03
20	Odisha	226,004	0	0	0	0.00
21	Punjab	3,358,232	71	6238	88	0.00
22	Rajasthan	680,960	15	1200	80	0.00
23	Sikkim	145,014	0	0	0	0.00

(continued)

Table 2.7 (continued)

Sl. No.	State	Unemployment allowance due	Unemployment allowance paid		Amount paid Rs. per day	% Days for which unemployment allowance paid
		No. of days	No. of days	Amount (in Rs.)		
24	Tamil Nadu	862,564	282	99,924	354	0.03
25	Tripura	74,405	6	600	100	0.01
26	Uttar Pradesh	690,635	218	24,620	113	0.03
27	Uttrakhand	6,012,677	7	430	61	0.00
28	West Bengal	18,409,904	759	16,574.5	22	0.00
	Total	48,361,667	2478	180,019	73	0.01

Source Data from NREGA website: http://nrega.nic.in

2.4 Performance of MGNREGA—Some Field Observations

In this section, we present some observations based on field survey data and group discussion carried out across seven states from the North, South and Western parts of the country. Table 2.8 presents a summary of the observations obtained from the surveyed states during the year 2009–10. According to the secondary sources, on average, around 40–50 days of employment was generated per household in each selected state. However, the selected households obtained more number of days compared to the estimates provided by the government sources. Among our selected households, 100 days employment was obtained by the households in Maharashtra, 94 days in Haryana, 92 days in Himachal Pradesh, above 80 days in Rajasthan and Gujarat, 76 days in Karnataka and 54 days in Punjab (Fig. 2.10).

The secondary sources indicated that out of all the projects taken up during the last three years (from 2008 to 2011), the completion rate varied from 17 to 60% in different states as the works undertaken involved 1–2 years, such as programmes like watershed management, water conservation and microirrigation. Those households who obtained work worked for few days to maximum of 100 days and the percentage of households who obtained work for 100 days varied from less than 2% in Punjab to 24% in Rajasthan (Fig. 2.11). The households who register for work under MGNREGA, if not provided work, are supposed to be compensated with unemployment allowance. But except a few cases in Maharashtra and Karnataka, none of the households were given unemployment allowance although in all the states the amount was reported to be due for payment for such households.

Now, turning to the observations obtained from the household survey, on an average, the size of the family working in MGNREGA averaged around 5 members out of which, 1–2 members were found working in MGNREGA for some time period. The share of female in the household members working in MGNREGA was less than half in some of the states while in others it was recorded more than half, e.g. in Rajasthan, Gujarat and Punjab. The percentage share of work obtained by the selected households under MGNREGA varied from 12% (lowest) to 25% (highest). Similarly, the share of wages obtained from MGNREGA in the total income of the beneficiary households was 9–28% (Fig. 2.12).

Thus, we find that MGNREGA succeeded in providing some livelihood security to the households at the crunch situation when getting work elsewhere becomes difficult because of the ongoing off-season in agriculture and related activities. Providing some employment opportunities to the households during such periods to maintain their food and livelihood security has been the basic objective of MGNREGA programme.

Although wage rate paid under MGNREGA was observed slightly less than the stipulated Minimum Wage Rate as declared by the legislation in different states, except Himachal Pradesh, there was no difference in the wage rate paid to the male and female workers (Fig. 2.13). On the other hand, wages in the open market differ quite substantially and female wage is sometimes found less than half of that

Table 2.8 Summary of finding in seven states—primary survey data

	Parameter	Karnataka	Maharashtra	Rajasthan	Himachal Pradesh	Gujarat	Haryana	Punjab
12	Family size (no of members per household) of beneficiaries	5.29	5.13	5.43	4.28	5.52	5.59	4.72
13	Proportion of household occupation from MGNREGA (%)	12.2	20.3	17.7	19.1	12.0	24.6	21.3
14	Proportion of household income from MGNREGA (%)	11.4	28.5	13.1	10.6	9.3	25.1	17.6
15	Total number of persons per household employed in MGNREGA	1.81	1.88	1.41	1.12	2.31	1.73	1.10
16	Number of female per household employed in MGNREGA	0.78	0.94	0.81	0.45	1.32	0.62	0.27
17	Number of days per household employed in MGNREGA	76	100	82	92	81	94	54
18	No of days female employed in MGNREGA	32	52	52	45	49	29	51
19	Percentage of selected households completed 100 days	24.9	30.7	44.5	42.5	5.0	48.5	–
20	Average wage rate in MGNREGA—Male	86.00	95.96	78.90	110	88.73	150	123
21	Average wage rate in MGNREGA—Female	85.00	87.60	80.00	110	86.51	150	123
22	Stipulated minimum wage	119	100–120	100	110	100	162	137
23	No of members migrated because not getting work in MGNREGA	0.08	0.31	0.44	0.19	0.06	0.00	0.00

(continued)

Table 2.8 (continued)

	Parameter	Karnataka	Maharashtra	Rajasthan	Himachal Pradesh	Gujarat	Haryana	Punjab
24	No of members migrated back after getting work in MGNREGA	0.07	0.11	0.18	0.05	0.05	0.00	0.00
25	HHs better off after migrating to work in MGNREGA (%)	63.6	67.7	50.0	100.0	77.8	–	–
26	MGNREGA successful in cutting down labour migration	44.9	37.3	75.0	100.0	41.5	84.5	34.0
26	MGNREGA successful in providing food security	54.7	77.5	99.5	100.0	48.0	67.0	42.0
27	MGNREGA successful in providing extra purchasing power	35.0	28.0	92.5	100.0	51.5	83.0	46.0
28	After MGNREGA there has been shortage of ag.labour (% of villages)	70.0	70.0	50.0	60.0	70.0	40.0	60.0
29	MGNREGA has led to increase in cost of agriculture production (% villages)	100.0	90.0	100.0	100.0	100.0	20.0	40.0

Source Field survey

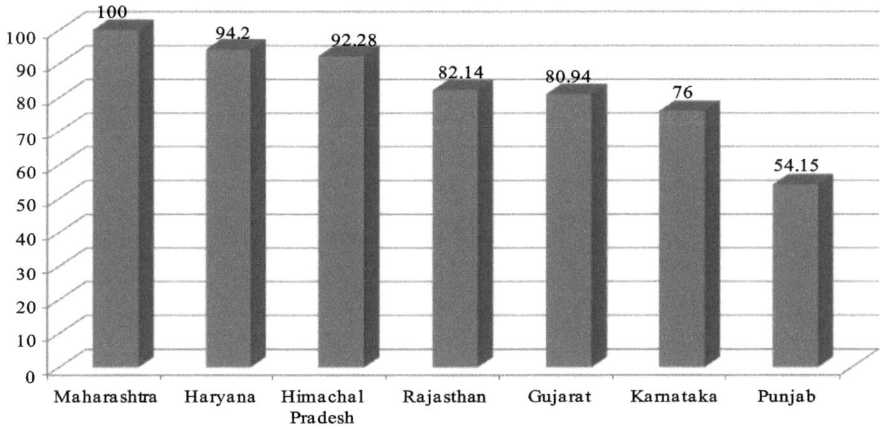

Fig. 2.10 Employment generated per household under MGNREGA (no of days). *Source* Field survey

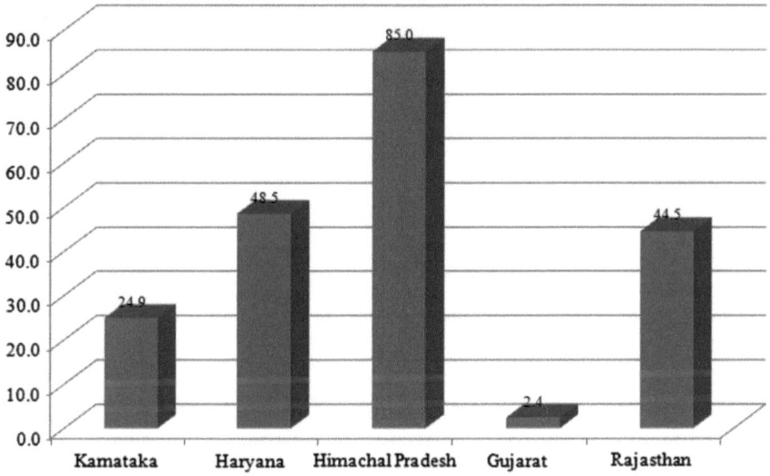

Fig. 2.11 Percentage of households employed 100 days. *Source* Field survey

obtained by the male for the same kind of activities. Thus, MGNREGA has succeeded in bringing down the incidence of exploitation of female labour on the work site by offering them equal remuneration as per that of male workers. Further, in order to check the impact of MGNEREGA on household migration from rural to urban areas, we enquired about the number of household members migrating to other places in search of job and whether there are incidences where members of these families are returning back to work under MGNREGA attracted by the availability of work within the residence premises and henceforth not migrating in search of job.

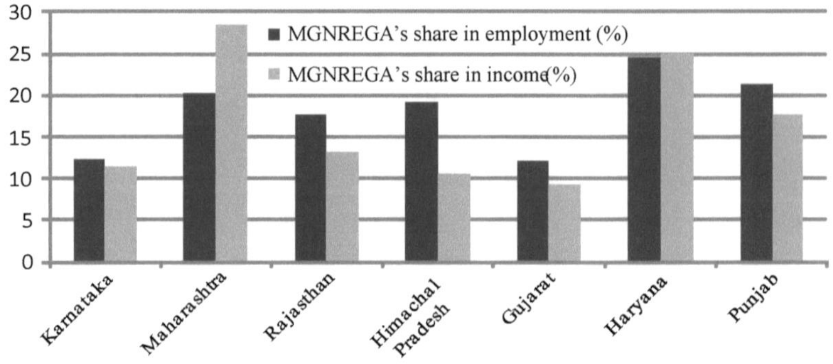

Fig. 2.12 MGNREGA's share in employment and income (%). *Source* Field survey

Fig. 2.13 Wage rate obtained under MGNREGA (Rs). *Source* Field survey

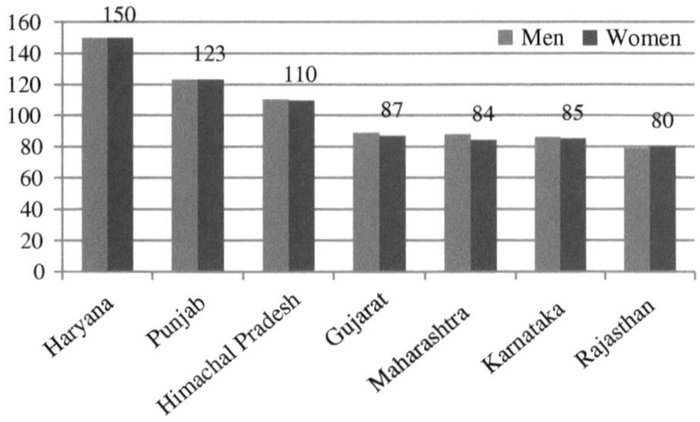

Our results showed that there are some instances where few members are still migrating to the city with the lure of getting better wage rate there. There were also instances where household members returned back to work under MGNREGA after employment opportunities were available within their villages. However, since the incidences of members migrating in search of a better job in cities and members returning back to the village to work in MGNREGA were found with no significant difference, it is difficult to conclude whether MGNREGA has been successful in arresting migration of households to cities in search of work. However, those members who returned back to work in MGNREGA after the beginning of this programme significantly indicated that they have been better off after relocating to the village and getting employment within the village.

In response to our question whether MGNREGA has been successful in providing food security to the households in the villages by providing them extra purchasing power, a majority of them agreed with their consent to the above question. This was also confirmed by the villagers with whom we had a special group discussion in each selected village. However, there was an overwhelming opposite view in the village against the MGNREGA programme.

The farming community in the village was of the opinion that since much of the local labour force is engaged by MGNREGA programme for working in non-farming activities, they were finding it difficult to get labour for agricultural purposes especially in the peak sowing and harvesting seasons. Majority of villagers indicated that after implementation of MGNREGA programme, there has been shortage of labour force in agriculture sector and thereby leading to an increase in labour and ultimately production cost in the agriculture sector that might affect adversely the food production and food security in the long run. The solution to the above problem is to undertake MGNREGA activities only during the lean agricultural season and bringing the farming related activities under the MGNREGA programme.

2.5 Concluding Remarks

In the three phases of MGNREGA implementation in India from 2006–07 to 2013–14 (up to October) 81 crore households were issued job cards across the states, out of which, around 34 crore households were provided employment averaging around 4.5 crore households. Indeed, this is a commendable achievement, as the coverage under MGNREGA constitutes roughly around 30% of the rural households in the country as a whole. A total number of 1.5 thousand crore man-days of employment was generated during the reference period.

Out of the total person days generated, the share of Scheduled Castes and Scheduled Tribes was 27 and 22%, respectively, while the share of women in the total employment was 48.0%. The undivided Andhra Pradesh topped in the generation of total person days, followed by Rajasthan, Uttar Pradesh Madhya Pradesh, Tamil Nadu and West Bengal. A total number of 45 person days of employment was provided under MGNREGA during the period, while the target set under the programme is 100 days of employment per household.

The surveyed villages present a mixed picture with some villages having perfect infrastructure like road, post office, bank, SHG, school, primary health centre, FPS, etc. while others had to travel some distance to approach the same. During the last ten years, there has been a slight change in the occupation structure in the selected villages. The prevailing wage rates in agriculture were fluctuating widely. Increase in wage rate in agriculture more than most of the other activities within the village indicate the enhanced demand for wage labourers due to employment works in MGNREGA that goes parallel with the agriculture sector thereby causing a competition in the labour market for the agriculture sector.

Increases in charges for agricultural operations per acre on an average were almost similar to increase in agricultural wages as overall wages observed an increase of around 49% compared to around 46% increase in the cost of per acre agricultural operations as per our group discussion data. A majority of the villages indicated shortage of agricultural labour, which has increased after the implementation of MGNREGA. In majority of the villages the shortage of labour was observed during the sowing and harvesting months of kharif and rabi seasons especially in the months of July, August and September and March and April. This was more so after the implementation of MGNREGA. A majority of villagers were of the view that after MGNREGA implementation cost of production in agriculture has increased by 10–20% because of the scarcity of labour.

On the question, whether workers who earlier migrated out of the village to work in the city are now coming back to work in MGNREGA, the trend of villagers returning back to the village to work in MGNREGA was found more prevalent in Himachal Pradesh and Karnataka while reverse was the case in Gujarat. But a majority of participants in the discussion indicated that MGNREGA has not made any significant changes in the migration pattern in the village.

Another point of debate was how the MGNREGA has affected living standards of villagers, a clear majority indicated that MGNREGA has not been successful in raising their living standards or their consumption level and the reasons was quoted that the programme has not provided enough numbers of days of work to make a significant dent on the poverty level, although a minority of them were of the view that MGNREGA has been successful in doing so, to some extent. The latter ones indicated that MGNREGA has improved living standards by providing work within the village and by ensuring same wage rate to female as equal to that of the male.

To another question, whether MGNREGA has changed the trend of attached labour in agriculture, a significant majority agreed on this, as people were getting better payments within the village compared to agricultural work so the trends of attached labour for the agricultural work were declining. However, MGNREGA has certainly increased peoples' awareness towards Government schemes through increase in the showcasing by television, newspaper, *Gram Panchayat* and *Gram* Sabhas and by other media. Among the selected states, in Rajasthan, Maharashtra and Gujarat, a clear majority of the discussants expressed that the household consumption, as well as enrollment of children in the school have increased after implementation of MGNREGA that has provided extra purchasing power in the hands of the villagers.

On the question of awareness, almost all states observed increased awareness of the households towards existing government schemes because of their participation in the Gram Sabha and also because of joint working opportunities in MGNREGA.

References

Adhikari, A., and K. Bhatia. 2010. Can we Bank on Banks? *Economic and Political Weekly*, xlv (1): 30–37.

Afridi, Farzana. 2008. Can community monitoring improve the accountability of public officials. *Economic and Political Weekly*, 43 (42): 35–40.

Aiyar, Y., and S. Samji. 2006. Improving the Effectiveness of National Rural Employment Guarantee Act. *Economic and Political Weekly* 41 (4): 320–326.

Aiyar, Y., and S. Samji. 2009. Transparency and Accountability in NREGA: A Case Study of Andhra Pradesh. Working Paper No 1, Accountability Initiative, Centre for Policy Research, Dharm Marg, Chanakyapuri, New Delhi, February.

Ambasta, P., V. Shankar, and M. Shah. 2008. Two Years of NREGA: The Road Ahead. *Economic and Political Weekly* XLIII (08): 41–50.

Anderson, Siwan, A. Kotwal, A. Kulkarni, and B. Ramaswami. 2013. Measuring the Impacts of Linking NREGA Payments to UID. Working Paper, International Growth Centre, London School of Economics and Political Science, London.

Basu, Arnab K. 2011. Impact of Rural Employment Guarantee Schemes on Seasonal Labor Markets: Optimum Compensation and Workers' Welfare. Discussion Paper No. 5701, ZEF, University of Bonn Germany and IZA, May 2011.

Berg, Erlend, Sambit Bhattacharyya, Rajasekhar Durgam, and Manjula Ramachandra. 2012. Can Rural Public Works Affect Agricultural Wages: Evidence from India. CSAE Working Paper WPS/2012–05, May 15, University of Oxford.

Bhatia, B., and J. Dreze. 2006. Employment Guarantee in Jharkhand: Ground Realities. *Economic and Political Weekly* 41 (29): 3198–3202.

CAG. 2008. Performance Audit of Implementation of National Rural Employment Guarantee Act. Report No. 11, Comptroller and Auditor General of India, Government of India.

Chakraborty, P. 2007. Implementation of Employment Guarantee: A Preliminary Apprisal. *Economic and Political Weekly* 42 (7): 548–551.

Dey, S. 2010. Evaluating India's National Rural Employment Guarantee Scheme: The Case of Birbhum District. West Bengal, Working Paper No 490, International Institute of Social Studies, The Netherlands.

Dreze, J., N. Dev, and R. Khera. 2008. Corruption in NREGA: Myths and Reality. The Hindu dated 22 January.

Dutta, P., R. Murgai, M. Ravallion, and D. van de Walle. 2012. Does India's Employment Guarantee Scheme Guarantee Employment. Working Paper No. 6003, World Bank Policy Research, March.

Imbert, C., and J. Papp. 2012. Equilibrium Distributional Impacts of Government Employment Programmes: Evidence from India's Employment Guarantee. Unpublished Manuscript, March.

Gaiha, R., V.S. Kulkarni, M.K. Pandey, and K.S. Imai. 2009. National Rural Employment Guarantee Scheme, Poverty and Prices in Rural India. ASARC Working Paper 2009/03.

Gopal, K.S. 2009. NREGA Social Audit: Myths and Reality. *Economic and Political Weekly* XLIV (03): 70–71.

ISWSD. 2008. Impact of National Rural Employment Guarantee Scheme on the Living and Working Conditions of Women in Rural India. Draft Report Based on field visits in December–February 2007–08 in Kerala, Karnataka, Jharkhand and Uttar Pradesh, Indian School Of Women's Studies Development, New Delhi.

Jacob, N. 2008. The Impact of NREGA on Rural-Urban Migration: Field Survey of Villupuram District, Tamil Nadu. CCS Working Paper No. 202, Summer Research Internship Programme, Centre for Civil Society.

Jha, R., S. Bhattacharya, R. Gaiha, and S. Shankar. 2009. Capture of Anti Poverty Programme: An Analysis of the National Rural Employment Guarantee Programme in India. *Journal of Asian Economics* 20 (4): 456–464.

Jha, R., S. Bhattacharya, and R. Gaiha. 2011. Social Safety Nets and Nutrient Deprivation: An Analysis of the National Rural Employment Guarantee Programme and the Public Distribution System in India. *Journal of Asian Economics* 22: 189–201.

Harish, B.G., N. Nagaraj, M.G. Chandrakanth, P.S. Srikantha Murthy, P.G. Chengappa, and G. Basavaraj. 2011. Impacts and Implications of MGNREGA on Labour Supply and Income Generation for Agriculture in Central Dry Zone of Karnataka. *Agricultural Economics Research Review* 24 (Conference Number) 2011: 485–494.

Kareemulla, K., S. Kumar, K.S. Reddy, C.A. Rama Rao, and B. Venketeswarlu. 2010. Impact of NREGS on Rural Livelihoods and Agricultural Capital Formation. *Indian Journal of Agricultural Economics* 65 (3): 524–539.

Khera, R. 2008. Employment Guarantee Act. *Economic and Political Weekly* 44 (43): 49–57.
Khera, R., and N. Nayak. 2009. Women Workers and Perceptions of the NREGA. *Economic and Political Weekly* 44 (43): 49–57.
Kumar, P., and S.K. Singh. in Press. Consumption Smoothing and Insurance Against the Income Risks: A Case of India. *Indian Economic Review* (Delhi School of Economics).
Liu, Y., and C.B. Barrett. 2013. Heterogeneous Pro Poor Targeting in National Rural Employment Guarantee Scheme. *Economic and Political Weekly* 48 (10): 46–53.
Mukherjee, D., and U.B. Sinha. 2011. Understanding NREGA: A Simple Theory and Some Facts. Working Paper No. 196, Centre for Development Economics, Department of Economics, Delhi School of Economics, Delhi.
NREGA. 2013. Mahatma Gandhi National Rural Employment Guarantee Scheme (MNREGA). Ministry of Rural Development (MRD), Government of India, New Delhi. http://nrega.nic.in/netnrega/home.aspx.
Shankar, S., R. Gaiha, and R. Jha. 2011. Information, Access and Targeting: The National Rural Employment Guarantee Scheme in India. *Oxford Development Studies* 39 (1): 69–95.
Sharma, A., P. Ghate, L. Joshi, and A. Sahu. 2009. Study on Evaluating Performance of National Rural Employment Guarantee Act. NCAER-PIF Publications.

Websites

www.rural.nic.in.
www.nrega.nic.in.
www.planningcommission.gov.in.
http://planningcommission.nic.in/plans/planrel/fiveyr/8th/vol2/8v2ch2.htm.

Chapter 3
MGNREGS Implementations and the Dynamics of Rural Labour Markets

D. Narasimha Reddy, A. Amarender Reddy, Madhusudan Bhattarai, N. Nagaraj and Cynthia Bantilan

3.1 Introduction

Recently, labour scarcity has emerged as one of the major constraints leading to an increase in agricultural production cost in India. Therefore, in this chapter, evaluation of differential impacts of MGNREGA on the extent of fulfilment of the basic entitlements such as days of employment, wages and earnings and the extent of coverage of social groups like *dalits, adivasis,* women members and poverty alleviation has been done. Then, this chapter also analyze state level data by disaggregating by

D. Narasimha Reddy
University of Hyderabad, Hyderabad, India

D. Narasimha Reddy
Institute of Human Development, Hyderabad, India
e-mail: duvvurunarasimha@gmail.com

A. Amarender Reddy (✉)
Center for Sustainable Agriculture, Monitoring and Evaluation, National Institute of Agricultural Extension Management (MANAGE), Rajendranagar, Hyderabad 500030, Telangana, India
e-mail: amarender@iari.res.in

M. Bhattarai
Jalsrot Vikas Sanstha (JVS), 20694, Kathmandu, Nepal
e-mail: madhu.bhattarai2010@gmail.com

M. Bhattarai
ICRISAT, Hyderabad, India

N. Nagaraj
GPS Institute of Agricultural Management, Bengaluru 560064, Karnataka, India
e-mail: nagaraj.nareppa@gmail.com

C. Bantilan
Research Program on Markets, Institutions and Policy, ICRISAT, Hyderabad, India
e-mail: cbantilan423@gmail.com

M. Bhattarai et al. (eds.), *Employment Guarantee Programme and Dynamics of Rural Transformation in India*, India Studies in Business and Economics,
https://doi.org/10.1007/978-981-10-6262-9_3

socials classes, men and women and to the factors that make a difference to the performance. Also, some micro-level findings and alternate scenarios are presented based on the findings based on a series of focus group discussions (FGDs) conducted in the villages of Andhra Pradesh. The secondary data presented on agriculture and rural labour markets are largely based on the official sources of data and from other studies made on different aspects of the scheme (Reddy et al. 2014).

Though, national economy of India has been growing at a rapid pace in the past two decades, there is a widely shared view that the increase in employment has not been commensurate with growth in the national economy. While faster growth of economy is beneficial to various stakeholders, the employment growth is more critical to reduce poverty in the economy. The policy initiatives directly addressing poverty reduction may be grouped into three types. They are:

(a) *Institutional measures* such as strengthening organization of the poor to enable them to acquire better capabilities like the promotion community based organizations (CBOs), provision of targeted credit, etc.
(b) *Transfer payments* which include direct cash transfers, pensions or indirect transfers like subsidized food and essentials through Public Distribution System (PDS).
(c) *Provision of self-employment* and wage employment programmes to the targeted group of population in the economy.

The experience of welfare programmes in India shows that considerable efforts have been made on all three modes in terms of effectiveness in their implementation and providing wider coverage to all the needed population. Here, we concentrate on one of the major initiatives, viz. Mahatma Gandhi National Rural Employment Guarantee Act (MGNREGA) of 2005, and the resultant Schemes and its implications on rural employment.

3.2 Fixation of Wages

The issue of wage rate for MGNREGS has been a subject of controversy since its initiation as an Act in 2005, because it is not fixed as a uniform daily wage rate applicable to all states at the same level. Nor it is linked to statutory minimum wages, which vary from State to State. Except in Himachal Pradesh, the wage payments under MGNREGS is done in terms of piece rate linked to the 'Standard Schedule of Rates' (SSRs) followed by the Public Works Departments, rather the MGNREGA wage varies from states to state due to the local economy-related factors. This brings-in the issues of fairness of rates, fair in time measurement, employment hours of work, etc. Details are in Boxes 3.1 and 3.2.

One of the basic principles followed is payment of an equal level of wages to male and female workers participating under the MGNREGA schemes. When the Scheme was launched in 2006, an indicative wage rate of ₹ 80 per person day was proposed. This meant that workers engaged under MGNREGS would be assigned physically measurable work equivalent to ₹ 80 as per the Standard Schedule of Rates followed in the state. Later, in 2009, the indicative wage rate was raised to ₹ 100 per person day, further, it was agreed to revise the base wage rate of ₹ 100 indexed on the basis of inflation rate in each of the states over the years.

Box 3.1: Payment of Wages

Assured minimum wages and timely payment of the same are basic entitlements under MGNREGS. But it turned out to be a controversial issue because of the complexity involved. The complexity is because of the choice of the mode of payment under MGNREGS. Except Himachal Pradesh, all states in the country are required to pay MGNREGS wages on piece rate basis, not on time rate or daily wages. This is the beginning of the problem. The assured minimum wage that is fixed under MGNREGS is to be realized through the physically measurable equivalent of work. This leads to the second problem of acceptable Standard Schedule of Rates (SSRs). The third problem is a timely measurement of work that is done. How frequently it should be done, who should do it and who should approve it, are the questions often raised. Fourth problem is who should pay wages? Implementing agency or an independent agency? How to integrate these steps? And at the end of it, how to ensure timely payment?

For instance, Andhra Pradesh government dealt with these problems systematically. Since the SSRs used in contract works involves machines, these rates are not comparable to solely manual work as stipulated under MGNREGS. The Engineering Staff College of India was commissioned by the Government of Andhra Pradesh to make work–time–motion studies and suggest amendments to SSRs to ensure minimum wages under MGNREGS. The results showed that according to existing SSRs, even after a day's work, the wages would be only one-third to one-half of the stipulated minimum wage under MGNREGS. Based on the study, the government of Andhra Pradesh revised the SSRs for MGNREGS by reducing the physical quantity by one-third to one-half. In fact, this change was accepted by the Union MoRD and was recommended to other States to follow a similar methodology. Still there were complaints that there were no rates in SSRs for certain tasks like, for example, 'tank silt', jungle and bush clearance, etc. The state government took the help of NGOs like Centre for Environment Concerns (CEC) to carry further studies, particularly focused on women's tasks in MGNREGS works. Based on the results of these studies the SSRs were further revised reducing the load of work to match one day's work to minimum wages.

The second problem of measurement is solved by the twin approaches of 'single-pit' or appropriate marking of the worksite and by fixing the visit of technical assistant on fixed day in a week for each cluster and logging the same in the muster. Recently, there has been further technological up gradation of the system by developing software to transfer measurements through cell phone.[1] The third problem of agency of payment was solved by opting for postoffices and banks for payment using latest technology including biometrics. For making the system work smoothly coordination meetings are held between the Divisional level postal officials and the District level rural development officials on a fixed schedule twice a month. All this also has been changing fast. Presently, AP has moved from payment through postoffice to payment by biometric smart card system operated by O-Mass Agency. At each Panchayat, the system is operated by a women candidate sponsored by the village organization of SHGs. Payments are made based on a biometric device which is linked to a bank by a cell phone. The system is amazingly simple and the village coordinators handle up to Rs. 2 lakh a peak payments day.[2] The Technical Support Unit (TSU) of the A.P State Employment Guarantee Council, of which the Chief Minister is the Chairman, took direct interest and initiated a few pilot projects to test different models and chose the one which ensures payment in less than a week. With a view to avoid bogus attendance and to check instances of tempering and misuse of muster rolls, the e-Muster system has been introduced. For smooth fund flows cross-systems, the electronic Fund Management System. (e-FMS) has been introduced recently. This also reduces delays in payment of wages. Likewise, kwage payments under MGNREGA has been now linked with Aadhaar numbers in 300 Direct Benefit Transfer (DBT) districts which will eliminate ghost beneficiaries and for a faster disbursement of wages. Under this new plan, wage payments will be routed directly into the accounts of the beneficiaries using electronic transfer systems.

[1]It is called Electronic Muster Measurement System (e-MMS). Under this system the Village Assistant records measurement every day and transfers the 'e-muster' through cell phone. The Technical Assistant takes the measurements every week and transfer the 'e-measurement' data to the mandal by cell phone. The Engineering Consultant (two or three for each mandal) makes 'e-check measurement' and the Mandal Programme Officer acts as the 'e-muste verification officer' with power to verify and consolidate the information.

[2]The person chosen is one of the Vice-Presidents of the Village Organization of SHGs. Often she is also an MGNREGS worker. She is paid a commission of Rs. 500 per Rs. 1 lakh.

Box 3.2: Wage Determination and Work Measurement Issues in Group Basedworks

A peculiar problem was observed in Rajasthan. Usually large numbers of workers were present at worksites, up to 50–70 persons and they were further divided into teams to undertake tasks (Khera 2008). Gender and caste-related issues surfaced in some cases. It was found that only some members of the group worked, while others shirked, assuming they would be paid anyway. As a result of this one could find 70 year olds and even some college students at the worksite during their summer holidays, not undertaking work but merely hanging around. In Tonk district were found some people playing cards at the worksite. Moreover, members of dominant communities such as Gujjar and Jat did not work, but threatened associates and officials to mark their attendance so that they could claim wages.

But there is also evidence to the contrary. In Andhra Pradesh, there were three instances where weak, elderly and female workers were allowed lighter tasks. Lactating mothers were also allowed to break in order to breastfeed. In these cases, wages were shared equally by consensus among the groups.

However, there were also cases where male labourers in a mixed group did not work hard, making women to do much of the work, and leading to female labourers preferring to work without men in their groups. The programme officer in charge of NREGA in Tonk District mentioned that they were experimenting by trying to make separate groups for males and females, but often this too was not preferred.

One of the reasons for low daily wages in Rajasthan is crowding at worksites. In one instance in Nadri Panchayat of Tonk District, an area with hard soil and rock, after the division of wages among workers, only Rs. 1 per day accrued to each of them due to the large number of workers, suboptimal work output and the outdated schedule of rates (SOR), specifying quantum of work to be completed to earn minimum wages. On the contrary, in another village where the numbers of 'sitting' labourers were few in number, wages were above Rs. 80.

Source Reddy et al. 2010.

Table 3.1 presents information on the average wage rate paid per person per day under MGNREGA scheme from 2006–07 to 2011–12. The average wage rates are derived by dividing the total MGNREGA wage expenditure in the state by the person days of employment provided in the state in the year concerned. The derived wage rate per person may not be adequate to conclude whether the concerned state is doing better or worse in terms of supplementing the earnings of rural households through the scheme. A better indicator is the total earnings per household under the scheme, which depends not only on the wage level but also the number of days of employment provided for the concerned year.

In almost all states, there has been a rise in money wage rates. But, given the fact that there has been a very high rate of inflation during these years, it would be more

Table 3.1 Average wages earned per person day and average annual earnings per household under MGNREGS during 2008–09 to 2011–12

Sl. No.	States	MGNREGS average level of wages per day (₹)			Average level of wages per day (₹)	Average level of wages per day (₹)	Average level of wages per day (₹)
		2006–07	2007–08	2008–09	2009–10	2010–11	2011–12
1	Andaman and Nicobar	–	–	124	144	185	174
2	Andhra Pradesh	86	83	83	92	100	101
3	Arunachal Pradesh	48	–	59	69	95	91
4	Assam	67	72	77	87	107	130
5	Bihar	70	70	85	98	101	133
6	Chandigarh	–	–	0	0	0	0
7	Chhattisgarh	62	68	73	82	104	120
8	Dadra & Nagar Haveli	–	–	1	112	116	0
9	Daman & Diu	–	–	0	0	0	0
10	Goa	–	–	0	95	139	161
11	Gujarat	56	63	68	89	97	112
12	Haryana	97	115	120	151	169	180
13	Himachal Pradesh	69	71	99	110	127	123
14	Jammu and Kashmir	69	70	68	93	113	124
15	Jharkhand	79	82	90	98	103	120
16	Karnataka	67	72	81	86	144	189
17	Kerala	121	118	120	121	133	147
18	Lakshadweep	–	–	80	112	138	152
19	Madhya Pradesh	60	63	73	84	98	122
20	Maharashtra	104	84	75	94	134	165
21	Manipur	75	81	78	78	93	125
22	Meghalaya	73	88	70	79	100	114
23	Mizoram	94	102	109	104	116	116
24	Nagaland	66	100	81	103	103	118
25	Odisha	53	76	92	106	96	123
26	Puducherry	–		79	76	91	116
27	Punjab	94	100	111	124	130	145
28	Rajasthan	51	61	88	87	75	90

(continued)

Table 3.1 (continued)

Sl. No.	States	MGNREGS average level of wages per day (₹)			Average level of wages per day (₹)	Average level of wages per day (₹)	Average level of wages per day (₹)
		2006–07	2007–08	2008–09	2009–10	2010–11	2011–12
29	Sikkim	87	88	92	95	100	117
30	Tamil Nadu	80	78	80	72	82	92
31	Tripura	60	71	86	101	103	118
32	Uttar Pradesh	56	90	99	99	105	120
33	Uttarakhand	72	73	85	99	102	127
34	West Bengal	70	79	78	90	107	138
	All states	64	74	84	90	100	117

Note For 2006–07 and 2007–08 average wage rates per person day refer to first phase districts only
Source 1. Kannan and Jain (2011) for 2006–07 and 2007–08
2. http://www.nrega.nic.in

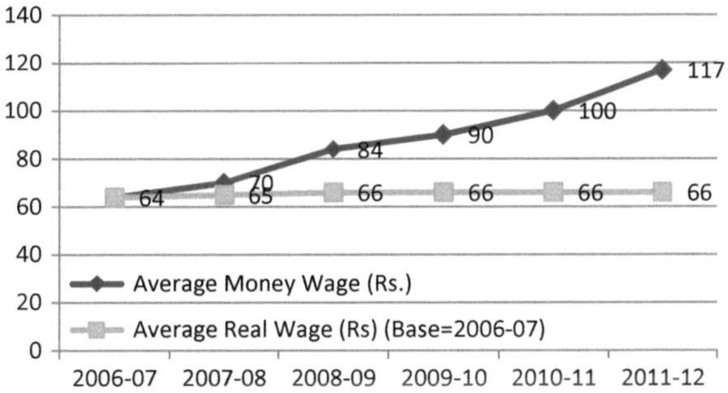

Fig. 3.1 MGNREGS national Average money and real wages per person day

appropriate to examine whether there has been any improvement in real wages realized under the scheme by deflating the money wages by Consumer Price Index for Rural Labour. Such an exercise is done by taking the national average wage rate per person day during the past 6 years and the results are presented in Fig. 3.1. It is clear from the results that though money wage rates have been rising over the years, the real wage rates have been virtually stagnant. But, if there were a decision to index the MGNREGS wage rate with the national inflation, there would have been a steep decline in real wage payments under the MGNREGS.

3.3 Impact of MGNRGA on Employment, Earning and Poverty

The overall performance of the scheme as a measure of social protection depends on not only ensuring better wages but also on achieving the objective of ensuring that more households are brought under the fold of hundred days of employment, at least as per the demand in the local areas. Table 3.1 shows that there is no state which had provided 100 days of employment even to 50% of the participating households in 2011–12.

Tripura, Mizoram and Manipur are the only states where at least one-third of the households had obtained 100 days of employment, but the size of their economy is very small compared to the economic size of the other major states of India. Of the other five states, which have reached more than 10%, three of them are Nagaland, Meghalaya and Sikkim. Among the large scale of States, only Andhra Pradesh (17.8%) and Maharashtra (11.3%) have achieved 100 days of employment per household crossing two digit levels under the MGNREGA programme activities.

The overall performance of providing employment under the scheme shows a tendency towards deceleration in recent years. The macro-picture of the average person days of employment captured in Fig. 3.2 shows a clear downward trend. An attempt is made here to estimate the impact of the earnings under the MGNREGS across the states. State-specific estimates of annual earnings of participating households are derived by dividing the total wage expenditure under MGNREGA work by the average person days of employment per participating household. Comparing the average household earnings from the scheme with the state-specific estimates of rural household poverty threshold expenditure would indicate the possible extent of the impact of the MGNREGS on rural poverty.

Table 3.2 provides the results of these estimates. For the country as a whole, the earnings from the scheme are a little over 12% of the poverty threshold income. These results suggest that in all those cases where the poverty gap is relatively low, there would have been a substantial reduction in rural poverty. Perhaps the steep decline in rural poverty in Tripura from 44.5% in 2004–05 to 19.8% in 2009–10 could be substantially attributed to MGNREGS.

Fig. 3.2 National average person days of employment per household. *Source* http://www.nrega.nic.in

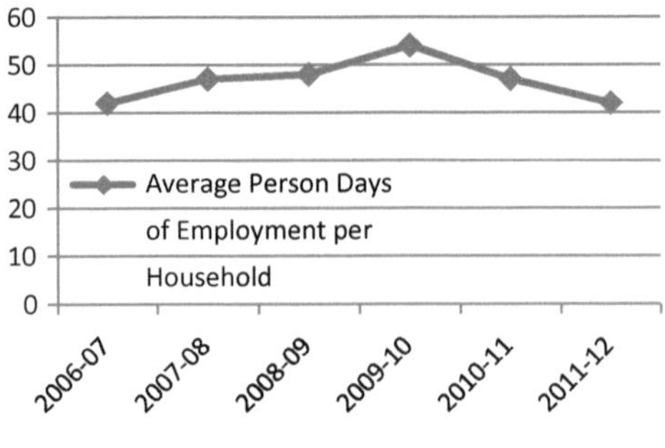

Table 3.2 Impact of MGNREGS on rural poverty (2009–10)

Sl. No.	States	Average earnings per household under MGNREGS (₹) 2009–10	Rural household poverty threshold income	MGNREGS earnings of % of poverty threshold income
1	Andhra Pradesh	6032	41,580	14.5
2	Arunachal Pradesh	1711	46,420	3.7
3	Assam	2982	41,500	7.2
4	Bihar	2687	39,336	6.8
5	Chhattisgarh	4228	37,038	11.4
6	Gujarat	3272	43,500	7.5
7	Haryana	5695	47,496	12.0
8	Himachal Pradesh	6276	42,480	14.8
9	Jammu and Kashmir	3573	43,374	8.2
10	Jharkhand	4834	36,398	13.1
11	Karnataka	4874	37,764	12.9
12	Kerala	4284	46,518	9.2
13	Madhya Pradesh	4659	37,914	12.3
14	Maharashtra	4814	44,622	10.8
15	Manipur	5681	52,260	10.9
16	Meghalaya	3901	41,214	9.5
17	Mizoram	9872	57,000	19.4
18	Nagaland	8987	61,008	14.7
19	Odisha	4196	34,026	12.3
20	Puducherry	1708	38,460	4.4
21	Punjab	3504	49,800	7.0
22	Rajasthan	6027	45,300	13.3
23	Sikkim	7625	43,734	17.4
24	Tamil Nadu	3912	38,340	10.2
25	Tripura	8028	39,804	20.2
26	Uttar Pradesh	6458	39,822	16.2
27	Uttarakhand	3455	43,170	8.0
28	West Bengal	4029	38,592	10.4
	All India	4870	40,368	12.1

Note Average earnings, per household under MGNREGS is derived by dividing the total wage expenditure by average person days of employment per household

1. Calculated on the basis of the state-specific poverty line threshold expenditure for 2009–10 based on the Tendulkar Committee revision and assuming household as comprising five consumption units

Source 1. http://www.nrega.nic.in

2. Upscportal.com for State-Specific Poverty Lines

The highest impact on households' earning is seen in Tripura state, where the household earnings from MGNREGS are as high as a little over 20% of the poverty threshold income. Mizoram is another high-performing state with the share as high as 19.4%. The performance of some of the relatively backward states like Odisha, Madhya Pradesh, Uttar Pradesh and Rajasthan was better than the national average. But, Bihar still lags much behind, which is also reflected in no decline in rural poverty in the state, which continued to be as high as 55% in 2009–10, the almost at same level of poverty as it was in 2004–05.

3.4 Impact of MGNREGS on Rural Labour Markets

3.4.1 Evidence from Across the Country

The search for information on the impact of MGNREGS on agricultural labour markets leads to some evidence on labour shortage, changes in wages, mechanization, peak season adjustment of work or adoption of MGNREGS calendar and migration. The available information, however, is sketchy and uneven across the regions. The implementation experiences also vary widely across the states. Yet some broad trends can be discerned.

With the exception of a few well-endowed regions, the pre-existing labour market in agriculture is characterized by surplus labour, low wages, high male–female wage differentials, and non-implementation of statutory minimum wages. The introduction of MGNREGS, with minimum and equal wages for male and female workers, has, in fact, brought not only an increase in the overall agricultural wages, but also reduction in the male–female wage gap of agricultural labour operation. For instance, agricultural wage increases were reported in a number of states right from Punjab and Haryana to Gujarat to West Bengal (Banerjee and Saha 2010). Even in tea gardens of Silchar, wage hikes are attributed to MGNREGS implementation in the state. That higher wages in the MGNREGS will divert workers from agriculture and create shortages of labour in agriculture is a theoretically valid proposition but the extent to which it will happen is an empirical question (Papola 2005).

This question assumes importance especially in the context where still substantial underemployment does prevail in rural areas. The earlier Maharashtra experience with the Employment Guarantee Scheme did put upward pressure on agricultural wages but there was no clear evidence of shortage of labour (Acharya 1990; Datt 1994). In agriculturally well-endowed regions, the level of agricultural wages was higher even before the MGNREGS was launched, where peak season labour demand was met by seasonal in-migration of labour from labour-surplus regions. The impact of MGNREGS on agricultural wages in such areas was not much, except in pockets where the migrant labour flow declined.

In the villages, most of the forward caste and large farmers are of the opinion that MGNREGS is the main reason for the labour shortage. While agricultural labourers and Schedule Castes and Schedule Tribe (SC/ST) communities are of the opinion that out-migration and work opportunities in non-farm sector are opening labour market for higher wage employment, and thereby they are demanding higher wages for agricultural sector. Hence, shortage of labour is not same for the farmers and agricultural labourers, and also among different social groups.

Recently, several previous studies in India have pointed out labour shortage not only in agriculture but also in non-agricultural activities that depend on rural casual labour.[3] These studies were from many states like Andhra Pradesh, Punjab, Haryana, UP and Tamil Nadu have pointed out that after the introduction of NREGA, there has been a shortage of labour during harvesting of crops like wheat and rice.[4] Labour shortage is also reported during peak paddy sowing season in Punjab,[5] and apple harvesting season in Himachal Pradesh.[6]

There are reports as to how with the shortage of labour, the bargaining power of migrant labour in Punjab had increased to the extent of not only raising wages but also in improvement in working conditions. One study in Punjab even reported 'Besides the TV, cooler, freshly cooked food and accommodation, the labourers are now welcome to live in the houses of farm-owners and not in some dilapidated tube-well room out in the farm. Wages have gone up threefold in some of these places. Farmers say seasonal payment of wages has increased from a mere ₹ 1,750 to ₹.5,000–₹. 6,250 per ha, in just about two years'.[7]

While farmers of these regions of Punjab (and other developed states) tend to blame implementation of MGNREGS in labour-surplus states like Bihar, U.P and Jharkhand, the Commissioner of Punjab Agriculture has a different explanation: 'Earlier, the labour force used to come to Punjab sometime by end of March, at the beginning of the harvesting season of wheat, and would stay there till paddy sowing operation was complete by end of July. This assured them ample opportunity of work for nearly four months. But increased mechanization of farm operations, especially in harvesting and threshing of wheat, has reduced the duration of employability for the migrant rural in Punjab, and predictability of the workforce migration to Punjab from Bihar has shown a dwindling trend from 2006–07 to 2011–12'.[8]

---

[3]"Aspirations within Misery: Labour Shortage in Agriculture", Sanhati, August 5, 2008.

[4]"NREGS lures labourers away from fields", The Pioneer, May 4, 2010.

[5]'Labour shortage affects paddy harvest', The Hindu, September 23, 2010.

[6]'Sugar mills go high-tech to beat labour shortage' Business Standard, August 14, 2011.

[7]"Farmers of Tamil Nadu, Andhra show the way", The Hindu, June 6, 2011.

[8]http://www.researchandmarkets.co/research/d5e163/indian_tractor-ind

3.4.2 Impact on Farm Mechanization

Recently, many studies have suggested that the shortage of labour in agriculture can be met by increased pace of farm mechanization. Farmers in the many villages of Gangetic belt of Uttar Pradesh (UP) have decided to go for mechanized harvesting of the wheat crop due to shortage of rural labour forces.[9] They have attributed the labour shortage to implementation of MGNREGS.

The use of combined harvesters for paddy harvesting in Pondicherry is also attributed to labour shortage resulting from the implementation of the MGNREGS.[10] Mechanization of sugarcane harvesting in Maharashtra and provision of heavy subsidies to harvesting machines are also shown as a consequence of MGNREGS.[11] In Andhra Pradesh, Tamil Nadu and Karnataka mechanization of paddy transplantation are promoted by providing subsidies on the machines.[12] Even in West Bengal, mechanization is being promoted to beat rising labour costs (Babu et al. 2010).

An interesting report on the significant rise in the tractor market in India in recent years has cited shortage of agricultural labour as one of the explanations for the need of speedy mechanization.[13] There is a danger that these reports could be read as if the MGNREGS is responsible for mechanization of Indian agriculture. It is a fact that introduction of combined harvesters, sugarcane harvesting machines and paddy transplanters have long preceded MGNREGS.

Some of these mechanization processes themselves, as observed by the Commissioner of Agriculture of Punjab cited above, disturbed the stable stream of labour supply. Tightening of agricultural labour market along with the state policy of subsidizing farm machinery ownership by farmers has been hastening agricultural mechanization, especially in agriculturally better-endowed regions, and the regions that are performing better in agriculture in the recent past.

Overall, the pace of growth rate in farm mechanization is faster in almost all the crops and states between 1997 and 2010 (Table 3.3). Growth rates in farm mechanization were above 10% per annum for paddy in Odisha and MP; for chickpea in UP; for cotton in AP and Karnataka; for maize in AP and Rajasthan.

The medium growth rate (from 5% to 10%) was observed for maize in Bihar; for chickpea in Haryana; for cotton in MP, Haryana, TN; for paddy in WB, UP, Bihar; for wheat in Bihar and MP. In the case of sugarcane, no state recorded more than 5% growth in farm mechanization. The growth rate in farm mechanization in

---

[9]The Financial Express, August 11, 2008 and The Asian Age, July 18, 2011.

[10]"Agriculture Ministry wants MGNREGA labour glitch uprooted", The Pioneer, July 24, 2011.

[11]A very detailed report on how male members of the household migrate to high paying factory work and women and elderly take to NREGS is reported as "MNREGS fails to curb distress migration in parts of Rajasthan", Business Standard, August 14, 2011.

[12]D.S. Rawat, Secretary General, ASSOCHAM in India Infoline News Service, June 26, 2011.

[13]D.K. Nair, Secretary General, Confederation of Indian Textile Industry (CITI) in SME Times, April 28, 2011.

Table 3.3 Machine labour (Rs/ha) triennium ending 2010

State	Maize	Chickpea	Cotton	Paddy	Wheat	Sugarcane	Total
AP	2094(11.51)		1838(12.69)	1894(0.46)		1475(−4.01)	1829(4.41)
Bihar	1509(6.13)	1770(1.81)		1564(9.14)	1983(6.06)	3091(1.04)	2076(5.48)
Gujarat			1993(2.52)		2952(3.04)		2473(2.82)
Haryana		2024(6.19)	2404(7.46)	3824(3.95)	5284(4.05)	1143(0.4)	2939(4.24)
Karnataka	1510(4.64)		964(14.53)			1872(0.46)	1447(2.96)
Maharashtra			1111(4.66)			7134(4.21)	4122(4.28)
MP	702(4.75)	2226(4.22)	663(8.44)	1023(11.19)	2808(5.25)		1488(5.00)
Odisha				742			742
Punjab			4525(3.03)	4852(2.01)	5507(4.57)		4961(3.25)
Rajasthan	1830(13.97)	1576(3.54)	1803(3.3)		3399(1.69)		2152(3.87)
TN			3126(7.35)			1449(3.02)	2300(3.42)
UP	1756(4.93)	2538(11.31)		2482(6.07)		1111(2.75)	1972(6.58)
WB				1279(7.10)			1279(7.10)
Total	1610(7.42)	1986(5.41)	2051(4.84)	2200(4.22)	3840(3.98)	2386(1.04)	2324(4.23)

Note Figures in parenthesis are ACGR (%) machine labour from 1997 to 2010
Source Difference publication of GOI

agricultural lagging states like Odisha, WB, UP, Bihar and MP were much higher than other states, which could be due to counting of growth rate from a lower base in these lagging states.

3.4.3 Adjustment Work Calendar of MGNREGA to Local Conditions

One of the local demand by farmers across the several places in India is to manage peak season agricultural labour demand by suspending MGNREGS work during peak farming seasons of sowing, transplanting and harvesting of paddy and wheat. Such a measure would not only help farmers to avoid labour shortage but also help workers to get more days of employment by way of peak season agricultural employment in farming, as well as, the lean season of employment from MGNREGS work. To address these public voices, in a number of states, the local Panchayat bodies were allowed, by mutual consent between farmers and agricultural workers, to work with a crop calendar that avoids commencement of MGNREGS work in peak farming season in the location.

This is also to ensure that it is implemented in the lean season only.[14] Such a calendar of work scheduled has been practiced even in the context of tea gardens in West Bengal, as one executive observed: 'The Government would do well, and it would be a win-win situation for all, if they keep MGNREGS work between November and March when we do not need the workers that way, even workers can make more money' (Bhagat 2010). The recent initiatives by the Union Ministry of Agriculture and the Planning Commission appear to be towards making such an MGNREGS calendar as an official part of the implementation of the programme.[15] For improving convergence with the other government rural development related departments (line agencies) and thereby to improve the quality of assets and infrastructure created under the MGNREGS, the State Convergence Plans have been formulated in many of the states.

There is also a focus from the present government in the centre on ensuring access to water to each agriculture farm by converging resources available under various rural development programmes such as water harvesting, conservation and management activities like MGNREGA, Integrated watershed Management Programme (IWMP) Command Area Development & Water Management (CAD&WM), Repair, Renovation & Restoration of water Bodies (RRR), etc. Accordingly, a comprehensive plan based on all available information on water sources, distribution network, water bodies, new potential for augmentation, efficient management system, etc., have been contemplated under Pradhan Mantri

[14]Fibre 2 Fashion (online) August 14, 2011.

[15]SME Times, May 7, 2011.

Krishi SinchaiYojana (PMKSY), as lunched late 2014, when the new government came to power in New Delhi in mid of 2014.

3.4.4 Asset Creation in Rural Areas

Although asset creation is not the primary aim of the MGNREGA scheme, in the recent years, asset creation related issues of the programme are gaining importance in public discourses. Recently, the Government of India and many other scholars working on rural development issues have proposed that at least 60% of the works to be taken up in a district in terms of cost shall be for the creation of productive assets directly linked to agriculture and allied activities through development of land, water and trees. It is proposed that the wage-material ratio for works taken up by agencies other than Gram Panchayat would be counted at the district level, and not at block level as practiced until now to facilitate for taking more durable assets under the MGNREGS programme (Government of India, Ministry of Rural development, Rajya Sabha, Unstirred question No-2044, answered on 16.03.2015, Performance of MGNREGA).

Likewise, for improving convergence with other line departments, and thereby to improve the quality of assets created under the MGNREGS programme, the State Convergence Plans need to be formulated. As noted earlier, there is a focus on ensuring access to water to each agriculture farm by converging resources available under various programmes undertaking water harvesting, conservation and management activities like integrated watershed programmes, command area development programmes, etc. Accordingly, a comprehensive plan based on all available information on water sources, distribution network, water bodies, new potential for augmentation, efficient management system, etc., is contemplated under Pradhan Mantri Krishi Sinchai Yojana (PMKSY), or is also called as Prime Minister Irrigation Plan. The impact of the programme (MGNREGS) is visible in many states in terms of increased water tables, reduction of fallow lands and increased land productivity, after the wider spread implementation of the MGNREGS.

3.4.5 Migration

By default on design of the programme, the MGNREGS, by ensuring work for hundred days at an assured minimum wage at the place of residence under the MGNREGS act in 2005, was expected to have a substantial impact on the reduction of distress migration. Though there are no studies yet in estimating the extent of decline in distress migration because of MGNREGS, there are a number of studies, which gathered the impression of participants on the impact of MGNREGS on migration.

The responses vary from state to state and between districts within a State. The available responses from these surveys from Uttarakhand (Singh and Nauriyal 2009), Odisha (Nayak), Andhra Pradesh and Karnataka (Kamath 2008), Tamil Nadu (IITM 2009) and Sikkim and Meghalaya (2009) show, by and large, there has been a sharp decline in distress migration, after successful implementation of MGNREGS in the places of these states, where the studies were carried out.

A study of select villages of Dhenkanal (Odisha), Bastar (Chattisgarh), Khunti and Gumla (Jharkhand) districts shows that earlier due to lack of employment opportunities within the villages, there was out-migration of large number of rural forces to agriculturally more advanced states like Punjab and Haryana (Banerjee and Saha 2010). The marginal and small farmers depended mostly on wage labour income, with very little earnings from the income from their farm operation, due to low yields in agriculture.

The commencement of MGNREGA works has ensured not only employment in their native places, but also afforded them an opportunity to save their labour forces for investment in their own farming activities that have resulted in higher yields. As a result, though out migration of labour has not been stopped entirely from these regions; the incidence of seasonal out-migration has come down sharply in the recent days.

A study with a specific focus on the impact of MGNREGS on Scheduled Tribes in Kandhamal and Koraput districts of Odisha shows that distress migration among the ST communities has declined by 72.5% among males and by 45.5% among females, after implementation of the programme activities in the states. And also, the average duration of migration of a labour household declined from 69 days in 2004–05 to 23 days per worker in 2001–12 (Rao et al. 2010). But a study of Purulia and Jalpaiguri in West Bengal shows only a marginal impact of MGNREGS on addressing distress migration, where the average number of days of migration declined only by about 10% (Babu et al. 2010). A study of five districts in Bihar finds that there was not much of incidence of migration in Siwan and Begusarai. Whereas, in Madhubani district, with an incidence of as high as 50% of out-migration of labour forces, only 11% felt that there was any significant impact of MGNREGS on rural labour wage markets. (Rao and Dheeraja 2010).

There are interesting instances of return migration of marginal and small farmers of Barmer district of Rajasthan who migrated to neighbouring Gujarat, Punjab and Haryana as wage labour due to water scarcity and depletion of groundwater (Paliwal 2011). In Barmer district, 47,779 'tankas' (small well-like structures made of concrete, cement and sand) and other water works were constructed under MGNREGS to collect rain water which improved groundwater table that enabled crop cultivation. The improved water supply has brought the small and marginal farmers back to agriculture from the seasonal labour work in other states.

Of course, migration is not a linear phenomenon, nor is its outcomes binary like good or bad. The impact would depend on the nature and context of migration. One study shows that improved irrigation facilities, soil conservation, and increase in area cultivated and crop diversification resulting in more employment-reduced migration by 60% in Sidhi district of Madhya Pradesh (CSE 2008a, b).

Reports from Dungarpur, Udaipur and Rajsamand districts show that rural men continue to migrate to factory work in Mumbai, Udaipur and Gujarat. In all these cases, the wages in these activities are higher than that of MGNREGS, and the duration of employment is for longer periods. These can hardly be called distress migration. From these households while men migrate for high-wage and relatively long duration non-agricultural work, women and elderly remain in the village to take to MGNREGS work, which certainly is an addition to overall household income. Nevertheless, to call this as a 'failure to curb distress migration' is misleading.[16]

The positive impacts of MGNREGS in reducing distress migration are evident in the reports from non-farm activities like textiles, jute mills, and a large number of small and medium enterprises (SMEs). The textile industry is dependent on migrant workers especially from Uttar Pradesh, Bihar and Odisha. Since schemes like MGNREGS provide livelihood to workers nearer home, it discourages labour migration from catchment areas to production centres. However, this cannot be read as the cause for labour shortage although it adds to the difficulties in mobilizing 'additional workforce' needed in this sector. The growth projections of the textile industry also earlier suggested that the labour demand would increase from the about 35 million in 2011–12 to 47 million by 2015.

Most of the workers earning about Rs. 7,000 a month are migratory in nature. They move from the agricultural sector to cities after the sowing season for half of the year, and get back to village when the harvest season starts. The MGNREGS is seen as discouraging migration of unskilled labour from rural to urban areas. but, there is no evidence that migration of labour for works that ensure higher wages and longer duration was discouraged by the implementation of MGNREGS in the rural areas.

The Secretary General of Confederation of Indian Textile Industry (CITI) observes that the problem in the textile industry is not losing workers, but the industry is not getting additional workers, especially skilled workers. 'The challenge will be to find enough workers and to train them. Though the training needs are neither complicated nor time consuming, the magnitude of the requirements would make it a herculean task'. Within the textile industry, it is claimed that jute mills in West Bengal pay the maximum daily wages with a fresher getting Rs. 227 per day and a skilled worker Rs. 404. These wages are two to four times MGNREGS wages.

Therefore, it is a widely held claim among many industrials and related stakeholders of jute mills there that shortage of labour in jute mills is due to MGNREGS, since MGNREGS activities in the villages have discouraged agricultural workers to

[16]It is reported that the draft proposal by the Planning Commission submitted to the Ministry of Rural Development suggests rechristening the Scheme as MNREGS-II so as to cover agricultural activities like sowing, harvesting, soil and compost preparation, irrigation and allied activities like tending livestock. It is also proposed that to begin with the farm activities will be allowed under the revised Scheme only in 2000 backward blocks, with a goal of putting back small-marginal farmers on their own farms. (The Pioneer, August 19, 2011 and Tehelka, August 20, 2011).

migrate from rural to urban areas. However, this does not reflect a true situation of migration behaviours of rural population. Similarly, the Indian Industries Association (IIA), Ghaziabad Chapter, has also reported that MGNREGS as the main culprit for labour shortage in small and medium industries in India now. Moreover, there are also several evidences and case studies from field across the places in India that migration for high-wage employment, especially male members of the household has not declined even after implementation of MGNREGS across India, but only distress migration of women and other vulnerable groups.

3.4.6 Youth and Educated

Educated and unemployed youth were more interested to migrate to work in urban/ non-agricultural works, even though there are opportunities to work in agriculture and MGNREGA. They are attracted neither to agricultural work nor to MGNREGA works. It is due to laborious nature and also due to low social status attributed to such agricultural work. Besides, a small farmer (especially youth) is not interested in agriculture because of the low income and insecurity of return from the land.

Farmers and rural youth are concerned that the hard work they put in agriculture may go waste, if there are natural calamities like drought, hail storms, frost, and insect-pest and disease infestations. Penetration of electronic media in the rural areas has changed the attitude of the youths and turned them against agriculture. Their interest in agriculture is further waning, because of low expected returns from agricultural produce. Youth of the village do not want to work in agriculture and MGNREGA works, because it is strenuous work for long durations and is a low paid job if opportunities exist outside. Hence, MGNREGS has less impact on stopping the migrant labour who moves for higher wage rates.

In short, the review of evidence shows that MGNREGS has certainly provided dent on following aspect of rural livelihoods.

- (i) reduced distress migration among rural poor,
- (ii) smoothened rural consumption in the lean season,
- (iii) set high standards and transparency in doing rural development even in hinder-land villages,
- (iv) addressed underemployment problem in vast tract of rural India,
- (v) created assets that improved livelihoods of rural poor,
- (vi) gave boost to the financial inclusion
- (vii) strengthened activities and functions of Gram Panchayats
- (viii) improved the wage levels in rural areas and thereby increasing the income levels of the poorest of poor
- (ix) set standards for decent working conditions and
- (x) Helped in bringing fallow lands into cultivation.

In fact, the MGNREGS programme has also faced several challenges on its implementations such as,

(i) delays in payment of wages
(ii) corrupt practices in implementation
(iii) denial of entitlements
(iv) poor technical capacity to implement large number of works and
(v) poor quality of assets created.

3.5 Impact of MGNREGS on Rural Labour Market in Telangana and Andhra Pradesh

One of the major and direct impacts of MGNREGS in rural Telangana and Andhra Pradesh, as in many other parts of the country, is felt in the rural labour market. Based on the series of focus group discussions (FGDs) spread over a fairly large number of villages (77), Table 3.4 presents some broad indicators of the change in the rural labour market as a result of implementations of MGNREGS in those villages. These indicators have to be interpreted in all their nuances to the extent the FGDs could capture them.

Table 3.4 Impact of MGNREGS on rural labour market in select villages in Telangana and Andhra Pradesh 2008–09[a]

Indicator	Increased	Decreased	No change	No clear response	All villages
1. Agricultural wages	70	Nil	2	5	77
2. Peak season shortage of agricultural labour	62	Nil	6	9	77
3. Male–female agricultural wage differential	Nil	71	Nil	6	77
4. Migration (a + b)	Nil	51	20	6	77
a) Villages with migration before NREGS	Nil	51	4	Nil	55
b) Villages with no migration before NREGS	Nil	Nil	12	Nil	12

[a]The evidence is based on reports of Focus Group Discussions (FGD) of 77 villages (panchayats) spread over 8 districts (Chittoor, Nalgonda, Medak, Ranga Reddy, Adilabad, Karimnagar and Kurnool). These FGD reports are part of the two projects: Galab et al. (2008) and Reddy et al. 2014)

3.5.1 Job Security

As a result of MGNREGA, not only did the rural labour have been able to obtain increased wage rates but also their holding of job cards has given them a sense of job security. The labours consider job cards as a measure of minimum security of job that will be offered to them in future, especially in the off-season of agriculture where the unemployment is rampant in all rural areas, especially in a dry region with less access to irrigation water to grow crops all rounds the year. Because of this perceived assurance of future availability of jobs and at assured wage rates, the labour is empowered with increased bargaining power for setting their wage rates even in other seasons than the case of without the minimum guarantee of employment as was the case before implementation of MGNREGS in 2006.

This increased bargaining power of the agricultural labour, at least in relative sense, is also one of the factors that the farmers community at large have felt their reduced says in setting the rural wage and hiring the labour forces in many parts of the year, and so has become a point of criticizing the MGNREGS activities by the farming communities. These points have been expressed by many farmers during the focus discussions with the farming communities regarding assessing the impact of the MGNREGS. However, a more thorough sociological and political economy related study on the topics may provide further insight on this social-cultural aspect of the age-old patronizing type of relationship between farming communities and agricultural labour forces in Indian sub-continent.

3.5.2 High Risk Perception of Farming

In general, a small farmer is not interested to depend on his all livelihood activities in agriculture because of the inadequate income from farming and an insecurity of return from the crop husbandry in general. In addition, the majority of the rural youth in India are concerned that the hard work they put in agriculture is not sufficient to sustain their livelihoods. In the case of any of the natural calamities like drought, hail storms, frost, and insect-pest and disease infestations, their labour and investments in farming would be wasted.

Likewise, penetration of electronic media in the rural areas has changed the attitude of the youths and turned them against agriculture. Their interest in agriculture is further waning, because of low expected returns from agricultural produces, and uncertainty in farm income. Therefore, for educated rural youth, farming is a strenuous work for long durations, and is a low paid job compared to alternate jobs for them in the non-farm sector. Thereby, in many parts of India, educated rural youth and women, even unemployed ones, are usually do not attracted to agricultural work due to drudgery and due to low social status attributed to agricultural work than services and other sector employment.

3.5.3 Perception of Different Social Groups

In the villages, at many times, large sections of the forward caste community of agricultural families have often complained that the MGNREGA is the main reason for the labour shortage in their communities. The authors have faced such feedback and remarks from farmers during their case studies and focus group discussions at several dryland villages in western and southern India. While agricultural labourers are of the opinion that out-migration and work opportunities in non-farm sector are opening labour market for higher wage employment, hence they are also demanding higher wages for the agricultural sector in the rural areas; otherwise, they prefer to go to non-farm sector jobs in the nearby cities. Hence, the notion of a shortage of labour in large part of the rural India is not same for the farmers and agricultural labourers and among different social groups within a rural community.

3.5.4 MGNREGA Wage Rates

In the first phase of MGNREGS, the minimum wage was fixed at ₹ 80 per day. It was increased in Andhra Pradesh to ₹ 100 in 2009. Since the MGNREGS wage is calculated on the basis of work done at the schedule of rates, the minimum wage level is only indicative and the wage level could be higher or lower depending on the nature of work and group efforts in completion of the work on time. But, in Kuppanagar, a village used here as a case study, the average wage level obtained has always been higher than the minimum indicated. Even in the earlier years when the minimum wage was ₹ 80, Kuppanagar workers logged wages ranging from ₹ 93 to ₹ 126.

The results of the household survey showed average wage rate of ₹ 103 in 2009–10. In Kuppanagar, as in other places in the state, work is allotted to a group calibrating the quantity equivalent to the schedule of rates that would fetch minimum wage to each member. Often, some members of the group do not turn up but yet the remaining ones complete the total allotted work and this increases the average wage to a level higher than an indicated minimum wage. Wherever, the workers are formed into Shrama Shakti Sangams (SSS), as in Kuppanagar, there is a better motivation to work as a team and complete the work allotted at a time, even if some members do not turn up. The result is the average wage of the group is then higher than the minimum wage.

Besides, the average wages are paid equally to men and women. The average MGNREGS wages logged by Kuppanagar workers are higher than local agricultural wages, especially for women. The impact of MGNREGS wages is felt in two ways. First, overall agricultural wages have increased. Male wages in agriculture increased from Rs. 80 before MGNREGS to ₹ 100 in 2008–09, and female agricultural wages increased from ₹ 50 to ₹ 80. The male–female wage gap has declined substantively. The hours of agricultural work also have declined and it is invariably half a day work at the wages mentioned above. In the second half of the day, the same agricultural labours have also worked on farm on piece rate basis. The net impact on agriculture is higher wage costs.

The feedbacks of farmers in the group discussions held by the authors have revealed an interesting pattern. Regardless of the social group, most of the MGNREGS workers are also small and marginal farmers and they too feel the impact of rising agricultural wages on their farms, but marginally, because of two reasons. First, their earnings, especially those of women, from MGNREGS are substantially higher now than the case of 5–6 years before the implementation of MGNREGS.

Second, they have substantially gained by way of improved productivity of their land due to MGNREGS sponsored land development works on their private lands. In many cases, after improvement of the land development work, even the value of land has become double within a year. Therefore, the small-marginal farmers do not complain much about rising wages recently, as they also get paid on increased wage rate now. The landless workers, in fact, acknowledge rising agricultural wages. However, their main complaint is about the steep rise in prices of essential commodities.

The response of relatively bigger farmers, normally non-participants in MGNREGS, is about the rising agricultural wages. Interestingly, in many villages, they do not complain about the MGNREGS as such, since most of them benefited from rising water table and increase in yield of their wells and bore wells due to MGNREGS works in the villages, especially due to de-silting of tanks and ponds and construction of a number of percolation tanks. These relatively bigger farmers have been repeatedly making a plea that half of their agricultural work and wages could be shared under MGNREGS. Paradoxically, they have developed a vested-interest in MGNREGS hoping their wage costs would be shared under the Scheme and, the political forces appear to be nursing this hope!

3.5.5 Agricultural Wages

At the time of the fieldwork during 2008–09, the MGNREGS minimum wage for both male and female workers was ₹ 80. In some of the villages, the male agricultural wage was equal or marginally more than the MGNREGS wage rate, but the female agricultural wage level was much lower in almost all the villages. The introduction of MGNREGS increased the demand for labour in rural areas and resulted in increase in agricultural wages for both male and female workers.

The rise in female agricultural wages, which were at much lower level, was much steeper than the rate of increase in male wage rates. As a result, the difference between male–female agricultural wages declined substantially in almost all villages (71) studied. An evaluation based on a large sample drawn from nine districts of Telangana and Andhra Pradesh shows 43% increase in wages in 2011–11 from the time when the inception of the scheme was done in 2005/06 (GoAP 2011).

The Telangana experience of the high, average and low performance in MGNREGS employment, wage rates and household earnings is highly instructive

Table 3.5 Employment and earnings under high, average and low MGNREGS performance in Telangana (2009–10)

Indicator	Kuppanagar Village (High)		State average	Makkarajpet village (Low)
	Sample households	All households		
1. Average person days of employment per household	161[a]	84	65	31
2. Average wage per person day (₹)	103	110	92	86
3. Average annual MGNREGS earnings per household (₹.)	16,137	9,240	5,980	2,781
4. MGNREGS earnings as % of poverty threshold income (Tendulkar poverty line)	40.0	23.0	14.9	6.9

[a]The high number of days is due to combining drought relief work with MGNREGS in the village during 2009–10

Source http://www.nrega.ap.gov.in and Household Sample Survey (Reddy 2011)

and worthwhile presenting here as a summary statement (Reddy 2011; Reddy et al. 2014). While, the relatively high average wage rate for the state as a whole could be attributed to state level political and administrative commitment and initiatives, the high and the low observed at the grassroots level is for most part a result of the presence or absence of participatory governance at the Panchayat level (Table 3.5).

3.5.6 Food Insecurity and MGNREGA

The experiences of Kuppanagar and Makkarajpet show what difference effective implementation of MGNREGS could make to food insecurity in dryland areas. While best performing Kuppanagar may show that hunger is a thing of the past, in poor performing Makkarajpet 85% still feel that they have to suffer the privation. While there has been an improvement in the consumption of food and reduced food insecurity, but everywhere there was growing concern about rising prices.

There are interesting instances reported in FGDs which reveal varying degrees of impact depending on the local conditions and the performance of MGNREGS. For instance, the five villages in Karimnagar district report that MGNREGS has no impact on food insecurity, meaning, Karimnagar, being agriculturally prosperous district did have higher levels of employment, wages and levels of consumption of food and hence MGNREGS did not make any difference. At the same time there is Adilabad, a relatively backward district but here too, ironically, MGNREGS did not make much difference to food insecurity. It is because of poor implementation of the MGNREGS in the district, no assured employment, low earnings from the scheme and continued migration which together perpetuate low levels of food consumption.

In contrast, in Khammam district, where there were villages with food deficit and hunger before MGNREGS, reports show complete turnaround in food consumption and security because of better implementation of MGNREGS, more employment, earnings and access to food. In most of the villages besides improved consumption levels in food, MGNREGS earnings have enabled the households to buy food in lump sum quantities. There is also change in food habits and some households have reported that they consume 'tiffin' for the breakfast.

A larger survey reports that large proportions of MGNREGS households are able to buy chicken and meat (68%) and vegetables (58%) and for 87% of these households MGNREGS has become a source of lean season employment. There are moving instances of livelihood dilemmas of the poor that before MGNREGS their incomes were too meagre to meet their own consumption requirements and therefore, neglected the needs of the aged members of the household. MGNREGS has enabled them to take better care of the aged parents. Some households reported that they provide pocket money to parents to buy toddy and beedies (local signature).

3.5.7 MGNREGA and Labour Shortage for Agriculture

Even before MGNREGS, in peak agricultural season labour shortage was experienced in many villages. Of course, there were a few dryland villages where it was shortage of work, than shortage of labour, which continues to be a problem. But after MGNREGS, 62 out of 68 villages reported increase in labour shortage. However, out 77 villages, only two villages reported that there was not any decline in area under cultivation due to rise in wages or shortage of labour in the peak season.

In Kupanagar village, there has actually been an increase in the area cultivated in the last 2 years, due to MGNREGS investment in fallow and rainfed lands of SCs. A number of strategies are being adopted to meet the changing labour market situations which in turn are also leading to many changes in the nature of rural and especially agricultural labour markets. Six villages reported labourbeing brought from outside the village by paying transport charges in addition to wages. In three villages wages were paid in advance to ensure labour supply in the peak season for agriculture. There has been growing tendency towards piece rate or contracting out of agricultural work than employing labour on daily wages.

Agricultural workers reported better bargaining power, better treatment at the farm, visible change in the form of respect and less pressure at the place of work. Besides a rise in wages, in most of the villages workers have been able to negotiate reduced duration of agricultural working day. And the growing shift towards piece rate or contract work on agriculture facilitated the change in the working day. There has been increasing tendency in the MGNREGS working day to begin early in the day by seven in the morning and terminate by one in the afternoon.

There are instances where the workers take to agricultural work in the afternoon, often on their own farms, after attending the MGNREGS work in the forenoon. There is an emergence, in some villages, a dual mode of work in a given day with MGNREGS work in the forenoon and agricultural work in the afternoon (Reddy 2011). The latter mostly on own farms. Such adjustments appear to soften the shortages of agricultural labour. And the very working day is being redefined due to changes in the labour market brought about by MGNREGS.

3.5.8 Group Work

There are important changes in the nature of work, duration of working hours and attitude to group work. Almost all work under MGNREGS is in the form of group work. The workers in many places, like in Kuppanagar, are oraganized into fixed labour groups called Shramik Shakti Sangams (SSSs). The group formation, imparting training to 'mates' of the groups and working together for over 2 years appears to promote better awareness, solidarity and motivation to perform better. The majority of groups with a few exceptions are groups of mixed castes.

There was considerable mutual understanding and sharing of work. The reaction of workers to group work reveals some of the finer elements of work, like work not being looked upon mere drudgery or exploitation but as a positive involvement. Worker's response was that under group work, which often involves the entire adult family members along with others, even hard work is not felt as difficult work. There is a sense of mutual sharing when old people and physically disabled are also part of the group. This has been possible because some stronger members compensate by taking more load and share wages equally. In the perception of workers, there is also certain amount of dignity associated with MGNREGS, since it is government work and no room for exploitation.

3.5.9 MGNREGS Calendar

Though there are reports elsewhere about mechanization of agriculture as a response to labour shortage, there is no such perceptible change towards mechanization as a response to MGNREGS in the villages of the eight districts discussed here. But there is a widespread demand by farmers for stopping MGNREGS work during the agricultural peak season. In fact, a number of Gram Panchayats have evolved, through mutual negotiation, work calendar that avoids MGNREGS work during the local agricultural peak season. Such adjustment is seen as a mutually beneficial measure that helps farmers to avoid labour shortage in the peak season and workers to get NREGS work in the lean season and thus increase the overall days of employment in a year.

3.5.10 Migration

Of the 77 villages reported in Table 3.11, in twelve villages there was no migration before or after MGNREGS. Of the remaining, in four villages there was not much change in the migration situation even after the scheme and in six other villages, there was no clarity in the information recorded. In the rest of the 55 villages, there were varying degrees of decline in migration. Most of the decline is in distress migration, but not in the emerging process of movement towards higher paying, relatively high productivity non-agricultural work and often, rural to urban mobility. At least four villages reported complete stoppage of distress migration.

Some villages in districts like Ranga Reddy reported decline in long-distance distress migration to Mumbai and Pune. This is similar to the decline in migration from drought-prone Mahabubnagar district which was well-documented elsewhere (Sainath 2008). In many other villages, the participants in discussions observed that there would be further decline in distress migration if MGNREGS work is provided for longer periods at a time and if wages are paid without much delay. Their arguments were well reasoned. They were conscious of the costs of migration including raising informal loans at high interest rates to meet the expenses of mobility, high rents and fuel costs in destinations, the ordeal of having to live in sub-human conditions and the risk of their children missing a chance to go to school.

The non-distress type of migration from these villages, which is not affected much by MGNREGS, is of three types. One is the migration of male members of the households for high paying non-agricultural work for relatively longer durations. For instance, from the villages of Kurnool district which borders Karnataka, male members of the households migrate to Bellary to work in construction, mining and other activities. The second type of non-distress migration that continues even after MGNREGS is rural to rural migration from dryland areas to fertile areas for agricultural work. For instance, from Mandals like Aspari in Kurnool district, entire household members migrate to Guntur district during June–August to work in the mirch (chilli) and tobacco fields where each migrating couple make as much as ₹ 500 per day.

These families return during September–October to their own villages to work in agriculture, and some, even in MGNREGS. The third type of continuing migration is—strictly speaking not migration—daily commuting to neighbouring towns. For instance, in Kurnool district members of some rural households commute to neighbouring towns like Allagadda to work in shops and other establishments where the wages are high. Interestingly, some work in MGNREGS in their villages in the forenoon, and commute in the afternoon to nearby towns to work in odd jobs including vegetable and fruit vending. Another independent survey cutting across 81 villages in nine districts of A.P reports 44% reduction in migration (GoAP 2011).

3.5.11 Extra Worker and Extra Employment Effect

A question often raised is, if there were to be substantial increase in employment under MGNREGS, what would be the impact on agriculture? Would there be shortage of labour for agriculture? Ora decline in the area cultivated due to shortage of labour? The experience of Kuppanagar village, suggests that though initially there were signs of shortage of labour, over the past three years there have been interesting developments in the working hours and the working day. Gradually there has been a shift in the daily work schedule of MGNREGS works. It is increasingly now tending to be confined to forenoon. With it, there is also a tendency on the part of workers who are engaged in the forenoon to take up either agriculture wage labour or own farm work in the afternoon.

As observed earlier, many workers earn MGNREGS wages in the forenoon and also earn on agriculture in the second half of the day, thereby doubling their day into two working and earning days. This is hard work but preferred by many workers since there is a substantial increase in income. This is a clear extra employment effect. The other factor contributing to extra worker effect is the inducement of relatively higher wages for women in MGNREGS compared to agriculture. Some women from certain social groups who did not perform wage labour are participating in MGNREGS work. It is because of being 'government' work, not work for a contractor or a landowner which carried a social stigma for certain social communities. Thus, the extra employment and worker effects together appear to keep labour supply to agriculture from being greatly disturbed.

3.5.12 Need for Improvement and e-FMS

However, there are number of complaints on the functioning of MGNREGS from the grassroots level participants. The complaints mainly relates to cases of job cards not provided, misappropriation of funds, engagement of contractors, forgery of muster roll, manipulation in job cards, underpayment of wages, non-payment of wages, corruption and other irregularities, use of machinery, delay in payments, etc., which needs to be addressed both at macro- and micro-level.

With a view to reduce above malpractices and to avoid bogus attendance and to check instances of tempering and misuse of muster rolls, the e-Muster system has been introduced. For smooth fund flow, the electronic Fund Management System (e-FMS) has been introduced which would also reduce delays in payment of wages. With a view to eliminate ghost beneficiaries and for a faster disbursement of wages, it has been decided to link the payments under MGNREGA to Aadhaar numbers 300 Direct Benefit Transfer (DBT) districts. Under this, payments will be routed directly into the accounts of the beneficiaries using the electronic system. Already, there are visible signs of reducing malpractices in a number of villages.

3.6 Concluding Observations

There is a growing evidence of an increase in agricultural wages across the country over the period between 2006–07 and 2011–12, in which the impact of MGNREGA is considerable. This review has also revealed a steep increase in female agriculture wages and a substantive decline in the male–female wage gap. The search for information on the impact of MGNREGA on agricultural labour markets leads to some evidence on labour shortage, changes in wages, speeding up mechanization process, peak season adjustment of work or adoption of MGNREGA calendar and migration.

The absolute decline in labour force in rural areas has tightened the rural labour market leading to shortage of labour for farm operations. Thus, labour scarcity has emerged as one of the major constraints to increase agricultural production in India. Furthermore, the tightened labour market has offered, better bargaining power to agricultural labourers, better treatment at the place of work, ability to negotiate the duration of the working day and has initiated a growing shift towards piece rate or contract work on agriculture facilitating change in the number of working days.

Based on macro-level results and micro-level evidence some policy interventions are suggested—such as development of labour saving technologies and machines to mitigate labour scarcity, an inclusive farm mechanization programme especially for women and youth, strengthening rural–urban connectivity, social protection for migrant labour and capacity building programmes for skill augmentation. Further, a revision of the time-frame of MGNREGA work to create more employment in the lean season has been recommended.

Based on the facts and figures presented earlier, some of the clear evidence on the impact of MGNREGS relates to labour market emerging out of the study are summarized as follows:

- Agricultural wages have increased across the country, in which the impact of MGNREGS is considerable.
- The rate of increase in the female agricultural wage has been much higher than male wages, and the historically high male-female differentials in agricultural wages have declined substantially.
- The peak period labour shortages in agriculture are observed in several regions and are resulting in a number of changes in working hours, working day and MGNREGS work calendar.
- The tightening labour market has offered better bargaining power to agricultural labourers, better treatment at the place of work and ability to negotiate the duration of the working day.
- The terms of wages are increasingly tending towards piece rate contracts.
- The ongoing process of agricultural mechanization is hastened especially in certain operations like ploughing and harvesting of paddy, chickpeas, wheat even in backward states.
- A clear response to peak season agriculture labour shortage is the negotiated MGNREGS calendar that avoids implementing works during agricultural peak

and provides developmental works during the lean season. And such a time schedule though not universal is welcomed by farmers as well as workers wherever adopted.

- There is no evidence that there has been marked a decline in the area cultivated either due to rise in agricultural wages or shortage of labour. On the contrary, there are counteracting forces by way of 'extra worker effect' by drawing especially women from certain social groups into the 'government employment' of MGNREGS wage work; and 'extra area effect' by making the some of the fallow lands of the poor more productive.
- There is clear evidence that rise in wages is one of the contributing factors, along with other rising input costs, to increasing costs of cultivation. While SC, ST and other small-marginal farmers who are also participants in the MGNREGS were not affected much, or in many cases gained considerably, the better off farmers could face the rising costs partly through mechanization.
- One of the salutary effects of MGNREGS on poor rural households is the drastic reduction in distress migration. But there is no reason to share the apprehension, as expressed by some (Farrington et al. 2007), that the scheme 'may discourage them from moving to more economically dynamic areas'. Just as in favour of decline in distress migration, there is equally strong evidence to show that migration for higher wage work that lasts for relatively longer period in a year remains unaffected and possibly would improve if skill formation and capacity building activities that would improve human capabilities are also brought under the MGNREGS.
- The worst affected are the small-marginal farmers who are neither participants in the MGNREGS work nor beneficiaries of works on their private lands. This section of the small-marginal farming community may not be small and face serious crisis. In this context the Planning Commission's proposal to make the scheme more farmer-friendly by extending the coverage to some of the agricultural operations, if designed properly, may address the problems of excluded small-marginal farmers.

Acknowledgments This chapter is a study which builds up on previous works of some co-authors, necessary permissions to reproduce parts of which have been received. Details of the papers are mentioned here. 'Impact of Mahatma Gandhi National Rural Employment Guarantee Act (MGNREGA) on Rural Labour Markets', Working Paper Series No. 58, ICRISAT Research Programme: Markets, Institutions and Policies, published in January 2014 by International Crops Research Institute for the Semi-Arid Tropics (ICRISAT), Patancheru, India; 'The Impact of Mahatma Gandhi National Rural Employment Guarantee Act (MGNREGA) on Rural Labor Markets and Agriculture' published in 2014 in volume 13, issue 3 of Taylor & Francis journal, *India Review*; and 'NREGS and Indian Agriculture: Opportunities and Challenges', Working Paper No. WP 01/2011, published by Institute for Human Development in 2011.

References

Acharya, S. 1990. *Maharashtra Employment Guarantee Scheme: A Study of Labour Market Intervention*. ILO-ARTEP: New Delhi.

Babu, V. Suresh., B. Dhanyashree., Joseph Abraham., and K. Hanumatha Rao. 2010. Impact of MGNREGS on Scheduled Castes in West Bengal, NIRD, Hyderabad (Processed).

Banerjee, Kaustav., and Partha. Saha. 2010. The NREGA, The Maoists and Development Woes of the Indian State. *Economic and Political Weekly* XLV (28), July 10.

Bhagat, Rasheeda. 2010. A World of Cultivated Taste. The Hindu Business Line, February 26.

Centre for Science and Environment (CSE). 2008a. *An Assessment of the Performance of the National Rural Employment Guarantee Programme in terms of its Potential for Creation of Natural Wealth in India's Villages*. New Delhi: CSE.

Centre for Science and Environment (CSE). 2008b. *NREGA—Opportunities and Challenges*. New Delhi, CSE, Policy Paper 2008.

Datt, Gaurav. 1994. Poverty Alleviation through Rural Public Works: The Experience of Maharashtra Employment Guarantee Scheme. *The Indian Journal of Labour Economics* 37 (4).

Farrington, J., R. Holmes, and R. Stater. 2007. *Linking Social Protection and the Productive Sectors, Briefing Paper 28*. London: Overseas Development Institute.

Galab S., Pruthvikar. Reddy, E. Revathi., and M. Ravi. 2008. Evaluation Report on the Impact of MGNREGS in Andhra Pradesh. *Centre for Economic and Social Studies*. Hyderabad (Processed).

GOAP. 2011. Impact of MGNREGS on Poverty and Levels of Living of Poor, (Akshara Livelihood Private Ltd.,), Department of Rural Development, GoAP, Hyderabad.

IITM. 2009. *Evaluation of National Rural Employment Guarantee Act*. IIT, Madras: Rural Technology and Business Incubator.

Kamath, R. 2008. *NREGA Surveys in Anantapur, Adilabad, Raichur and Gulbarga (2007–08) (MoRD and UNDP Sponsored)*. Bangalore: Indian Institute of Management.

Kannan, K.P., and Varinder, Jain. 2011. Implementation of NREGA Across Indian States: A Phase-wise Analysis. In *Paper presented at Final Workshop under CDS-ASSR Project on Monitoring the Implementation of Social Security for the Working Poor in India's Informal Economy*. Centre for Development Studies (CDS), Thiruvananthapuram.

Khera, R. 2008, "Empowerment Guarantee Act", *Economic and Political Weekly,* 43 (35), 8–10.

Nayak, N.C. ND. Appraisal Processes and Procedures of NREGS in Orissa: A Study of Mayurbhanj and Balasore District. Kharagpur, Indian Institute of Technology.

Paliwal, Ankur. 2011. Water Turns the Tide. *Down to Earth*, April 15.

Papola, T.S. 2005. A Universal Programme is Feasible. *Economic and Political Weekly*, February 12.

Rao, K. Hanumantha., S. Subrahmanyam., C.S. Murthy., and V. Suresh Babu. 2010. Impact of MGNREGS on Scheduled Tribes in Orissa. NIRD, Hyderabad (Processed).

Rao, K. Hanumantha, and C. Dheeraja. 2010. *Changing Gender Relations through MGNREGS: Bihar State Report*. Hyderabad (Processed): NIRD.

Reddy, D.N., C. Upendranath., Rukmini, Tankha., and Alakh Sharma et al. 2011. Institutions and Innovations in the Implementation Process of Mahatma Gandhi National Rural Employment Guarantee Scheme (MGNREGS) in India. *Centre for Social Protection Research Report 09*. Sussex, UK: Institute of Development Studies.

Reddy, D.N. 2011. Functioning of National Rural Employment Guarantee Scheme (MGNREGS) in Andhra Pradesh. In *Paper presented at Final Workshop under CDS-ASSR Project on Monitoring the Implementation of Social Security for the Working Poor in India's Informal Economy*. Thiruvananthapuram: Centre for Development Studies.

Reddy, D.N., R. Tankha, C. Upendranadh, and A.N. Sharma. 2010. National Rural Employment Guarantee as Social Protection. *IDS Bulletin* 41 (4): 63–76.

Reddy, D.N., Reddy, A.A., and Bantilan M.C.S. 2014. The Impact of Mahatma Gandhi National Rural Employment Guarantee Act (MGNREGA) on Rural Labor Markets and Agriculture. *India Review* 07/2014; 13(3).

Sainath, P. 2008. NREGA: A Fine Balance. Source: http://www.indiatogether.org/2008/jul/psa-finebal.htm.

Singh, S.P., and D.K. Nauriyal. 2009. *System and Process Review and Impact Assessment of NREGS in the State of Uttarakhand*. Roorkee: Indian Institute of Technology.

Chapter 4
Beyond Digging and Filling Holes: Maximizing the Net Positive Impact of MGNREGA

Shilp Verma and Tushaar Shah

4.1 Background

The Mahatma Gandhi National Rural Employment Guarantee Act (MGNREGA) was enacted by the Indian Parliament in 2005. Starting with the 200 most 'backward' districts, the implementation of the programme spread to an additional 130 districts by 2007–08 and to all the districts of India by 2008–09. In 2013-14, MGNREGA generated 2.3 billion person-days of employment for over 50 million rural households; more than half the person-days went to women and more than 40 per cent to the SC and ST population (see Table 4.1). With the annual outlay of over US$ 6 billion, MGNREGA is arguably the world's largest employment guarantee programme. It may as well be the world's largest rural water security programme, as over half the MGNREGA funds are being invested in water-related works (Shah et al. 2011).

MGNREGA was introduced as a flagship social security programme of the Government of India but instances of large-scale corruption, political favouritism and poor quality of assets have resulted in fierce criticism and disenchantment with the programme. One of the biggest strengths of MGNREGA is believed to be its self-targeting design. This implies that unless there is widespread systemic corruption, the programme's benefits can be expected to reach its desired beneficiaries as the rural elite are unlikely to be willing to do unskilled manual labour at minimum wages.

However, this strength might also turn against the programme for two reasons. One, such a targeted programme might get branded as '*raahat kaam*' (relief work)

S. Verma (✉)
IWMI—Tata Water Policy Program, International Water Management Institute (IWMI), Anand, Gujarat, India
e-mail: shilpv@gmail.com

T. Shah
International Water Management Institute (IWMI), Anand, Gujarat, India
e-mail: t.shah@cgiar.org

M. Bhattarai et al. (eds.), *Employment Guarantee Programme and Dynamics of Rural Transformation in India*, India Studies in Business and Economics,
https://doi.org/10.1007/978-981-10-6262-9_4

Table 4.1 MGNREGA performance over the years

Parameters	Units	2006-07	2007–08	2008–09	2009–10	2010–11	2011–12	2012–13	2013–14	2014–15
Number of job cards issued	Million	37.85	64.74	100.15	112.55	119.82	122.75	130.61	130.57	123.03
Number of HHs that demanded employment	Million	21.19	34.33	45.52	52.86	55.76	50.35	45.61	53.93	45.27
Number of HHs that were provided employment	Million	21.02	33.91	45.12	52.53	54.95	49.86	45.58	50.06	45.19
Person-days of employment generated	Billion	0.91	1.44	2.16	2.84	2.57	2.11	2.30	2.30	1.60
Share of women in employment person-days	per cent	40.65%	42.52%	47.88%	48.10%	47.73%	48.18%	51.30%	51.86%	53.94%
Share of SC/ST in employment person-days	per cent	61.81%	56.71%	54.72%	51.20%	51.48%	40.20%	40.01%	42.47%	40.39%
Total expenditure (₹)	Billion ₹	88.23	158.58	272.51	379.10	393.77	375.49	368.52	370.78	317.77
Total expenditure (US$[a])	Billion US$	1.47	2.64	4.54	6.32	6.56	6.26	6.14	6.18	5.30
Total expenditure per person-day employment[b]	$/day	$1.62	$1.84	$2.10	$2.23	$2.55	$2.96	$2.66	$2.69	$3.32

Source: MoRD (2015) http://nrega.nic.in/netnrega/home.aspx

[a]Calculated assuming average exchange rate over the years as: 1 US$ = ₹ 60

[b]Authors' estimate based on total expenditure and person-days of employment generated

in the minds of its intended beneficiaries as well as the implementing agency. Worse, the beneficiaries may come to view it as a precursor to a future unconditional entitlement. Two, the programme may completely bypass and is likely to be overlooked by the better-off farmers and the rich rural elite, who, either officially via the *Gram Panchayat* or unofficially via strong socio-cultural networks, tend to be the opinion makers in the village.

It is therefore important to distinguish between the programme's wage and non-wage benefits and to understand that, while the poor may benefit from both, the better-off in the village would be interested primarily in the latter. The challenge is to enhance the stake of both groups in maximizing the net positive impacts (Shah 2009).

4.1.1 Studies and Methods

In 2009–10, and then again in 2010 and 2010–11, the International Water Management Institute (IWMI) worked with masters students from the Institute of Rural Management, Anand (IRMA) to: (a) understand how MGNREGA and village labour markets interact; and (b) document case studies of over 140 best-performing MGNREGA water assets (Fig. 4.1). Detailed tables are in annexure: Tables 4.5, 4.6 and 4.7).

In 2009–10, 35 students were asked to provide a qualitative overview of MGNREGA implementation in their village while collecting specific data on MGNREGA works. This was largely an exploratory study to understand the dynamics of MGNREGA implementation; students were given a common village schedule which they were asked to fill-up based on focussed group discussions with villagers.

Fig. 4.1 Study Locations. **a** Districts covered in exploratory study on MGNREGA, 2009–10 **b** Districts covered in study of MGNREGA—labour market interactions, 2010 **c** Districts covered in case studies of best-performing MGNREGA water assets, 2010–11

In 2010, 27 students undertook fieldwork with specific research questions and hypotheses to explore the interactions between MGNREGA and rural labour markets. The students used a common research framework and were asked to explore the following aspects of labour market interactions with MGNREGA. They were

a. Has MGNREGA implementation had an additive or substitutive impact in the village;
b. How have local wage rates changed;
c. Has there been any segmentation in the village labour market;
d. What is the role played by the MGNREGA work supervisors;
e. Has there been any change in the incidence of shared cropping and land leasing; and
f. What has been the impact of MGNREGA on migration?

Further, in 2010–11, eight students spent 10 weeks and surveyed more than 600 landless and marginal farmers and nearly 350 medium and large farmers; they also conducted 143 case studies of best-performing MGNREGA water assets in 75 villages across four states (see Table 4.2). For the case studies of MGNREGA assets, the students followed a common case study protocol. For the survey of village leaders, labourers and farmers, village schedules and structured questionnaires were used.

In addition to these, the authors also undertook fieldwork in Rajasthan, Madhya Pradesh, Gujarat, Haryana, Punjab, Uttar Pradesh, and West Bengal (Shah and Indu 2009; Verma 2010; Verma and Schwan 2012).

In Sect. 4.2 of this chapter, we discuss how prevailing conditions in rural labour markets influence MGNREGA implementation. In Sect. 4.3, the impact of MGNREGA implementation on rural labour markets is presented. Section 4.4 focuses on the views, attitudes, and perceptions about MGNREGA among rich and poor villagers. Section 4.5 discusses the case studies of 143 best-performing MGNREGA assets. In Sect. 4.6, we try to draw inferences and lessons from all the studies and fieldwork and enumerate some practical suggestions for improving the net positive returns from MGNREGA. We conclude in Sect. 4.7 with a discussion on the emerging new context of MGNREGA.

4.2 How Do Local Labour Markets Influence MGNREGA Implementation?

The design of MGNREGA assumes that every village has poor people who demand more work than is locally available at the government-determined minimum wage rate. While this might broadly be true for India as a whole, it is certainly not true everywhere. In all, we found four distinct situations of MGNREGA's interaction with local, especially agricultural, labour markets (Table 4.3).

Table 4.2 Sample sizes in each of the four states covered in 2010–11

State	District	No. of assets studied	No. of villages covered	Field Surveys (No. of respondents)		Student reports
				Landless and marginal farmers	Medium and large farmers	
Bihar	Bhojpur	10	08	51	41	Kumar and Chandra (2010)
	Nalanda	15	10	92	49	
	Vaishali	10	05	43	25	
Gujarat	Junagadh	16	13	65	72	Gaur and Chandel (2010)
	Sabarkantha	18	08	80	29	
Kerala	Palaghat	40	12	98	56	Nair and Sanju (2010)
Rajasthan	Dungarpur	21	09	85	35	Singh and Modi (2010)
	Tonk	13	10	90	40	
Total		143	75	604	347	
				951		

Table 4.3 Four distinct types of MGNREGA labour market interactions

	Type I—Misfit	Type II—Insignificant	Type III—Potentially significant	Type IV—Significant
Wage rates	$W_{LOCAL} > W_{MGNREGA}$	$W_{MGNREGA} > W_{LOCAL}$	$W_{MGNREGA} > W_{LOCAL}$	$W_{MGNREGA} > W_{LOCAL}$
Conditions	Booming local labour market offering much greater opportunities	MGNREGA work insignificant vis-à-vis local demand	MGNREGA potentially significant but poorly implemented	MGNREGA significant vis-à-vis local demand
Examples	Kutch (Gujarat), Uttarkashi (Uttarakhand), Kangra (Himachal Pradesh)	Godda (Jharkhand), Koraput (Orissa), Nalanda (Bihar), Narmada (Gujarat)	Narmada (Gujarat), Mandla (Madhya Pradesh)	Dholpur (Rajasthan), Palakkad (Kerala), Chittoor (Andhra Pradesh), Jalna (Maharashtra)

Source Authors' conceptualization

4.2.1 Type I: Misfit

In this case, a booming local labour market, with work going aplenty at much higher than the official minimum wages, makes MGNREGA a 'misfit' and difficult to implement for lack of demand. There was neither interest in the scheme's wage benefit nor in its non-wage benefits.

Shah et al. (2011) provide a glimpse into this from the field studies in Mundra, Kutch district in Gujarat, where people have hit jackpots by selling their land at very high prices and were able to access limitless work opportunities at twice the MGNREGA wage rate or more. There were no work-seekers; yet the block and district administration were relentlessly pressurizing the *Panchayat* leaders to find people to work in the programme. Somewhat similar were Uttarakhand and Himachal Pradesh villages, where the prevailing agricultural wages were equal to or far above the minimum wages resulting in a general indifference towards the programme; and it required an unusually enthusiastic *Panchayat* leadership to goad people into joiningMGNREGA works.

4.2.2 Type II: Insignificant

This is the situation of no or insignificant interaction between MGNREGA and the local labour markets. In other words, MGNREGA neither had any impact on the functioning of the local labour markets; nor did the labour markets significantly affect the programme's implementation. In Godda (Jharkhand), Koraput (Orissa) and Nalanda (Bihar) villages, the volume of MGNREGA work on offer was too small compared to the demand and the total size of the labour market. Here, MGNREGA had no perceptible impact on the working of the local labour markets, nor was the scheme able to substantially animate the village community.

4.2.3 Type III: Potentially Significant

This is the situation where MGNREGA wages were significantly higher than local wages and the volume of potential MGNREGA work was also significant and yet, MGNREGA invoked a lukewarm response from the community owing to administrative bottlenecks, distrust, systemic corruption, lack luster implementation or lack of awareness.

In Narmada (Gujarat), the prevailing local agricultural wages were roughly a third of the MGNREGA wages on offer. The local Panchayat rallied to initiate MGNREGA works in the village but was discouraged by a passive block administration.

When they finally managed to initiate some work, there were long delays in the payment of wages prompting villagers to give up on MGNREGA and return to the residual labour market, which paid out cash wages instantaneously (Verma 2010). Likewise, in Mandla, people initially took to MGNREGA enthusiastically but shifted back to lower paying works as MGNREGA wage payments took as long as 6 months.

4.2.4 *Type IV: Significant*

This is the situation in which MGNREGA presence is large enough to catalyze widespread interest in the community and to significantly alter the structure, conduct and performance of agricultural labour markets. We found this, to some extent, in Dholpur (Rajasthan) and to a much greater extent, in Palakkad (Kerala), Chittoor (Andhra Pradesh) and Jalna (Maharashtra) villages.

Thus the prevailing labour market conditions define how village communities react and respond to MGNREGA. In labour-scarce regions, MGNREGA is unlikely to find many enthusiastic takers as the prevailing market wage rate would be higher than the MGNREGA wages. However, in labour-surplus conditions with depressed market wage rates, a well-implemented MGNREGA is likely to bring huge relief to the labourers.

4.3 How Does MGNREGA Influence Local Labour Markets?

Bhalla (2004) argued that the unemployment rate among the poorest—the agricultural workers—was only 1 per cent and therefore, MGNREGA was unlikely to benefit them much, especially since it offers work at low (minimum) wages. However, the response to MGNREGA and the scale of its implementation has been overwhelming, with significant and possibly irreversible impacts.

According to the official statistics released by the Ministry of Rural Development (MoRD), till date MGNREGA has spent US$ 51.7 billion[1] and generated more than 19.6 billion person-days of employment for roughly 50 million participating households. A large part of this employment accrues to women and SC/ST participants (Fig. 4.2). Bhalla (2010), however, argues that the official figures of employment generation are gross over-estimates and that the actual figures are likely to be closer to half these numbers.

[1]Assuming an average exchange rate over the years as: 1 US$ = ₹ 60.

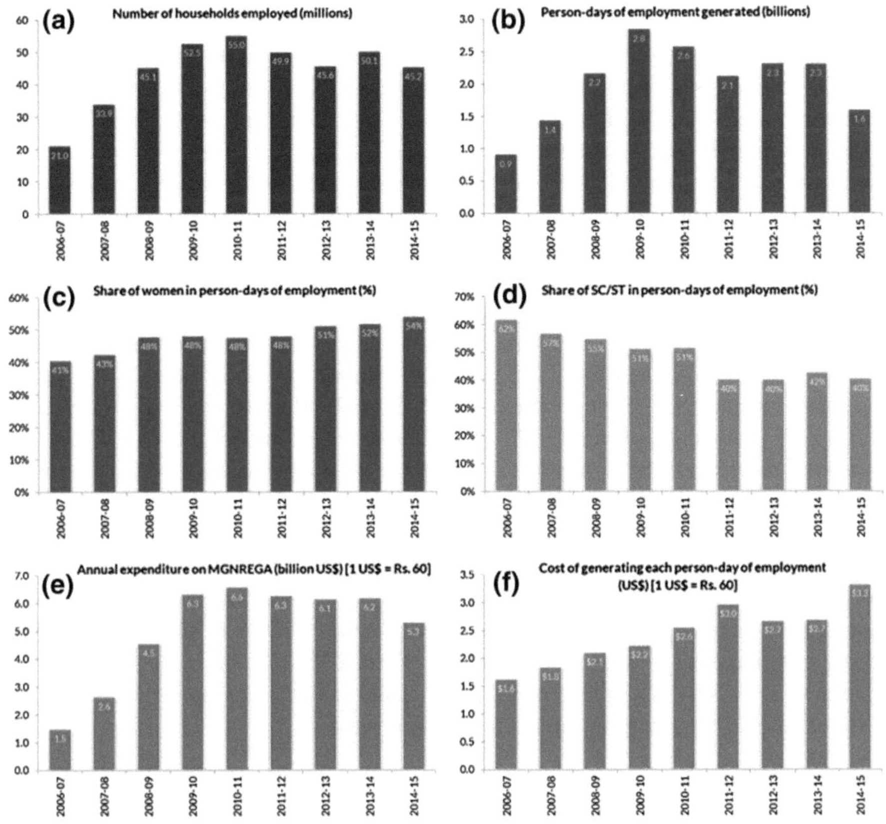

Fig. 4.2 Performance of MGNREGA over the years. *Source* MoRD (2015)

4.3.1 Tighter and Segmented Labour Markets

Where the interaction between MGNREGA and labour markets has been significant, it has altered the local labour markets in several ways. It has increased work participation rates by offering attractive, accessible and convenient work opportunities, thereby shifting the labour supply curve outward.

It has partitioned the pre-MGNREGA labour market into two: the MGNREGA market and the residual labour market. By removing a block of labour supply from the residual labour market, MGNREGA has created labour shortages and pushed up wage rates in the residual market.

Further, administrative pressures to implement MGNREGA works can create incentives for site supervisors and managers to be lenient in work measurement. This would mean that the MGNREGA segment of the rural labour market, over time, become less productivity-sensitive vis-à-vis the residual market. This, among other factors, has attracted women and less-able men to MGNREGA works.

For MGNREGA to have major impact on farm labour markets, it is critical that the volume of work offered under the scheme is substantial during the peak agricultural season. In Dholpur (Rajasthan), much MGNREGA work was scheduled during summer when farm labour demand was low; therefore, the scheme's impact on labour market was relatively small. Here, MGNREGA work was additive; it expanded the labour market by attracting new labour to the work force without drawing away a significant chunk of workers from the residual market.

Similar results were reported from Bikaner and Rajsamand (Rajasthan); Idukki and Trivandrum (Kerala); West Sikkim District (Sikkim); and Chittoor (Andhra Pradesh). In Palakkad (Kerala), however, the plantation economy demands farm labour throughout the year; and here, MGNREGA offered nearly 100 days of work to anyone who asked; as a result, the scheme's impact on labour market was broad and deep, raising female wage rates from ₹ 60 to ₹ 90 and male wage rates from ₹ 100 to anywhere between ₹ 150 and 225/day. The impact of MGNREGA in Palakkad, therefore, was substitutive; it withdrew a sizeable, mostly female, work force from agriculture. To make up, farm wage rates had to go up 50–70 per cent.

Several parallel effects seem to be in operation here. The scheme puts into the hands of poor people significant amount of cash that reduces the need for distress or forced labour. Our survey of landless and marginal farmers across 75 villages in four states found that, on average, MGNREGA workers experienced more than 50 per cent increase in income from labour; from ₹ 9,177 to ₹ 14,551 per annum. Where MGNREGA is implemented on full scale, farm and non-farm labour markets become tighter, putting pressure on wage rates.

4.3.2 Increased Women Participation and Reduced Male-Female Wage Ratio

MGNREGA work has found particular appeal among poor women who find the wages attractive and the facilities at the work site—such as crèche and shade—particularly convenient. Finding work close to their home also increases the scheme's appeal. In Bambara village of Adilabad, the Panchayat also offered flexi-time on MGNREGA works which enhanced its appeal even further.

The convenience and appeal of MGNREGA—besides the general impression of MGNREGA work being light and poorly monitored—also attracts relatively less poor rural women to the scheme, some entering the labour market for the first time. In a Dholpur village (Rajasthan), it was noted that when SC/ST women first joined the MGNREGA work force, *Thakur* women stayed aloof; but soon, they too joined and got away with shirking work while the SC/ST women did the hard labour. Likewise, in Idukki (Kerala), we found that almost all economically inactive middle class women joined the MGNREGA labour force.

Since the residual labour markets pay significantly higher wages to male workers than to their female counterparts, MGNREGA sites were doubly more attractive to

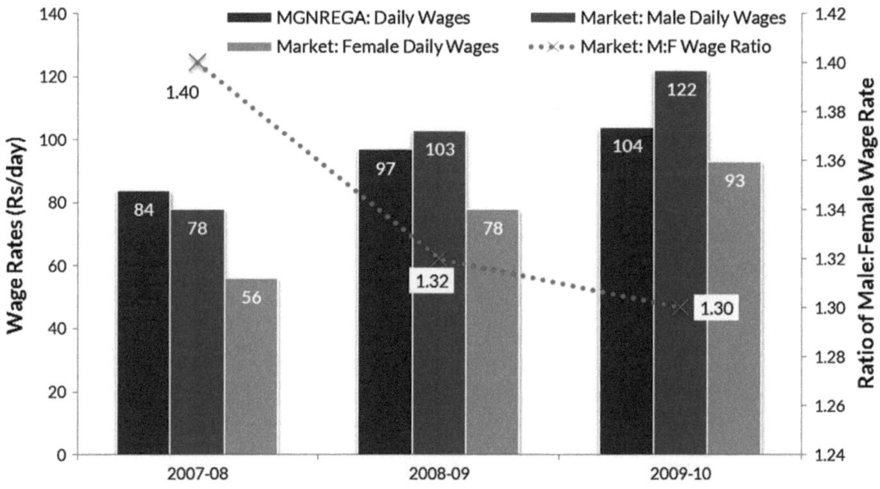

Fig. 4.3 Impact of MGNREGA implementation on Male and Female wage rates. *Source* IWMI-IRMA village surveys in 2010–11

women workers. In Palakkad villages, the labour market got vertically segmented: women, old and the infirm choosing MGNREGA but able-bodied men demanding higher wages in farm jobs.

Likewise in Rajsamand and Dungarpur (Rajasthan) where migration to urban centres like Udaipur, Ahmedabad and Surat offers lucrative opportunities for men, much of the MGNREGA workers were found to be women and older men who had discontinued migration. Women found MGNREGA work attractive since it gave them extra cash they could spend on themselves and on household items. For which they earlier had to depend on their husbands/male family members and had to wait for them to return home during festivals (Verma 2010).

Wage data from our surveys in 75 villages shows that not only have the wages in the residual market been rising steadily, the ratio of male wages to female wages has been declining (Fig. 4.3). This is a positive outcome of the pressure MGNREGA exerts on the residual labour markets.

4.3.3 Less Clear Impact on Migration

Surveys revealed that farmers in popular migrant destinations repeatedly complained about reduction in the inflow of migrants and the demand for higher wages and better facilities by the migrant workers. At the same time, in migrant-source locations, we found no significant reduction in out-migration.

Shah and Indu (2009) reported that in many villages of Punjab and Haryana, MGNREGA was seen reducing the inflow of migrant labour; and even those workers who come often prefer to work on MGNREGA works. In Rithal village of Rohtak district in Haryana, farmers depended heavily on migrant labour from Madhya Pradesh. These migrants however started working on MGNREGA works in Rohtak. Farmers felt that poor people and migrants prefer MGNREGA work at ₹ 135 per day rather than farm work at ₹ 200 per day, because, the former is lighter and less rigorously supervised. Farmers are now using JCBs to get their earth work done.

Our overall impression was that while MGNREGA implementation reduced distress migration, opportunistic migration continued as before. MGNREGA wages could not match up to the wages able-bodied men could earn by migrating to urban centres where the wages are much higher. Moreover, administrative bottlenecks might have tempered any potential impact on out-migration. In Mandla (Madhya Pradesh), MGNREGA implementation initially reduced out-migration but delays in payment of MNGREGA wages led the people back to their migrant ways. Similar delays were also reported elsewhere.

4.4 Attitude of the Rich and the Poor

The principal-agent problem comes to full play in MGNREGA. Moral hazard is openly evident, so is adverse selection. A working hypothesis we had was that works on private lands would be better monitored compared to works related to development/rejuvenation of common pool resources (CPR).

For instance, in some villages of 24-Paraganas district in West Bengal, Shah and Indu (2009) found MGNREGA work on private fishing ponds was supervised well, all funds available were utilized and wages were paid promptly. Shah and Indu (2009) also reported that people applying and then not reporting for work was emerging as a big issue in Punjab and Haryana villages.

In one village near Rohtak town, the *Pardhan* got a MGNREGA project to get irrigation drains de-silted, but most people who applied for work refused to come despite cajoling and coercing; so children, old people and anyone who would work, were to be persuaded to complete the work.

Large land owners are at the receiving end of MGNREGA. Subodh Saha, a large farmer who migrated from Bangladesh on the basis of land exchange, asserted that MGNREGA was government's plan to finish off the farmers. '*When people got ₹ 80 for doing 'nothing', why would they do hard farm labour for me?*' he asked (Shah and Indu 2009).

Similar sentiments were portrayed in eastern UP, south Rajasthan and West Bengal. Growing labour scarcity and the consequent rise in wages were the obvious grouses, so were the growing laziness of labourers and a decline in the work ethic. Our survey in 75 villages of Bihar, Gujarat, Kerala and Rajasthan tried to better understand the perceptions of the rich and poor regarding MGNREGA and its various aspects.

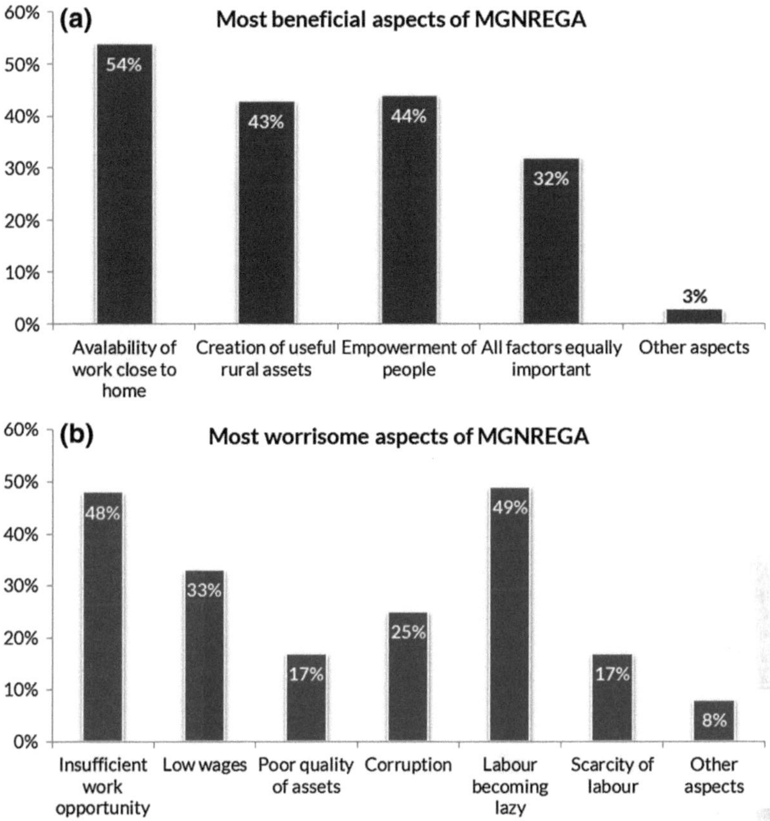

Fig. 4.4 Most beneficial and worrisome aspects of MGNREGA. *Source* IWMI-IRMA village surveys in 2010–11. *Note* The values on the *y*-axis represent the percentage of villages that chose the particular variable

In focused group discussions, we asked about the most beneficial and most worrisome aspects of MGNREGA in each village (Fig. 4.4). Not surprisingly, most groups mentioned 'availability of work close to home' as the most beneficial aspect of MGNREGA; 'empowerment of village communities, including women' was second; closely followed by 'creation of useful rural assets'.

In terms of the worrisome aspects, the most prominent was a dilution in work ethic expressed as 'labour becoming lazy'. Nearly half the groups complained about the 'lack of sufficient work' and one-third felt that MGNREGA offered 'low wages'. These groups demanded that MGNREGA be implemented more forcefully and at a larger scale. Interestingly, corruption and malpractices in MGNREGA did not figure prominently; and were reported by only one-fourth of the groups as worrisome.

As shown in Table 4.1, we surveyed around 600 landless and marginal farmers and around 350 medium and large farmers. The landless and marginal farmers are

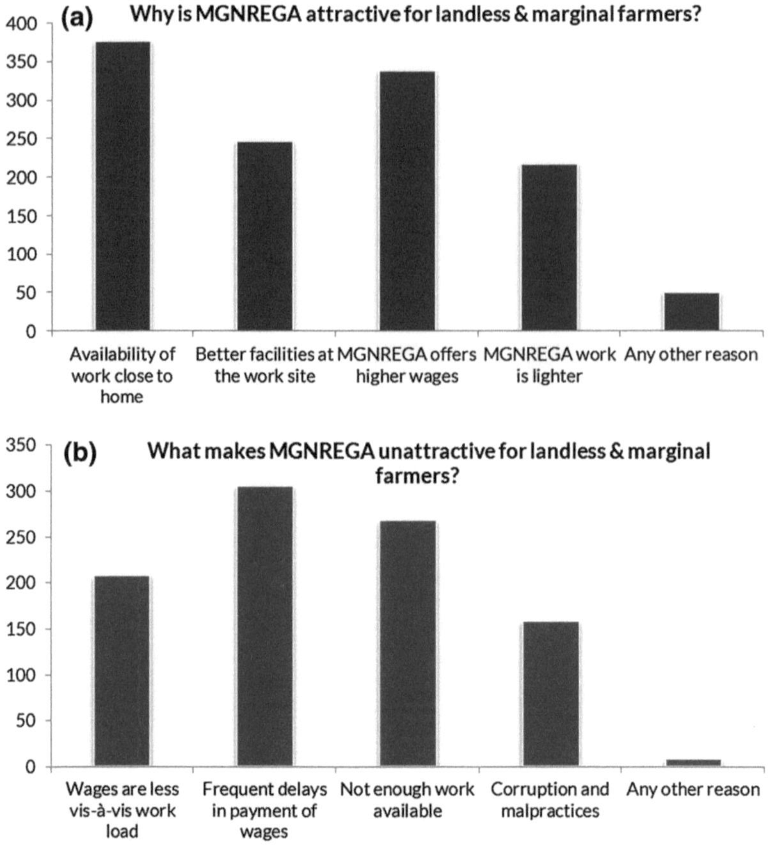

Fig. 4.5 Reasons why MGNREGA work is attractive and unattractive for labourers. *Source* IWMI-IRMA village surveys in 2010–11. *Note* The values on the *y*-axis represent a composite index based on ranks given by the respondent to the different variables

the most likely beneficiaries of the wage benefits of MGNREGA; we asked them reasons why they found it attractive; and reasons that made MGNREGA unattractive to them (Fig. 4.5).

As in the group discussions, 'availability of work close to home' was found to be the most attractive aspect of MGNREGA. This was followed by 'higher wages' than the prevailing residual market wage rates; somewhat contradicting the results from the group discussions. Labourers acknowledged that MGNREGA wages acted as the new wage floor and offered negotiating power to the labourers vis-à-vis their employers.

The labourers also appreciated the 'improved work-site facilities'; putting pressure on residual labour market to provide the same. Several labourers, especially women, acknowledged that 'MGNREGA work is lighter' compared to the residual farm labour market. Our respondents reported frequent delays in

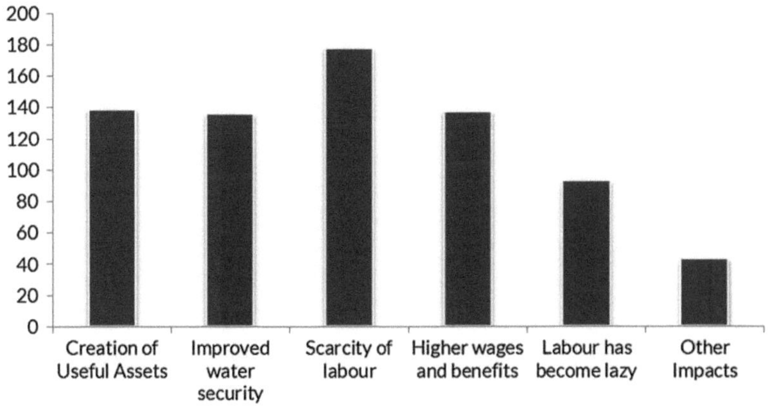

Fig. 4.6 Key impacts of MGNREGA for medium and large land-owning farmers. *Source* IWMI-IRMA village surveys in 2010-11. *Note* The values on the *y*-axis represent a composite index based on ranks given by the respondent to the different variables

MGNREGA wage payments and the non-availability of sufficient quantum of work as the most unattractive aspects of the scheme; several labourers were also unhappy with the unclear/arbitrary manner in which actual wages were calculated, leading to suspicions of corruption and malpractices. In some villages, labourers suspected that large farmers colluded with the MGNREGA administration to ensure that no works were carried out during the peak agricultural season. This significantly reduced their bargaining power.

In our interviews with medium and large farmers, the people most likely to hire labourers to work on their farms, we discussed their perceptions about the impact of MGNREGA implementation in their village (Fig. 4.6). These farmers, not surprisingly, thought that the biggest impacts of MGNREGA have been the growing scarcity of labour and the resultant hike in wages and benefits. Several of them acknowledged improvements in local water security and appreciated the creation of useful rural assets. The erosion of work ethics among labourers and their growing laziness was another key impact that they reported.

4.5 Overview of Best-Performing MGNREGA Water Assets

Our sampling of MGNREGA assets was purposive: in each state, the students selected the study villages after a review of secondary data and discussions with local MGNREGA officials. The objective was to document, through case studies, some of the best-performing MGNREGA water assets.

A common case study protocol was used (with slight modifications to suit the specificities of assets being studied). Of the 143 best-performing MGNREGA water

Table 4.4 Sample size of best-performing MGNREGA water asset case studies

State	District	Types of assets	No. of assets	No. of villages	Ownership	
					Public	Private
Bihar	Bhojpur	Pyne micro-canals; Ponds; wells	10	08	5	5
	Nalanda		15	10	14	1
	Vaishali		10	05	7	3
Gujarat	Junagadh	Ponds; check dams; wells	16	13	11	5
	Sabarkantha		18	08	13	5
Kerala	Palaghat	Public and private ponds	40	12	23	17
Rajasthan	Dungarpur	Anicuts; farm ponds, wells	21	09	17	4
	Tonk		13	10	9	4
Total				75	99	44
					143	

assets we studied (see Table 4.4), 46 were village ponds, 29 check dams and anicuts, 26 private ponds and farm ponds, 21 micro-canal works, 20 private wells and 1 river works. 60 of the studied assets were constructed afresh while 83 works involved renovation and/or capacity enhancement of existing infrastructure. 100 of the 143 works were completed before March 2009, while 40 of the remaining 43 were undertaken in 2009–10 and the remaining three, in 2010–11. With the exception of five works, all others were completed well within the budgeted cost estimates.

On average, each work created more than 2000 person-days of employment amounting to roughly 700 days of labour created per lakh rupees investment. However, there was huge disparity in the size of works as indicated by the range of land area that they influenced, from 0.18 to 100 ha. A majority of these works were undertaken with the primary objective of creating and enhancing irrigation potential. Other objectives included augmenting groundwater recharge, addressing domestic water requirements and livestock needs, fishing and pisciculture. Taken together, the 117 assets (for which detailed quantitative data on costs and benefits was calculated by us) generated annual gross value equal to their cost (see Figs. 4.7 and 4.8).

Traditional inundation canal systems (*pyne*) that serve the dual-purpose of irrigation and drainage in conjunction with embankments (*ahar*) have been prevalent in Bihar for centuries. According to Pant, these indigenous systems were used to irrigate nearly a million hectares in Bihar in 1930.

However, due to various reasons—including the abolition of zamindari and rapid development of groundwater irrigation—the area irrigated by these systems declined to half by 1997 (Pant 1998). Kumar and Chandra (2010) found in their study villages that these systems were near-completely dysfunctional before they were taken up for renovation and revival under MGNREGA.

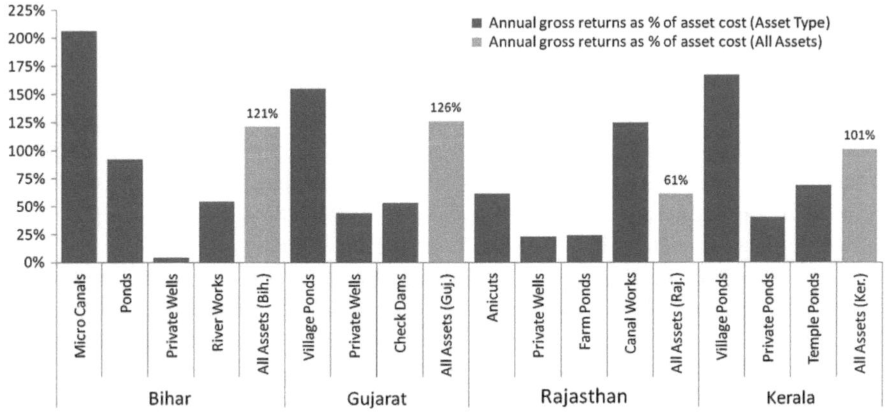

Fig. 4.7 Gross returns from one year of use as a proportion of investment made in different states. *Source* Bihar: Kumar and Chandra (2010); Gujarat: Gaur and Chandel (2010); Kerala: Nair and Sanju (2010); Rajasthan: Singh and Modi (2010)

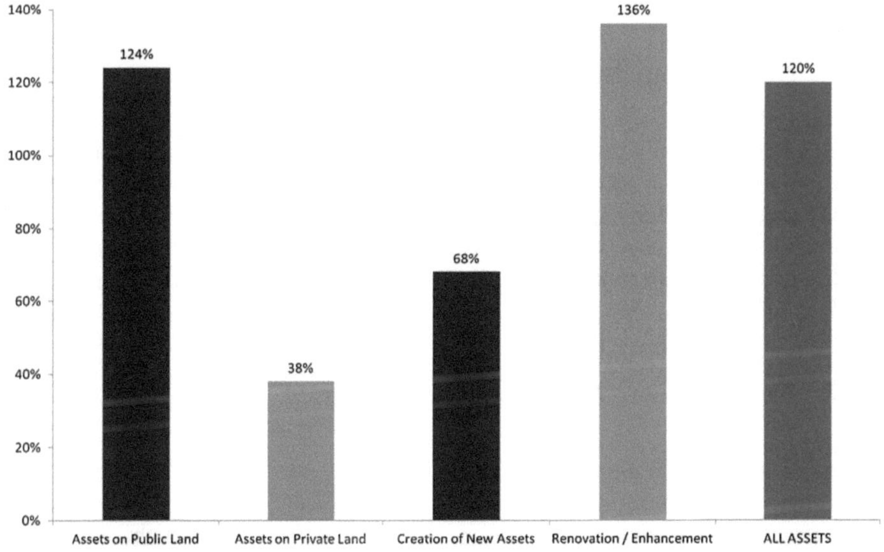

Fig. 4.8 Benefits from one year of use as a proportion of investment made in different asset-types. *Source* Bihar: Kumar and Chandra (2010); Gujarat: Gaur and Chandel (2010); Kerala: Nair and Sanju (2010); Rajasthan: Singh and Modi (2010)

The 19 case studies of MGNREGA works on micro-canal systems turned out to be the most promising across the four states in terms of gross returns. The assets required little investment in renovation and allowed farmers to provide 3–6 additional watering to their paddy crops. Bulk of the benefit to farmers came in the form of diesel-saving. Kumar and Chandra (2010) also found that while ponds were demanded primarily for irrigation, an important share of their benefits accrued from pisciculture.

In Gujarat, Gaur and Chandel (2010) found that most of the public assets created under MGNREGA were check dams, not used directly for irrigation but undertaken to augment groundwater recharge. They also reported that while the gross returns from MGNREGA assets on private land were significantly lower, their provision had exemplary impact on the livelihoods of the beneficiaries.

The field study in Rajasthan (Singh and Modi 2010) offered an interesting comparison between MGNREGA implementation in a predominantly tribal district (Dungarpur) and a non-tribal district (Tonk). Despite a more proactive and better staffed MGNREGA administration in Dungarpur, the productivity of assets was significantly higher in Tonk. While the ratio of gross returns to MGNREGA investment in anicuts was 102 per cent in Tonk, it was a much lower 37 per cent in Dungarpur. This may partly be attributable to the physical factors (undulating terrain, poor soil quality, etc.) and partly to the fact that the farmers in Tonk were far more experienced and better connected to markets.

4.6 Lessons from Best-Performing MGNREGA Assets

The 143 best-performing MGNREGA assets were purposively selected to understand the potential of MGNREGA in meeting its dual objectives of livelihood security and rural water security. However, they do not seem to depict the general situation of MGNREGA works across the country. We offer eight propositions which will ensure than more, if not all, MGNREGA assets perform exceptionally.

4.6.1 Pick the Low Hanging Fruits First

The estimates of gross return from our case studies illustrate two important points. First, that purely in terms of returns on investment, the best bet would be enhancement, renovation or revival of existing village water bodies that may have fallen into disrepair as the socio-economic context of communities changed over time. *Pynes* in Bihar is a case in point but there might be others—cleaning of irrigation canals and channels; de-silting and deepening of tanks and ponds to enhance storage and augment groundwater recharge; de-silting of small and large irrigation reservoirs to rejuvenate their storage capacity, etc.

Second, although the annual economic returns from MGNREGA assets on private lands might be lower, when implemented well, they make significant improvements in the lives of beneficiaries—who invariably belong to the poorest households and the most marginalized communities. The feverish demand for

Kapildhara[2] wells in Madhya Pradesh also illustrates this point. The distinct advantage of implementing works on private lands is that their ownership is clearly defined; and beneficiaries either themselves work in the construction process or provide additional supervision and oversight to ensure superior quality of work.

4.6.2 Keep MGNREGA Demand-Driven

One of the concerns with MGNREGA was that its success would depend on villagers internalizing the fact that MGNREGA offers an 'entitlement' to demand work and is not a relief programme. However, we found several instances where the implementation of MGNREGA was driven not by an overwhelming demand for wage labour but by the MGNREGA administration at various levels. It did not always appear as if the administration itself understood well the difference between MGNREGA and other centrally sponsored schemes.

The *Sarpanchs* (president, *Gram Panchayat*) viewed MGNREGA as an opportunity to gain political mileage and enhance their social clout at the expense of the national government. The Block and District administration set spending targets for themselves in order for the State to take advantage of a centrally sponsored programme with near-unlimited access to funds. The MGNREGA administration at the Centre did not help either by awarding districts that managed to *generate* more days of employment, and in effect, spend more money. While this enthusiasm might have led to some high-quality assets, in several cases this also led the administration to ignore work quality and focus exclusively on employment creation.

In 2009–10, the then Gujarat Chief Minister (CM) declared his wish to undertake the construction of *boribandhs* under MGNREGA. An overzealous administration took up the wish of the CM in a mission mode and more than 250,000 *boribandhs* were constructed. Little did the administration realize that the construction of effective *boribandhs* required a thorough understanding of local stream hydrology or that it needed to be done in a small time window—when the stream flow was neither too much nor too low.

Not surprisingly, studies found that more than 85 per cent of the *boribandhs* were rendered useless in no time (Shah and Mistry 2012). Our surveys also revealed that MGNREGA assets performed best where they were most required and where the decision to undertake the works was taken by the village communities, rather than by the *Sarpanch* or the MGNREGA administration.

[2]*Kapil dhara yojana* in Madhya Pradesh was initiated with the objective of stabilizing agricultural production and improving farmers' livelihood by providing irrigation facilities including digging of new wells.

4.6.3 Recognize the Importance of Assets

A common perception under the previous UPA national government was that MGNREGA was primarily a conduit for doling out extra cash to people and that the focus on MGNREGA's non-wage benefits was often missing. Apparently, MGNREGA has an elaborate system of reporting, much of which is done near-real-time. However, none of the parameters in the management information system (MIS) seem to focus on the quality of assets, the benefits people can derive from them, or on their sustainability. Once a work is declared *complete*, the MIS stops tracking it.

Admittedly, almost in every state, we found that the local MGNREGA staff was over-burdened by the rush to initiate 'new works' or to complete the ongoing ones. Field engineers in several states reported that each of them was looking after 6–10 *Gram Panchayats*, which could easily mean more than 100 ongoing works at a time.

In Andhra Pradesh, we found engineers eagerly looking forward to vacancies being filled in the hope of easing their burden; in Madhya Pradesh, we found that MGNREGA engineers were also looking after non-MGNREGA works; and some of them 'informally trained and hired' local villagers to help them out.

They suggested that MGNREGA Mates should be given some technical training to assist them better. The MGNREGA Mates are fairly well qualified and can easily be trained into *barefoot engineers*. Doing this would not only provide some much-needed relief and assistance to the engineers; but will also train a cadre of young villagers in practical aspects of civil engineering.

Another issue is the high dropout rate of engineers and this came up repeatedly in our discussions in Madhya Pradesh. The open market offers significantly higher salaries to engineers and it is therefore, difficult for MGNREGA to retain the best ones. The field engineers candidly admitted that the quality of assets suffered due to poor supervision and lack of proper technical inputs but also described their inability to do anything about it.

Singh and Modi (2010) found that the difference in the work load of Junior Technical Assistants correlated well with difference in the quality of assets between Dungarpur and Tonk. Gaur and Chandel (2010), on the other hand, reported that a smart system of incentives in place for MGNREGA Mates in Gujarat led to healthy competition among them on who could create the best-performing assets. Shah (2009) argued that it is the non-wage benefits of MGNREGA that afford it a clear advantage over a cash transfer scheme. Conversely, if the quality of MGNREGA assets were to be consistently poor, it would end up being nothing more than a poor substitute for a cash transfer programme.

4.6.4 Fix Responsibility for Maintenance

Our surveys reported that even in the case of best-performing public assets, maintenance was an issue and the life expectancy of assets was woefully low. In Kerala, of the 23 public ponds we surveyed, only one was being maintained by the community. Villagers, including those who were directly benefiting from the assets, felt that it was the responsibility of the *Gram Panchayat* to regularly clean and maintain the ponds.

In some cases, the user-community used to carry out some kind of annual maintenance work before it was taken up under MGNREGA. Ever since, the user-community stopped the maintenance activities and expected the government or the *Gram Panchayat* to shoulder the responsibility. Likewise in Gujarat, Gaur and Chandel (2010) suggested that because the benefits from public assets were diffused over a larger group of beneficiaries, there was little interest in maintenance among individual users.

Singh and Modi (2010) noted that in Rajasthan, while communities were *vigilant* about the maintenance of public assets, they were either incapable (in Dungarpur) or unwilling (Tonk) to contribute monetarily towards asset maintenance. Likewise in Bihar, Kumar and Chandra (2010) recommended that special provisions should be made for the *Gram Panchayats* to undertake repair and maintenance works on a regular basis.

Even in Madhya Pradesh, where the implementing agencies are required to identify user groups and hand over the assets to them on completion, maintenance was an issue. The then MGNREGA Commissioner in Bhopal, Dr. Pastore suggested that it is futile to hand over assets to user groups that are identified after the works have been implemented. He suggested that the user groups should be identified before construction begins and should be involved in the planning, design, procurement and implementation of the works. Only then would they assume ownership and responsibility for the asset (Verma and Schwan 2012).

The relatively better work-supervision and maintenance of MGNREGA assets on private lands suggests that if the assets built are useful and effective. The users have clearly defined ownership, and if it is clear to them that neither MGNREGA, nor the *Gram Panchayat*, nor any other programme of the government would take up the responsibility of maintaining the assets. The users should see self-interest in proper maintenance of assets on their own land. The problem with assets on common land is that their ownership is not clearly defined and their benefits are too diffused.

There is unlikely to be any one institutional model for maintenance that would work everywhere. MGNREGA must therefore offer flexibility and actively seek out local institutional arrangements. The MGNREGA administration, on its part, should include asset quality parameters in the MIS and initiate a routine of regular inspection of works even after their construction has been completed.

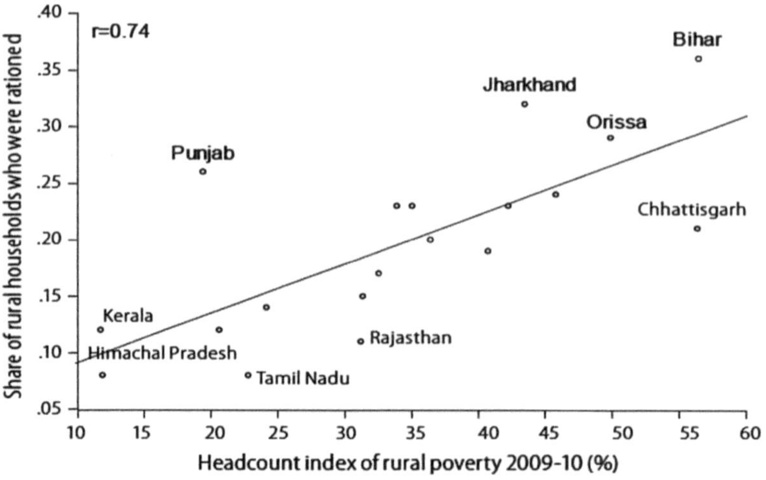

Fig. 4.9 Rural poverty and unmet demand for MGNREGA work. *Source* Dutta et al. (2012), p. 58

4.6.5 Better Equip MGNREGA Administration, Especially in Poor Areas

Through an analysis of the National Sample Survey data for 2009–10, Dutta et al. (2012; p. 57) show that '*poorer states have greater unmet demand*' for MGNREGA work (see Fig. 4.9). Thus, MGNREGA implementation becomes a function of the ability of the administration rather than of the demand, as originally envisaged.

The administration in better-off states, districts and villages tends to be better equipped in implementing MGNREGA in a supply-push mode even when the effective demand might be relatively low. Poor communities, on the other hand, are likely to be less resourceful and have less effective MGNREGA administration. They are also more likely to have less effective, less informed and less empowered *Gram Panchayats*. There is, therefore, a need to pay special attention to ensuring that MGNREGA administration at all levels is well trained and equipped.

4.6.6 Build Capacities of PRIs and Help Them Become Better Demand Systems

Among the four states where we conducted asset case studies, Kerala and Rajasthan seemed to be performing better, but for different reasons. Singh and Modi (2010) suggested that the MGNREGA awareness levels in Rajasthan were quite high and people were quite aware about the provisions and processes of MGNREGA.

In Kerala, where *Kudumbashree* is involved in MGNREGA implementation, the programme was able to reach out to women much more than anywhere else. This explains the very high participation of women in MGNREGA in Kerala. Impressions from Gujarat were mixed. While PRIs in Junagadh and Sabarkantha districts seemed to be doing quite well, their performance in tribal south Gujarat was largely disappointing.

In Narmada district, the wages offered by MGNREGA were more than twice the prevailing market rates. Tribal communities were initially quite upbeat about MGNREGA, but an indifferent block and district administration caused long delays in the works approval and wage payment processes and a poor performance in both quantity of employment generated and quality of assets; leaving the village communities feeling helpless, dejected and cynical.

4.6.7 Avoid Alienating Better-off Farmers, but not by Constraining Wage Benefits

In several states, we found that the better-off farmers viewed MGNREGA as a headache; several of them even called it a conspiracy against farmers. In several places, farmers complained about scarcity of agricultural labour, rising wages, deteriorating work ethic, labour demanding improved working conditions and better facilities, etc. They argued that just as MGNREGA was trying to help the labourers; it must also benefit the farmers—who are at the receiving end of the tightened labour markets.

In Kerala and Andhra Pradesh, there was a forceful demand for allowing MGNREGA workers to work on the private land of farmers, especially for labour intensive agricultural operations, such as paddy harvesting. In Anand (Gujarat), the labourers complained that the rich farmers were colluding with the *Gram Panchayat* and block administration to ensure that MGNREGA works are frozen during the peak agricultural season. This was also reflected in the demand by the then Agriculture Minister to freeze MGNREGA works (Tiwari 2011). Doing this would undo much of the gains that MGNREGA workers might have picked up so far.

It was observed by many that the rise in agricultural wage rates, the setting of a new wage floor, the greater bargaining power and the better working conditions—all of these would vanish if the competition between MGNREGA and agricultural labour is eliminated.

We believe that such demands from farmers stem from two sources: (1) in places where the agricultural labour market is already tight, a supply-push implementation of MGNREGA unreasonably distorts the market. If MGNREGA is allowed to retain its intended demand-pull character, much of these complaints would vanish; (2) where farmers have not experienced non-wage benefits of MGNREGA, they perceive MGNREGA only for its negative consequences.

If MGNREGA assets improve local water security; enhance connectivity to input and output markets; and improve village amenities, the entire agrarian economy would get a boost. Instead of tweaking MGNREGA to reduce its wage benefits, efforts should be made to enhance its non-wage benefits so that the better-off farmers acquire a stake in its effective implementation.

4.6.8 Get Performance Measurement Right and Plan an Exit

As discussed earlier, the current MIS of MGNREGA unintentionally creates perverse incentives for the administration to focus on spending. If we want to maximize the non-wage benefits of MGNREGA, the parameters on which MGNREGA implementation is measured will have to be carefully revised. Popular articles and news reports also see a reduction in MGNREGA spending—year on year—as a sign of deteriorating performance or a lapse on the part of the local MGNREGA administration instead of celebrating a decline in demand for minimum-wage labours a positive (see Deccan Herald 2012; ToI 2012).

MGNREGA has a huge database down to the level of each individual job card. This goldmine of data needs to be carefully analysed. If the same households and the same people keep returning to work at minimum-wage year-after-year, MGNREGA cannot be said to have fulfilled its objectives. A perpetual MGNREGA will, in all probability, be a poor one.

In the long run, the success of MGNREGA may be measurable in terms of its reduced demand. Regions and people that require MGNREGA work today should be able to improve their economic condition and enhance their access to opportunities through it and this should reduce their demand for unskilled labour employment over years. This will happen only if the assets created under MGNREGA are effectively able to enhance the profitability of agriculture by improving land productivity, providing enhanced water security, connecting villages to input and output markets and improving rural infrastructure to lift people and places out of poverty.

4.7 Conclusion

Recent discussions on the fate of MGNREGA have tended to focus on operational guidelines—labour-material ratio, wage rates, use of machines, etc.—and on the question of targeting its implementation to a few poor districts. Our field studies highlight how, in spite of all its shortcomings, MGNREGA is transforming rural India through its wage and non-wage benefits.

As labour markets tighten and become segmented, they are also becoming more appealing and equal for women. Village communities identify opportunities of finding 'work close to home', 'empowerment' of labourers and 'useful rural assets' as among the most beneficial aspects of MGNREGA while also raising concerns about deteriorating '*work ethic*' and delays in wage payments.

Although MGNREGA is designed to be self-targeting at the individual level, at the community level, it relies heavily on the capabilities of local institutions. Unless these institutions are strengthened, it is likely that the districts, regions and villages that most need the benefits of MGNREGA will remain deprived. For the rural elite, MGNREGA-induced labour scarcity and higher wages are areas of concern but where implemented well, rich farmers do recognize the value of MGNREGA assets.

Our case studies of best-performing assets highlight the potential of MGNREGA as a water security programme. Under the right conditions, the incremental gross value created with the help of these assets can surpass their costs in a little over a year. However, these conditions are rarely met. The case studies also highlight potential convergence opportunities with the ambitious *Pradhan Mantri Krishi Sinchai Yojana* (PMKSY) which promises '*harkhetkopaani*'.

Mainstreaming the creation of high-performing assets is the key to MGNREGA success. We have offered eight practical suggestions for maximizing MGNREGA's net positive impact. Broadly, our propositions reflect four principles: *prioritization, capacities, incentives* and *exit*. By '*exit*' we imply a gradual decline in demand for work under MGNREGA. We argue that focusing on non-wage benefits of MGNREGA can elevate its performance; and, in the process, build stakes for rural communities.

Doing this will require significant capacity-building investments in local institutions (PRIs, block and district administration) and creative, context-specific arrangements for ensuring sustainability of assets. There is also an urgent need to build capacities and enhance opportunities in the non-farm sector.

MGNREGA work should not and cannot be a permanent occupation for poor households. Over years, the dependence of poor households on MGNREGA and the willingness of people to work at government-prescribed minimum wages must decline. This would be a robust indicator of MGNREGA's success. This can be done by building high-performing assets that help uplift the village economy to a level of prosperity which crowds out the need for minimum-wage work.

Acknowledgements Earlier versions of this chapter were presented at a seminar in Pretoria, South Africa (Verma 2012) and at IWMI-Tata Programme's 2012 Partners' Meet in Anand, Gujarat, India (Verma and Shah 2012a, 2012b).

Annexure

(see Tables 4.5, 4.6 and 4.7)

Table 4.5 List of students who worked with IWMI in 2009–10

State	Districts	Students
Andhra Pradesh	Adilabad	Anjanayulin M., Sindhura A., Sarah S. and Pravin Y
Bihar	Nalanda	Gaurav Kumar and Pratik Gupta
Gujarat	Kutch	Manoharsinh Chauhan, Pavan Chandel, VR Patel and ZailsinhMaharaul
Jharkhand	Godda	Ahmad Fawaz and SumanAcharjee
Kerala	Palakad	Nisha Nair, Gayathri Devi, J P Sara, M. Arulmani and T R Karthik
Maharashtra	Nandurbar	NitinPai and Utsav Mishra
Orissa	Koraput	Anshuman K Gupta
Rajasthan	Dholpur	Abhishek Tiwari, Deepali, Dipin Gupta, Rajat Bhatia, Rajesh Sihag, Suyash Raj and Sunil Yadav
	Bhilwara	Karanpret Singh, Mukesh Mehta and Yash Menaria
Uttarakhand	Uttarkashi	Archit Gupta, Govindkumar Rai and Vineet Khokhar
	Bageshwar	Nitya Chanana and Priyanka Sah

Table 4.6 List of students who worked with IWMI in 2010

State	Districts	Students
Andhra Pradesh	Chittoor	Ramachandra Rani and Premkumar Loganathan
Gujarat	Narmada	Uchit Desai and Mehul Srivastava
Himachal Pradesh	Kangra	Pushpendra Sharan
Kerala	Idukki	Annu Ann Alexander and Milli Anthony
	Trivandrum	Rahul, K. and Vyas Sreenivas
Madhya Pradesh	Mandla	Abhishek Gupta, Ashish Patil, Gandharv Paliwal. Krati Vyas, Shubham Dwivedi and Rohit Bhatnagar
Maharashtra	Jalna	Manoj Prabhakar Sonawane and Shaikh Ateeque Abdul
Orissa	Mayurbhanj	Amrita Chandra and Avantika Garg
Rajasthan	Bikaner	Jaywardhen Tiwari and Shakti Singh Sekhawat
	Rajsamand	Gaurav Jain and Rahul Soni
Sikkim	Sikkim West	Ankit Saxena, Sankalp Patnaik, Shantanu and Vishnu Raghunathan

Table 4.7 List of students who worked with IWMI in 2010–11

State	Districts	Students
Bihar	Bhojpur, Nalanda and Vaishali	Anshuman Kumarand Gopal Chandra
Gujarat	Junagadh and Sabarkantha	Pavan Chandel and Pulkit Gaur
Kerala	Palaghat	Nisha Nair and Sanju S.
Rajasthan	Dungarpur and Tonk	Aparna Singh and Rashi Modi

References

Bhalla, S.S. 2004. Corruption with a human face. *Business Standard*, 11th December. http://www.business-standard.com/article/opinion/surjit-s-bhalla-corruption-with-a-human-face-104121101048_1.html.

Bhalla, S.S. 2010. Does NREGA really work? *Business Standard*, 27th March. http://www.business-standard.com/article/opinion/surjit-bhalla-does-nrega-really-work-110032700029_1.html.

Deccan Herald. 2012. MPs upset with unspent NREGA funds. *Deccan Herald*, 19th November. http://www.deccanherald.com/content/293058/mps-upset-unspent-nrega-funds.html.

Dutta, P., R. Murgai, M. Ravallion, and D. van de Walle. 2012. Does India's employment guarantee scheme guarantee employment? *Economic and Political Weekly*, XLVII (16): 55–64.

Gaur, P., and P. Chandel. 2010. *Effectiveness and ownership of irrigation assets created under NREGS and effect on labour market in Gujarat*. Anand: Institute of Rural Management, MTS report.

Kumar, A., and G. Chandra. 2010. *Effectiveness and ownership of irrigation assets created under MNREGA and labour market dynamics in Bihar*. Anand: Institute of Rural Management, MTS report.

MoRD. 2015. Website of the Mahatma Gandhi National Rural Employment Guarantee Act 2005. Ministry of Rural Development (MoRD), Government of India. http://nrega.nic.in/netnrega/home.aspx.

Nair, N., and S. Sanju. 2010. *Water conservation and irrigation asset creation under NREGS in Kerala: Understanding the ownership and effectiveness of the assets created and its influence on labour dynamics*. Anand: Institute of Rural Management, MTS report.

Pant, N. 1998. Indigenous irrigation in south Bihar: A case of congruence of boundaries. *Economic and Political Weekly* 33 (49): 3132–3138.

Shah, T. 2009. Money for Nothing: Cash transfer is a flawed alternative to NREGS. *The Times of India*, p 12. Ahmedabad, 5th November.

Shah, T., and R. Indu. 2009. MGNREGA in Indo-Gangetic Basin: Fieldnotes from Here and There. Anand: International Water Management Institute.

Shah, H., and P. Mistry. 2012. The invisible bags: A case study of Bori Bandhs constructed under MGNREGA in Gujarat. February, Ahmedabad: DISHA. http://mgnrega-disha.org/the_invisible_bags.pdf.

Shah, T., S. Verma, R. Indu, and H. Pullabothla. 2011. *Asset Creation through Employment Guarantee?: Synthesis of Student Case Studies in 12 states of India*. Anand: International Water Management Institute.

Singh, A., and R. Modi. 2010. *Effectiveness and ownership of assets created under NREGS in Rajasthan*. Anand: Institute of Rural Management, MTS report.

Tiwari, R. 2011. Farms hit, freeze NREG for 3 months/yr: Pawar to PM. *The Indian Express*, 9th December. http://www.indianexpress.com/news/farms-hit-freeze-nreg-for-3-monthsyr-pawar-to-pm/885796.

ToI. 2012. MNREGS has few takers in Warangal. *The Times of India*, Hyderabad, 18th Jan. http://timesofindia.indiatimes.com/city/hyderabad/MNREGS-has-few-takers-in-Warangal/articleshow/11531360.cms.

Verma, S. 2010. *Labor market dynamics in post-NREGS rural India: Field notes from tribal South Gujarat and Southern Rajasthan*. International Water Management Institute: Unpublished field notes, Anand.

Verma, S. 2012. Water asset creation in MGNREGS, India. Invited presentation at seminar organized by the Water Research Commission of South Africa (WRC), International Water Management Institute (IWMI) and Trade and Industrial Policy Strategies (TIPS) International. Pretoria: 14th August.

Verma, S., and T. Shah. 2012a. Labor market dynamics in post-MGNREGA rural India. Water Policy Research Highlight# 8. Anand: IWMI-Tata Water Policy Program.

Verma, S. and T. Shah. 2012b. Beyond digging and filling holes: Lessons from case studies of best-performing MGNREGA assets. Water Policy Research Highlight# 42, Anand: IWMI-Tata Water Policy Program.

Verma, S., and S. Schwan. 2012. Field notes from field trips in Bhopal and Betul, Madhya Pradesh. Unpublished field notes. New Delhi: Deutsche Gesellschaftfür Internationale Zusammenarbeit (GIZ), Indo-German Technical Cooperation.

Chapter 5
Has Profitability of Foodgrain Production Declined After Implementation of MGNREGS in India?

A. Narayanamoorthy, Madhusudan Bhattarai and R. Suresh

5.1 Introduction

The major objective of this study is to find out whether the Mahatma Gandhi National Rural Employment Guarantee Scheme (MGNREGS) has affected the profitability of crops cultivated in different parts of India. Several scholars have argued vehemently in recent days that 'MGNREGS has "pushed up" the average wage of casual workers and distorted the rural labour markets by diverting large number of labour from agriculture to non-farm rural jobs, thus creating an artificial labour shortage and raising the cost of production of agricultural commodities' (Gulati et al. 2013a, b, c, p. 9). As a result of increased cost of production, the profitability of different crops reportedly has declined.

A. Narayanamoorthy (✉) · R. Suresh
Department of Economics and Rural Development, Alagappa University, Karaikudi 630003, Tamil Nadu, India
e-mail: narayana64@gmail.com; na_narayana@hotmail.com

M. Bhattarai
Jalsrot Vikas Sanstha (JVS), 20694, Kathmandu, Nepal
e-mail: madhu.bhattarai2010@gmail.com

M. Bhattarai
ICRISAT, Hyderabad, India

M. Bhattarai et al. (eds.), *Employment Guarantee Programme and Dynamics of Rural Transformation in India*, India Studies in Business and Economics,
https://doi.org/10.1007/978-981-10-6262-9_5

Several studies and reports published in various sources, including vernacular dailies,[1] especially those published in south India, have reported declining profitability of farmers due to the introduction of National Rural Employment Guarantee Scheme (MGNREGS). Some of the past studies have shown that it helps getting the assured wage rate and employment to rural poor in most of the states where it is implemented effectively (Shah 2009; Mukherjee and Sinha 2011; Dutta et al. 2012; MoRD 2012; Mann and Ramesh 2013). But, other studies have shown the contradictory evidence as well (Gulati et al. 2013a, b, c).

Several past studies have also reported that since implementation of the MGNREGS, the growth of agricultural sector declined that has already been passing through a serious crisis since the early 1990s because of increased cost of cultivation and poor remuneration from crop cultivation (Harish et al. 2011; Narayanamoorthy and Alli 2013; Gulati et al. 2013a, b, c). In many places, this scheme is operated throughout the year including in the busy seasons of agriculture. As a result, it has created unusual labour scarcity in the rural areas which resulted in steep increase in the wage rate of agricultural labourers (Shah 2009; Dutta et al. 2012; Berg et al. 2012; Gulati 2013a, b, c).

Likewise, some studies have also reported that introduction of MGNREGS has also reportedly deteriorated the quality of labour uses in several parts of the country, considerably, meaning that the effective working hours of labour has reduced which is ultimately increasing the labour requirement for the given operation (Verma and Shah 2012). Both the increased wage rate and requirement of labour have reportedly increased the cost of cultivation of different crops substantially since the introduction of MGNREGS (Chandrasekar and Ghosh 2011).

As the farm output prices are not fixed in consonance with the rise in the cost of cultivation in India, the losses from crops cultivation reportedly increased for farmers. Importantly, citing increased wage rate due to MGNREGS in agriculture, farmers belonging to the fertile region of Andhra Pradesh have even declared 'paddy crop holiday' in the large area during Kharif season 2011 (GoAP 2011; Narayanamoorthy and Alli 2012).

The farm wage rate and cost of cultivation are determined by irrigation coverage and host of other factors which vary widely from one region to another in India. Given the wide variation in determining factors, is it correct to say that the MGNREGS is increasing farm wage rate which results in increased cost of cultivation uniformly across different crops and states in India? Even if one accepts the

[1]A large number of news reports have been published in various national and state level news papers covering the issue of NREGS's impact on crop cultivation and its profitability since the introduction of the national rural employment scheme. Most news reports have highlighted the sufferings of the farmers due to non-availability of labour and increased wage rate after the introduction of NREGS. For instance, *Dinamani*, a popular news paper in South India, has brought out many reports on this issue during 2009 (August 6, August 23, September 11, November 5), 2010 (January 1, February 11, September 25, November, 27), 2011 (January 25 and 31) and also during 2012 (April 24 and August 17). Many news reports focusing on this same issue have also been published during 2013 and 2014 in various news papers.

argument that MGNREGS increases the farm wage rate, will the impact of it on wage rate and cost of cultivation be the same across high and low irrigated states? Quite a few studies have analysed the implementation, equity and governance aspects of MGNREGS after the implementation of this scheme (Aiyar and Samji 2006; Bhatia and Dreze 2006; Chakraborty 2007; Gopal 2009; Khera and Nayak 2009; Adhikari and Bhatia 2010; Jha et al. 2009, 2011; Imbert and Papp 2011; Liu and Barrett 2013).

Several studies have shown that the MGNREGS has been relatively successful since it directly provides more employment opportunities and wage to the poor in the rural areas (Dutta et al. 2012; MoRD 2012). Although the employment guarantee scheme has multiplier impacts on village economy that help in ameliorating the standards of living, it is also expected to cause a hike in agricultural wages (Berg et al. 2012; Hirway et al. 2008).

Gulati et al. (2012) reported that by distorting the rural labour markets through creating an artificial labour shortage, the employment scheme has reportedly raised the cost of production of agricultural commodities. As a result, farmers have been facing an adverse effect on the farm profitability in major crops (Narayanamoorthy 2013; Reddy and Reddy 2007).

Although a large number of studies have analysed the impact of the employment scheme on farm wage rate particularly, not many detailed studies are available as to what happened to the profitability of crops covering major states and major crops of India. Given the absence of detailed macro-level data-based studies, one cannot come to a conclusion that MGNREGS has reduced the profitability of the crops uniformly across states.

Moreover, the surplus labour available is less in the irrigated regions as compared to un-irrigated regions and therefore, the impact of MGNREGS on the cost of human labour will not be the same between the two regions. Irrigation coverage to the cropped area, cropping pattern, intensity of crop cultivation, availability of labour and rural infrastructure facilities widely vary across the states. Accordingly, the crop profitability is also a function of irrigation, infrastructure and other input factors noted above (Vishandass and Lukka 2013), the impact of MGNREGS on the profitability of crops may not be the same across the states.

Keeping this in view, an attempt is made in this study to find out the impact of MGNREGS on the cost of cultivation as well as the profitability of different major crops, utilising the cost of cultivation survey data. The specific objectives of the study are:

1. To analyse change in the cost of human labour in different operations of selected crops before and after the introduction of rural employment guarantee scheme,
2. To examine the change on the overall pattern of the cost of cultivation in different crops before and after the introduction of rural employment guarantee scheme.
3. To estimate the profitability in different crops also including imputed value of family labour cost (cost C2) before and after the introduction of rural employment guarantee scheme.

5.2 Data and Methodology

The entire study has been carried out utilising crop-wise cost of cultivation survey data covering the period from 2000–01 to 2010–11.[2] The Commission for Agricultural Costs and Prices (CACP) has been publishing valuable time series data on operation-wise costs, productivity, income, etc., for various important crops over the years. For studying the profitability of crops cultivation, all the costs and income related data have been compiled from various CACP's publications and also from its website.

The labour and other inputs required for the cultivation of different crops are not the same, which is also expected to be varied in different states depending upon the intensity of crops cultivation. The intensity of input use in high productivity states will be totally different from the states that are producing relatively low productivity in any crop.

Profit level is also expected to be different for different crops because of nature and market conditions. One of the objectives of the study is to find out whether the profitability of crop varies with the states having high and low productivity. Keeping this in view, a total of five foodgrain crops, namely, paddy, wheat, jowar, gram and tur have been considered for the study. Based on the productivity data of Triennium Ending 2010–11, for each crop, two states belonging to the category of high area with high productivity (HAHP) and high area with low productivity (HALP) have been considered for studying the profitability of crops. The details of crops and the states selected for the analysis are presented in (Table 5.1). States have been selected based on the cultivated area and productivity of the crops.

As regards the method of profit calculation, CACP has been using nine different cost concepts (A1, A2, A2 + FL, B1, B2, C1, C2, C2* and C3) for measuring the economics of various crops cultivation. Details on each of the cost types are provided in the appendix section. For this study, cost C2 has been considered for computing the profitability of various crops as it covers the entire variable and fixed costs needed for crop cultivation.

The objective is to study whether or not the profitability in different crops cultivated in different states had increased after the introduction of MGNREGS. For this, all the costs and income related data have been converted into constant prices using Consumer Price Index of Agricultural Labour (CPIAL) deflator at 1986–87 prices. Profit level of the crop is computed by deducting the cost C2 from the value of output. For purpose of analysis, the study period has been divided into two sub-periods as pre-MGNREGS (2000–01 to 2005–06) and post-MGNREGS (2005–06 to 2010–11) to capture the impact of the national rural employment scheme on the cost of cultivation and profitability.

---

[2]In order to capture the very latest development in the profitability of different crops, we ideally wanted to cover the data up to 2012–13. But, unfortunately the CACP has published cost and income related data of different crops only up to 2010–11 as on July 2014.

Table 5.1 Details of crops and states selected for the study

Crops	States selected for study	Category of state selected	Area (mha)		Yield (kg/ha)	
			TE 2005–06	TE 2010–11	TE 2005–06	TE 2010–11
1. Paddy	Andhra Pradesh	HAHP	3.35 (9.12)	4.19 (11.08)	3,020	3,114
	Odisha	HALP	4.48 (10.26)	4.35 (9.87)	1,491	1,577
2. Wheat	Punjab	HAHP	3.46 (13.10)	3.52 (12.07)	4,202	4,487
	Madhya Pradesh	HALP	3.97 (13.94)	4.13 (14.93)	1,716	1,816
3. Jowar	Karnataka	HAHP	1.63 (17.53)	1.33 (16.80)	806	1,129
	Maharashtra	HALP	4.65 (54.67)	4.10 (55.01)	745	862
4. Gram	Madhya Pradesh	HAHP	2.70 (36.94)	3.01 (33.84)	927	972
	Rajasthan	HALP	1.08 (15.58)	1.31 (19.37)	607	760
5. Tur	Maharashtra	HAHP	1.08 (30.73)	1.13 (29.75)	664	730
	Karnataka	HALP	0.57 (16.76)	0.70 (20.37)	539	529

Notes: *HAHP* High area with high productivity, *HALP* High area with low productivity, *TE* Triennium ending; Figures in brackets are percentage to India's total area
Sources Computed utilising data and www.dacnet.nic.in

5.3 Analysis and Discussion

As reported earlier, this study covers five different foodgrain crops for analysis. These five selected crops are not the same in terms of its duration, coverage of irrigation, productivity, value of output, etc. The states that are selected for the analysis of each crop are also not the same. Therefore, it is prudent to analyse the profitability of each crop separately rather than taking all the crops together. First analysis of the profitability of paddy crop before and after the introduction of MGNREGS is done.

5.3.1 Profitability in Paddy

Paddy is one among the important and labour-intensive crops cultivated in most parts of India. It has been reported especially in south India that the introduction of National Rural Employment Scheme has created artificial demand for labour which resulted in increased labour cost required for crop cultivation.

As generally human labour cost accounts for close to one-third of cultivation cost in paddy, this increased labour cost has reportedly increased the gross cost of cultivation that eventually affected the profitability of paddy crop.

Is it correct to say that the human labour cost required for paddy cultivation has increased after the introduction of rural employment scheme? What is the increase in labour cost vis-à-vis the costs of other operations? Will the profitability be affected only due to the increase in labour cost that occurred because of rural employment scheme? What was the state of labour cost in paddy cultivation before the introduction of the employment scheme? There is need to find out answers to these questions to make any judgment as to whether or not the rural employment programme has made any impact on the profitability of paddy crop.

Profitability of any crop is directly linked with its productivity, which is highlighted by many studies (Bhalla and Singh 2012). Therefore, as mentioned in the methodology section, two states having the characteristics of high area with high productivity (HAHP) and high area with low productivity (HALP) have been selected for the analysis. While Andhra Pradesh has been considered as HAHP state, Odisha has been selected as HALP state in paddy crop for the detailed analysis.

Table 5.2 presents the trends in operation-wise cost, productivity, value of output and profit for paddy crops for the two selected states for pre and post-MGNREGS period. For the purpose of analysis, the operation-wise cost has been classified into five categories, namely cost on human labour, cost of bullock labour, machine labour cost, costs on yield increasing inputs and other costs. This classification is done in order to find out the pattern of human labour cost in comparison to other operations of paddy cultivation.

It is clear from Table 5.2 that there has been a substantial variation in the operation-wise cost of cultivation between the two periods considered for the analysis. This is particularly true in the case of cost of human labour, which is discussed widely as a serious issue after the introduction of national rural employment programme.

The cost of human labour has increased at a rate of 6.13% per annum in HAHP state during post-MGNREGS period, but the same grew at a negative rate of −1.84% during pre-MGNREGS period. What is interesting here is that this has happened despite significant increase in the cost of machine labour which grew at a rate of 7.50% per annum during post-MGNREGS period. It is generally expected that the cost of human labour would decline when farmers spend more cost on the machine labour. But, this has not happened in the case of HAHP state in paddy cultivation.

This implies that the wage rate paid for the human labour used for paddy cultivation has increased substantially possibly due to the introduction of the national rural employment programme. The growth rate in human labour cost is also found to be much higher as compared to the costs of all other major operations during the post-MGNREGS period. As a result of fast increase in cost of human labour and machine labour, the gross cost of cultivation (cost C2) of paddy has also

Table 5.2 Cost and profitability of paddy cultivation from 2000–01 to 2010–11 (values in Rs. at 1986–87 prices)

Parameters	Particulars	Andhra Pradesh (HAHP)			Odisha (HALP)		
		2000–01 to 2005–06	2006–07 to 2010–11	2000–01 to 2010–11	2000–01 to 2005–06	2006–07 to 2010–11	2000–01 to 2010–11
Human labour	Cost (Rs.)	2,709	3,157	2,913	2,034	2,141	2,083
	CGR (%)	−1.84	6.13	1.33	1.05	4.19	2.18
	Share (%)	31.25	34.14	32.30	38.59	39.37	39.07
Bullock labour	Cost (Rs.)	281	158	223	636	562	598
	CGR (%)	−0.39	−10.09	−4.73	1.55	−1.03	−0.40
	Share (%)	3.25	1.71	2.47	12.06	10.43	11.22
Machine labour	Cost (Rs.)	550	851	705	121	153	136
	CGR (%)	4.24	7.50	6.46	12.42	0.44	6.70
	Share (%)	6.34	9.21	7.81	2.30	2.83	2.55
Yield enhancing inputs	Cost (Rs.)	2,005	1,765	1,850	850	766	806
	CGR (%)	2.22	−2.17	−2.85	0.32	−2.96	−1.55
	Share (%)	23.13	19.09	20.52	16.12	14.22	15.12
Other cost (fixed costs)	Cost (Rs.)	3,220	3,501	3,381	1,630	1,786	1,708
	CGR (%)	1.00	1.13	0.62	1.06	−0.24	−0.04
	Share (%)	37.16	37.85	37.49	30.93	33.15	32.04
Cost C2	Cost (Rs.)	8,667	9,248	9,018	5,271	5,389	5,331
	CGR (%)	−0.58	2.62	0.57	1.21	1.12	0.76
	Share (%)	100.00	100.00	100.00	100.00	100.00	100.00
Value of output	VOP (Rs.)	8,810	10,030	9,507	4,088	4,851	4,501
	CGR (%)	0.48	1.58	0.95	0.19	2.60	1.13
Yield (qtl/ha)		50.49	53.29	52.04	29.42	30.64	30.01
Profit (VOP-C2)		143	782	489	−1,182	−538	−829
Number of years profit realised		4/6	4/5	8/11	0/6	0/5	0/11

Notes: *CGR* Compound growth rate percent/per annum, *HAHP* High area with high productivity and *HALP* High area with low productivity

Sources Computed using data from CACP (various years)

increased at a rate of 2.62% per annum during post-MGNREGS period, which was not the case during pre-MGNREGS period.

The pattern of cultivation of crops is not the same across the states in India. Some states have been following intensive agriculture by adopting modern technological inputs, while other states are following different forms of cultivation practices. Therefore, one may not be able to firmly conclude that what is happening in one state is same in all other states. Specifically, the labour use pattern and the wage rate are widely varied across the states.

In view of this, another state namely Odisha has been selected under the category of HALP so as to find out whether or not the pattern of operation-wise cost of cultivation is same in comparison to HAHP state. As expected, the pattern of operation-wise cost including the cost of human labour in HALP state varied from the HAHP state during both pre and post-MGNREGS period.

However, the cost of human labour, which is one of our main focuses in the paper, has increased at a faster pace during post-MGNREGS period as compared to its previous time period considered for the analysis. For instance, the cost of human labour increased at a rate of 4.19% per annum during post-MGNREGS period, but the same has increased only at a rate of 1.05% per annum during pre-MGNREGS period.

In contrast to the human labour cost, the growth rate in machine labour cost has decelerated sharply after the introduction of rural employment scheme, which is something unexpected. The gross cost of cultivation (cost C2) too has decelerated in HALP state during post-MGNREGS period because of the slow pace of growth in the cost of all other operations except the human labour cost.

Overall, what is clear from the analysis of operation-wise cost is that although the cost pattern is not the same between the two states, the cost of human labour has increased at relatively faster pace in both the states after the introduction of rural employment scheme.

One of the major objectives of the study is to find out whether the profitability in crops cultivation has affected after MGNREGS. It has been argued in the recent years that the rural employment scheme introduced throughout the country has created artificial demand for labour which resulted in increased cost of human labour.

After studying operation-wise cost of cultivation, the focus is towards the profitability of paddy crop. It is to be noted here that the profitability of any crop is determined not only by the cost of cultivation but also by the factors such as productivity of the crop, market price, etc.

The results presented in Table 5.2 shows that the average value of paddy output increased from ₹ 8,810/ha in 2000–06 to ₹ 10,030/ha in 2006–11 (output measured at market prices only) in HAHP states, showing a much faster pace of growth rate during post-MGNREGS period. As a result of the faster growth in VOP, the profitability from paddy increased from ₹ 143 to ₹ 782/ha during the period 2001–06 and 2006–11.

Although the absolute profitability is very meager, it increased manifold during post-MGNREGS period as compared to its earlier period. Not only has the profitability increased after the introduction of employment scheme, but the number of years profit realised by the farmers have also increased during post-MGNREGS period in HAHP state (see, Fig. 5.1).

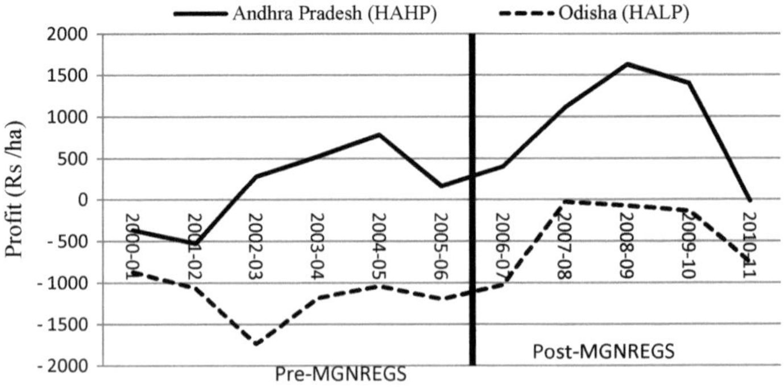

Fig. 5.1 Profitability in paddy cultivation at 1986–87 price

The profitability scenario of HALP state is totally different from HAHP state. While no significant increase is noticed in VOP between pre and post-MGNREGS period, the losses incurred by the farmers in cultivating paddy have reduced from ₹ 1,182 to ₹ 538/ha during this period.

Surprisingly, farmers belonging to HALP state could not reap profit even in single year during the entire period of analysis from 2000–01 to 2010–11. Although the cost of cultivation is very low in HALP as compared to HAHP state, farmers are unable to reap any profit from paddy cultivation possibly because of low productivity. This suggests that it is difficult to increase the profitability without increasing its productivity.

5.3.2 Profitability in Wheat

Wheat is an important foodgrain crop cultivated predominantly during rabi season in different parts of the country. It accounts for about 24% of India's total foodgrains area and about 37% in India's gross production of foodgrains during 2011–12. Similar to paddy crop, it is also cultivated mostly under irrigated conditions where the cost of cultivation is generally higher; human labour cost accounts for about 10–17% of cost C2 of wheat crop.

Therefore, the introduction of MGNREGS may have made some impact on the profitability of wheat crop through increased human labour cost in different states. In order to study the profitability in wheat crop, two states have been selected having the characteristics of HAHP and HALP. Punjab (the highest productivity state in wheat in India) has been considered as HAHP state, while Madhya Pradesh (MP) has been selected as HALP state for the analysis.

The details of operation-wise cost, gross cost of cultivation, value of output and profit pertaining to wheat crop for the two selected states are presented in Table 5.3. The pattern of profitability in HAHP state is studied first. It is expected that the human labour cost would have gone up considerably after the introduction of MGNRES in wheat crop.

But against the expectation, the human labour cost has increased only marginally. For instance, the average human labour cost during pre-MGNREGS period was ₹ 757/ha, which has increased to ₹ 831/ha during post-MGNREGS period. The growth rate computed for pre and post-MGNREGS period also shows that the cost of human labour incurred for the cultivation of wheat crop in Punjab has decelerated (−1.67%) during post-MGNREGS period as compared to its previous period (−1.00%). This happened despite deceleration in the cost of machine labour during post-MGNREGS period. Interestingly, the real cost of all other operations has also decelerated during post-MGNREGS period, which is something not noticed in the case of paddy crop.

On the whole, the analysis on HAHP state shows that the real cost of human labour incurred for the cultivation of wheat crop has not increased during post-MGNREGS period. What happened to the profitability of wheat crop after the introduction of MGNREGS is the next key question probed in the study. As per the data of CACP, the gross cost of cultivation (C2) has increased marginally from ₹ 7,249 to ₹ 7,773/ha between 2000–06 and 2006–11 in Punjab. But, in spite of the

Table 5.3 Cost and profitability of wheat cultivation from 2000–01 to 2010–11 (values in Rs. at 1986–87 prices)

Parameters	Particulars	Punjab (HAHP)			Madhya Pradesh (HALP)		
		2000–01 to 2005–06	2006–07 to 2010–11	2000–01 to 2010–11	2000–01 to 2005–06	2006–07 to 2010–11	2000–01 to 2010–11
Human labour	Cost (Rs.)	757	831	790	738	787	760
	CGR (%)	−1.00	−1.67	−0.83	0.24	1.01	0.64
	Share (%)	10.44	10.69	10.56	16.89	15.78	16.35
Bullock labour	Cost (Rs.)	27	17	23	238	148	197
	CGR (%)	−10.10	−14.01	−9.63	0.52	−13.12	−5.40
	Share (%)	0.38	0.22	0.30	5.44	2.96	4.23
Machine labour	Cost (Rs.)	1,064	1,169	1,112	426	601	506
	CGR (%)	3.67	−0.60	1.73	7.99	4.63	6.26
	Share (%)	14.68	15.04	14.85	9.77	12.05	10.88
Yield enhancing inputs	Cost (Rs.)	1,665	1,394	1,542	1,202	1,180	1,192
	CGR (%)	1.26	−5.07	−2.36	2.73	−3.86	0.31
	Share (%)	22.97	17.94	20.59	27.54	23.65	25.64
Other costs (fixed costs)	Cost (Rs.)	3,736	4,348	4,014	1,762	2,272	1,994
	CGR (%)	−0.45	0.66	0.92	4.36	−0.57	2.94
	Share (%)	51.54	55.94	53.62	40.36	45.55	42.89
Cost C2	Cost (Rs.)	7,249	7,773	7,487	4,366	4,989	4,649
	CGR (%)	0.39	−0.67	0.28	3.41	−0.86	1.98
	Share (%)	100.00	100.00	100.00	100.00	100.00	100.00
Value of output	VOP (Rs.)	8,450	7,918	8,209	4,234	6,240	5,146
	CGR (%)	−2.25	−0.96	−0.57	6.84	0.70	5.54
Yield (qtl/ha)		43.19	42.49	42.87	19.83	24.81	22.09
Profit (VOP-C2)		1,202	1,887	1,513	−132.19	1,251.37	496.70
Number of years profit realised		6/6	5/5	11/11	3/6	5/5	8/11

Notes and Sources Same as in Table 5.2

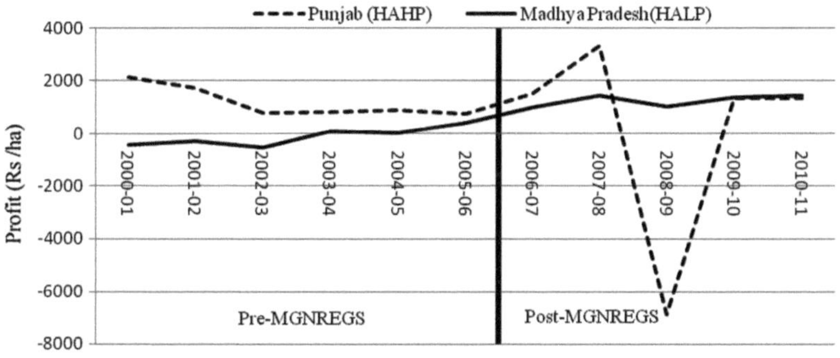

Fig. 5.2 Profitability in wheat cultivation at 1986–87 price

marginal increase in cost C2, the profitability from wheat cultivation has increased from ₹ 1,202 to ₹ 1,887/ha during this period.

The results of wheat crop discussed above in relation with HAHP state are in many ways different from HALP state (Madhya Pradesh). In spite of substantial growth in machine labour cost during post-MGNREGS period (4.63%), the human labour cost spent for the cultivation of wheat has increased at a rate of 1.01% per annum during this period. This is different from the results arrived above with HALP state. This seems to suggest that although the national rural employment programme has been in operation across all the states in India, the impact of it on labour cost is not the same in all the states because the factors determining the wage cost of agricultural labour are not the same.

Whatever may be the reasons for the increased wage cost, the results from HALP state show that the profitability from wheat crop has increased dramatically from Rs. −132 to ₹ 1,251/ha between pre and post-MGNRES period in HALP state. This raise in profit is mainly due to increased productivity of wheat which had increased from 19.83 to 24.81 qtl/ha between the two periods.

This analysis of wheat crop, on the whole, suggests that the introduction of MGNREGS has not affected the profitability in both the high and low productivity states as the number of years profit realised by the farmers have increased after its introduction (Fig. 5.2).

5.3.3 *Profitability in Jowar*

Jowar is another food grain crop which is considered for the analysis for two reasons. First, unlike paddy and wheat crops, jowar is cultivated predominantly under rainfed condition.[3] Second, it is generally treated as a low-value crop in comparison to paddy and wheat crops.

[3]The coverage of irrigation in jowar crop is very low in India; it increased only from 3.60% in 1960–61 to 8.70 in 2011–12. This is very low when compared to the crops like paddy and wheat where the coverage of irrigation is 58.60 and 92.10%, respectively, during 2010–11.

Therefore, studying the profitability of this crop would give some interesting results that will be useful to compare with other high value cereal crops. As followed earlier, two states namely Karnataka and Maharashtra have been considered for the analysis of jowar crop. While Karnataka has been selected as HAHP state, Maharashtra has been considered as HALP state for the purpose of analysis.

First, the analysis of the profitability of jowar crop is done by taking data from HAHP state. It is evident from Table 5.4 that the cost of human labour incurred for cultivating jowar has increased at a faster rate after MGNRGES. The real human labour cost increased at a rate of 10.24% per annum from 2006–07 to 2010–11, whereas the same was almost constant (0.01%) during pre-MGNRGES period.

In terms of value, an average of ₹ 850/ha was incurred on account of human labour during post-MGNRGES period which was only ₹ 567/ha during pre-MGNRGES period. It is generally expected that the machine labour cost would be less wherever the human labour cost is higher for any crop cultivation. But contrary to this, the machine labour cost too has increased at a much faster rate (9.36% per annum) after the introduction of employment scheme in Karnataka which is an interesting result.

The increased human as well as machine labour cost has also made substantial impact on the gross cost of cultivation (C2) after the introduction of employment scheme. Despite substantial reduction in the cost on yield increasing inputs, the cost C2 increased at a rate of 4.15% per annum during post-MGNRGES period as against the negative rate of −0.31% per annum during pre-MGNRGES period.

However, the increased labour cost as well as the gross cost (C2) have not made any big impact on the profitability of jowar in HAHP state; the average profit in relation to cost C2 was negative during both pre and post-MGNRGES period. It appears that although the cost of cultivation in jowar has increased after the employment scheme, it has not made any significant damages on its profitability (Fig. 5.3).

The profitability of jowar in HALP state (Maharashtra) is somewhat different from its counterpart state of HAHP. The results show that the real human labour cost increased at a rate of 8.70% per annum during post-MGNRGES period as against the negative growth of −1.44% during pre-MGNRGES period. This is almost matching with the result of HAHP state. The cost of machine labour too increased at an appreciable rate (6.66%) during post-MGNRGES period which also increased at a rate of 7.49% per annum during pre-MGNRGES period. Possibly because of slower increase of machine labour cost, the gross cost of cultivation has increased at a rate of 3.62% per annum, which is little lower (2.83%) than the increase experienced during pre-MGNRGES period.

As observed in HAHP state, the changes observed in cost of cultivation during pre and post-MGNRGES period have not made any impact on the profitability of jowar. Profitability is found to be negative at both periods considered for the analysis. The only difference noted between the two periods is the magnitude of losses (in relation cost C2) incurred by jowar farmers is relatively less during post-MGNREGS period as compared to pre-MGNRGES period.

Table 5.4 Cost and profitability of Jowar cultivation from 2000–01 to 2010–11 (values in ₹ at 1986–87 prices)

Cost/Profit	Particulars	Karnataka (HAHP)			Maharashtra (HALP)		
		2000–01 to 2005–06	2006–07 to 2010–11	2000–01 to 2010–11	2000–01 to 2005–06	2006–07 to 2010–11	2000–01 to 2010–11
Human labour	Cost (Rs.)	567	850	695	1,055	1,240	1,139
	CGR (%)	0.01	10.24	4.33	−1.44	8.70	2.24
	Share (%)	28.32	36.63	32.40	28.09	28.69	28.38
Bullock labour	Cost (Rs.)	452	348	404	855	930	889
	CGR (%)	4.25	−7.33	−1.76	10.61	−4.14	3.04
	Share (%)	22.57	14.98	18.84	22.78	21.51	22.16
Machine labour	Cost (Rs.)	111	160	134	220	296	255
	CGR (%)	−3.80	9.36	2.35	7.49	6.66	5.49
	Share (%)	5.55	6.91	6.22	5.86	6.86	6.35
Yield enhancing inputs	Cost (Rs.)	310	276	295	557	532	546
	CGR (%)	−5.56	−8.65	−4.99	0.49	−2.43	−1.89
	Share (%)	15.50	11.89	13.73	14.83	12.31	13.59
Other costs (fixed costs)	Cost (Rs.)	561	687	618	1,068	1,323	1,184
	CGR (%)	0.10	7.62	2.71	2.44	6.01	3.83
	Share (%)	28.05	29.59	28.81	28.45	30.63	29.51
Cost C2	Cost (Rs.)	2,001	2,321	2,146	3,756	4,321	4,013
	CGR (%)	−0.31	4.15	1.63	2.83	3.62	2.50
	Share (%)	100.00	100.00	100.00	100.00	100.00	100.00
Value of output	VOP (Rs.)	1,358	1,951	1,627	2,221	3,034	2,590
	CGR (%)	1.93	10.08	5.73	2.93	6.20	5.79
Yield (qtl/ha)		6.95	7.75	7.32	12.72	14.24	13.41
Profit (VOP-C2)		−643	−370	−519	−1,535	−1,287	−1,423
Number of years profit realised		0/6	1/5	1/11	0/6	0/5	0/11

Notes and Sources Same as in Table 5.2

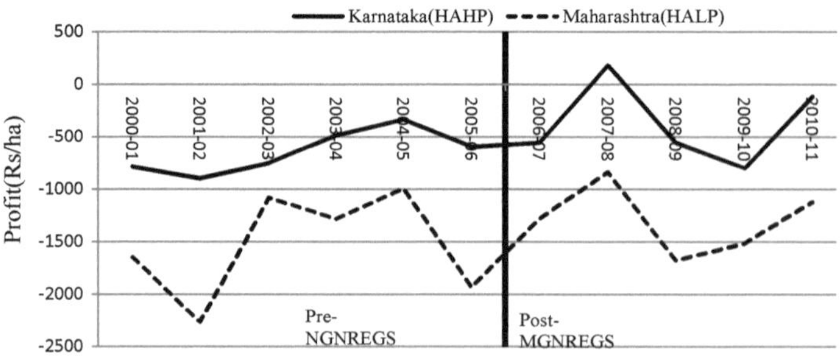

Fig. 5.3 Profitability in Jowar cultivation at 1986–87 price

5.3.4 Profitability in Gram

After studying the profitability of three cereal crops, the focus is turned towards the pulse crops which accounted for about 13% (24.46 million ha) of the cropped area as of 2011–12 in India. Although various pulse crops have been traditionally cultivated in India, two major pulse crops namely gram (Bengal gram) and tur (red gram) have been considered for the purpose of analysis as these two crops together accounted for about 52% of India's total pulses area in 2011–12.

Since gram and tur are different in many ways, it is not prudent to analyse the profitability of these two crops together. Therefore, here profitability of Gram analysed first and then tur. As followed earlier, two states namely Madhya Pradesh (HAHP state) and Rajasthan (HALP state) have been considered for the study. It clearly emerges from Table 5.5 that the cost incurred and profit realised from gram is not the same between the two states. In the case of HAHP state, the cost on human labour has increased substantially after the introduction of employment scheme. The real human labour cost grew at a rate of 4.36% per annum during post-MGNREGS period, but the same grew at a negative rate of −1.58% per annum during pre-MGNREGS period, suggesting a fast increase of human labour cost after the employment scheme.

However, the machine labour cost has surprisingly not increased substantially during post-MGNREGS period (2.87%) as compared to its previous period (2.81%). Because of negative growth in bullock labour cost as well as in the cost of yield increasing inputs, the gross cost of cultivation on gram has declined at a rate of −3.88% per annum during post-MGNREGS period.

As regards the profitability, although the average value of output has increased to ₹ 4,730/ha during post-MGNREGS period from its pre-MGNREGS period value of ₹ 4,397/ha, the growth rate of VOP during post-MGNREGS period was negative (−6.67% per annum). Notwithstanding this, the average profit realised by the farmers belonging to HAHP state during post-MGNREGS period increased to ₹ 1,034/ha, which was only about ₹ 800/ha during its previous period.

It was expected that the pattern of operation-wise cost of cultivation and profitability of gram in HALP state would be different from that of HAHP state. But the

Table 5.5 Cost and profitability of gram cultivation from 2000–01 to 2010–11 (values in ₹ at 1986–87 prices)

Costs/Profit	Particulars	Madhya Pradesh (HAHP)			Rajasthan (HALP)		
		2000–01 to 2005–06	2006–07 to 2010–11	2000–01 to 2010–11	2000–01 to 2005–06	2006–07 to 2010–11	2000–01 to 2010–11
Human labour	Cost (Rs.)	552	587	568	815	725	774
	CGR (%)	−1.58	4.36	0.45	−3.92	4.41	−1.02
	Share (%)	15.35	15.87	15.59	26.77	23.56	25.30
Bullock labour	Cost (Rs.)	201	113	161	155	88	125
	CGR (%)	1.02	−10.78	−7.48	−9.45	−27.15	−19.78
	Share (%)	5.60	3.06	4.43	5.11	2.86	4.08
Machine labour	Cost (Rs.)	338	450	389	316	320	318
	CGR (%)	2.81	2.87	3.64	1.25	0.64	0.23
	Share (%)	9.38	12.18	10.67	10.39	10.40	10.39
Yield enhancing inputs	Cost (Rs.)	882	914	897	672	748	707
	CGR (%)	2.22	−7.26	−1.49	3.20	−15.20	−3.57
	Share (%)	24.53	24.72	24.62	22.09	24.30	1,137
Other cost (fixed costs)	Cost (Rs.)	1,624	1,632	1,628	1,086	1,197	3,060
	CGR (%)	1.83	−6.16	−1.66	0.51	−10.22	−2.74
	Share (%)	45.14	44.16	44.69	35.68	38.88	37.14
Cost C2	Cost (Rs.)	3,597	3,696	3,642	3,044	3,079	3,060
	CGR (%)	1.44	−3.88	−0.85	−0.38	−7.24	−2.53
	Share (%)	100.00	100.00	100.00	100.00	100.00	100.00
Value of output	VOP (Rs.)	4,397	4,730	4,548	3,631	4,102	3,845
	CGR (%)	2.14	−6.67	−1.09	−0.42	−11.71	−3.19
Yield (qtl/ha)		9.89	10.08	9.98	6.62	8.25	7.36
Profit (VOP-C2)		800	1,034	906	587	1,023	785
Number of years profit realised		6/6	5/5	11/11	6/6	5/5	11/11

Notes and Sources Same as in Table 5.2

results presented in Table 5.5 depict not much difference in profit and other major parameters. Similar to HAHP state, the cost of human labour has increased at a faster rate during post-MGNREGS period as compared to its previous period. The growth in gross cost of cultivation (C2) has sharply declined during post-MGNREGS period, which was also observed with HAHP state. Due to the increase in yield of gram from 6.62 to 8.25 qtl/ha between the two periods, the profitability has increased from ₹ 587 to ₹ 1,023/ha between pre and post-MGNREGS period.

Again the increase in profitability in gram cultivation between HAHP state and HALP state is more or less same after the introduction of employment scheme (Fig. 5.4). The number of years profit realised by the farmers through the cultivation of gram is also same for both the states selected for the analysis. It appears

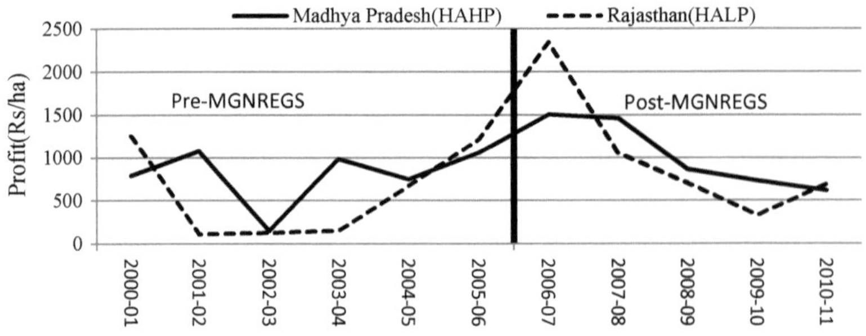

Fig. 5.4 Profitability in gram cultivation at 1986–87 price

from the analysis that although the human labour cost has increased at a faster rate after the introduction of national employment scheme, it has not made any severe impact on the profitability of gram in both HAHP and HALP.

5.3.5 *Profitability in Tur*

As mentioned earlier, tur is another important pulse crop selected for the analysis along with gram. Tur is cultivated predominantly under rainfed condition in various parts of India. Because of increased demand for tur, its area increased from 2.43 million ha in 1960–61 to 4.01 million ha in 2011–12, an increase of about 65%.

But, its productivity has not increased appreciably despite various efforts taken by the government which has been a serious concern among the policy makers.[4] In order to study the profitability of tur crop during pre and post-MGNREGS period, two states namely Maharashtra (HAHP state) and Karnataka (HALP state) have been considered as these two are cultivating tur under large area over the years. In fact, about 50% of India's total tur crop area was found only from these two states during 2011–12.

Given the variation in productivity of tur between the two states selected for the analysis, it is expected that the profitability would also be different among them. It is evident from Table 5.6 that the cost of human labour has increased substantially in HAHP state after the introduction of the NREGS. Not only has the average of cost of human labour increased from ₹ 1,082 to ₹ 1,827/ha between the two periods but its growth also registered at a high rate of 14.08% per annum during post-MGNREGS period, which is much higher the same registered during pre-MGNREGS period (7.23%).

[4]Considering the increased demand for tur, the government of India has substantially increased its minimum support price (MSP) especially in the recent years. The MSP announced for tur was only Rs. 1,105 per quintal during 1999–2000, but it increased to Rs. 3,850 per quintal during 2012–13. The hike in MSP for tur crop is very high as compared to many important foodgrain crops cultivated in India.

Table 5.6 Cost and profitability of tur cultivation from 2000–01 to 2010–11 (values in ₹ at 1986–87 prices)

Costs/Profit	Particulars	Maharashtra (HAHP)			Karnataka (HALP)		
		2000–01 to 2005–06	2006–07 to 2010–11	2000–01 to 2010–11	2000–01 to 2005–06	2006–07 to 2010–11	2000–01 to 2010–11
Human labour	Cost (Rs.)	1,082	1,827	1,421	709	972	828
	CGR (%)	7.23	14.08	9.78	4.89	12.03	6.23
	Share (%)	26.66	28.65	27.78	23.17	27.39	25.24
Bullock labour	Cost (Rs.)	879	1,178	1,015	438	347	397
	CGR (%)	26.37	−4.72	11.47	9.34	−10.08	−1.37
	Share (%)	21.65	18.47	19.85	14.33	9.77	12.09
Machine labour	Cost (Rs.)	137	320	221	183	223	202
	CGR (%)	14.40	19.98	17.25	4.53	29.24	9.50
	Share (%)	3.38	5.02	4.31	6.00	6.30	6.14
Yield enhancing inputs	Cost (Rs.)	471	970	698	783	751	768
	CGR (%)	11.71	14.82	13.63	−0.87	−0.93	0.74
	Share (%)	11.60	15.20	13.64	25.61	21.14	23.42
Other cost (fixed costs)	Cost (Rs.)	1,490	2,083	1,760	945	1,257	1,087
	CGR (%)	5.42	9.37	6.33	5.01	5.45	4.06
	Share (%)	36.72	32.65	34.41	30.89	35.40	33.11
Cost C2	Cost (Rs.)	4,058	6,379	5,113	3,058	3,550	3,282
	CGR (%)	10.45	9.19	9.63	4.07	5.33	3.78
	Share (%)	100.00	100.00	100.00	100.00	100.00	100.00
Value of output	VOP (Rs.)	4,671	7,314	5,872	3,098	4,622	3,791
	CGR (%)	8.04	9.55	7.85	7.11	8.01	5.70
Yield (qtl/ha)		9.81	11.33	759	6.01	7.08	6.50
Profit (VOP-C2)		612	935	247	40	1,072	509
Number of years profit realised		6/6	4/5	10/11	3/6	5/5	8/11

Notes and Sources Same as in Table 5.2

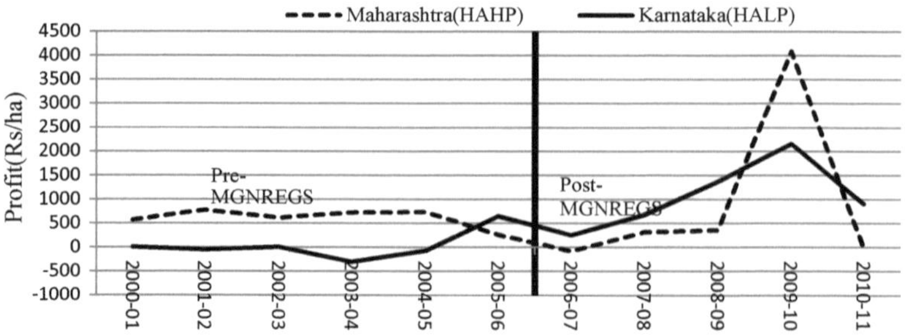

Fig. 5.5 Profitability in tur cultivation at 1986–87 price

Interestingly, this substantial increase in labour cost is seen in spite of considerable increase in the machine labour cost (19.98% per annum) during post-MGNREGS period. This kind of faster growth in labour cost has not been observed in any of the crops analysed so far.

Along with the labour cost, the costs of yield increasing inputs have also increased considerably during post-MGNREGS period which resulted in increased gross cost of cultivation (C2) between the two periods; increased from ₹ 4,058 to ₹ 6,379/ha. But, this steep increase in cost C2 has not affected the profitability of tur which in fact has increased from ₹ 612 to ₹ 935/ha between the two periods mainly because of increased value of output. One can say certainly from the analysis that the profitability of tur in HAHP state would have been much better if the cost of human labour has not increased substantially after the introduction of MGNREGS.

It is expected that the cost of cultivation and profitability of tur in HALP state would be totally different from that of HAHP state because of variation in productivity. But both the cost of human labour and the machine labour have increased at a pace which is almost similar to HAHP state (Table 5.6). While the human labour cost grew at a rate of 12.03% per annum during post-MGNREGS period, the same grew only at about 4.50% per annum during pre-MGNREGS period.

The cost of yield increasing inputs registered negative growth during both periods of analysis in HALP state which is different from HAHP state. However, despite a considerable increase in gross cost of cultivation, the profitability of tur has increased from ₹ 40 to ₹ 1,072/ha between the two periods in HALP state. Increased value of output and the slower increase in the gross cost of cultivation have helped the farmers cultivating tur to realise better profit during post-MGNREGS period (Fig. 5.5).

5.4 Conclusions and Suggestions

An attempt has been made in this study to analyse the impact of MGNREGS on the profitability of five foodgrain crops utilising cost of cultivation survey data from 2000–01 to 2010–11 covering different states. The results of the study have shown mixed results; not completely supported the argument that the profitability of crops has declined after the introduction of NRGES. This is not only true with HAHP states but also with HALP states.

Supporting the earlier studies that the farm wage rate has increased due to the introduction of employment scheme, this study results also showed that the real cost of human labour has increased considerably in all five crops in both HAHP and HALP states after its introduction (2006–07 to 2010–11).

However, it has not made any deleterious impact on the profitability. The profitability, which is calculated by deducting the value of output from cost C2, has increased in all five crops in HAHP states, whereas either the profitability has increased or the losses reduced in HALP states. Besides, the number of years profit realised by the farmers have also increased in most crops during the post-MGNREGS period as compared to pre-MGNREGS period (2000–01 to 2005–06).

While there is no distinct pattern emerging in profitability between cereals and pulse crops, the level of increase in profitability is found to be relatively better among the pulse crops after the introduction of NRGES. Increased productivity in most crops has one way or the other helped to negate the increase in human labour cost which also facilitated to increase profitability.

Although there is no clear evidence from this study that the profitability of crops has declined during post-MGNREGS period, this may not be true in all regions/ states in India. Regions where the employment scheme have been operated intensively may have increased the farm wage rate at a faster rate which might have affected the profitability of crops.

It is difficult to capture this effect through the cost of cultivation survey data which is used in this study. Detailed studies using farm level collected from different regions need to be carried out to verify the results of this study. The study finds that wherever the productivity of crop has increased during post-MGNREGS period, the profitability has not been affected despite considerable increase in human labour cost. Therefore, concerted efforts are needed to increase the productivity of crops and then the gross value of output to negate the cost increase in human labour.

This study clearly reveals that the gross cost of cultivation (C2) has increased substantially in most crops as compared to the increase that is observed in value of output in both HAHP and HALP states after the launch of rural employment programme. Farmers would have earned appreciable profit during post-MGNREGS period, if the cost of human labour had not increased appreciably.

The relatively less increase in the value of output in most crops suggests that the farmers are not getting the price for their produce in consonance with cost of cultivation. The National Commission on Farmers has suggested that the government should announce the minimum support price (MSP) for crops at 50% more than the actual cost of production (Cost C3). Minimum support prices announced every year for various crops should also be linked with the wholesale price index so as to protect the farmers from the possible inflationary pressure.

The cost of human labour incurred for cultivating different crops in south Indian states like Andhra Pradesh and Karnataka has registered high growth rate as compared to other selected states especially after the introduction of MGNREGS. This has either dampened the profitability of the crop or created losses for farmers in relation to cost C2. One needs to find out as to why have these happened specifically in south Indian states? Is it due to labour scarcity that was accentuated by the proper implementation of rural employment programme in these states?

The Mohan Kanda Committee (GoAP 2011) appointed for studying the reasons for crop holiday in East Godavari region in Andhra Pradesh pointed out that 'Non-availability of labour in the peak season of agricultural operation on account of MGNREGS' as one of the reasons for the distress call made by the farmers. Our analysis based on the cost of cultivation survey data also seems to indicate that the labour scarcity accentuated due to MGNREGS may have increased the cost of human labour at a faster pace. Therefore, arrangements may be made to link up MGNREGS with agricultural operations to reduce the labour scarcity and also to improve the profitability in crops cultivation.

Acknowledgments This paper is part of a project on 'Impacts of MGNREGA on Food Security and Rural Livelihoods in Selected States of India', funded by CGIAR Research Programme on Policies Institutions and Market (CRP-PIM) and implemented by ICRISAT, Hyderabad (India) with several partners in India, including Alagappa University, Tamil Nadu. This is a revised version of the paper which authors had earlier published as a Discussion Series Paper Number 25 titled as 'Has MGNREGS Affected the Farmers Profitability? An Assessment based on Cost of Cultivation Data', under the Research Programme on Policies, Institutions and Markets of International Crops Research Institute for the Semi-Arid Tropics (ICRISAT). The authors acknowledge ICRISAT and CRP-PIM for providing funding support for this study.

The authors are also thankful to N. Gayadhri Devi and Susanto Kumar Beero for their research assistance in completing this paper.

Appendix Note 1

CACP has been using nine different cost concepts. These are the followings:

(a) Cost A1 = All actual expenses in cash and kind incurred in production by owner.
(b) Cost A2 = Cost A1 + rent paid for leased-in land.
(c) Cost A2 + FL = Cost A2 + imputed value of family labour.
(d) Cost B1 = Cost A1 + interest on value of owned capital assets (excluding land).
(e) Cost B2 = Cost B1 + rental value of owned land (net of land revenue) and rent paid for leased-in land.
(f) Cost C1 = Cost B1 + imputed value of family labour.
(g) Cost C2 = Cost B2 + imputed value of family labour.
(h) Cost C2* = Cost C2 estimated by taking into account statutory minimum or actual wage whichever is higher.

(i) Cost C3 = Cost C2* + 10% of cost C2* on account of managerial.
(j) Functions performed by farmer.

Source Narayanamoorthy (2013).

References

Adhikari, A., and K. Bhatia. 2010. NREGA Wage Payments: Can We Bank on Banks? *Economic and Political Weekly* 42 (1): 30–37.

Aiyar, Y., and S. Samji. 2006. Improving the Effectiveness of National Rural Employment Guarantee Act. *Economic and Political Weekly* 41 (4): 320–326.

Berg, E., S. Bhattacharyya, R. Durg, and M. Ramachandra. 2012. *Can Rural Public Works Affect Agriculture Wage: Evidence from India*. CSAE Working Paper WPS/2012–05, Centre for the Study of African Economies, University of Oxford, Oxford, UK.

Bhalla, G.S., and G. Singh. 2012. *Economic Liberalisation and Indian Agriculture: A District-Level Study*. New Delhi: Sage Publications India Private Limited.

Bhatia, B., and J. Dreze. 2006. Employment Guarantee in Jharkhand: Ground Realities. *Economic and Political Weekly* 41 (29): 3198–3202.

Chakraborty, P. 2007. Implementation of Employment Guarantee: A Preliminary Appraisal. *Economic and Political Weekly* 42 (7): 548–551.

Chandrasekar, C.P., and J. Ghosh. 2011. Public Works and Wages in India, January 11. www.thehindubusinessline.com.

Dutta, P., R. Murgai, M. Ravallion, and D. Van de Walle. 2012. *Does India's Employment Guarantee Scheme Guarantee Employment?* Policy Research Working Paper No. 6003, The World Bank, Washington, USA.

GoAP. 2011. *Report of State Level Committee to Study the Problems of Farmers in Crop Holiday Affected Mandals of East Godavari District of Andhra Pradesh*. Mohan Kanda, Chairman, Government of Andhra Pradesh.

Gopal, K.S. 2009. NREGA Social Audit: Myths and Reality. *Economic and Political Weekly* 44 (3): 70–71.

Gulati, A., J. Gujral, and T. Nandakumar. 2012. *National Food Security Bill Challenges and Options*. Discussion Paper No. 2, Commission for Agricultural Costs and Prices, Department of Agriculture and Cooperation, Ministry of agriculture, Government of India, New Delhi.

Gulati, A., S. Jain, and A. Hoda. 2013a. *Farm Trade: Tapping the Hidden Potential*. Discussion Paper No. 3, Commission for Agricultural Costs and Prices, Department of Agriculture and Cooperation, Ministry of agriculture, Government of India, New Delhi.

Gulati, A., S. Jain, and N. Satija. 2013b. *Rising Farm Wages in India the 'Pull' and 'Push' Factors*. Discussion Paper No. 5, Commission for Agricultural Costs and Prices, Department of Agriculture and Cooperation, Ministry of Agriculture, Government of India, New Delhi.

Gulati, A., S. Saini, and S. Jain. 2013c. *Monsoon 2013: Estimating the Impact on Agriculture*. Discussion Paper No. 8, Commission for Agricultural Costs and Prices, Department of Agriculture and Cooperation, Ministry of agriculture, Government of India, New Delhi.

Harish, B.G., N. Nagaraj, M.G. Chandrakanth, S.P.P. Murthy, P.G. Chengappa, and G. Basavaraj. 2011. Impacts and Implications of MGNREGA on Labour Supply and Income Generation for Agriculture in Central Dry Zone of Karnataka. *Agricultural Economics Research Review* 24 (5): 485–494.

Hirway, I., M.R. Saluja, and B. Yadav. 2008. Impact of Employment Guarantee Programmes on Gender Equality and Pro-poor Economic Development. Background Paper No. 1, *Reducing Unpaid Work in the Village of NanaKotda, Gujarat: An Economic Impact Analysis of Works Undertaken Under the National Rural Employment Guarantee Act (NREGA): Research Project No. 34*, supported by Gender Team, Bureau of Development Policy and UNDP, New York.

Imbert, C., and J. Papp. 2011. *Equilibrium Distributional Impacts of Government Employment Programs: Evidence from India's Employment Guarantee.* Working Paper No. 2012–14, Paris School of Economics, Paris.

Jha, R., S. Bhattacharyya, and R. Gaiha. 2011. Social Safety Nets and Nutrient Deprivation: An Analysis of the National Rural Employment Guarantee Program and the Public Distribution System in India. *Journal of Asian Economics* 22: 189–201.

Jha, R., S. Bhattacharyya, R. Gaiha, and S. Shankar. 2009. Capture of Anti-poverty Programs: An Analysis of the National Rural Employment Guarantee Program in India. *Journal of Asian Economics* 20 (4): 456–464.

Khera, R., and N. Nayak. 2009. Women Workers and Perceptions of the NREGA. *Economic and Political Weekly* 44 (43): 49–57.

Liu, Y., and C.B. Barrett. 2013. Heterogeneous Pro-poor Targeting in the National Rural Employment Guarantee Scheme. *Economic and Political Weekly* 48 (10): 46–53.

Mann, N., and J. Ramesh. 2013. Rising Farm Wages will Lift all Boats. *The Hindu*, May 14.

MoRD. 2012. *MGNREGA Sameeksha: An Anthology of Research Studies on the Mahatma Gandhi National Rural Employment Guarantee Act, 2005, 2006–2012*, ed. Mihir Shah, Neelakshi Mann, and Varad Pande. New Delhi: Ministry of Rural Development, New Delhi and Orient BlackSwan.

Mukherjee, D., and U.B. Sinha. 2011. *Understanding NREGA: A Simple Theory and Some Facts.* Working Paper No. 196, Centre for Development Economics, Delhi School of Economics, Delhi.

Narayanamoorthy, A. 2013. Profitability in Crops Cultivation in India: Some Evidence from Cost of Cultivation Survey Data. *Indian Journal of Agricultural Economics* 68 (1): 104–121.

Narayanamoorthy, A., and P. Alli. 2012. India's New Food Security Worries: From Crop Holiday to Declining Foodgrains Area. *Indian Journal of Agricultural Economics* 67 (3): 487–498.

Narayanamoorthy, A., and P. Alli. 2013. Rural Job Scheme Sows Misery. *The Hindu Business Line*, February 9.

Reddy, V.R., and P.P. Reddy. 2007. Increasing Costs in Agriculture: Agrarian Crisis and Rural Labour in India. *Indian Journal of Labour Economics* 50 (2): 273–292.

Shah, M. 2009. Multiplier Accelerator Synergy in NREGA. *The Hindu*, April 30.

Verma, S., and T. Shah. 2012. Labour Market Dynamics in Post-MGNREGA Rural, Water Policy Research Highlight No. 8, IWMI-Tata Water Policy Programme, Anand, Gujarat. Accessed from www.iwmi.org/iwmi-tata/apm2012.

Vishandass, A., and B. Lukka. 2013. *Pricing, Costs, Returns and Productivity in Indian Crop Sector During 2000s.* Discussion Paper No. 7, Commission for Agricultural Costs and Prices, Department of Agriculture and Cooperation, Ministry of Agriculture, Government of India, New Delhi.

Part II
MGNREGA: State Level Experiences and Outcomes

Chapter 6
From EGS to MGNREGS in Maharashtra: Were the Programme Potentials Achieved?

Jayanti Kajale and Sangeeta Shroff

6.1 Introduction

Agriculture is the mainstay of the Indian economy because of its high share in employment and livelihood creation. While India's agricultural sector has an impressive record of taking the country out of severe food crisis to that of self-sufficiency, the recent past speaks of lack of dynamism in this sector. The contribution of agriculture to the gross domestic product (GDP) had declined from 36.4% in 1982–83 to 13.7% in 2012–13. Besides the declining contribution of agriculture to GDP, the growth rate of the agriculture sector has also shown dismal performance in recent years than in the preceding decades.

During the Tenth Plan period, the growth rate of GDP was 7.6% per annum, whereas the growth of agricultural sector was only 2.4% per annum. In contrast, industry and service sectors grew at a little more than 9% per annum. The Eleventh Plan (2007–12) target of growth of 4% per annum in the agricultural sector has also not been achieved as the average growth rate of this sector for this plan period was 3.3%.

While the slower growth of GDP in agriculture compared to other sectors is expected, the main failure has been the inability to reduce dependence of the workforce on agriculture significantly by creating enough non-farm opportunities to absorb surplus labour in rural areas. The agricultural sector is also characterised by the dominance of small and marginal farmers and a decline in the size of holdings which is not able to provide sufficient income to farmers.

J. Kajale (✉) · S. Shroff
Gokhale Institute of Politics and Economics, Pune, Maharashtra, India
e-mail: jayanti@gipe.ac.in

S. Shroff
e-mail: sangeeta@gipe.ac.in

M. Bhattarai et al. (eds.), *Employment Guarantee Programme and Dynamics of Rural Transformation in India*, India Studies in Business and Economics,
https://doi.org/10.1007/978-981-10-6262-9_6

In view of the stagnancy in agriculture in the post-2000 period, intervention by the government certainly has an important role to play. One such intervention has been the implementation of the Mahatma Gandhi National Rural Employment Guarantee Scheme (MGNREGS) in 2006, which aims at enhancing livelihood security of the households in rural areas of the country as agriculture has under-performed and is unable to sustain the huge workforce dependent upon it. In this context, we present here Maharashtra state experience relating to implementation and performance of MGNREGS and also compare it with the implementation and performance of EGS (i.e. Maharashtra EGS, or MEGS), the social Safety Net programme for rural poor, which is in fact precedent of MGNREGS in India.

The implementation of MGNREGS by the central government since 2006 is considered to be a landmark policy decision in terms of its socio-economic implications across rural India. At all India level, MGNREGS was implemented in February 2006 in the most backward 200 districts. It was extended to 130 additional districts in 2007-08 in its second phase. Finally in the third phase in 2008–09, the scheme was implemented in the remaining districts. It was thus implemented in all the 615 districts of the country since April 2008. By the end of 2014, the MGNREGS had provided over 2.2 billion person days of employment benefiting over 50 million households per annum. At all India level, an average wage employment of 46 person days was provided in the year 2013–14 with an outlay of ₹ 330 billion in a year (or USD 5.5 billion per year). With wages indexed to the consumer price index for agricultural labour, the average wage under the scheme had increased from ₹ 65 per day in the year 2006–07 to ₹ 132 in 2013–14, (Economic Survey of India, 2013–14, Govt. of India publications).

Reports from different regions (states) of the country reflect a positive outcome of the scheme as far as employment generation is concerned (see, Khera 2008; Khera and Nayak 2009). Likewise, past studies on the impact of MGNREGS in states, such as Rajasthan, Gujarat and Maharashtra revealed that the scheme had made a positive impact on the employment generated and food security in these states. Several empirical studies have reported that the rural poor would like a continuation of the scheme in the respective states (Swain and Sharma 2011; Shah and Makwana 2011; Kajale and Shroff 2011).

Nonetheless, there are studies and media reports which point out flaws in the system and the need for strengthening the same (Bhatia and Dreze 2006; Chakraborty 2007; Siddhartha 2008; NCAER 2009). Corruption, noncompliance with the provisions of the Act in terms of delays in providing employment as well as in making wage payments, problems relating to monitoring of the works, overburdening and shortage of permanent staff at the *Panchayat* level, the existing method of wage calculation were some of the major administrative issues believed to have affected creation of employment on one hand and generation of demand for the works on the other. These studies thus showed apprehensions on the potential of MGNREGS to bring about positive changes in rural areas and highlighted the need for carrying out administrative reforms.

Moreover, it is now increasingly being recognised at various levels that there is an urgent need to shift the focus from employment generation to creation of durable assets along with generation of employment. The Economic Survey of India (2013–14) suggested 'an urgent need to revamp the MGNREGA to prevent its misuse and make it a development oriented programme creating tangible and meaningful assets and infrastructure including tourism—related infrastructure or some large agriculture-related activities' (GoI 2014, p. 253).

The state of Maharashtra had pioneered in launching the employment guarantee scheme (EGS) to the rural poor during the drought years of the early 1970s. The Maharashtra Employment Guarantee Scheme (i.e. MEGS) Act came into existence in 1977 and continued to provide a supplementary source of employment and income to the rural poor of the state. After the implementation of MGNREGS in 2006, both the schemes are being implemented in Maharashtra simultaneously. This has also provided the authors an opportunity to compare implementation and performances of two alternate schemes in the same location of a state.

Maharashtra is one of the leading states as far as industrialization is concerned. However, a major characteristic feature of the state is its urban centric growth which has taken place around the districts of Thane, Mumbai and Pune, which are located in western part of Maharashtra. The economic activities of these three districts together contribute more than 30% to the state income.

Around 50% of the state population is mainly dependent on the agricultural sector as cultivators and agricultural labourers for livelihood. The agricultural sector of the state to a large extent is characterised by low level of irrigation and therefore rainfed farming. Currently, only 18% of the gross cropped area in the state is under irrigation[1] (Economic Survey of Maharashtra, 2013–14), resulting into lower crop productivity in the state. The state experienced agricultural stagnation and agrarian crisis that manifested in suicides of farmers across various regions especially after 2000. Under such circumstances, it is extremely important to increase and sustain growth rate of the agricultural sector of the state not only for maintaining food security and improving the standard of living of the rural population, but also for sustaining growth in rural employment and income.

One major component of sustainable development of agriculture is increasing productivity of land resources by creation of assets and increasing absorptive capacity of the sector. In this context, it is argued that MGNREGS, with aims to create employment and generate assets in rural areas, has potential for creating a base for sustainable development of the agricultural sector of the country as a whole.

[1]Data relating to irrigated area under crops are available till 2000–01 only.

6.2 Objectives and Methodology

The main objective of this chapter is to study the employment profile of the state run EGS and centrally sponsored MGNREGS in Maharashtra. It analyses phase wise performance of MGNREGS, extent of employment generated, assets created and expenditure incurred on the works carried out during 2008–09 and 2012–13. Various factors responsible for the poor performance of the scheme till 2010–11 are also examined. Finally, the chapter discusses limitations and potentials of the scheme as well as policy implications. The study is based on secondary data, mainly collected from the MGNREGS website. This is supported by discussions and qualitative data collected from the field by the authors.

Section 6.3 of the chapter discusses characteristic features of the state run EGS and the centrally supported MGNREGS and the employment generated under these schemes. Next, in Sect. 6.4, trends in phase wise employment generated as well as assets created under MGNREGS during 2008–09 to 2012–13 are analysed. Section 6.5 discusses insights from the field and problems encountered during implementation of the scheme at the grass root level. Conclusions and the emerging policy implications are discussed in Sect. 6.6.

6.3 Employment Guarantee Schemes in Maharashtra: EGS and MGNREGS

The state of Maharashtra was the first state to provide guarantee of employment to the rural poor during the drought years of early 1970s. In fact, a pilot employment guarantee scheme was implemented way back in 1965 and was later extended to all rural areas and areas of 'C' class Municipal Councils of Maharashtra in 1972. Finally, the EGS Act came into existence in 1977, and was implemented all over rural areas of Maharashtra as an act since 1979.

The EGS intended to provide unskilled manual employment on demand. Since its inception till 2005–06, Maharashtra EGS had generated 427.7 crores (or 4.28 billions) person days of employment thus making it one of the largest public works programmes in the world. Several studies in the past have reported a significant impact of the EGS programme on the socio-economic status of the rural poor in Maharashtra, and that it performed better than several other poverty alleviation programmes in India like National Rural Employment Programme, Rural Landless Employment Guarantee Programme and Integrated Rural Development Programme (Acharya 1990; Government of India 2005).

The broad pattern of expenditure and employment generated under EGS over the years has shown a strong correlation with droughts and bad harvests. Similarly, higher EGS employment levels were found to be related to seasonality, i.e. with the slack agricultural season. The composition of employment under EGS shows that it

Table 6.1 Employment generated and expenditure under EGS in Maharashtra state

Year	Man days of employment generated (in crores)	Expenditure under EGS (in ₹ crores)	Expenditure per man day of employment generated (₹)
2001–02	16.17	914.62	56.56
2002–03	15.45	889.00	57.54
2003–04	18.53	1050.71	56.70
2004–05	22.18	1256.47	56.65
2005–06	11.64	983.24	84.47

Source www.mahaegs.nic.in

has been successful in providing considerable employment to women workers and tribal population (Vatsa 2005).

From 2001–02 till 2005–06, on an average of over 15 crores mandays of employment were generated annually under EGS (Table 6.1). Besides, EGS has also been a very successful drought relief employment generating programme, as it has provided employment whenever the need arose in the state of Maharashtra. 4,30,000 works were started since beginning of EGS till March 2002, and over 4,08,000 works were completed till that time (Department of planning, Govt of Maharashtra).

In the beginning, majority (93% in terms of expenditure) of the works under EGS were related to drought proofing (Vatsa 2005). In the post 1990 period, there has been a shift in favour of individual asset building schemes such as wells and plantations (horticultural linked EGS). This has benefited individual farmers and the horticultural sector of the state. However, this does not seem to have increased availability of water over the years that would enhance overall productivity of the agricultural sector and create durable assets in the long run. This underlines the need for creation of good quality assets and mechanism for their maintenance. It was rightly pointed out that professional and management support was needed for creation of good quality assets under EGS Vatsa 2005).

In the light of implementation of the central act—MGNREGS, the Government of Maharashtra decided to amend its EGS Act, 1977 and enlarge its scope to remove parts that were inconsistent and less favourable and to accommodate essential features of the Central Act. MGNREGS that is implemented today is a combination of two schemes. Guarantee of employment for 100 days per household as well as the expenditure incurred for the same is provided by the central government. IT based reporting and monitoring, social auditing, provision of job cards are some of the distinguishing features of the central scheme.

Expenditure incurred for the employment generation exceeding 100 days is contributed from EGS by the state government. Also, under EGS, the state government provides subsidies for the individual benefit schemes such as Jawahar (Dhadak) Sinchan Well Scheme, and horticulture linked EGS. Hence, data relating to employment generation is now reported only under the central scheme, i.e. under MGNREGS.

Table 6.2 Status of implementation of MGNREGS in Maharashtra

No.	Indicators	2008–09	2009–10	2010–11	2011–12	2012–13
1	Households provided employment (lakhs)	9.06	5.36	4.5	13.8	15.5
2	Households provided employment/ households demanded employment (%)	99.8	99.9	99.3	98.5	97.9
3	Employment days (crores)	4.1	2.7	2.00	6.5	8.1
4	Average employment per household (days)	46.2	51.1	44.3	47.3	52.6
5	Households completing 100 days of employment (0000)	32	22	28	15	21
6	Share of SC employment (%)	16.5	25.6	22	5.8	6.9
7	Share of ST employment (%)	44.2	33.1	25.5	17.1	14.6
8	Share of women employment (%)	46.2	39.6	45.8	45.9	44.4

Source District's implementation report on www.nrega.nic.in

After the implementation of MGNREGS, with increasing expenditure and inability of MGNREGS to generate employment in the state comparable to that under EGS (before implementation of MGNREGS) (Table 6.2), questions were raised about sustainability of MGNREGS in the future. Discussions with the officials of the EGS and Water Conservation Department revealed that the continuous decline in employment days generated was a consequence of difficulties faced in the initial days by the administrative machinery when two schemes were being implemented simultaneously. The decline, however, was arrested and since 2011–12, the employment generated has started rising as is clear from Table 6.2.

Table 6.2 shows the implementation status of MGNREGS in Maharashtra since 2008–09, when the scheme became fully opertationalised. Almost all the households which demanded employment in Maharashtra were provided work under the scheme. However, the share of such households had slightly declined over time. In the year 2008–09, 4.19 crores days of employment were created in the state under the MGNREGS.

The employment days created under the programme started to decline since 2009–10. The data for later years showed that the situation improved in 2011–12 with 6.51 crores employment days being generated. However, this number is less than the employment generated under the EGS per annual basis prior to implementation of the MGNREGS in the state. A similar pattern is noticed for average employment per household and households completing 100 days of employment. The share of scheduled caste (SC) and scheduled tribe (ST) population in total employment generated, however, has not shown any encouraging trend. Share of the women employment also has shown a decline.

The share of the state in the total employment generated at all India level was 1.94% in 2008–09 and in the consecutive years, it declined to less than 1%. The figures for the year 2010–11 show that 219 crores and 1.33 crores (0.6% of the all India level) days of employment have been generated at the national and state level respectively. In the consecutive years (2011–12 and 2012–13), however, Maharashtra's share in total employment generated increased up to 3%. Thus, data for the later years reveals gradually increasing importance of the scheme in the state.

6.4 Employment Generated and Assets Created Under MGNREGS in Maharashtra

6.4.1 Employment Generated

In the first year of implementation (phase I) in 2006–07, the scheme of MGNREGA was implemented only in twelve most backward districts of the state. These are the districts with considerable tribal population and together contribute around 45% to the state ST population. In the second year (phase II), six additional districts were included. These eighteen districts are the districts with per capita net district domestic product (NDDP) (at current prices) less than the state average in 2012–13 (Economic Survey of Maharashtra, 2012–13). The scheme was then fully operationalized in 2008–09 (phase III) with the inclusion of remaining fifteen districts. These 15 districts included in phase III are also the most developed districts with higher per capita NDDP (at current prices) in 2012–13 (Economic Survey of Maharashtra, 2012–13). The names of the districts of Maharashtra included under MGNREGS in phased manner are provided Appendix Table 6.7.

Table 6.3 shows that in 2008–09 when MGNREGS became fully operational, the share of phase I districts in total employment generated in the state under the scheme was 75%. It went on increasing till 2010–11. It is observed that share of phase II and III districts has increased considerably only after 2011–12. This indicates that the demand for employment under this scheme was negligible in those districts which came under the Act in the third phase. In fact, in eight districts in Phase III, there was no employment generated under MGNREGS and five districts had a share of less than 1%.

According to the media reports, in some of the phase III developed districts, employment could not be provided to the registered families. This shows that there was a demand for MGNREGS work which could not be satisfied. There was a feeling that lack of provision of work under MGNREGS was closely related to the objective of maintaining stability in the agricultural sector in terms of adequate availability of labour and lower wage rates, particularly in the sugarcane belt of the state. Overall, it appears that MGNREGS has created demand for work mainly in the most backward districts of the state where it was implemented in phase I.

This situation completely reversed, however, since 2011–12. It can be seen that the number of days of employment generated at the state level almost doubled in 2011–12 and further increased in 2012–13. The combined share of second and third phase districts which was less than 20% increased to more than 40%. As has been

Table 6.3 Phase wise number (in lakhs) and share of person days of employment generated (in percentage) under MGNREGS in Maharashtra

Phase	2008–09	2009–10	2010–11	2011–12	2012–13
Phase I	312.38 (74.41)	213.46 (77.81)	172.44 (86.22)	362.05 (55.6)	430.91 (49.39)
Phase II	80.62 (19.2)	23.08 (8.41)	7.07 (3.54)	94.89 (14.57)	132.82 (15.22)
Phase III	26.82 (6.39)	37.81 (13.78)	20.49 (10.25)	194.27 (29.83)	308.66 (35.38)
State	419.82 (100)	274.35 (100)	200 (100)	651.21 (100)	872.39 (100)

Note Figures in the parenthesis indicate percentage share of employment generated to total
Source District's Implementation Report on www.nrega.nic.in

stated earlier, concerted efforts to revitalise the scheme were carried out by the department of Water Conservation and EGS. As a result, the outreach of the scheme increased and all the districts came to be covered by the scheme.

6.4.2 Assets Created

Apart from the number of days of employment generated, another important indicator for assessing the outcome of MGNREGS is the number of works completed. The list of permissible works under MGNREGS are:

(i) Water conservation and water harvesting;
(ii) Drought proofing, including afforestation and tree plantation;
(iii) Irrigation canals, including micro and minor irrigation works;
(iv) Provision of irrigation facility, plantation, horticulture, land development to land owned by households belonging to the SC/ST, or to land of the beneficiaries of land reforms, or to land of the beneficiaries under the Indira AwasYojana/BPL families;
(v) Renovation of traditional water bodies, including de-silting of tanks;
(vi) land development;
(vii) Flood-control and protection works, including drainage in waterlogged areas;
(viii) Rural connectivity to provide all-weather access.
(ix) Any other work that may be notified by the Central Government in consultation with the State Government.

From the list of work, it is obvious that the focus is more on enriching water resource base and land development. The works get classified as completed works and ongoing/suspended works. Table 6.4 presents phase wise data relating to assets created under MGNREGS. It can be seen that the number of works completed had raised for phase I and phase II districts till 2010–11. But, there was a marked fall in the same in the year 2011–12 and again a rise in the year 2012–13.

In the developed districts of phase III, the performance of the scheme was very poor in the initial years. In 2012–13, however, 54% of the total works completed

Table 6.4 Physical performance indicating assets created-number of completed and ongoing works under *MGNREGS* in Maharashtra

Phase	No. of completed works					No. of ongoing work/suspended work				
	2008–09	2009–10	2010–11	2011–12	2012–13	2008–09	2009–10	2010–11	2011–12	2012–13
Phase I	6209 (57.6)	5656 (53.3)	13,445 (71.9)	3293 (51.2)	23,407 (30.36)	10,962 (76.7)	9655 (67.5)	12,591 (41.3)	110,519 (44.4)	131,069 (44.91)
Phase II	3997 (37.1)	4488 (42.3)	4759 (25.4)	1876 (29.2)	12,428 (16.12)	1866 (13.1)	1952 (13.6)	9901 (32.5)	54,026 (21.7)	57,350 (19.65)
Phase III	572 (5.3)	469 (4.4)	503 (2.7)	1264 (19.7)	41,249 (53.51)	1470 (10.3)	2706 (18.9)	8006 (26.3)	84,235 (33.9)	103,376 (3542)
State	10,778	10,613	18,707	6433	77,084	14,298	14,313	30,498	248,780	291,795

Note Figures in the parenthesis are percentages to the total
Source District's implementation report on nrega.nic.in

Table 6.5 Percentage of completed MGNREGS works to previous year's ongoing MGNREGS works in Maharashtra

Phase	CW 2009–10 to OW in 2008–09	CW 2010–11 to OW in 2009–10	CW 2011–12 to OW in 2010–11	CW 2012–13 to OW in 2011–12
Phase I	51.60	139.25	26.15	21.18
Phase II	240.51	243.80	18.95	23.0
Phase III	31.90	18.59	15.79	48.97
State	74.23	130.70	21.09	30.98

CW completed works, *OW* ongoing work
Source Based on data collected from District's Implementation Report on nrega.nic.in

were from these districts. The extent of MGNREGS activities started increasing after 2011–12 in these districts. The number of works completed has risen by more than 72 times in 2012–13 as compared to the initial year. It is observed that at the state level, the number of works completed during the period has increased by more than 600%.

However, considering the number of inhabited villages (40,959 as per the Economic Survey of Maharashtra, 2012–13) and the number of completed works (77,084), the number of works completed per village in the year was less than 2 (1.88). The data on ongoing works shows that their number was increasing over the years both at the district and state levels. The number of ongoing works was higher by almost 26 times in 2012–13. Throughout the period, phase I districts have maintained higher share in the ongoing works.

Table 6.5 shows the percentage of the completed works in a year to the ongoing works of the previous year. This percentage was relatively higher in the initial years for all the districts. In fact, completed works were more than the ongoing works of the previous years for phase I and II districts. This proportion had fallen in the latter years. In 2012–13, only 31% of the works of the earlier year could be completed at the state level. Thus, the data suggests that a number of works could have remained incomplete whereas some might have been suspended for certain reasons. However, the fact remains that resources have been spent on these works (Table 6.6).

The government had to take the challenge of completing a maximum of 2.91 lakh (ongoing/suspended) works of the previous years in the financial year 2013–14. Though the overall performance of the scheme improved in the latter years, the extent of incomplete/suspended works was also increasing (see, Tables 6.4, 6.5, and 6.1).

Table 6.6 presents the expenditure on total works completed as well as on the ongoing/suspended works in Maharashtra under the MGNREGS. The year wise pattern of expenditure is similar to that relating to the number of MGNREGS works completed. The expenditure on completed as well as ongoing works declined at the state level till 2010–11 and has shown increasing trend since 2011–12. It can be noted that in 2008–09 around 97% of the expenditure on the ongoing projects was incurred in phase III districts (mainly only on one district, i.e. Raigad).

Table 6.6 Expenditure on completed and ongoing MGNREGS works in Maharashtra

Phase	Expenditure on completed works (₹ lakhs)					Expenditure on ongoing/suspended works (₹ lakhs)				
	2008–09	2009–10	2010–11	2011–12	2012–13	2008–09	2009–10	2010–11	2011–12	2012—13
Phase I	6104.8 (.93)	7315.9 (62.)	1563.8 (76.)	19,429 (74.)	34,283.54 (43.93)	16,827.7 (2.7)	16,253.4 (87.7)	17,717.0 (89.)	83,773.8 (57.0)	65,590.85 (50.64)
Phase II	7590.3 (1.2)	3891.1 (33.)	20.21 (13.4)	160.2 (6.)	10 257.9 (13.14)	1404.7 (.2)	984.1 (5.3)	747.7 (3.8)	19,626.1 (13.43)	22,896.83 (17.67)
Phase III	639,911.7 (97.9)	596.1 (5.1)	18.3 (10.6)	524.39 (20.)	33,485.81 (42.91)	615,100.6 (97.1)	1290.8 (7.)	1451.8 (7.3)	43,496.6 (29.6)	41,029 (31.67)
State	653,606.8	11,803.1	1602.5	2627.4	78,027.25	633333.	18,528.4	19,916.5	146,896.5	129,516.7

Note Figures in the parenthesis are percentages the state total

Source District's implementation report (monthly progress report on performance indicating asset created) on nrega.nic.in

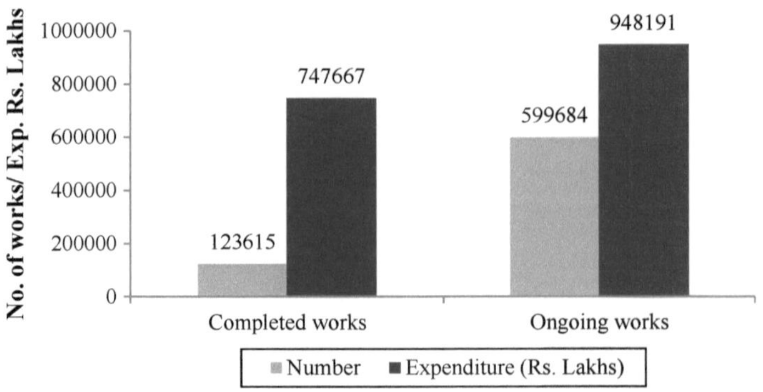

Fig. 6.1 Number of works and expenditure incurred by MGNREGS in Maharashtra during 2008–09 and 2012–13. *Note* Figures in the table are cumulative figures for the entire period. *Source* District's Implementation Report (monthly progress report on performance indicating assets created) on nrega.nic.in

In the remaining years, however, more than 50% was spent on phase I districts. Since 2011–12, share of phase III districts had increased again. It is 41% for the completed works and 36% for the ongoing works in 2012–13. It is worth noting here that large amount of resources have been spent on ongoing works. In 2012–13, the number of ongoing works was 29,1795 and the amount spent was ₹ 129,517 lakhs.

Figure 6.1 shows the total number of completed and ongoing works and expenditure during the concerned five year period. Considering the total number of works that were ongoing and completed every year during 2008–09 and 2012–13, it appears that only around 21% of the total ongoing/suspended works were completed. Taking together the data relating to employment generated and assets created in Maharashtra over the last five years, it may be observed that though there has been an improvement in the performance in terms of employment generated, the scheme seems to have underperformed in terms of asset creation given the extent of resources that have been spent on ongoing and suspended works.

The total expenditure under EGS in 2005–06 was ₹ 98,324 million (Table 6.1). In 2008–09, when MGNREGS was fully operationalized, the expenditure on completed works was ₹ 65,360.6 million. Besides, expenditure was also incurred on ongoing works (Table 6.6). Thus, the funds available as well as expenditure incurred under MGNREGS are many times higher than those under EGS before implementation of MGNREGS.

However, as discussed above, the performance of MGNREGS in the initial years of implementation was not satisfactory and the employment generated was less than that created under EGS. It was only since 2011–12 that the performance of MGNREGS started improving. Efficiency in the usage of funds allocated for generation of employment and creation of assets would go a long way in tapping the potential of MGNREGS to improve the resource base of the agricultural sector.

6.5 Employment and Assets Created Under MGNREGS: Insights from the Field

A survey was conducted for understanding the working of MGNREGS in five representative districts of Maharashtra, viz., Nandurbar, Gondia (phase I districts), erstwhile district Thane[2] (phase II district) and Jalna and Kolhapur (phase III districts). From each district, data was collected from two villages, one near the district headquarters and the other away from it. From a total of 10 villages, 205 participant households were selected for field survey (Kajale and Shroff 2011). A structured schedule for the participant households and a village schedule to be filled in by the village officials were designed.

The data was collected for the year 2008–09. It was revealed that in 2008–09, a large number of works were undertaken by the government and participation of households in this particular year was impressive. However, it was noted that that the employment was generated mainly in the backward and tribal districts such as Thane and Nandurbar as well as in the interior parts of Jalna (see Boxes 6.1 and 6.2).

The survey clearly brought out that in dry areas as well as in areas with hardly any employment opportunities, seasonal migration was the only livelihood strategy. In these areas, MGNREGS proved to be a better livelihood option for the rural households. In fact, majority of the households reported that during the period when enough work was available, participation in the scheme enhanced their standard of living and ensured food security. However, in contrast to the backward and tribal districts, developed sample districts of the state such as Kolhapur registered negligible demand for MGNREGS work as ample employment opportunities were available for the rural poor (see Box 6.2).

Box 6.1: MGNREGS in the Backward Districts

Situated in the northern hilly part of Thane District, Jawhar is one of the interior-most talukas of the district. About 96% of the rural population belongs to the ST community. It was reported that 2008 and 2009 were the years when adequate work under MGNREGS was available and generally the households were satisfied with the same. Majority of the agriculture based households in the villages participated in MGNREGS in these two years. Since the beginning of 2010, the extent of work available at the village had declined. This affected the economic status of the households. The month of May was especially difficult as agricultural work was also not available. In such cases, the workers migrated temporarily to nearby towns/cities to get

[2]Thane, located in the western Maharashtra region was divided and a new district 'Palghar' was carved out of talukas of Palghar, Vada, Vikramgad, Jawhar, Mokhada, DahanuTalasari, and Vasai-Virar in August 2014. In view of non-availability of data for the newly created district Palghar, this study is based on erstwhile district Thane with 15 talukas including Palghar.

employed as casual daily labourers. The poor households survived on food grains from their own farms and food grains available under the Public Distribution System.

Mohadi was one of the sample villages—a Banjara village, situated in the hilly areas of district Jalna. Discussions with the villagers revealed that they were in need of work within the village and generally were reluctant to migrate in search of work and would willingly take up physically rigorous work under MGNREGS. However, according to the *Sarpanch*, the estimate of proposed work under MGNREGS could not be prepared due to non-availability of the technical officer either because the posts did not get filled or because the selected candidates did not join. In such cases, the existing technicians were to shoulder responsibilities of additional *gram panchayats*. In another village—Malkhed in Jalna, it was reported that being a dry area, large scale migration took place in the nearby Aurangabad district. However, implementation of MGNREGS had reduced the flow of migration from this village.

Source Kajale and Shroff (2011) (unpublished report, Agro-Economic Research Centre, Gokhale Institute of Politics and Economics, Pune).

The analysis of the field level data underlines the important role of MGNREGS in areas where agricultural and non-farm sectors have failed to provide livelihood support to the households. These are the areas where work under MGNREGS was undertaken in the slack season and the households could participate in the scheme after the busy season in the village was over. MGNREGS thus has shown potential to introduce positive changes in the village economies, traditionally dependent on subsistence and dry agriculture, provided that work is available whenever needed.

Box 6.2: MGNREGS in Kolhapur

Among the five sample districts, Kolhapur was the most developed district in terms of its agricultural performance. The soil here is fertile and cropping pattern is varied. The land ownership pattern was dominated by small and marginal land holders and the proportion of landless population was very low. Discussions with the households revealed that demand for MGNREGS work was very low during the concerned period as people were not used to and willing to participate in rigorous physical activity. They preferred to cultivate their own land, get income from the livestock (at least 2 cows) and work as agricultural labour (to supplement income and for getting fodder). The agricultural labourers were paid in cash and got advance if needed. Under MGNREGS however, the payment was made through Bank/Post Office after 15 days. On this background, the households did not prefer to work on this scheme. It was found during the survey that women specifically from the SC community were the main participants of the scheme.

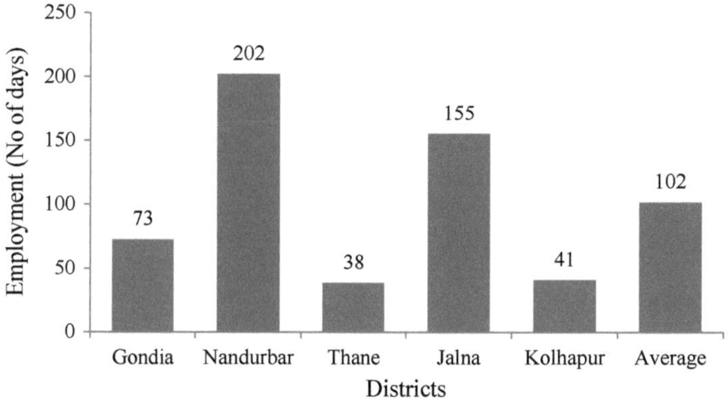

Fig. 6.2 MGNREGS employment days (nos.) generated per sample household in 2008–09. *Source* Kajale and Shroff (2011)

Source Kajale and Shroff (2011) (unpublished report, Agro-Economic Research Centre, Gokhale Institute of Politics and Economics, Pune).

Figure 6.2 shows the number of days of employment generated under MGNREGS per household in the sampled districts. It was higher in case of Nandurbar (202) and Jalna (155) followed by Gondia (73). It was found that in Jalna and Gondia, the MGNREGS work was undertaken on large scale in the villages located farther from the district headquarters than those which were comparatively nearer. In Nandurbar also, which is a tribal district, in both the villages, MGNREGS works were taken up on large scale. In these villages, many household members got employment individually up to 100 days. The number of days was very low in Thane. This was probably because of participation of almost the whole village in MGNREGS work. In Kolhapur, a number of employment days per household was very low.

6.5.1 Nature of Assets Created Under MGNREGS and Their Durability

Provision of work under MGNREGS leads to the creation of assets such as farm ponds, tanks, check dams, roads, etc. As mentioned earlier, the focus of the works is on enriching the water resource base and on land development. A substantial amount of money is spent on labour and other components while the assets are being created. It is therefore important that the assets that are created are of good quality and serve the purpose for a longer period. The field surveys showed that majority of the households were employed under water conservation/harvesting

(75%), micro irrigation works (8.1%) and road connectivity (10%). This pattern is similar to that observed at the district level as well as at the state level.

At the aggregate level, majority of the sample households, i.e. 60% reported that the quality of assets generated was good. About 34% of the households reported that the quality was very good. However, here, the perception of the village official, who coordinated various MGNREGS activities, was different (Box 6.3). The above discussion shows that MGNREGS has potential to enhance the quality of agriculture in a particular region provided that the assets created are of good quality and are durable.

Box 6.3: Perception of a Gramsevak in a Village in District Thane regarding Asset Creation

Thane District receives heavy rainfall during monsoons but because of hill slopes, it becomes difficult to store water at low costs. Hence the households face water shortage and considerable time is spent in searching and collecting water especially during summer. The topography of this region hinders successful watershed and soil conservation strategies and due to lack of any protective irrigation, rabi cultivation is difficult. The gramsevak of one of the sample villages of Jawahar (district Thane) reported that some of the bunds/bandharas or such other structures constructed under MGNREGS before the arrival of monsoon, for storing water, got washed away due to heavy rains and it was difficult to get sanction for the same work in the next financial year. Thus, unless the quality of work is superior (both on account of technical assistance and adequate investment), the asset created would not be durable and would lead to wastage of resources.

Source Kajale and Shroff (2011) (unpublished report, Agro-Economic Research Centre, Gokhale Institute of Politics and Economics, Pune).

Discussions with the village officials also revealed some of the problems associated with working of the scheme. In the initial year of MGNREGS, labourers were paid wages in cash. However, they were reluctant to participate when it became mandatory for them to receive payments through banks or post offices. Often the post office or the bank was located far way and the households also found it cumbersome to open an account. It was also revealed that for the village officials, planning for new works on a continuous basis in each and every village so as to provide 100 days of work was not technically feasible.

Similarly, many farmers were reluctant to give their land for construction of farm ponds or other MGNREGS activities. Some of the line departments such as forest department or PWD did not have enough land to start new activities. This served as a constraint on the work that could be created and employment that could have been generated. Workers sometimes migrated to nearby urban areas for few months for construction and other non-farm work as wages in non-farm sector were two to three times higher than MGNREGS wages. One of the main problems reported by the officials was that with the implementation of MGNREGS, the system had come under tremendous pressure and this had largely affected the efficiency of the *panchayat* level officials and the *gramsevak.*

In view of various problems faced at the village level in implementing the scheme, it is possible that MGNREGS had a set back after 2008–09, i.e. in 2009–10 and 2010–11. At the state level, as has already been mentioned, it was revealed that the continuous decline in employment generated was a consequence of difficulties faced in the initial days by the administrative machinery when two schemes (EGS and MGNREGS) were being implemented simultaneously. The decline, however, was arrested and the performance of MGNREGS started showing indications of recovery since 2011–12.

6.6 Conclusions and Implications

MGNREGS is indeed a policy decision which has a huge impact on the socio-economic and poverty dynamics in rural India so the state of Maharashtra. In 2008–09, when MGNREGS was fully operationalised all over Maharashtra, about 4.20 crores person days of employment were generated in Maharashtra which, however, felled to only 2.74 crores person days of employment generated in the following year. The same pattern was observed in all most all districts of Maharashtra. The number of districts brought under the purview of MGNREGS in phase III had negligible or no demand for work, rather the work was mainly provided in the most backward districts where it was in great demand (mostly in districts included in phase 1). The decline in employment generation under MGNREGS was apparently due to certain limitations in the implementation of the scheme, as such. Planning for work in every village was always not feasible and farmers were also reluctant to give their land for work under MGNREGS.

The programme participants were also reluctant to open an account in the bank or post office for receiving cashless payment, rather they preferred cash payment on the spot, as was practiced in other forms of employments. It was also reported by the officials of the EGS department that problems were faced by the administrative machinery due to simultaneous implementation of both schemes of EGS and MGNREGS in the state, especially in the initial years of the implementation.

It is clear that EGS which was implemented since 1979, was successful in creating employment. However, it appears that it has not been able to create durable assets for drought mitigation and infrastructure for agricultural development during the 35 years since its inception and before the implementation of MGNREGS. Our analysis of MGNREGS also shows that though the scheme has started expanding since 2011–12, its performance relating to asset creation does not present a satisfactory picture. It still has not been able to match the extent of annual employment that was generated under EGS before 2005–06. The funds allocated for MGNREGS are many times higher than those allocated for EGS. So far, a massive amount of resources have been spent not only on completed works but also on works that are ongoing or suspended under MGNREGS.

Our analysis of MGNREGS also shows that though the employment generation schemes and EGS have started expanding to large areas since 2011–12, its performance relating to asset creation does not provide a satisfactory level of achievements. In case of Maharashtra, MGNREGS has still not been able to match the extent of annual employment that was generated under EGS before 2005–06. The funds allocated for MGNREGS are many times higher than those allocated for EGS. Massive amount of resources have been spent not only on completed works but also on works that are ongoing or some are also suspended half ways.

Moreover, the activities under MGNREGS will continue to be successful in terms of participation if beneficiaries demanding work are provided within the locality at appropriate time and at comparable wage rates as that of alternate sources of employment. It is noted that there is a need for locating newer and appropriate types of works and innovative ways of undertaking works under MGNREGS to ensure timely provision of work especially in slack seasons of agricultural activities. Possibilities of working on private lands under MGNREGs can also be explored to generate more number of work and employments in the rural areas, but it needs pilot testing and experiment for assessing the success of the evidence.

Provision of timely and adequate technical help to all the *Gram Panchayats* to ensure timely starting of the MGNREGS activities is another step for strengthening local capacity for effective implementation of the schemes. Such technical back up may also expand potential demand for MGNREGS work. Similarly, this would also help in timely starting the work activities when they are needed most and ensuring quality of assets generated at the local level. Careful planning and timely completion of the works is extremely essential also to reduce frequent suspension of works at the middle stage of implementation.

In sum, the activities under MGNREGS will be sustainable and successful if they lead to creation of durable assets and efficient management of scarce water resources locally, which ultimately would also lead to increasing productivity of the state agricultural sector. Efficiency in the usage of funds allocated for generation of employment and creation of assets would go a long way in tapping the potential of MGNREGS to improve resource base of the agricultural sector, and bring about transformation of the rural economy by development of allied sectors as well as non-farm activities in rural areas.

Acknowledgements The paper largely draws on the report titled 'Impact of NREGA on Wage Rates, Food Security and Rural Urban Migration in Maharashtra', 2011, submitted to the Ministry of Agriculture, GoI New Delhi, by the authors.

Appendix

See Table 6.7.

Table 6.7 Name of districts in Maharashtra that were included under MGNREGA by phases

Phase	Name of districts
Phase I	Ahmednagar, Amravati, Aurangabad, Bhandara, Chandrapur, Dhule, Gadchiroli, Gondia, Nanded, Nandurbar, Yavatmal, Hingoli
Phase II	Akola, Buldhana, Usmanabad, Thane, Wardha, Washim
Phase III	Beed, Jalgaon, Jalna, Kolhapur, Latur, Nagpur, Nasik, Parbhani, Pune, Raigad, Ratnagiri, Sangli, Satara, Sindhudurg, Solapur

References

Acharya, S. 1990. *Maharashtra Employment Guarantee Scheme: A Study of Labour Market Intervention*. New Delhi: ILO-ARTEP.

Bhatia, B., and J. Dreze. 2006. Employment Guarantee in Jharkhand: Ground Realities. *Economic and Political Weekly* 41 (29): 3198–3202.

Chakraborty, P. 2007. Implementation of Employment Guarantee: A Preliminary Appraisal. *Economic and Political Weekly* 42 (7): 548–551.

Government of India. 2005. *Maharashtra Development Report*. New Delhi: Planning Commission.

Government of India. 2014. *Economic Survey of India, 2013–14*. New Delhi: Ministry of Finance.

Kajale, J., and S. Shroff. 2011. *Impact of NREGA on Wage Rates, Food Security and Rural Urban Migration in Maharashtra*. Unpublished report. Pune: Agro-Economic Research Centre. Gokhale Institute of Politics and Economics.

Khera, R. 2008. Empowerment Guarantee Act. *Economic and Political Weekly* 43 (35): 8–10.

Khera, R., and N. Nayak. 2009. Women Workers and Perceptions of the National Rural Employment Guarantee Act. *Economic and Political Weekly*. 44 (43): 49–57.

NCAER. 2009. *Evaluating Performance of National Rural Employment Guarantee Act*. New Delhi.

Shah and Makwana. 2011. *Impact of NREGA on Wage Rates, Food Security and Rural Urban Migration in Gujarat*. Unpublished report, Agro-Economic Research Centre, Sardar Patel University, Vallabh Vidyanagar.

Siddhartha, A.Vanaik. 2008. CAG report on NREGA: Fact and fiction. *Economic and Political Weekly* 43 (17): 39–45.

Swain and Sharma. 2011. *Impact of NREGA on Wage Rates, Food Security and Rural Urban Migration in Rajasthan*. Unpublished report, Agro-Economic Research Centre, Sardar Patel University, Vallabh Vidyanagar.

Vatsa, K.S. (2005). Employment guarantee scheme in Maharashtra: Its impact on drought, poverty and vulnerability. *Paper presented at International Conference on Employment and Income Security in India*, 6–8 April, 2005, organized by Institute for Human Development, New Delhi.

Chapter 7
Asset Creation Under MGNREGA and Sustainable Agriculture Growth: Impacts of Convergence Initiatives in Odisha and West Bengal

Pulak Mishra and Saswat Kishore Mishra

7.1 Introduction

Mahatma Gandhi National Rural Employment Guarantee Act (MGNREGA), implemented by the Government of India is a landmark legislation in the history of India's development initiatives, particularly towards the creation of employment security and rural livelihood opportunities to mass population of India. Execution of the Act has helped in promoting employment and livelihood security in rural India (Jha and Gaiha 2012), increasing purchasing power of the poor (Vijayananda and Jithendra 2008), boosting rural wages and labour force participation (Azam 2012), empowering women (Khera and Nayak 2009) and creating pressure on rural economy towards better terms of trade in favour of agriculture (Panda 2013). Along with indexing wages with inflation, more than 10 crore new bank/post office accounts have been opened with around 80% of payments being made through this route within 5 years of its initiation (Shah 2012). Besides, the share of female in employment generated has also increased (Azam 2012) along with that of the STs and the SCs (Prasad 2012).

It is observed that majority of the works undertaken for asset creation have not been completed and quality of assets created has been poor lacking desired potential (GoI 2014; ILO 2014). In many cases, quality of the assets created in general

P. Mishra (✉) · S.K. Mishra
Department of Humanities and Social Sciences, Indian Institute of Technology, Kharagpur, India
e-mail: pmishra@hss.iitkgp.ernet.in

S.K. Mishra
e-mail: saswat@asci.org.in

M. Bhattarai et al. (eds.), *Employment Guarantee Programme and Dynamics of Rural Transformation in India*, India Studies in Business and Economics,
https://doi.org/10.1007/978-981-10-6262-9_7

'leaves much to be desired' (Dreze and Khera 2009).[1] While the necessity of such assets cannot be discarded, planning for and designing of assets, their maintenance and efficient utilization need special attention.

In order to overcome the constraints as well as to realize better outcomes, the concept of *'convergence planning'* was introduced in 2009. The Ministry of Rural Development designed the guidelines for convergence. Presently, the major participating ministries/organizations in the convergence initiatives include Ministry of Agriculture, the Ministry of Environment and Forests, the Ministry of Water Resources, the Department of Land Resources and Indian Council for Agricultural Research (ICAR).[2]

It is expected that inter-sectoral convergence of development programmes would lead to optimum utilization of public fund and maximum returns on public investments. Besides, such an effort is also crucial for conservation and management of natural resources and creation of assets that would help in mitigating adverse effects of climate change. Thus, convergence initiatives can be seen largely as efforts towards sustainable and inclusive development of rural India.

In this perspective, this Chapter is an attempt to understand the experience of initiatives towards convergence of the MGNREGA with other developmental schemes in the Indian states of Odisha and West Bengal. More specifically, the Chapter addresses the following issues: What are the different types of convergence models that have been initiated in Odisha and West Bengal? How have the joint efforts of various line departments contributed to conservation and management of natural resources? Are assets created under convergence initiatives sustainable in the long-run? How have these assets contributed to agriculture sector, particularly in respect of increase in production and yield? Can the existing institutions contribute to management and utilization of these assets? If not, what institutional supports are necessary in this regard?

The relevance of the study in the context of Odisha and West Bengal arises as agriculture is both a predominant occupation as well as an economic lifeline in these states. Although contribution of agriculture to the respective Gross State Domestic Product (GSDP) had declined over the years,[3] the sector still provides

---

[1]For example, the *kuchcha* structures in Bihar were often incomplete when the monsoon arrived and many check dams were left without "dressing" making them vulnerable to soil erosion. Besides, roads did not have adequate top layer and the location of many of these assets was often inappropriate (Dreze and Khera 2009).

[2]Accordingly, the major programmes covered under the convergence initiatives include Watershed Programmes, National Agriculture Development Programme, National Horticulture Mission, Scheme of Artificial Recharge of Ground Water through Dug well, Accelerated Irrigation Benefit Programme, Backward Region Grant Fund, Pradhan Mantri Gram Sadak Yojana (PMGSY), Swarnjayanti Gram Swarozgar Yojana (SGSY), National Afforestation Programme (NAP), etc.

[3]While the share of agriculture and allied activities in GSDP of Odisha(at constant prices 2004–05 prices) declined from 19.08 to 16.38%, that in West Bengal declined from 20.43 to 16.92%. For details in this regard, see *'Data Report for the use of Deputy Chairman, Planning Commission, 4th August, 2014'* (sourced from http://planningcommission.gov.in).

employment to about 68 and 56% of the rural workforce in Odisha and West Bengal, respectively.[4]

Thus, revival of agriculture through inter-sectoral convergence is imperative to arrest widespread distress and persistent rural poverty in these two states.[5] Further, there is huge difference between the two states in respect of convergence plans received over the years. For example, while contribution of line departments in total convergence plans of West Bengal was 68.38% in 2014–15, it was only 19.28 % for Odisha.

The study uses secondary data and information gathered from various reports and case studies on convergence initiatives at block/village levels in the Indian states of Odisha and West Bengal. The secondary data are sourced from the Official Website of the Ministry of Rural Development, Government of India (i.e. http://nrega.nic.in/netnrega/home.aspx).

The present paper also examines the impact of convergence initiatives undertaken in the Sankrail block of Paschim Medinipur district of West Bengal. It is one of the tribal-dominated and backward blocks in West Bengal. Necessary data/information for this case study is gathered from related reports on the block. Analysis of experiences using secondary data has been carried out at all India level with special emphasis on Odisha and West Bengal. The findings are supplemented with experiences from the cases of convergence in different places of Sankrail block of West Bengal.

The Chapter is divided into six sections including introduction. The second section discusses the role of convergence as an institution in facilitating the growth of Indian agriculture sector. An overview of performance of the MGNREGA in Odisha and West Bengal is given in section three. Convergence initiatives under the MGNREGA in Odisha and West Bengal are discussed in the fourth section. The fifth section examines the experience of convergence initiatives and their impact for a selected case in West Bengal. Section six summarizes the major findings with necessary policy suggestions.

7.2 Convergence as Institution for Sustainable Growth of Agriculture

While growth of non-farm sector is imperative during economic transition, a substantial body of literature also suggests that agricultural growth is a precondition for the sustainable and inclusive development of an economy. Economies of the West with faster agriculture growth developed more rapidly in the nineteenth century (Adelman and Morris 1988). Similarly, industrial revolution of Europe including its offshore and Japan followed green revolution in these countries (Allen 1994; Bairoch 1973; Crafts 1985; Lipton 1977; Ohkawa and Rosovsky 1960;

[4]For details see 66th NSSO Round, 2009–10.

[5]While rural poverty in Odisha is 60.8% (highest in the country) that in West Bengal is 38.2%. For details in this regard, see *'Data Report for the use of Deputy Chairman, Planning Commission, 14th March, 2013'* (sourced from http://planningcommission.gov.in).

Overton 1996; Rostow 1960). The post-war industrialization of Taiwan and South Korea was also largely facilitated by pre-war agricultural growth (Kang and Ramachandran 1999). Even rapid growth of China in recent years is considered as an outcome of reforms in agriculture and rural areas (Fan and Gulati 2008).[6] Many of the developed countries have followed government led agrarian transformation resulting in rapid growth of industry sector and reduction in poverty (Bezemer and Headey 2008).

In India, policies to enhance agricultural growth focus on large-scale investment in irrigation and other infrastructure (Vaidyanathan 2010) and issues relating to technology, environment and institutions are largely ignored. It is found that intensive use of fertilizer and pesticides has resulted in lower land productivity, ground water depletion and pollution and health hazards (Reddy 1995; Reddy and Galab 2006). Further, application of modern technologies and cultivation of water intensive crops have increased use of water resulting in desertification and drying up of wells in many states such as Punjab, Haryana, Andhra Pradesh, Maharashtra and some parts of Uttar Pradesh.

More specifically, retarded growth of Indian agriculture can be seen as market, policy and institutional failures (Behera and Mishra 2007). For enhancing its growth requires institutional framework based on competition, transaction costs, and efficiency and bounded rationality among various agents with enough bargaining power for rural people. Such institutions can significantly influence growth and socio-economic development across countries (Acemoglu and Robinson 2008 and 2012). This is crucial as a failure of markets causes the emergence of outliers during the course of development, creating the necessity of state intervention (Krueger 1990). Further, inclusion of socially marginalized sections into the mainstream development process requires institutional framework with a well-functioning political order.

Asset creation through the convergence of various line departments under the MGNREGA is one such institutional framework that can lead to optimum utilization of public investments in conservation and management of natural resources through synergy amongst different government programmes. Such efforts can also help in mitigating the adverse effects of climate change and creating conditions for sustainable development of the rural economy. Besides, given the decentralized nature of implementation of the MGNREGA, convergence measures can enhance people's participation and provide necessary flexibility that suit to the local conditions while ensuring optimum utilization of public fund (Nayak et al. 2011).

However, since investment in common lands may not generate optimal outcomes primarily because of free rider problems, convergence initiatives in private/individual lands are very important. This is so because people use environmental resources largely depending on property rights governing these resources

[6]Experience from a broader subset of less developed countries (LDCs) also suggest that agricultural transformation is important at the early stages of development, especially for breaking down the barriers to growth in traditional rural societies (Adelman and Morris 1988; Adelman 1984).

(Tietenberg 1994; Williamson 2000). There are evidence of massive degradation of natural resources due to lack of well-defined and secure property rights (Panayotou 1993; Pearce and Warford 1993). Privatization of natural resources among potential users can lead to efficient use and allocation through market forces (Demsetz 1967).

Thus, sustainable management of resources and acceleration of agricultural growth require an integrated approach to link natural resources and people through institutions and convergence initiatives implemented through *Panchayati Raj* Institutions (PRIs) can play a crucial role in this regard.[7] Although traditionally West Bengal is known for its success in *panchayati raj* implementation, the state needs to improve on three basic parameters of devolution including framework, finances, and functionaries concerning the *panchayats* (Table 7.1). While West Bengal just about manages to perform as much as the 20 major states taken together in terms of adhering to the basic provisions of the Constitution (74th Amendment) Act 1992, Odisha fares much higher on this account.

The extent of fiscal transfers, availability of funds and the expenditures incurred by *panchayats* is by and large the same in both these states. Although the extent of physical infrastructure, e-connectivity and capable manpower deployed to the *panchayats* in West Bengal is much better than that in Odisha, yet there is enough scope for further improvement. Moreover enhancing the knowledge and skills of elected representatives and *panchayat* officials at the local level is critical in case of Odisha.

Hence, the institution of convergence has the potential to facilitate the sustained growth of agriculture through asset creation that provides capacity to withstand shocks and uncertainties. The critical mass of these assets may vary from a limited (e.g. economic) to a wider set (e.g. personal, cultural, social and political).

Table 7.1 Panchayat devolution index and sub-indices

States	West Bengal	Odisha	Average of 20 major states[a]	All India
1. Framework	56.84	66.50	55.22	51.40
2. Functions	50.57	51.46	40.53	34.06
3. Finances	35.41	35.11	32.25	29.45
4. Functionaries	37.67	28.55	39.56	36.99
5. Capacity	81.18	19.14	53.98	49.33
6. Accountability	53.96	53.04	48.92	43.33
7. Overall score	49.81	40.01	42.57	38.52
8. Overall rank	6	11	–	–

Note [a]Excluding four North Eastern States and four Union Territories
Source Alok, V. N. (2013)

[7]So far, the PRIs, especially the Gram Panchayats (GPs) have played a crucial role in people's participation in the MGNREGA. For example, social audits by the GPs has increased awareness of the workers regarding their rights and entitlements and contributed to their increased ability of bargaining power.

In addition to coping with stresses and shocks, such institutional approach can also enable the farmers to gain required economic, political and social bargaining power and freedom that are crucial for boosting agricultural growth and facilitating the economic transition. Given this backdrop, what follows next is an attempt to give an overview of the MGNREGA in the Indian state of Odisha and West Bengal.

7.3 Performance of MGNREGA in Odisha and West Bengal: An Overview

The MGNREGA is one of the largest social security and public works initiative in India. While the overall impact of the Act in terms of employment generation is satisfactory, outcomes of the works undertaken (mostly related to water and soil conservation) appear to be largely redundant.[8] Further, the performance of the MGNREGA has deteriorated over the years (Jha and Gaiha 2012). However, the experiences at the state level have been mixed (Mishra and Mishra 2015). It is observed that higher utilization of available funds in these states did not have any significant impact on physical performance of the scheme (Table 7.2).

The average person days of employment generated per household and percentage of households provided with 100 days employment are fairly lower in Odisha and West Bengal despite substantially higher fund utilization ratio there as compared to the national average. The situation is more critical for West Bengal which spends in excess of the available funds while providing hardly 3% of the households with 100 days employment. Work completion rate, in general, is also quite low in both the states. More than 50% of the works initiated under the MGNREGA are not completed in West Bengal, whereas the work completion rate is only 22% in Odisha.

Besides, share of both the SCs and the STs in employment has sharply fallen in West Bengal during 2008–14 (Table 7.3). In case of Odisha, although participation of the STs has increased, that of the SCs has declined during the same period. However, contrary to nearly the same share of the SCs in the rural population, their inclusion in the MGNREGA in Odisha is lower than that at all India level. Unlike in Odisha, share of women in employment generated has increased in West Bengal. However, low rate of women participation in both the states *vis-a-vis* that at all India level is a matter of serious concern.

The overall work completion rate of major asset creation projects related to agriculture undertaken during 2007–13 was also not very encouraging (Table 7.4). The average work completion rate in West Bengal declined sharply across all major projects during this period. The average completion rate in Odisha increased steeply

[8]The audit report tabled by the Comptroller and Auditor General (CAG) in the Parliament on 23rd April, 2013 finds that while more than 22 million works were taken up under the programme during 2007–08 to 2011–12, close to 70% of these works were never completed.

Table 7.2 Performance of MGNREGA in Odisha and West Bengal, 2008–09 to 2013–14

	Odisha	West Bengal	All India[a]
1. Total expenditure (Lakh Rs.)	651114.26	1553353.92	21453597.9
2. Total person days of employment generated (Lakh)	3674.8	9637.28	1,41,926
3. Expenditure incurred per unit lakh person days of employment generated	177.18	161.18	151.16
4. Actual expenditure against total available fund (%)	92.79	101.05	74.06
5. Share in country's total expenditure (%)	3.03	7.24	–
6. Average person days of employment per household	39	33	47
7. Share in country's total person days of employment generated (%)	2.59	6.79	–
8. Percentage of households getting 100 days employment	6.31	2.58	10.91
9. Completed work against planned work (%)	21.63	47.84	32.37

Note [a]for all the 34 states and union territories of the country
Source Official Website of MGREGS, Ministry of Rural Development, Government of India

across all project categories, there is scope for further improvement. It is observed that more than 70% of the works initiated towards creation of assets related to agriculture sector is not completed.

Although the impact of the works completed on production and yield is yet to be explored, slower pace seems to have restricted growth of production and yield in Odisha and West Bengal (Table 7.5).[9]

Production of food grain and non-food grains in these states have either remained by and large the same or increased only by limited extent. However, production of horticulture crops in West Bengal has increased during 2011–12 and 2013–14 contrary to its stagnated production in Odisha (Table 7.6).

Thus, the experience of the MGNREGA in Odisha and West Bengal over the years suggests that the quantum of assets created does not match with the quantum of expenditure. Furthermore, even when assets are generated, their potential towards yielding sustainable livelihood for the rural poor creates doubt. In this perspective, the Ministry of Rural Development initiated convergence of various development programmes with the MGNREGA to create sustainable productive assets at the household and community levels, promote better cohesion across sectors/departments, lower transaction and administrative costs and ensure effective utilization of resources. It is expected that the convergence initiatives will facilitate the growth of agriculture, diversify occupational structure and enhance economic

[9]This is particularly so as the works relating to agriculture has potential of improving soil fertility, restricting land degradation and top soil erosion and mitigating against droughts.

Table 7.3 Social inclusion under MGNREGA across caste category and for women in Odisha and West Bengal

State/All India	Percentage share of SC person days		SC in rural population (%)	Percentage share of ST person days		ST in rural population (%)	Percentage share of women person days		Women in rural population (%)
	2008–09	2013–14	2011 Census	2008–09	2013–14	2011 Census	2008–09	2013–14	2011 Census
Odisha	20.24	16.36	17.8	35.81	40.82	25.7	37.58	33.57	49.71
West Bengal	37.45	32.98	27.5	14.81	9.45	7.8	26.53	35.45	48.79
All India[a]	29.29	22.6	18.5	25.43	17.19	11.3	47.88	52.84	48.69

Note [a]for all the 34 states and union territories of the country
Source Official Website of MGREGS, Ministry of Rural Development, Government of India

Table 7.4 Work completion rate of major asset creation projects in Odisha and West Bengal

Activities/works related to	Odisha		West Bengal		All India	
	2007–09	2011–13	2007–09	2011–13	2007–09	2011–13
1. Rural connectivity	20.34	28.09	60.86	42.91	47.02	37.03
2. Flood control	17.28	29.74	66.76	48.23	59.35	41.22
3. Water conservation and water harvesting	14.33	30.52	46.74	48.21	47.11	22.15
4. Drought proofing	9.13	24.08	61.14	48.59	35.91	17.54
5. Micro-irrigation	19.82	19.46	56.89	49.10	45.49	40.45
6. Provision of irrigation facility	13.21	35.26	57.98	38.05	39.75	25.33
7. Renovation of traditional water bodies	12.47	29.31	52.73	45.50	35.85	39.12
8. Land development	21.89	33.71	61.21	48.44	54.10	46.11
9. Any other activity approved by MRD	21.07	18.22	9.72	42.86	61.46	29.10
10. Others[a]	NPU[b]	9.77	NPU	11.41	NPU	17.90
Total	16.62	28.34	52.67	44.94	47.34	28.22

Note [a]includes the average completion rate of all projects namely under Bharat Nirman, Coastal areas, Rural drinking water, Fisheries, Rural sanitation, Aanganbadi and Play ground. [b]No projects undertaken

Source Official Website of MGREGS, Ministry of Rural Development, Government of India

Table 7.5 Production of food grains and major non-food grains in Odisha and West Bengal

	Odisha		West Bengal		All India	
	2007–09	2011–13	2007–09	2011–13	2007–09	2011–13
1. Food grains (in 000' tonnes per 100 sq km)	4.94	4.83	18.06	18.59	6.93	7.92
2. Non-food grains (in 000' tonnes per 100 sq km)	0.76	0.97	11.91	11.81	11.29	12.86
3. Yield of total food grains (In Kgs/Hectare)	1414.67	1514.33	2513.33	2693.33	1855.67	2099.33

Source Agricultural Statistics at a Glance 2014, Ministry of Agriculture, Government of India

opportunities. The following section critically accounts for the convergence initiatives undertaken in Odisha and West Bengal and their possible implications.

7.4 Convergence Initiatives in Odisha and West Bengal

The concept of convergence is not new in development literature. The conventional hypothesis has emphasized primarily on interregional convergence within and across countries. Many past empirical researches have treated convergence as an

Table 7.6 Production of horticulture crops[a] (000'MT per 100 Sq. Km.) During 2011–12 and 2013–14

States/All India	2011–12	2013–14
Odisha	7.86	7.95
West Bengal	30.45	33.55
All India	7.83	8.54

Note [a]includes Fruits, Vegetables, Flowers, Aromatic/Medicinal Plants and Spices

Source Agricultural Statistics at a Glance 2014, Ministry of Agriculture, Government of India

outcome in itself rather than a process. There are attempts to undertake convergence initiatives in rural development programmes (Mukherjee and Kuruda 2002).

As regards convergence under the MGNREGA, Uttar Pradesh, Haryana and Chhattisgarh are the leading ones in terms of share in the total convergence plans received during 2014–15 followed by Gujarat, Maharashtra, Karnataka and Odisha (Table 7.7). On contrary, West Bengal lies at the bottom end with roughly 4% share in total convergence plans. However, the contribution from the line departments in total project costs is high in West Bengal and quite less in Odisha.

While the states like Maharashtra and Gujarat have been able to garner large number of convergence plans with a financial contribution from the line departments, Odisha and West Bengal showcase contrary positions in this regard. It is therefore, necessary to understand the extent of assets creation through convergence and models of convergence initiated. What follows next is an attempt in this direction?

Although the number of works approved for convergence as a proportion of total approved works in both the states is by and large the same, proportion of works for convergence under implementation is less in Odisha as compared to West Bengal (Table 7.8). The same is true in respect of their share of expenditure incurred on the ongoing works. While the share of works completed under convergence is miserably low in Odisha both in terms of number and expenditure incurred, it is evenly poised for West Bengal, possibly due to the intensive approach of convergence initiative in the state. Further, Odisha has performed poorly in terms of work completion rate under convergence.

The convergence models adopted in Odisha and West Bengal have subtle differences in their approaches towards the planning, implementation and monitoring of the projects (Table 7.9). Unlike what is observed at the state level, these models of convergence appear to be fairly successful in addressing their objectives in the target districts of Odisha.

The gliding path of convergence initiatives in the state largely include: active community participation at every stage of project implementation, community evaluation of project activities, vigorous social mobilization processes and mass public campaigns about the benefits of the interventions, imparting of training and dissemination of information to the targeted beneficiaries about skill-sensitive practices coupled with marketing of the output.

Table 7.7 Convergence plans received so far by the Ministry for the year 2014–15

State	No. of convergence partner Ministries/Department	Share in the country's total plans received (%)	Total project cost (Rs. In Cr.)	Contribution from line departments in the total project cost of the state (%)
1. Andaman and Nicobar	11	6.88	12.80	4.38
2. Chhattisgarh	13	8.13	975.85	39.03
3. Gujarat	11	6.88	789.30	64.30
4. Haryana	14	8.75	199.54	37.40
5. Himachal Pradesh	8	5.00	209.07	58.98
6. Karnataka	10	6.25	1258.91	35.93
7. Madhya Pradesh	7	4.38	10,529	14.85
8. Maharashtra	10	6.25	1438.01	78.59
9. Meghalaya	9	5.63	182.12	68.94
10. Mizoram	4	2.50	82.32	31.01
11. Odisha	10	6.25	1166.12	19.28
12. Rajasthan	8	5.00	747.99	45.44
13. Sikkim	3	1.88	101.40	67.22
14. Tamil Nadu	7	4.38	1765.04	25.15
15. Tripura	10	6.25	567.34	40.00
16. Uttar Pradesh	19	11.88	102.06	36.28
17. West Bengal	6	3.75	4159.06	68.38
Total	160		24285.90	35.00

Note Major line departments include Agriculture, Animal Husbandry, Irrigation, Horticulture, Forestry, Fishery, Drinking Water & Sanitation, PWD, Women& Child Welfare
Source Official Website of MGREGS, Ministry of Rural Development, Government of India

Table 7.8 Percentage share of no. of works with convergence in total works approved, ongoing and completed in Odisha and West Bengal

Status of Works[a]	Odisha	West Bengal	All India
Approved	11.08	11.62	9.16
Ongoing	6.23 (0.24)	8.78 (3.93)	11.34 (3.80)
Completed	5.16 (1.39)	50.28 (31.98)	7.10 (4.86)
Work completion rate	0.70 (2.80)	2.81 (6.30)	3.90 (2.90)

Note Figure in the parentheses show the percentage share of expenditure on works with convergence in total expenditure
[a]These works include Drought Proofing, Flood Control and Protection, Development of Land, Micro-Irrigation Works, Renovation of traditional water bodies, Rural Connectivity, Rural Drinking Water, Water Conservation and Water Harvesting, Fisheries, and Works on Individuals Land (Category IV)
Source Official Website of MGREGS, Ministry of Rural Development, Government of India

Table 7.9 Selected successful convergence interventions in Odisha and West Bengal

States	Districts	**Line Departments Involved**[a] Programmes Converged	Objective(s) [b]Activities	Impact(s)
Odisha	Koraput	**Horticulture and Soil Conservation**[a] Land Development and Commercial Plantation	(1) Land development [b]Transformation of muddy hilly patches of land into cultivable agricultural land resources [b]Changing the existing cropping style and pattern and promoting high value cash crops [b]Promoting plantation of commercial horticulture species	[c]Shift from subsistence agricultural crops to high value crops like mango, cashew, aromatic plants and coffee [c]Development of 1940 hectares of forest land [c]Accruing of Rs. 12,300 per hectare on an average per crop to the beneficiaries [c]Improvement in the standard of living particularly of ST community [c]Aroused consciousness about the effectiveness of democratic decentralized planning of development works
	Kandhamal	**NGOs**[a] Land and Water Management—Integrated Natural Resources Management (INRM)	(1) Restoration and management of natural resources [b]Bring in community culture of effective natural resource management [b]Improve the productivity of agriculture and allied sector	[c]Attracted attention as 70–80% of wage seeker households now work for more than 80 days per household per year. [c]Villagers resorted to cultivation of vegetables in their model plot and fishery in farm ponds [c]Helped the community in promoting execution of INRM related works under MGNREGA by creating productive assets
	Mayurbhanj	**HSC, Integrated Tribal Development Agency (ITDA), Agriculture, Odisha Livelihood Mission, Lift Irrigation** [a]National Horticulture Mission (NHM), JalNidhi, BijuKrishakKalyanYojana (BKKY)	(1) Creation of sustainable assets that also generate livelihoods [b]Land development and excavation for raising commercial crops [b]Planning the intercropping in plantation patches [b]Building social capital & train the beneficiaries on crop rearing	[c]Regular irrigation for most of the areas through bore wells, farm ponds, drip irrigation [c]Survival rate of plantation is currently 96% [c]The average estimated income per beneficiary from these plantations is Rs. 30,000 pa from the fourth year [c]Mango and other fruits planted in around 8226 hectares area on the lands of 12,556 individual beneficiaries under MGNREGA

(continued)

Table 7.9 (continued)

States	Districts	**Line Departments Involved**[a] Programmes Converged	Objective(s) [b]Activities	Impact(s)
West Bengal	24 Parganas	**Forest Dept. along with members of women SHGs**	(1) Forest Cover [b]Restoration of mangrove cover in 6000 hectares of forest area in the Sunderbans [b]Secure lives of people against natural calamity [b]Arrest outward migration during the lean season	[c]Plantation of over one crore mangrove seedlings over an area of 2485 hectares [c]Restoration of the ecological lifelines of river embankments and earthen dams with mangrove plantation [c]Participation of a large number of women drawn from local women SHGs [c]Women getting 100 days of assured employment from rearing mangrove saplings [c]Arrested distress migration of labourers by generating more than 3.5 lakh person days in the lean season
	Bankura	**Horticulture Dept., Food Processing Industries &Horticulture** [a]National Horticulture Mission (NHM), National Rural Livelihood Mission (NRLM), National Mission for Micro-Irrigation	(1) Transformation of wasteland into productive agricultural land	[c]Provided unskilled wage employment to wage seekers but also has created durable assets [c]Nearly 392 hectares of non-productive wasteland have been transformed into productive assets [c]Plantation of mango trees ensured arrest of large-scale soil erosion of the area [c]Small ponds (Hapas) and cattle-proof trenches have helped in retaining surface runoffs leading to adequate water percolation and ground water recharge [c]Developed potential for investment for the food processing industries
	Burdwan (Banks of	**Irrigation dept.**	(1) Flood proofing [b]Restoration of rural livelihoods by constructing sustainable flood proofing	[c]The project work is still in progress

(continued)

Table 7.9 (continued)

States	Districts	**Line Departments Involved**[a] Programmes Converged	Objective(s) [b]Activities	Impact(s)
	the river Damodar)		structures & strengthening agricultural irrigation channels [b]Improve height of river embankment above the train line and national highway level [b]Road for providing market linkages	[c]Till October 2013, Rs. 4.60 Crore has been spent and 1.55 Lakh person days have been generated
	Burdwan (Bhatar block)	**Agriculture and Horticulture Department (AHD)**	(1) Building livelihoods around a pond [b]Ensure effective water intake capacity [b]Prevent soil erosion and provide livelihoods to families	[c]The land surrounding the pond owned by the GP was developed [c]Fruit saplings including Banana, Guava and Mango, were planted in the area [c]40 rural households are not only maintaining this asset but also earning their livelihoods through fruit orchards and pisciculture

Note [a]refers to programmes converged; [b]refers to specific activities carried out under the programme; [c]refers to impact(s) of the programme
Source Report on—Enhancing Sustainable Livelihoods of the Poor through Convergence of Mahatma Gandhi NREGA with Various Schemes, Ministry of Rural Development, Government of India

While such initiatives have ensured enhanced purchasing power and improved standard of living of the people through transformation of agricultural practices in Koraput (Odisha), there has also been large-scale local participation in planning for and execution of the works. This has further opened up avenues for a sustainable livelihood by the creation of productive assets in the backward districts of Kandhamal and Mayurbhanj in Odisha.

In case of West Bengal, the approaches to the convergence interventions include undertaking need-based work programmes (unlike resource endowment-based projects undertaken in Odisha), larger involvement of local institutions such as the PRIs, Self-Help Groups (SHGs), Civil Society Organizations (CSOs), etc. While the coverage appears to be more intensive in the state, the focus has largely been towards attaining sustained livelihood opportunities and self-sufficiency and creating infrastructure for disaster preparedness in rural areas. Given these broad observations, the next section attempts to analyze selected convergence initiatives undertaken in Odisha and West Bengal on the livelihood of the local community and agriculture and allied sectors.

7.5 Impact of Convergence: Experience of Selected Cases

As mentioned above, the models of convergence initiatives and their outcomes are likely to vary depending on socio-economic and ecological settings and institutional dynamics at the local level. On realizing these aspects, an attempt was made by Nayak et al. (2011) to understand the convergence initiatives in Odisha. The study finds three broad models of convergence of various rural development projects with the MGNREGA in the state.

In the first model, rejuvenation of community tanks for fisheries is linked with plantation, irrigation, and water conservation. In the second model, watershed development projects undertaken under the MGNREGA are linked with irrigation, social forestry, plantation, soil and water conservation and animal husbandry. The third convergence model relates to conversion of rural connectivity projects under the MGNREGA to black-topped roads along with soil conservation through plantation and water conservation by digging water channels on both sides of the roads.

The joint efforts of the various line departments have resulted in better conservation and management of natural resources. It is observed that with excavation of tanks, de-siltation of existing water bodies, and building of strong embankments around them, availability of water for irrigation has increased and groundwater level has improved considerably. This has enabled the farmers to go for multiple cropping in the catchment areas. At the same time, plantation of trees along the embankment of these water bodies has also helped in checking soil erosion.

Given the experience, the present section examines the implications of convergence initiatives by analyzing selected cases from the Sankrail Block under Paschim Medinipur district West Bengal. The block comprises of 10 GPs spread across 287 villages, covering an area of 275.68 km^2. While the sex ratio is 973 females per 1000 males, the share of the STs and the SCs in the total population is 23.07 and 15.92%, respectively (Census of India 2011). In some parts of the block, soil is highly productive and alluvial in nature. The rest of the area is used mostly for cultivation. The workforce constitutes mainly cultivators and agricultural labourers. A number of MGNREGA schemes have been converged with various other programmes enhancing livelihood opportunity for the local people by harnessing agriculture and allied sectors. Three such cases are discussed below:

7.5.1 Case I: Convergence of the MGNREGA with Fisheries and Horticulture

During the last 7 years, a large number of water bodies (about 5000) have been excavated and/or renovated under the MGNREGA in the Sankrail block. However, extensive excavation of pond was implemented from the year 2012–13 for the BPL marginal farmers in their own land. The objective was of twofold: (a) to conserve maximum water through natural watersheds and (b) to introduce scientific excavation method conducive for fish netting and pisciculture. Table 7.10 presents the further details in this regard.

7.5.1.1 Rationale for Water Conservation Under the MGNREGA

Most part of the block is covered with laterite soil having low water retention capacity resulting in steady depletion of the water table, and thus limiting growth and diversification of agriculture.

7.5.1.2 Impact

This project is found successful by increasing water table. Availability of water has broadened the scope as well as scale of vegetation in the area. In addition to the creation of physical assets, wage expenditure also ensured increase in income of local workforce.

7.5.1.3 Convergence Intervention

In order to address the objective of fish cultivation, the Department of Fisheries (Govt. of WB) had prepared a detailed model plan with the involvement of the Department of Agriculture & Cooperation (GoI). The National Horticulture Mission (NHM) was also converged with the MGNREGA. While the Department of

Table 7.10 The MGNREGA in convergence with water conservation and fish cultivation

District/ Block	**Line Departments involved**[a] Programmes Converged	Objective(s) [b]Activities	Financial component	Impact(s)/Present Status
Paschim Medinipur (Sankrail Block)	**Fishery Department (GoWB)** **Department of Agriculture & Cooperation (GoI)**[a] National Horticulture Mission (NHM)	(1) Conservation of natural water and scientific excavation conducive for fish netting and pisciculture activities [b]Excavation/renovation of ponds [b]Lime application [b]Cow dung application [b]Fish seedling distribution [b]Banana and other horticulture garden generation	Total cost—Rs. 217.19 lakh Share in total expenditure (%) ▪ MGNREGA (77.62) ▪ Fishery Dept. (20.54) ▪ NHM (1.84)	[c]Person days already created and activities from fishery department are ongoing • 183 No. Of Ponds excavated in FY 2013–14 (across two GPs) covering 8 ha area and involving wage expenditure of Rs. 1,45,98,592 [c]Million gallon increase in the level of water table [c]Development of vegetation [c]Nearly 10,000 banana and 5500 pineapple tree seeds supplied [c]400 model ponds (out of 500 created under MGNREGA) selected for fish cultivation • Projected net income of Rs. 24,045 from unit area of 0.1 ha. (and above water area) • Projected net income of Rs. 13,398 from unit area of 0.04 ha. (and above water area)

Note [a]refers to programmes converged; [b]refers to specific activities carried out under the programme; [c]refers to impact(s) of the programme
Source Office of the Block Development Officer, Sankrail

Fisheries has provided fully subsidized fishery inputs along with technical training, awareness and frequent exposure visits, the NHM has distributed various horticulture saplings.

7.5.1.4 Rationale for Fish Cultivation Under Convergence

The fundamental reasons for exploiting water bodies created under the MGNREGA include the following: (a) the fishermen and fish farmers in the Sankrail block are poverty-ridden and cannot afford desired expenses for fish culture, (b) there is huge potential for high fish production given the alluvial nature of soil, and (c) huge population and domestic market offers enormous incentives for higher production. Also, limited application of manure and technical know-how on the part of the fish farmers had resulted in sub-optimal fish production over the years.

7.5.1.5 Impact

Since contemporary means of fish cultivation is expensive, farmers either mostly confine their economic activities to agriculture or follow traditional methods of pisciculture. The convergence initiatives have motivated local people to take up pisciculture as an alternative livelihood option. Provision of training has enabled the fish farmers to follow more progressive and professional approach towards fish cultivation. The once economically downtrodden people have started producing as well as consuming protein-rich food while their projected annual net income showed healthy signs (Table 7.10). Support from the NHM has further expanded opportunities and strengthened livelihood of the beneficiaries.

7.5.2 Case II: Convergence of the MGNREGA with Agriculture, Horticulture and Eco-Tourism

This project was proposed to come up at Kodopal, a tribal-dominated area located about 4 km away from the block headquarters and spread across around 400 acres. Forest wood collections and seasonal wage labour are the main source of livelihood of the local people. In order to provide greater livelihood opportunity to the local workforce, the block administration has undertaken convergence initiatives in barren land. Although the primary aim of this initiative is to guarantee extra livelihood, the plan was also to extend it to a comprehensive eco-tourism project. Around 400 acres of delta land at the confluence of Subarnarekha and Dulung has been identified for this purpose.

7.5.2.1 Rationale

Prior to 2013, the area was covered with bushy hedges and undulating sandy plants. Earlier interventions through the MGNREGA such as trench cutting, field binding, field mulching and land preparation lacked proper planning and technicality despite engaging more than 400 labourers daily. The detailed comprehensive plan has been drawn for convergence of the MGNREGA with horticulture, agriculture and self-help group and self-employment related works (Table 7.11).

7.5.2.2 Impact

About 10% of the allocated fund under convergence has been spent generating 11,000 man days of work. While the MGNREGA works have been directed for road development, building social forestry, vermicompost units and orchard saplings, the Horticulture Department has provided technical support for orchard raising and material oriented components, such as irrigation system, pump mechanization, initial sapling and medicinal plantation. The Agriculture Department has given demonstration on cultivation of seasonal vegetables that have greater scope for extra livelihood generation. The human resources engaged under the MGNREGA have been brought for extensive planning through district resource persons (DRPs/RPs and other resource persons). This has facilitated financial inclusion through opening of bank accounts and completion of group formation for a new model of tribal-cooperative farming.

7.5.3 Case III: The MGNREGA in Convergence with Sericulture

The aim of this project is to enhance the livelihood of local people through Sericulture across two regions each under the GPs of Pathra and Khudmarai.

7.5.3.1 Impact

The initiatives could generate employment of more than 9000 unskilled man days with substantial wage expenditure ₹ 13.49 lakh (Table 7.12). Besides, additional projected employment of 4000 man days with projected average earnings of ₹ 34,000 per beneficiary per annum are very also encouraging.

Table 7.11 The MGNREGA in convergence with eco-tourism and socio-economic development

District/Block	**Line Departments involved**[a] Programmes Converged	Objective(s) [b]Activities	[c]Financial component	[d]Impact(s)/Present status
Kodopal (Sankrail Block)	**Ministry of Health & Family Welfare Department (GoI)**[a] National Mission on Medicinal plants (NMMP) **Department of Agriculture & Cooperation (GoI)**[a] National Horticulture Mission (NHM) **Ministry of Rural Development (GoI)**[a] National Rural Livelihoods Mission (NRLM)[a] Integrated Action Plan (IAP) **NG0 (assisted by NABARD)**	(1) Eco-tourism and socio-economic development project [b]Land development and land preparation [b]Flood protection work [b]Intercropping at orchard plots [b]Fruit orchard installation [b]Installation of vermicompost units [b]Inter plot connecting roads development [b]Social forestry and flower bearing trees [b]Installation of micro-irrigation system, medicinal garden, cottages [b]Installation of unconventional power generation [b]Construction of approach roads	[c]Total Cost —Rs. 269 lakh [c]Share in total expenditure (%) ■ MGNREGA (50.99) ■ NMMP (11.48) ■ Tourism (22.30) ■ NHM (2.97) ■ NLRM (1.49) ■ NGO (1.30) ■ IAP (9.29)	[d]Fund of Rs. 26.5 lakh already utilized and 11,000 man days already created [d]Bank accounts opened and group formation completed for tribal-cooperative farming [d]Proposed plans and components under MGNREGA • Development of 26 km of main road, approach road and inter plot roads • Nursery building of social forestry and orchard saplings • Vermicompost units building and azola pit formation • Orchard raising plot-wise [d]Proposed plans and components under Horticulture [d]Technical support for orchard raising • Material oriented components like irrigation system, pump mechanization and initial sapling through NHM • Medicinal plantation using NHM fund [d]Proposed plans and components under Agriculture • Plots for agriculture demonstration • Scope for extra livelihood generation through cultivation of seasonal vegetables

Note [a]refers to programmes converged; [b]refers to objective(s) of the programme; [c]refers to financial component; [d]refers to impact(s) of the programme
Source Office of the Block Development Officer, Sankrail

Table 7.12 The MGNREGA in convergence with sericulture

District/Block/GP	**Line Departments involved**[a] Programmes Converged	Objective(s) *Activities	[c]Financial component	[d]Impact(s)/Present status
Pathra and Khudmarai GPs (Sankrail Block)	**Department of Sericulture Ministry of Rural Development (GoI)**[a] Integrated Action Plan (IAP)	(1) Providing livelihood through sericulture [b]Land development and land preparation [b]Protection trench cutting [b]Internal drainage development and road development [b]Creation of water body [b]Training and cultivation of Tussar [b]Marketing of production	[c]Total Cost —Rs. 53.55 lakh [c]Share in total expenditure (%) ▪ MGNREGA (91.88) ▪ Dept. Of Sericulture (3.45) ▪ IAP (4.67)	[d]9000 no. of unskilled man days completed with a wage expenditure of Rs. 13.49 lakh under MGNREGA [d]Over 4000 no. of unskilled man days projected to be generated [d]Average earnings per beneficiary per annum projected at Rs. 34, 000

Note [a]refers to programmes converged; [b]refers to objective(s) of the programme; [c]refers to financial component; [d]refers to impact(s) of the programme
Source Office of the Block Development Officer, Sankrail

7.6 Summary and Conclusions

This Chapter assesses and document experience of convergence planning related initiatives under the MGNREGA in the states of Odisha and West Bengal towards sustainable growth of agriculture. The assessment suggests that West Bengal has performed better than Odisha in terms of the physical performance of the MGNREGA on most of the criteria of assessments. Odisha, on the contrary, has followed an extensive approach in terms of coverage whereby the average person days generated and households provided with 100 days employment are higher. Nonetheless, there is a huge potential for improvement. Convergence initiatives have yielded better output in West Bengal than in Odisha possibly due to the efficacy of *Panchayati Raj* Institutions (PRIs) in the state.

The convergence initiatives taken in Odisha and West Bengal have immense potential in achieving sustainable agriculture growth and enhancing livelihoods opportunities. For example, works relating to soil conservation and land development can increase agriculture production and yield, whereas commercial plantation is likely to diversify occupational structure of the local workforce.

Similarly, convergence with National Horticulture Mission, National Rural Livelihood Mission and National Mission for Micro-irrigation is expected to result in transformation of wasteland into productive agricultural land. However, reaping the potential benefits require more coordinated approach by the line departments towards convergence as lack of clarity on nature and extent of participation by them can hinder such efforts. Besides, too many formalities and differences in priorities of the line departments can also limit the success of convergence.

Simplified procedures, unity of command, greater involvement of organizations like Krishi Vigyan Kendras, incentives for the functionaries and appropriate legislative structure are required to enhance the success. Further, while monitoring/evaluation of planning and maintaining quality of assets created may be outsourced, the *Panchayati Raj* Institutions (PRIs) should have larger role to play as planner and executor of decisions. Assigning property rights of the assets is an another critical aspect as lack of well-defined property rights may result in their overutilization and social conflicts. Greater success of convergence initiatives also requires active participation of the line departments and other stakeholders in planning, management and execution of the works.

References

Acemoglu, D., and J.A. Robinson. 2008. The Role of Institutions in Growth and Development. Commission on Growth and Development, Working Paper No. 10, Commission on Growth and Development, Washington, DC: The World Bank.

Adelman, I. 1984. Beyond Export-led Growth. *World Development* 12 (9): 937–949.

Adelman, I., and C. Morris. 1988. *Comparative Patterns of Economic Development, 1850–1914*. Baltimore: John Hopkins University Press.

Allen, R.C. 1994. Agriculture During the Industrial Revolution, 1700–1850. In R Floud and D N McCloskey (ed.), *The Economic History of Britain Since 1700* (2nd ed.). Cambridge UK: Cambridge University Press.

Alok, V.N. 2013. Strengthening of Panchayats in India: Comparing Devolution Across States. Empirical Assessment—2012–13, The Indian Institute of Public Administration.

Azam, M. 2012. The Impact of Indian Job Guarantee Scheme on Labour Market Outcomes: Evidence from a Natural Experiment, Institute for the Study of Labor (IZA) Discussion Paper Series No. 6548. Bonn: IZA.

Behera, B., and P. Mishra. 2007. Acceleration of Agricultural Growth in India: Suggestive Policy Framework. *Economic and Political Weekly* 42 (42): 4268–4271.

Bezemer, D., and D. Heady. 2008. Agriculture Development and Urban Bias. *World Development* 36 (8): 1342–1364.

Bairoch, Pal. 1973. Agriculture and Industrial Revolution C Cipolla (ed.), *The Fontana Economic History of Europe*, vol. III, 452–506. London, Fontana: The industrial Revolution.

Census of India. 2011. Office of the Registrar General & Census Commissioner, Ministry of Home Affairs, Government of India, New Delhi.

Crafts, N.F. 1985. *British Economic Growth During the Industrial Revolution*. Oxford: Clarendon.

Demsetz, H. 1967. Towards a Theory of Property Rights. *American Economic Review* 57: 347–359.

Dreze, J., and R. Khera. 2009. The Battle for Employment Guarantee. *Frontline* 26 (1): 3–16.

Fan, S., and A. Gulati. 2008. The Dragon and the Elephant: Learning from Agriculture and Rural Reforms in India and China. *Economic and Political Weekly* 43 (26): 137–144.

GOI. 2014. Discussion paper on quality of assets created under MGNREGA. Letter No. 'D.O. No. AS (RD)/MGNREGS/14/FTS 36607', dated 31st May, 2014. Office of the Additional Secretary, Ministry of Rural Development, Government of India, New Delhi.

ILO. 2014. Employment and Livelihood Security Through MGNREGA: A Case of a Right-Based Social Protection Floor in India. *Report of the International Labour Organization (ILO)*. Retrieved from http://www.ilo.org/beirut/events/WCMS_246596/lang–en/index.htm on August 10, 2014.

Jha, R., and R. Gaiha. 2012. NREGS: Interpreting the Official Statistics. *Economic and Political Weekly* 57 (40): 18–22.

Kang, K., and V. Ramachandran. 1999. Economic Transformation in Korea: Rapid Growth Without an Agricultural Revolution? *Economic Development and Cultural Change* 47 (4): 783–801.

Khera, R., and N. Nayak. 2009. Women Workers and Perceptions of the National Rural Employment Guarantee Act. *Economic & Political Weekly* 44 (43): 49–57.

Krueger, A.O. 1990. Government Failure and Development. *The Journal of Economic Perspectives* 4 (3): 9–13.

Lipton, M. 1977. *Why Poor People Stay Poor: A Study of Urban Bias in World Development*. London: Temple Smith.

Mishra, P., and S.K. Mishra. 2015. Strategies and Policies for Alleviation of Rural Poverty in India: Experience of Mahatma Gandhi National Rural Employment Guarantee Scheme. *Review of Development and Change* 19 (2): 43–76.

Mukherjee, A.N., and Y. Kuroda. 2002. Convergence in Rural Development: Evidence from India. *Journal of Asian Economics* 13: 385–398.

Nayak, N.C., B. Behera, and P. Mishra. 2011. *Monitoring Convergence between NREGS and Ongoing Schemes of the other Ministries in Orissa*. New Delhi: Project Report Submitted to the UNDP.

Ohkawa, K. and Rosovsky, Henry. 1960. The Role of Agriculture in Modern Japanees Economic Development. *Economic Development and Cultural Change,* 9,1, Part II, Oct, 43–68.

Overton, M. 1996. *Agricultural Revolution in England: Transformation of the Agrarian Economy* 1500–1850. Cambridge university Press, XIV, 258.

Panayotou, T. 1993. *Green Market: The Economics of Sustainable Development*. California: Institute for Contemporary Studies Sans Francisco.

Panda, B. 2013. MGNREGA: A No 'Dole' Tale. The Shillong Times, May 22.

Pearce, D.W., and J. JWarford. 1993. *World Without End: Economics, Environment and Sustainable Development*. New York: Oxford University Press.

Prasad, K.V.S. 2012. Performance of Mahatma Gandhi National Rural Employment Guarantee Act (MGNREGA): An Overview. *International Journal of Management & Business Studies* 2 (4): 99–103.

Reddy, V.R. 1995. Environment and Sustainable Agricultural Development: Conflicts and Contradictions. *Economic and Political Weekly* 30 (12): A21–A27.

Reddy, V.R., and S. Galab. 2006. Agrarian Crisis: Looking Beyond the Debt Trap. *Economic and Political Weekly* 41 (19): 1838–1841.

Rostow, W.W. 1960. *The Stages of Economic Growth: A Non-Communist Manifesto*. Cambridge UK: Cambridge University Press.

Shah, M. 2012. *Report of the Committee for Revision of MGNREGA Operational Guidelines*. New Delhi: Mihir Shah Committee Report Submitted to Ministry of Rural Development, Government of India.

Tietenberg, T. 1994. *Environmental Economics and Policy*. New York: Harper Collins College.
Vaidyanathan, A. 2010. *Agricultural Growth in India: Role of Technology, Incentives and Institutions*. New Delhi: Oxford University Press.
Vijayanand, S.M. and V.N. Jithendra. 2008. Implementation of NREGA: Experience in Kerala. In *International Seminar on National Rural Employment Guarantee Scheme in India,* New Delhi, September 16–17.
Williamson, O. 2000. The New Institutional Economics: Taking Stock, Looking Ahead. *Journal of Economic Literature* 38: 595–613.

Chapter 8
MGNREGS: Political Economy, Local Governance and Asset Creation in South India

Vinoj Abraham

8.1 Introduction

The rural economy of India was reeling under a severe agrarian crisis marked by declining agricultural productivity, stagnating real wages, and fluctuating prices for agricultural products since late 1990s, which worsened the living conditions of the rural poor, otherwise faced with rising unemployment, distress migration, and farmer suicides. It was in this background that the National Rural Employment Guarantee Act (2005) and the subsequent Mahatma Gandhi National Rural Employment Guarantee Scheme (MGNREGS) were implemented since 2006. Arguably, the world's largest workfare programme, the scheme, aimed at enhancing the livelihood security of the households in rural areas of India.

This scheme in its spirit aims to ameliorate the worsening conditions of living of the rural poor and recharge the rural sector by increasing the purchasing power, and at the same time reverse the trends in rural sector by building assets that would increase productivity in agriculture specifically and upkeep the rural common properties. While a large number of studies have looked into the nature and progress of employment creation under the scheme, there have been very few studies looking into the equally important issue of asset creation under the scheme.

The study contained in this chapter is an attempt to understand the process of asset creation under the MGNREGS. Though it is a centrally sponsored scheme, the responsibility of its implementation is vested with the local government bodies, including gram, block and district panchayats. The functioning of these bodies, their approach to the scheme and the influence of the local socio-political forces largely shape the process of asset creation at the local level. This chapter looks into the process of asset creation from within the above-said framework.

V. Abraham (✉)
Centre for Development Studies (CDS), Prasanth Nagar, Medical College,
Trivandrum P.O. 695011, Kerala, India
e-mail: vinoj@cds.ac.in; vinojabraham@gmail.com

M. Bhattarai et al. (eds.), *Employment Guarantee Programme and Dynamics of Rural Transformation in India*, India Studies in Business and Economics,
https://doi.org/10.1007/978-981-10-6262-9_8

This chapter is based on a set of field-based surveys conducted in the four south Indian states, Andhra Pradesh (erstwhile), Kerala, Karnataka and Tamil Nadu, as part of an evaluation of MGNREGS funded by Planning Commission and Government of India. In the four states, fourteen districts were chosen to cover: districts on the basis of regional representativeness within the states; phase-wise implementation of MGNREGS; and districts that had incurred the highest expenditure in MGNREGS within each state.[1] Primary surveys of MGNREGS workers, beneficiaries of assets created, verification of assets, focus group discussions, etc. were also conducted as part of the field study. The data collection at the field sites was done during the period April to October 2013 for the reference year 2011–12.

The first section presents the introduction to the paper. The next section (Sect. 8.2) provides a comparative overview of the local governance and political economy of the four southern states and contextualizes MGNREGS within this frame. Then Sect. 8.3 provides an analysis of the processes and outcomes of asset building under the scheme. Likewise, the selection of project and type of assets to be created under the scheme, and its implications on project expenditure on assets created are described in Sects. 8.4 and 8.5. Then, ownership type, asset quality and importance of the assets created under the programmes are provided in Sects. 8.6, 8.7 and 8.8. The last section (Sect. 8.9) provides the broad conclusions and policy implications of the study.

8.2 Local-Level Governance, Politics and MGNREGS

The implementation of MGNREGS scheme at the local level is essentially pillared on the panchayat Raj and it envisages exploiting the various tiers of panchayat Raj system in administering the programme. The panchayat Raj institutions (PRI) are involved in both concurrent planning and execution of MGNREG scheme. Given the central role played by the gram panchayat in MGNREGS, the execution of the scheme is closely linked to the structure and efficiency of these local bodies.

In preparing the MGNREG annual work plan for the impending year, the gram panchayats undertake the functions, viz., (a) receive applications for job cards from households; (b) generate the estimate of labour demand for the year; and (c) generate the shelf of projects (assets) to be created for the year to be prepared and prioritized as passed in the gram sabha.

In executing the scheme, the gram panchayats perform the functions, such as issuing job cards to households after due verification; executing the projects using the labour and materials with the help of the programme officer of MGNREGS; providing worksite facilities and conducting social audit. Work demand and asset

[1]For details of the survey, please see Report of the Evaluation of the MGNREGS cluster 6, Centre for Development Studies, Thiruvananthapuram.

demand are generated from the grass roots level through the gram panchayat and gram sabha meetings. Essentially, this flow is managed and organized by the representatives of people at the gram panchayat level.

At the block panchayat, the demand for assets and its technical specifications and the actual days of works generated are recommended. From this level, the demands which represent the opinion of the local people flow to the District Programme Officer, who is also the Collector of the District. The responsibility for implementation of the scheme, after receiving the approval from the District Programme Officer, goes back to the gram panchayat. The execution of the programme is largely overseen by the gram panchayat secretary, under whom separate MGNREGS staff is appointed to administer the programme implementation.

The above-mentioned two aspects, i.e. planning and execution at the local level, are affected by the following factors. First, the coordination between the two branches of the local government, the bureaucracy and the elected representatives; Second, deepening of the democratic process within the local governments, and third, local social-economic structure that shape the local polity. In what follows, a discussion of the above three aspects in the four southern states is presented to understand the context under which MGNREGS was implemented in these states.

The three-tier panchayat Raj system, instituted through the 73rd amendment of the Indian Constitution, has been in place in all states of the country. Since the amendment in 1993, the South Indian states, viz., Andhra Pradesh, Karnataka, Kerala and Tamil Nadu had undertaken various legislations and had been in the forefront of implementing the scheme. However, the functioning of these local bodies has been guided by the powers devolved to it by the respective state governments, and their relation with traditional local-level axes of power.

Narayana (2005) had argued that the transformation of the gram panchayats from being extensions of the state agencies to fully functional local governments varied widely across the states depending on the willingness to give up power of those who draw power from the existing state structures. Also, the traditional village councils, which are rooted in traditional practices, values and power relations, coexist with the elected gram panchayats acting as parallel structures of governance with their writs running over the elected gram panchayats (Ananth Pur 2007).

This apart, the elected representatives of the local governments are often local elites and proxy members of the elites who control the local governments. Their motives and attitudes towards the gram panchayats and local community in general could shape the processes and outcomes of the gram panchayat. Besley et al. (2007) had shown that in South India, politicians in the gram sabha were social elites in terms of education, land ownership and with a history of political representation in their households. Furthermore, the political elites participated and benefited more from various social welfare and workfare schemes than the local public.

In *Andhra Pradesh*, the economic reforms initiated by the Telugu Desam Party (TDP) since 1993–94 with funding from the World Bank, DFID and advisory support from the McKinsey embarked on a centralized technocratic governance structure, which ironically for greater governance efficiency weakened the local bodies.[2]

Since 2006, there had been no panchayat level elections. In fact, after 2006, the next election was held only in 2014 after a gap of 8 years. The panchayat elections were not held because of the very volatile political conditions in the wake of the demand for a separate state of Telengana. In the absence of the panchayat level elections, the gram panchayat was virtually non-functional. Though a gram panchayat president did exist, their influence was considerably weakened as their legitimate tenure of 5 years was over and their local support was weakened.

Moreover, the state government had followed its tradition of technocratic governance established during the early 1990s and was successful in reaching governance to the grassroots level, ironically by establishing more centralized technocratic governance bypassing the local bodies at the gram panchayat level, thus, considerably weakening the position of local bodies in the governance structure of the state (Kumar 2009).

The MGNREG scheme, as in the case of other development programmes in Andhra Pradesh, was largely administered as a technocratic centralized scheme mostly bypassing the local-level government at the panchayat level in a top-down approach. With a weakened GP system, the bureaucracy along with the technocrats at block and the district-level panchayats became the dominant actors in administering the scheme.

Karnataka was one of the first states to experiment with devolution of power to the local level starting in the late 1980s. The strengthening of the local governments by transferring of functions, funds and functionaries were successfully conducted in Karnataka and is widely considered to be a success story of decentralization. However, the influence of the local elites run deep and many gram panchayats experience parallel systems of traditional governance in the gram panchayats. In Karnataka, the co-existence and involvement of such traditional village councils in the elected gram panchayats were documented well by Ananth Pur (2007) and Ananth Pur and Moore (2010). Manor (2007) had noted that in rural Karnataka, the influence of caste system and other social institutions was on the decline in creating material opportunities, but individuals, who operated through local politics, were becoming more important.

With changes in the economic structure of rural Karnataka, which was fast transforming to non-agriculture occupations, the traditional dominant classes had to give way for new emerging individuals who rose as political elites in the emerging political horizon of Karnataka. Local elites who were wealthy and relatively high in

---

[2]It is argued that while TDP ruled the state during 1993–04, the local bodies were largely held by the Congress, and hence there was great reluctance for the state to pass on power to the local bodies (Kumar 2009).

the caste hierarchy were also more educated and closer to political power in the GP than the rest of the villagers. Their domination in the village life helped them control the resources and capture programmes and policies that were implemented within the GP. Multiple government schemes were contracted out to these local elites for many years, which encouraged them to invest heavily in this direction.

At the state level, the Congress-JD(S) alliance which won the election in 2004 was toppled in 2006 for a BJP-JD(S) alliance ministry. It was during the tenure of the BJP-JD(S) alliance in the Karnataka state government that the MGNREGS was implemented for the first time in Karnataka. In the next tenure starting from 2008, the BJP had formed the government with support of only six independents. While BJP was ruling the state, it was the lead opposition against the Congress-led central government during the same period.

The political will to implement a programme in its full import that was initiated by the Congress was perhaps not forthcoming from the BJP-led state government. The lack of political will from the state government along with strong local political elite ensured the dominance of the local elites in development and welfare schemes administered through the gram panchayats, including the MGNREGS.

Kerala embarked on decentralization and strengthening of the local governments by institution building and legislative reforms in the early 1990s. The state offered as the laboratory of the unique experiment of decentralized people's planning since 1997 (Isaac and Harilal 1997). The local government in Kerala is relatively autonomous compared to similar bodies in other states. It is not controlled by upper bodies and generates its own revenue and budgets (Narayana 2005). Given the strong decision and implementing powers of the gram panchayat, they have become agents of development and change in Kerala. The autonomy granted to the gram panchayats made these bodies very important in the rural governance.

Drawing on a large section of the population of the state, the left dominant LDF government in early 2000s initiated the grass root level planning for the ninth plan under the Kerala State Planning Board. Scholars report that Kerala's decentralized governance is different from the rest of India as it moved ahead of others to devolve powers, responsibilities and funds (Oommen 2014).

The representatives in the gram panchayats continued to be dominated by political elites in Kerala as in the case of other states. However, the high level of political awareness and higher participation of the people in *gram sabhas* and *gram panchayats* as well as the higher level of average level of education among the representatives have created a condition wherein, though political elite capture was present, the extent and intensity of the developmental programmes captured by these elites are at minimal level in Kerala than other states of India (Narayana 2005; Heller et al. 2007).

Nevertheless, even in Kerala, the dominance of middle-level and upper level bureaucracy over the elected representatives is widespread across the state. For instance, Chathukulam and John (2002) noted that while during the LDF regime the synergies between the elected representatives and bureaucracy were maintained, the bureaucracy was not reined into being part of the decentralization process in Kerala. Oommen (2014) had noted that the decentralized planning which held much promise in its early stages in Kerala has now become a routine exercise at the local level, bereft of the spirit of inclusion. It is not anymore a shield against issues of vital concern such as '...endemic vested interests, communalism, clientelism, alcoholism and several other negative factors that envelop Kerala society today' (Oommen 2014, p. 45).

A committee appointed by the state government of Kerala to evaluate the progress of the decentralized planning and development (GoK 2009) had observed that the Beneficiary Committee system, to counter clientilistic behavior, and elite capture of programmes were not successful. In fact many project mode programmes, aimed at individual households, were being used as tools of vote bank politics by the elected members of the local bodies. In case of MGNREGS too, it was observed in our study that while elite capture and corruption of the programme were minimal in Kerala, vote bank politics seemed to play an important role in the running of the programme at the gram panchayat level.

In *Tamil Nadu*, the Panchayat Raj Act was passed in 1994. Tamil Nadu, which had a long history of traditional village councils administering the villages, however, had a weak institutional setup for the implementation of the Act in its spirit. Narayana (2005, p. 2822) noted that 'the government was reluctant to give powers to local bodies as it issues executive orders instead of notifications on the 29 subjects mentioned in the Tamil Nadu Panchayats Act, 1994. As executive orders do not have legal validity that notifications have, the bureaucracy ignores them and local bodies remain mere agents of the government'. Kumar (2009) remarks that probably this poor devolution of powers to the local governments stem from the fact that regional parties like DMK and AIADMK hold way at the state-level politics.

Regional parties see local governments as a dilution of their powers and would like to guard their interests at the state level. Regional parties often view decentralization as a means of the central government to bypass their powers to reach the grass root levels. Yet, despite poor devolution of powers to the local bodies, various centrally sponsored and state-sponsored welfare and development programmes were successfully implemented in the state, mainly due to the direct role of the bureaucracy supported by newer technologies, such as Information Communication Technology (ICT), Geographical Positioning System (GPS), etc.

While implementation of development programmes in a top-down manner had been by and large successful in Tamil Nadu, there has been growing resentment amongst the landlords and industrialists against such initiatives, mainly due to their losing control over labour. Harriss et al. (2010) in a village study noted that while the traditional village councils have weakened and are probably non-existent, the landlord's power and reach have persisted to the present times.

With the increasing levels of education among the agricultural workers, implementations of the schemes like the 'One rupee rice scheme' and 'NREGA' tensions between the landlord and the farm workers have escalated. The sharp caste divisions in land holding groups and agricultural workers have led to polarization and political identity formations around caste groups. De Neve and Carswell (2011) have argued that these rising tensions have led to protests among the landed and landless, leading to the formation of new political parties with considerable influence.

In the recent past, a number of exclusively caste-based parties and new Dalit parties have sprung across Tamil Nadu, such as PMK, the Dalit Panthers, Puthiya Tamizhagam, KNMK, etc. De Neve and Carswell (2011) finds that the involvement of local parties' and politics is entrenched in MGNREGS and the local elected representatives use the scheme for strengthening patron–client relationships.

From the above discussion, for the sake of analytical abstraction, one could contrast the four states as having the following features of local governance. Andhra Pradesh is marked by the dominance of the techno-bureaucratic administration and weak people's representation at the local level. Karnataka is marked by dominance of local-level institutions of decentralization over the bureaucracy; however, the local-level institutions have been captured by traditional social and political elites.

Kerala too is marked by the dominance of local-level institutions. Though role of traditional elites had declined in Kerala, vote bank politics had invaded these institutions. Tamil Nadu is again marked by dominance of the techno-bureaucratic administration at the local level and weak institutional arrangement for local governance. Additionally, the emergence of identity-based politics at the village level has a strong impact on local-level programme implementation.

From the above premise of the local polity and governance structure, now we embark on the question of asset creation under the MGNREGS scheme. The endeavor here is to argue the case that the type of asset creation, methods of asset creation and maintenance and benefits accrued by the local people are largely influenced by the local polity, local governance structure and democratic practices at the local level.

8.3 Asset Creation Under MGNREGS

The MGNREGS guidelines provide for construction of various types of assets under the scheme.[3] Within these various asset types, the MGNREGS mission of the respective state governments prioritize the asset types based on demand for assets and local requirements. Finally, gram sabha of each gram panchayat in their meetings puts forward the yearly demand for construction of various assets from the list of asset types provided by the national guidelines and prioritized by the state governments.

All these assets are aimed at improving the rural livelihoods, particularly improving rural infrastructure, and improving agricultural performance by enhancing the quality of land and increasing the availability of water through water management methods. It can be noted that the importance given to the type of asset created reflects the local economic needs of the region (Table 8.1).

For instance, in Tamil Nadu, where many traditional water bodies have disappeared and have caused deleterious consequences on agriculture, the restoration of

[3]See Table 8.1 for the broad list of type of assets that is taken up under MGNREGS.

Table 8.1 Distribution of number of assets completed 2006–07 to 2011–12 (in %)

Type of asset	2006–07	2007–08	2008–09	2009–10	2010–11	2011–12
Andhra Pradesh						
Rural connectivity	0.2	1.0	4.2	2.9	7.1	1.6
Flood control and protection	0.0	1.9	0.7	0.8	0.6	3.5
Water conservation	47.9	29.8	30.6	35.2	36.1	57.0
Drought proofing	10.4	3.7	4.1	4.0	1.9	4.8
Micro-irrigation	4.2	7.2	10.6	14.1	15.3	30.3
Provision of irrigation to SC/ST	0.2	3.6	12.7	9.2	10.1	0.7
RTWB	6.2	5.5	6.0	6.6	11.0	1.6
Land development	30.9	47.2	30.9	27.1	17.9	0.5
Any other activity	0.0	0.0	0.0	0.0	0.0	0.0
Bharat Nirman RGSK	0.0	0.0	0.0	0.0	0.0	0.0
Total	100	100	100	100	100	100.0
Karnataka						
Rural connectivity	26.2	16.3	12.2	8.0	11.7	12.6
Flood control and protection	6.2	5.9	10.0	6.0	10.4	11.5
Water conservation	34.7	29.4	28.0	17.1	10.4	16.1
Drought proofing	6.1	19.0	13.7	11.9	17.4	13.3
Micro-irrigation	3.6	2.5	4.9	7.4	4.2	5.2
Provision of irrigation to SC/ST	7.3	9.4	9.1	18.9	17.8	12.1
RTWB	5.1	6.1	11.6	4.8	4.4	4.6
Land development	2.1	11.4	10.4	20.9	20.6	19.4
Any other activity	8.8	0.0	0.1	5.1	3.2	5.2
Bharat Nirman RGSK	0	0.0	0.0	0.0	0.0	0.1
Total	100	100.0	100.0	100.0	100.0	100.0
Kerala						
Rural connectivity	0	6.5	2.8	3.4	3.2	2.8
Flood control and protection	0	27.4	42.8	36.5	26.6	21.0
Water conservation	0	22.5	10.0	8.8	13.2	15.6
Drought proofing	0	1.6	2.3	4.0	3.3	2.8
Micro-irrigation	0	13.4	13.8	12.2	8.5	8.0
Provision of irrigation to SC/ST	0	0.9	1.1	3.9	4.2	3.9
RTWB	0	12.3	16.3	16.5	14.1	10.5
Land development	0	15.3	10.9	13.8	26.4	34.9
Any other activity	0	0.1	0.0	0.9	0.4	0.6
Bharat Nirman RGSK.	0	0.0	0.0	0.0	0.0	0.0
Total	0	100.0	100.0	100.0	100.0	100.0

(continued)

Table 8.1 (continued)

Type of asset	2006–07	2007–08	2008–09	2009–10	2010–11	2011–12
Tamil Nadu						
Rural connectivity	12.2	11.9	19.9	23.1	24.8	27.8
Flood control and protection	0.3	0.6	0.7	0.7	1.5	0.5
Water conservation	27.3	20.4	14.9	12.4	14.0	17.8
Drought proofing	0.3	0.0	0.0	0.0	0.0	0.0
Micro-irrigation	16.7	20.3	19.0	18.6	13.0	13.4
Provision of irrigation to SC/ST	0.0	0.0	0.0	0.0	0.0	0.0
RTWB	43.1	46.9	45.5	45.1	46.7	40.2
Land development	0.0	0.0	0.0	0.1	0.0	0.2
Any other activity	0.0	0.0	0.0	0.0	0.0	0.0
Bharat Nirman RGSK	0.0	0.0	0.0	0.0	0.0	0.0
Total	100.0	100.0	100.0	100.0	100.0	100.0
All Southern States						
Rural connectivity	5.3	3.0	5.2	4.4	7.6	5.5
Flood control and protection	1.2	3.6	8.3	5.3	3.9	7.6
Water conservation	45.0	29.0	26.3	28.8	31.1	40.4
Drought proofing	9.4	4.7	4.3	5.2	3.3	5.6
Micro-irrigation	4.4	7.6	11.1	12.9	13.7	21.1
Provision of irrigation	1.5	3.8	10.0	10.1	9.9	3.2
RTWB	6.8	7.5	9.9	8.4	11.7	6.2
Land development	24.9	40.8	24.8	24.0	18.4	9.5
Any other activity	1.6	0.0	0.0	1.0	0.3	1.0
Bharat Nirman RGSK	0.0	0.0	0.0	0.0	0.0	0.0
Total	100.0	100.0	100.0	100.0	100.0	100.0

Source MIS, MGNREGS website

these bodies received the maximum attention. While in Kerala which is affected by incessant rains, flood control and flood protection have been one of the most important asset types created. Similarly, the semi-arid regions of Karnataka and Andhra Pradesh opted for drought proofing and water conservation as important type of assets created.

During the initial phase of the programme, land development and water conservation were the two most important types of assets constructed in south India accounting for more than 70% of the assets created in the year 2006–07 (Table 8.1). Though water conservation still continues to be an important type of asset being built in the recent years also. The prominence of land development has declined substantially and its place has been taken up by works on micro-irrigations. This is mainly because of the decline in the land development assets created in Andhra Pradesh which declined from 47% in 2007–08 to just 0.5% in 2011–12 (Table 8.1). While in Kerala and Karnataka, Land Development[4] continues to be an important type of asset. In Tamil Nadu, Land Development works were hardly taken up.

Though the state governments provide priority lists, the actual works done could vary according to the demands rising from the gram sabha. It can be inferred that the state priority ranking and ranking of actual works done will have greater congruence if the priority list have a more dominant role in deciding the actual works being done than the works demand generated by the local-level bodies and vice versa.

A simple rank correlation done between the state priority ranking and the ranking of actual works done for the period 2006–07 to 2011–12 in Andhra Pradesh shows moderately high degree of correlation (0.57), while in the other three states, the coefficient of rank correlation was very small and not significant. This probably signals that in Andhra Pradesh the directions from the MGNREGS mission at the state level are implemented at the grass root level to a considerable extent without being interfered at the local level, while in other states this is not the case.[5] It also points that probably the weak local-level bodies in Andhra Pradesh have made it easier for a bureaucratic implementation of the directions of the state mission from top.

In Tamil Nadu, while apparently the choice of assets is aimed at reviving agriculture sector, the prioritization of certain assets and exclusion of certain assets seemed to be aimed at keeping the local power relations in balance. Among the various asset types, in Tamil Nadu, the share of assets under Restoration of Traditional Water Bodies (RTWB) was the highest, accounting for nearly 50% of all assets completed throughout the period 2006–07 to 2011–12.

During the same period, however, asset types that benefited the SC/STs, i.e. provision for irrigation for SC/ST land, were the least important. Assets created under land development, which also benefits SC/ST land, and small and marginal land holdings were also almost completely absent. The priority list of assets notified by the Tamil Nadu NREGS mission also gives the highest priority to RTWB while the irrigation provision for SC/ST and Land Development do not appear in the

---

[4]Unlike in Andhra Pradesh, where one of the prominent assets to be developed was 'Investing on Scheduled Caste/Scheduled Tribe lands for irrigation and land development duly fulfilling Special Component Plan/Tribal Sub-Plan norms in each Mandal', this item was conspicuous by its absence. http://karnregs.kar.nic.in/Resource/KREGS_Scheme_Eng.pdf, accessed on 3 January 2015.

[5]In Tamil Nadu, the priority list does not match directly with the MGNREGS guidelines, so the exercise is limited to the other three states.

priority list.[6]The choice of assets ensured that options of self-employment for the poor would not open up through the scheme.

Within RTWB, tanks and ponds built for irrigation purposes are the most important. Studies show that irrigation tanks were traditionally managed by the upper caste dominant landlords in local collectivities in rural Tamil Nadu (Sivasubramaniyan 2006). Tanks form the second most important source of irrigation after wells and Tube wells in Tamil Nadu. Tanks were not private properties, but the gains from the usage of the tanks had a large class component. The importance of these tanks in irrigation, agriculture and thereby to the local landlords is self-evident. The prioritization of assets and the completion of assets under the scheme thus seem to maintain the power relations between the landless agricultural workers, majority of them being scheduled castes and the landlords.

8.3.1 *Project Selection Under MGNREGS*

The sample survey conducted by us also corroborates the above arguments. As can be seen from Table 8.2, in all other states, an overwhelming majority stated that the choice of projects was as per local people's needs. In Andhra Pradesh, 12.5% of the beneficiaries stated that there was no specific way to choose, whereas another 12.3% stated that they did not know how the choice was made. Only 66% of the sample responded that the choice of projects was according to the need of the local people.

In Kerala and Karnataka, nearly 90% of the sample claimed that the choice was according to the needs of the local people. It may be noted here that these are the two states that have fairly well-developed local government institutions, as mentioned earlier. It is probably the influence of these local institutions in project decision-making that have led to the selection of projects and asset types that represented the local needs.

In Tamil Nadu, project selection was influenced to an extent by the local leadership. About 20% of the beneficiaries stated that project selection was as per the need of the local leader. Another 10% responded as either not knowing the method of selection or having no particular method of selection in a place.

Similar evidences that support the above arguments are visible on the role of gram sabha in asset choice. Majority of the respondents (87%) from all the states reported that all MGNREGS works are being approved in gram sabha (Table 8.3). In Tamil Nadu and Andhra Pradesh, about 18 and 15% of the respondents,

---

[6]Priority of works for Tamil Nadu are as follows: (a) Formation of new ponds. (b) Renovation of existing Ponds, Kuttais, Kulams, Ooranies, Temple tanks, etc. (c) Desilting of channels. (d) Desilting and strengthening of bunds of irrigation tanks. (e) Formation of new roads. (f) Other water conservation/soil conservation measures/flood protection measures. http://www.tnrd.gov.in/schemes/nrega.html, accessed on 3 January 2015.

Table 8.2 How projects are selected across the selected states

	AP (n = 440)	KL (347)	KN (528)	TN (440)	Total (1755)
As per need of local people (%)	65.68	89.91	78.6	69.32	75.27
As per need of leader (%)	9.32	2.02	11.55	20.45	11.34
No specific way to choose (%)	12.5	0.58	0.57	7.05	5.19
Don't know (%)	12.27	2.88	8.33	2.27	6.72
Others (%)	0.23	4.61	0.95	0.91	1.48
Total (%)	100	100	100	100	100

Source Primary survey of asset beneficiaries, 2013
Note AP—corresponds to Andhra Pradesh, KN—Karnataka, KL—Kerala and TN—Tamil Nadu

Table 8.3 Whether the NREGA works are being approved in gram sabha: state-wise

Responses\states	Unit	AP (n = 459)	KL (n = 345)	KN (n = 560)	TN (n = 414)	Total (n = 1,778)
Yes	%	85.84	97.39	94.64	75.12	88.36
No	%	9.8	2.32	4.82	18.12	8.72
Gram Sabha does not exist	%	4.36	0.29	0.54	6.76	2.92
Total	%	100	100	100	100	100

Source Primary survey, 2013

respectively, stated that the works were not being approved in gram sabha, whereas, in Kerala and Karnataka, more than 95% respondents stated that the works were passed in the gram sabha.

8.4 Project Implementation

The interaction between the elected bodies and the bureaucratic executive body reduces at the implementation stage. The implementation is done by the executive body at the panchayat level with the panchayat secretary playing an active role taking additional charge as the NREGS Programme Officer at the panchayat level. The scheme design does not require the participation of the elected bodies in implementation of the same. Some members of the GP, but at times, oversaw the worksites and enquired the welfare of the workers. In general, however, involvement was limited to expressing their views on the programme, often critically.

In Andhra Pradesh, at this stage, the implementation is directly from the Mandals (blocks) and below which there are field assistants and mates and hence, there was hardly any interference of the elected bodies at the implementation stage. On the contrary, in Tamil Nadu, some of the elected members of the panchayat took interest in the implementation of the scheme in their personal and political interests.[7] In Kerala, though the NREGS mission was responsible for implementation of the scheme, the GP members also took active interest in this. However, they were also critical of the scheme in many instances.

In Karnataka, also there is very active involvement of the GP elected members in the scheme. However, their involvement in the scheme is due to the peculiar way the scheme was interpreted at the local level. In many parts of Karnataka, the scheme lost one of its most important characteristics, namely, self-targeting of beneficiaries. In many parts of Karnataka, the scheme was interpreted as a targeted asset building scheme. The GP members were informally entrusted with targets to achieve through the scheme. Moreover, the GP members often represented, or themselves, were the local elites, caste leaders or landlords.

Locally dominant elite weakened the powers of the local-level bureaucracy considerably while the needs of the elite were addressed in the implementation of the MGNREGS projects. The dominance of the local elites in the gram panchayats led to considerable amount of elite capture of the programme in parts of Karnataka. Table 8.4 shows that 25% of the workers claimed that there were contractors involved in the MGNREGS works in Karnataka. This is the response received to a direct query on contractors' involvement in the scheme.

The actual figures could be much higher. During the field visit, it became evident that in some parts of Karnataka, there were local elites owning machinery, like Road Rollers, JCB excavators, etc., whose only utility was to be rented out to run various government schemes. Many members of these families are trained to enter the system, through education. For instance, we met a household who had three of their kins including children being civil engineers with contract license from the state government. They were involved in running many government schemes including asset building under the MGNREGS within the GP. They were also the richest and the household head was the virtual gram panchayat president, his wife being the titular president.

Though in general Karnataka had a high share of contract involvement, there were exceptions such as Bilagi block in Bagalkote (see Table 8.5). As can be noticed, contractors are not completely absent in any of the districts, and in all cases are higher than the state averages of all other states. But there is a greater presence of such contractors in Belgaum and Mysore.[8]

---

[7]For instance in a GP in Tanjavur district of Tamil Nadu, we came across a very industrious GP president who, along with all the elected members of the GP and his supporters, regularly featured in the worksites as MGNREGS workers. They also worked and gave directions at worksites and ensured that along with the workers the GP also gained by building some useful assets. This interaction and active involvement of the GP leadership in the scheme made the scheme hugely popular in the GP and was successfully used as an asset building as well as rural livelihood scheme. But in other GPs the elected members were wary that the scheme was depriving the agriculturists of their labour and making agriculture unviable.

[8]However, it may be noted that at the GP level, there were claims of contractor involvements even in States with aggregate low levels of contractor interference. Byson Valley GP in Kerala, for instance, had 40% respondents claiming there was contract involvement.

Table 8.4 Agents performing NREGA work in the gram panchayat across the states surveyed, 2013

		AP (n = 454)	KL (355)	KN (539)	TN (444)	Total (1,792)
Contract	%	2.64	7.04	25.05	2.25	10.16
Gram panchayat	%	94.71	69.3	67.72	97.3	82.2
Others	%	2.64	23.66	7.24	0.45	7.65
Total	%	100	100	100	100	100

Source Primary survey of MGNREGS workers, 2013

Table 8.5 Percentage share of workers response to who are carrying out the NREGA work in the gram panchayat (GP) across the districts surveyed in Karnataka

District	Contract	Gram panchayat	Others	Total
Bagalkote (1)	13.21	84.28	2.52	100.0
Belgaum (4)	43.97	43.97	12.07	100.0
Chitradurga (10)	11.49	79.05	9.46	100.0
Mysore (22)	39.66	54.31	6.03	100.0
Total	25.05	67.72	7.24	100.0

Source Primary survey of MGNREGS workers, 2013

For the programme to be run on target-based contractor-driven mode, the assets that were prioritized under the guidelines were probably not sufficiently attractive. The modus operandi was to re-interpret the asset types and build large assets that could utilize large machinery. For instance, constructions of temple walls, school walls and market walls were common across different districts, yet they would appear in the MIS as flood control, flood protection, land development, etc. Re-interpretation of asset types was not unique to Karnataka. Kerala is another state that had involved in interpreting asset types, but that was under the completely different premises of interpretation of the labour cost–material cost ratio in asset creation.

The MGNREGS guidelines stipulate that the ratio of labour cost to material cost cannot be below a ratio of 60:40, implying that at least 60% of the spending on asset creation should be of labour cost. This stipulation was essentially aimed at keeping the works as much as possible labour intensive and also to reduce involvement of contractors and middlemen. This ratio should be applied preferably at the gram panchayat, block and district levels, while the 60:40 ratio was maintained in all the states, where it differed was the unit at which this ratio was maintained.

In Andhra Pradesh and Karnataka, the labour material ratio was interpreted as the share of the total budget at the district level. In Tamil Nadu, it was interpreted as the ratio to be followed for each project. In Kerala too, this was essentially the interpretation. In Kerala, additionally, all works involving materials were discouraged so much that there were hardly any projects that included material involvement. From the field visits, interviews and Focus Group discussions, it was repeatedly heard that complete avoidance of material costs in Kerala essentially led to a situation where the shelf of activities that could be taken up under the scheme was very limited.

This, along with other factors, led to the interpretation of asset types in Kerala. For instance, a channel clearance near a road would be termed as flood protection, while the same activity may appear as water conservation with cosmetic changes in another region. This, though will not affect the overarching goal of employment provisioning, led to very similar type of assets/activities being taken up under different names in Kerala.

8.5 Assessment of Expenditure Incurred on Assets

To assess the appropriateness of the expenditure on the assets, data was collected on the actual expenditure on assets and an assessment made by a competent person (usually an engineer) on the expenditure that could have incurred on the asset. The cost of asset is assessed in terms of both material and total expenditures. Table 8.6 shows the average ratio of actual material expenditure to that of the material expenditure that the engineer had estimated to be ideal. A ratio of above one suggests that there is over expenditure and a ratio of less than one would mean that there is under expenditure. This query was responded from very few assets only.

Here we have analyzed the data for all the assets for which we got responses. In Andhra Pradesh, the actual expenditure on materials was more or less the same as assessed by the engineer, while in Kerala there was severe under expenditure on materials. In Kerala, material expenses were completely discouraged; hence, it can be expected that there was under expenditure.

In Karnataka, on the other hand, there was an overshoot of material expenditure by 50% more than the ideal expenditure that the engineer estimated to be ideal. This again is explainable as the involvement of informal contractors and skilled workers could have led to scaling up of material use in asset building. We were not able to get any data of Tamil Nadu, and hence cannot comment about Tamil Nadu on this (Table 8.6).

Table 8.6 Estimates of expenditure on material for the project by engineer ideally versus actual material expenses in rupees

State	Mean	Std. dev.	Freq.
Andhra Pradesh	1.02	0.05	11
Kerala	0.55	0.13	6
Karnataka	1.55	2.28	16
Tamil Nadu			
Total	1.19	1.61	33

Source Primary survey of MGNREGS, 2013

Table 8.7 Ratio of estimates of total expenditure for the project by engineer ideally versus actual expenses

State	Mean	Std. dev.	Freq.
Andhra Pradesh	0.62	0.51	101
Kerala	1.18	1.58	59
Karnataka	0.83	0.41	40
Tamil Nadu	0.99	1.21	60
Total	0.87	1.04	260

Source Primary survey of MGNREGS, 2013

Table 8.7 shows the average ratio of actual total expenditure to that of the total expenditure that the engineer had estimated to be ideal. This shows the divergence between actual and ideals. It may be noted that overall the actual and ideal were nearly the same. In Andhra Pradesh, there was considerable under expenditure while in Kerala, there was some marginal over expenditure. In Tamil Nadu and Karnataka, the overall expenditure was more or less equal to the ideal expenditure as estimated by the engineer. Thus, it may be stated that in general there were no large cost overruns, and the actual expenditure was more or less close to the ideal expenditure.

However, Tables 8.6 and 8.7 may be interpreted only with caution, as, it can be seen, a large share of the asset survey respondents chose not to answer these questions relating to actual and ideal spending.

8.6 Ownership Type of Assets

The MGNREGS scheme accommodates the creation of both public and private assets. Public assets are those whose benefits are not derived by any exclusive individual or group specifically; rather the benefits are drawn by the local community in general. Though MGNREGS is a public-funded programme, it does allow for private asset creation in some cases such as works on the land owned by SC/ST or works on small and marginal farmers.

In our study, we define private assets as those assets whose major beneficiaries are private individuals or an exclusive group. To arrive at the ownership nature of the asset if there was a claim of ownership over the land or the benefits of the assets by an individual or a group, then it was identified as private asset, or else it was classified as public assets.

From our sample, in Tamil Nadu (100%) and Karnataka (90%), most works done were public in nature where the asset became a common village property (see Fig. 8.2). In Kerala, nearly 65% of the assets were public in nature while in Andhra Pradesh, more than 86% of the assets created were private in nature. Private assets were created in Andhra Pradesh as most of the activities conducted were in private lands as land development activities.[9]

In Kerala too, a large share of works (35%) were done in private lands. This was especially true in case of Idukki district where most works were private in nature.[10] In Kerala and Andhra Pradesh, land development activities were taken up in large scale and land development activities were aimed at rejuvenating agriculture in these regions. Most land development activities in Andhra were related to Jhuliflora clearance and putting fresh soil. In Kerala, most land development activities were related to clearance of unused land and preparation for agriculture. In Karnataka and Tamil Nadu, such activities were not encouraged. Activities which had a clear public nature were only taken up in these states (see Fig. 8.1).

Andhra Pradesh was able to utilize the provision of land development and irrigation works for the private individuals through the prioritization of the scheme and provisioning it to SC/ST and small land holders. But in Kerala, the provisioning for private assets was largely specific to the hill district of Idukki, while in Thiruvananthapuram district, there were hardly any private assets being created. Idukki district has a plantation crop based agricultural economy.

Though the district has a plantation economy, a large share of these plantations is small and marginal land holdings. There is a large presence of scheduled tribes and castes but they are largely landless population in the region. Christian migrants from the mid-Travancore region, which form the major vote bank for the Kerala Congress (M), a local regional party with considerable power in the state-level multiparty coalition of the Congress-led UDF, are the dominant small and marginal farmers in the region. In this region, most MGNREGS works taken up were in private lands, such as preparation of land for next agricultural season or doing the initial works for the next crop, mainly Cardamom and other spices cultivation.

From the field interviews, it was clear that the groups formed for MGNREGS were essentially 'exchange labour groups'[11] that were already prevalent in the region. These MGNREGS groups were essentially working on their own farms or neighborhood farms and thus were benefitting a wage subsidy through MGNREGS on the farm work. The scheme probably would not have achieved same level of success in Idukki had it been designed as total public works programme. The

---

[9]Though most works done in Andhra Pradesh were private in nature, two GPs in Ibrahimpatnamblock of Krishna district and the three GPs in Vidapanakkal block of Anantapur had about 30–40% respondents claiming that assets were public.

[10]In Kerala, there were specific GPs that did complete private works, while some had a mix of both private and public; and some had only public works. In Idukki district, Kanchiyar and Kattapana were two GPs that had very high share of private works, in all other GPs private works were not the majority of the works. In both these GPs, KC (M) was ruling in coalition with the Congress, while in other panchayats their role was in the opposition or marginal.

[11]Exchange labour system is a traditional system of labour sharing, wherein the small farmers pool their labour together and work in each other's farms. This practice, which was waning earlier, had resurged in the recent past due to rising wages of wage labour and unavailability of unskilled labour in the local labour markets in Idukki.

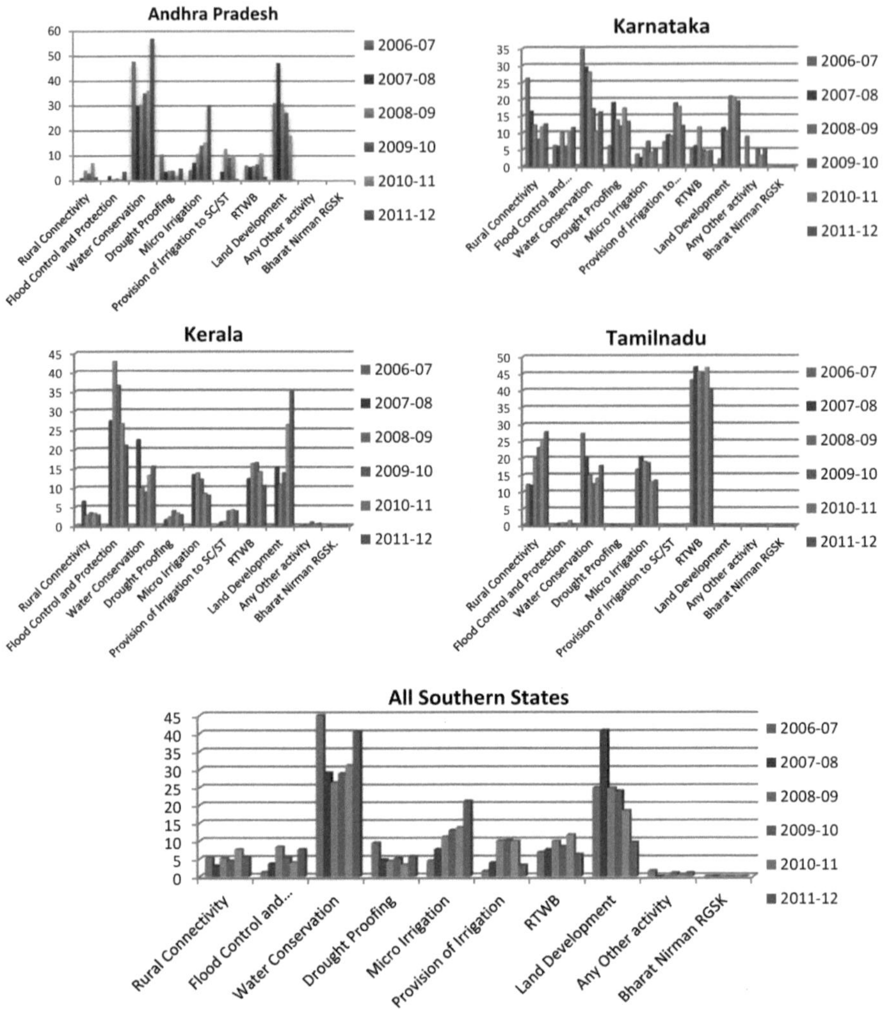

Fig. 8.1 Distribution of number of assets completed from 2006–07 to 2011–12 (%). *Source* MIS, MGNREGS

attraction of the programme in Idukki, despite lower MGNREGS wages than private wage works, is the associated private gains in asset creation.

In Tamil Nadu, private works were discouraged completely, even when the MGNREGS provisions allowed this, probably, as argued earlier, i.e. to maintain the power relations within the local economy. In Karnataka too, private works were discouraged as private works empower the SC/ST and the small and marginal farmers. Moreover, within the present arrangement, wherein there was elite capture of the programme, public works provided better gains to the elites, while private works which benefitted only the poor and marginalized were unwelcome.

8.7 Asset Quality and Durability

For creating durable and good quality assets, each state follows a protocol manual that describes the technical specifications of the assets to be created. This protocol manual usually is drawn from either the Central Public Works Department or the Local Public Works Department. To ensure the quality of assets at the field level, engineers or technically competent supervisors are appointed at the block level or gram panchayat level who conducts feasibility studies prior to the work. There are also monitoring and evaluation bodies at different levels of bureaucracy that visits the assets routinely.

From the field visits it was evident that despite the clear guidelines laid down for asset creation, the quality of assets created varied vastly across various projects and states. From the asset level survey we conducted, nearly 70% of all assets were constructed as per the specification of the CPWD or local PWD manual (see Fig. 8.3). In Kerala, 81% of the assets were created as per the specifications laid out.

In Andhra Pradesh and Karnataka, the provisions of the CPWD specifications were followed in case of 77% of the assets. From the field interviews, the asset beneficiaries in Andhra Pradesh and Kerala also perceived that the quality of assets created under MGNREGA was as per specifications. In Tamil Nadu, however, only 60% of the assets were built as per specifications.

The relatively higher level of following the specification in Andhra Pradesh and Kerala could be due to the fact that many of these were private works. In such cases, probably there is a greater incentive for the private owner to encourage and ensure that the work is done in good quality. The low performance in Tamil Nadu where the public works were the maximum also supports this argument. But Karnataka, which also did mostly public works, had performed well in this respect, unlike Tamil Nadu. From our field verification visits, we had noted that some of the better assets among the four states that we surveyed were constructed in Karnataka (see Fig. 8.2).

But it is also the fact that Andhra Pradesh had introduced Global Positioning System (GPS)-based work measurement and wage payment system. This essentially ensured that the works were completed as per the technical specification and there was no space for human manipulations or errors. In none of the other states, GPS-based measurement system was followed except in parts of Tamil Nadu. While a technological solution ensured specifications in Andhra Pradesh, it was the vigilant and active gram panchayat that enabled the creation of a strong social audit process that ensured the specification of assets in Kerala.

At the time of survey, in 2013, Kerala had a very vibrant local social audit mechanism established at the gram panchayat level, with members drawn from different walks of life in the social audit team. In Tamil Nadu, an independent social audit mechanism at the village level did not exist in the early years of implementation, and it was only in 2012–13 that a permanent social audit mechanism was

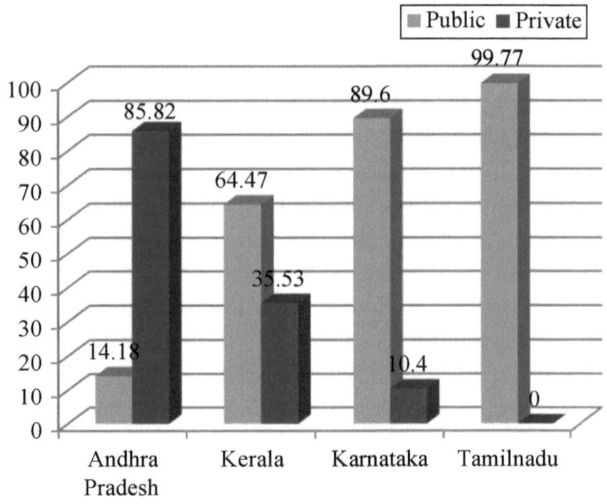

Fig. 8.2 Type of Asset Created: State wise *Source* Primary Survey of MGNREGS, 2013

structured and audit was conducted in two blocks in Tamil Nadu.[12] In Karnataka, social audit mechanism was in place early but it had been subject to elite capture, like the rest of the programme (Rajasekhar et al. 2013).

This apart, there was a politics of the quality of asset building in southern states. Quality of asset was linked to follow the stipulated specification of the assets. And specification of assets was to be measured by the competent authority, based on which the wages were to be paid. MGNREGS allows discretion to follow either piece rate or time rate wages.

In case of piece rate wages, completion of work as per specification is the norm for wage payment and in case of daily wages, a daily productivity norm, determined by the implementing agency, is the basis for wage payment.

The wage payment system followed in different states varied, for instance, while Tamil Nadu and Andhra Pradesh followed the piece rate method, and Kerala and Karnataka followed the daily wage method. In both cases, however, measurements of the completed assets were to be carried out to ensure fulfillment of the specification.

In Andhra Pradesh and Tamil Nadu, where the practice of piece rate was followed, the average daily wage was in general less than the minimum wages declared by the state to be paid for MGNREGS works. In Andhra Pradesh, the GPS-based measurement yielded many works that were not completed to specification, leading to under payment of wages. But in Tamil Nadu, which had a more severe case of under—payment compared to Andhra Pradesh, yet did not have GPS-based measurement of wages was accomplished through manual

[12]Minutes of the meeting of the Empowered Committee to scrutinize and discuss Anticipated Labour Demand of Tamil Nadu for 2013–14, 15 February 2013, http://nrega.nic.in/Netnrega/WriteReaddata/Circulars/Minute_TN_meeting15Feb13.pdf, accessed on 7 January 2015.

measurement. The manual measurement of wages was implemented by local supervisors or overseers who were temporary appointees under the scheme.

The measurement of assets created was strictly imposed owing to the pressures from the local landlords. In many places in Tamil Nadu, it was stated in interviews with the workers that local landlords were enthusiastic about measurement of assets and payment being made accordingly. This probably was a tactic to keep the MGNREGS wages lower than the agricultural wages, thus dis-incentivising participation in MGNREGS.

In Kerala, where daily wage payment was followed, measurement of assets was opposed by workers collectives in many parts. Any attempt to impose measurement-based wages was opposed by the worker's collectives and was supported by the local political leadership, such that in our survey, there was hardly any worker who received wages less than the minimum wages stipulated.

In many parts of Karnataka, though daily wage system was followed, there was no conflict between the local elites, workers and the implementing agencies as the assets created were as per the specifications, while the works were done by skilled workers using machinery. The agricultural workers who cooperated with the arrangement and doubled up as MGNREGS workers got an additional small sum of money as payment for the arrangement. Thus, while the scheme got captured and its main objective of providing rural livelihood opportunities got diluted, Karnataka was able to build assets that were according to specifications and also that were durable.

Though overall, the assets created were claimed to be as per specifications, and many of these assets were not durable. Durability of these assets was dependent on multiple factors including implementing the technical asset specifications, durable materials used in asset creation, weather conditions and most importantly periodic maintenance of these assets.

Since in Kerala and Tamil Nadu use of material components was completely discouraged, most of the assets created were used with non-durable materials and the nature of the work themselves non-durable. Given the climatic conditions of Kerala which has very heavy rainfall, these assets almost completely disappear after a cycle of rains. Also, many of the private works taken up in the agriculture land were seasonal works which would not sustain to the next cycle of crops. Interviews with the stakeholders show that in Tamil Nadu also, the works done were not of permanent nature, though they were relatively more durable. Most of the works done were pond cleaning or road cleaning, which were not asset creations, but doing maintenance works of assets already existing, through MGNREGS.

While asset creation was designed within the MGNREGS scheme, there was no provision for maintenance of the assets created. Lack of maintenance of the assets was an important concern raised by all stakeholders alike, including workers, asset beneficiaries and the panchayat officials in almost all GPs of the states. The nature of the works taken up under MGNREGS is such that for sustenance of the assets large maintenance cost needs to be incurred or else assets would deteriorate in a short time.

Though a large majority of the assets created under MGNREGS require maintenance, as noted above, however, in practice, only 33% of the assets were being maintained regularly (Table 8.8). More than 67% of the assets were not having any maintenance. In Tamil Nadu, more than 78% of the assets were not receiving any maintenance. While in Kerala, nearly 69% were not receiving any maintenance.

During interviews with workers, it was revealed that MGNREGA helped to create good quality assets, and it has been maintained well. But some felt that quality of assets created is very poor and maintenance of assets is not addressed well in Tamil Nadu; more than 79% of the workers opined that the assets were not maintained properly. While in Andhra Pradesh 79% stated that assets were maintained properly.

In Kerala too, nearly 67% claimed that the assets were maintained properly. This divergence between Tamil Nadu on the one side and Kerala and Andhra Pradesh on the other is probably due to the incentive problem. In Tamil Nadu, as noted earlier, most works were public in nature, and since there were no funds allotted for maintenance, maintenance was not done, while in Andhra Pradesh and Kerala, many of the works were private in nature, thus incentivizing private maintenance, even if there were no funds available for it.

This private versus public asset dimension can be seen in case of involvement of local people in maintenance as well. As can be seen from Table 8.8 in Andhra Pradesh, more than 90% of workers stated that local people were involved in maintenance, which is due to the involvement of the owners of the private assets themselves. In Kerala too, where there was a large share of private assets, the involvement of local people was substantial in maintenance, while in Tamil Nadu where the assets were public in nature, more than 96% of the workers stated that local people were not involved in the maintenance of the assets.

8.8 Importance of the Asset Constructed for the Locality

In Tamil Nadu, 58% of the asset beneficiaries claimed that the asset that constructed in the locality was very important (see Table 8.9). In Kerala, 48% stated that the asset was very important for the locality. While in Andhra Pradesh, only 22.5% considered it to be very important and in Karnataka only 7% considered it to be very important. In none of the states, the assets built were considered to be unimportant.

In Andhra Pradesh and Karnataka, the largest share of respondents considered these assets to be important. Thus it can be concluded that the assets created were necessary for the locality to most regions of the various states. But Kerala and Tamil Nadu were able to identify assets that were most important for the regions. This probably has to do with better functioning of the Panchayat Raj system in these states.

In Andhra Pradesh, due to the lack of elections at the GP level during the last 5 years, people's representation in asset selection might have been weak. In Karnataka,

Table 8.8 Aspects on maintenance of assets: state-wise

	AP	KL	KN	TN	Total
Regular maintenance carried out	41.79	37.29	28.85	7.41	32.68
Proper maintenance done	79.01	66.57	44.3	2.05	46.54
Local people helping to protect and maintain the assets	90.62	50.15	65.18	3.67	53.15

Source Primary survey of MGNREGS, 2013

Table 8.9 Importance of the selected asset in the locality surveyed across the states

	Unit	AP (n = 440)	KL (346)	KN (514)	TN (439)	Total (1739)
Not important	%	1.82	6.36	6.42	2.51	4.26
Important	%	75.68	45.66	86.19	39.86	63.77
Very important	%	22.50	47.98	7.39	57.63	31.97
Total	%	100	100	100	100	100

Numbers of beneficiaries are in percent share

since the scheme was interpreted and implemented differently from the objectives and plan of the scheme, it might have led to poor selection of assets as compared to other regions. Since contractors could get involved in asset building, many of the assets chosen would be of the nature that there could be greater use of material, skilled workers and machinery and hence, may be some of the local issues at grass roots level that may have got sidelined.

8.9 Concluding Observations

Though the MGNREGS was a centrally sponsored scheme, with clear guidelines on the implementation at each level of governance, there were considerable variations across states in planning and implementation of asset creation. Depending on the local economic, political and social structure, planning and implementation of asset creation under the scheme was redesigned, re-interpreted and implemented to accommodate the interests of the various interest groups.

To generalize if there were a strong and functioning gram panchayat and gram sabha system at the village level, then there was greater representation in demand generated for work and assets at the local level. But if functioning of the GP system is compromised, then it is possible that at this stage, either a dominant bureaucratic executive branch could make the decisions, which may not be representative of the people, or dominant local political lobbies could exploit the programme for political clientelism, or dominant elites could capture the programme for economic gains, which may represent only the needs of the elites in the society.

Technocratic solutions to corruption did yield outcomes that were largely un captured by various interest groups, but the top-down approach of such technocratic planning also left the scheme without participation in choice of assets, and local level ownership in planning and implementation at the grass root level. Central to the efficient functioning of such public programmes is the bottom-up planning and implementation of projects. It is the active local representative bodies that voice the grass roots that can transform such public programmes into transformational agents in development.

Appendix

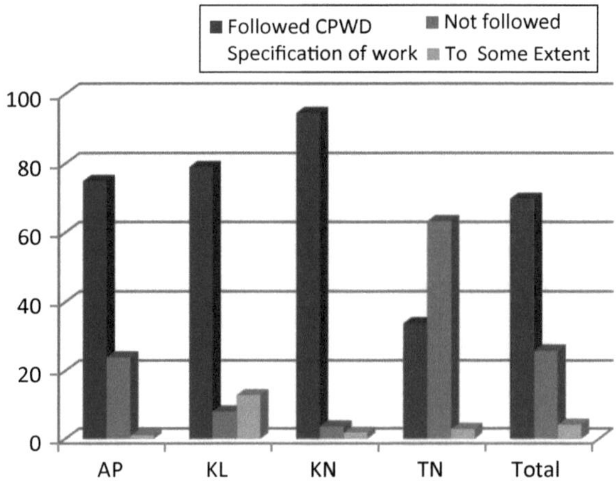

Fig. 8.3 Specification of work as per of C.P.W.D or Local P.W.D Manual: State wise

References

Ananth Pur, K., and M. Moore. 2010. Ambiguous Institutions: Traditional Governance and Local Democracy in Rural South India. *Journal of Development Studies* 46 (4): 603–623.

Ananth Pur, K. 2007. Dynamics of Local Governance in Karnataka. *Economic and Political Weekly*, Feb 24.

Besley, T., R. Pande, and V. Rao. 2007. Political Economy of Panchayats in South India. *Economic and Political Weekly*, Feb 24.

Chathukulam, J., and M.S. John. 2002. Five Years of Participatory Planning in Kerala: Rhetoric and Reality. *Economic and Political Weekly*, Dec 7.

De Neve, G., and G. Carswell. 2011. NREGA and the Return of Identity Politics in Western Tamil Nadu, India. *Forum for Development Studies* 38 (2): 205–210.

GoK. 2009. Report on Committee for Evaluation of Decentralized Planning and Development, Government of Kerala, Thiruvananthapuram.

Harriss, J., J. Jeyaranjan, and K. Nagaraj. 2010. Land, Labour and Caste Politics in Rural Tamil Nadu in the 20th Century: Iruvelpattu (1916-2008). *Economic & Political Weekly*, July 31, 45 (31): 47–61.

Heller, P., K. N. Harilal, and S. Chaudhuri. 2007. Building Local Democracy: Evaluating the Impact of Decentralization in Kerala, India. *World development* 35 (4): 626–648.

Isaac, Thomas T.V., and K.N. Harilal. 1997. Planning for Empowerment People's Campaign for Decentralised Planning in Kerala. *Economic and Political Weekly*, Jan 4–11, 32 (1/2): 53–58.

Kumar, V.A. 2009. Federalism and Decentralisation in India: Andhra Pradesh and Tamil Nadu. Working paper 208, Institute for Social and Economic Change, Bangalore.

Manor, J. 2007. Change in Karnataka over the Last Generation: Villages and the Wider Context. *Economic and Political Weekly*, Feb 24, 42 (8): 653–660.

Narayana, D. 2005. Local Governance without Capacity Building: Ten Years of Panchayati Raj. *Economic and Political Weekly*, June 25, 40 (26): 2822–2832.

Oommen, M.A. 2014. Deepening Democracy and Local Governance Challenges before Kerala. *Economic and Political Weekly*, June 21, 49 (25).

Rajasekhar, D., S. Lakha, and R. Manjula. 2013. How Effective are Social Audits under MGNREGS? Lessons from Karnataka. Working Paper No. 294, Institute for Social and Economic Change, Bangalore.

Sivasubramaniyan, K. 2006. Sustainable Development of Small Water Bodies in Tamil Nadu. *Economic and Political Weekly*, June 30, XLI (6).

Chapter 9
MGNREGA and Inclusive Development: A Case Study in Tripura, Northeast India

Indraneel Bhowmik, Pritam Bose, Samrat Goswami and Pradip Chouhan

9.1 Introduction

Tripura is the second smallest state in the northeastern region of India. Its economy is predominantly rural-based and is characterised by a heterogeneous mix of tribal and non-tribal population. Tripura's hilly topography has been a prime deterrent to development as it impairs the transportation and communication network within the state as well as with other states. Moreover, unemployment, poverty, low capital formation, poor infrastructure facilities, and lack of private sector employment[1] add to problems in the development process.

Under these circumstances, the state government, being the largest employer in the state, is also an important economic player. In case of Tripura, the state government has taken an active role in the implementation of MGNREGA. Recently, one of the state ministers in the Legislative Assembly has demanded the provision of 200 person-days per household per annum, under the scheme of MGNREGA in the areas.

---

[1]In Tripura, 42% of the total main workers in the state are engaged in agriculture, of which 23% are cultivators and the remaining 18.74% are agricultural labourers.

I. Bhowmik (✉) · P. Bose · P. Chouhan
Department of Economics, Tripura University, Agartala, Tripura, India
e-mail: indraneel@tripurauniv.in

P. Bose
e-mail: pritambose2008@gmail.com

P. Chouhan
e-mail: pradipchouhan08@gmail.com

S. Goswami
Department of Rural Studies, Tripura University, Agartala, Tripura, India
e-mail: sam449@gmail.com

M. Bhattarai et al. (eds.), *Employment Guarantee Programme and Dynamics of Rural Transformation in India*, India Studies in Business and Economics,
https://doi.org/10.1007/978-981-10-6262-9_9

As a result of high commitment from state government, Tripura is one of the best performers of MGNREGS in the country by creating employment of highest average person-days per household per year consequently for last 3 years (2011–12, 2012–13 and 2013–14). Moreover, Unankoti district of Tripura has also been awarded by the central government for best utilisation of funds for the year 2013–14 (which has utilised 98% of allotment fund).

The social safety net benefit to the vulnerable groups of society (like SC, ST and Women) of MGNREGA is a major factor for the state support, as it is akin to the political ideology of the Communist Party Of India (M)-led state government. Inclusiveness has been an inherent objective of the programme, as it is attested by the fact that SCs and STs account for appropriated 29 and 32% of the total man-days generated under MGNREGA nationally in the initial years of inception. In this context, we provide the impact of the MGNREGA in Tripura, one of the smaller states in northeast India.

It is beyond doubt that MGNREGS is having an impact on the livelihood of the rural people. However, the studies on effectiveness and impact of MGNREGS in the past have provided conflicting results, and the findings widely varied across studies, the regions and states covered. For example, the impacts of the programme have widely varied across the states (Dreze and Khera 2009).

The effectiveness of the scheme is seen to have a significant relationship with good governance at state level (Sen Roy and Samanta 2009). On the contrary, Jha and Gaiha (2012) evaluating the official statistics of the scheme provided a very meagre impact and performance of MGNREGA in most of the states. Further, Usami and Rawal (2012) finds notable discrepancies between the NSSO data and the Management Information Systems (MIS) data regarding the number of households having job cards and the number of job cards that are officially recorded as issued.

Moreover, numerous critics have reported about corruption, fund embezzlement, and malpractices in course of the functioning of the scheme. Thus, with the inception of National Democratic Alliance government at the Centre, the scheme, considered as a product of the earlier United Progressive Alliance regime, was reportedly in trouble (EPW 2014) following the stringent release of funds for individual states.

The argument in favour of the scheme stems from the various studies showing positive outcomes, like income security to the rural poor, creation of productive assets, high level of women participation and also the higher bargaining power of the rural labourers, has, however, led to the continuance of the scheme albeit small changes focussing on greater linkage to agriculture and improved asset quality through convergence, in accordance with the priorities of the new government.

It is important to note here that Tripura's performance has been credited particularly for higher average person-days employment generation per household (Dreze and Oldiges 2007; Usami and Rawal 2012; The Shillong Times, 2012). The scheme is supposed to improve the agriculture, poor irrigation system and poor road connectivity (Roy 2010) in the state.

Further, the equity aspect of the scheme has also been found to be in the right direction as participation of women and socially excluded groups are higher in Tripura (Talukdar 2008; Bhowmik 2013). In Dhalai district, the scheme has been found to be positively contributing to the income, employment generation, value addition in education, food consumption pattern, investment on assets, and savings pattern of the beneficiaries (Roy 2012).

In this background, the Chapter presents the impact of the scheme on the participating households especially on the STs, who are generally considered to be at the lower extreme in the ladder of social exclusion. Nonetheless, for the present context, the specific objective of the study is to examine the impact of the scheme on the participating households of the Dhalai district of Tripura with a particular focus on the ST households. Dhalai is the remotest and the most backward district of the state with a majority (55%) of the population belonging to Scheduled Tribes category.

The study uses both secondary and primary data. Secondary data on employment, physical assets, and financial investments was collected from the official website of the MGNREGA. The primary data was collected through a household survey using a structured schedule. A representative sample of 100 households selected purposively from the two *Gram Panchayats* (GPs) of Dhalai district in between June and July 2015.

One Rural Development (RD) Block was selected in the district randomly—Durga Chowmuhani—and from the selected RD Block, two gram panchayats, viz., Kalachari and Dhan Chandra Para, were selected randomly. From each *Gram Panchayat*, 50 households participating in the scheme were selected randomly and were surveyed through a structured schedule.

It should be noted here that Kalachari GP is situated on the major district road connecting the district headquarter Ambassa to the Subdivisional (Taluk) headquarters Kamalpur. Categorised as a Census Town by Census 2011, Kalachari is predominantly inhabited by people belonging to the scheduled castes community, though sizeable number of people from other communities including religious minorities and scheduled tribes also live there.

Dhan Chandra (DC) Para, situated on the road connecting ManikBhander to Fatikroy in Unakoti district, beyond the Durga Chowmuhuni RD Block headquarters, is predominantly inhabited by scheduled tribes belonging to the Tripuri community with a few households belonging to the scheduled castes also. Among the two villages, Kalachari is more vibrant economically owing to its geographical advantages while DC Para being in the hinterlands has limited economic opportunities. A revisit to the study area was made in November 2015 to understand the implications of the recent changes in the MGNREGS framework and its implementation.

Standard statistical analysis of the data has been undertaken to fulfil the stated objective. Paired sample *t* test has been used to examine the changes in income.

Real income of pre-MGNREGS period was obtained using the GSDP deflator. Moreover, in order to measure the extent of inclusiveness, 'Allotment ratio'[2] was calculated to see the issue of inclusiveness:

$$\textbf{Allotment ratio}; = \text{Proportion of Person-days generated for a community (category)/Proportion of Job card holdings by that community (category)}.$$

A score of 1 or above suggest greater inclusion of people in the scheme, while less than 1 means lesser inclusion. Moreover, an 'asset ownership index'[3] was constructed on the basis of information relating to the ownership of six assets (land, bicycle, DVD, TV, motor bike and fan). Possession was recorded as 1, while it was 0 for non-possession. The correlation coefficients between the monthly income of the workers and ownership of these assets were taken as weights (Thapa, 2012) to obtain the asset index as below:

$$\textbf{Asset Ownership Index} = [(r_1 * \text{land}) + (r_2 * \text{bicycle}) + (r_3 * \text{mobile}) + (r_4 * \text{dvd}) + (r_5 * \text{tv}) + (r_6 * \text{fan})]/6]$$

where, r_1, r_2, r_3, r_4, r_5 and r_6 are the value of correlation between monthly income and the possession of the respective asset. The value of the asset index was normalised using the following formula:

$$(\textbf{Observed value} - \textbf{Minimum value})/(\textbf{Maximum value} - \textbf{Minimum value}).$$

The chapter is divided into five sections including the introduction. Section 9.2 presents a brief profile of MGNREGS in Dhalai district, while Sect. 9.3 deals with observation on the basis of field survey. Section 9.4 provides a discussion on the nature and impact of the recent changes in the scheme, while Sect. 9.5 provides the summary of the findings along with concluding remarks.

9.2 An Overview of MGNREGS in Dhalai District

Dhalai is considered to be the most remote and backward of the eight districts of Tripura though it has emerged as the largest in the state, with a geographical coverage of 2400 km^2, owing to the administrative reorganisation made by the state government in 2012. It is the only tribal dominant district with 55% of the population belonging to Scheduled Tribes (STs). Moreover, 17% of the district population of 3.78 lakhs belong to the Scheduled Castes (SCs) category. Dhalai is the

[2]Refer to Bhowmik (2013) for greater detail.

[3]Refer to Thapa (2012) for greater detail.

least urbanised district of the state with 90% of the district population residing in rural areas.

The overall literacy rate is 85.72%, while the work participation rate is 41.20%. The female literacy rate and work participation rate in the district are 79.79 and 27.32%, respectively. The district is predominantly agrarian, where Jhum cultivation has been the main source of livelihood for the tribal households dwelling in tiny hamlets across the district for a long period. Developmental plans and welfare initiatives by the state government are the major contributors to the district economy as the contribution from the industrial sector is negligible.

Dhalai also has the distinction of being the only district of Tripura to be included among the 200 backward districts of India when MGNREGS was first launched. The district had almost 80,000 households with MGNREGS job cards in 2013–14 and accounts for 10–13% of the total job cards issued in the state as shown in Table 9.1. More than 95% of the enrolled households have demanded job all throughout the period and as a result, the district exhibits a marginally higher share among the total households demanding employment.

The share of the district in terms of person-days generated (figures in parentheses in the third row of Table 9.1) has been much higher than the share of households in 2008–09, but declined in 2009–10 and thereafter has been higher than the share of employment demanding houses for all successive years. The share has reached 15.21% in 2014–15, which is highest after 2010–11. Such a scenario attests to the overall backwardness of the district as well as dependence on the scheme among the people of the district as also higher degree activism than some other districts.

The success of a programme can be measured through the performance of the programme and the performance of a programme can well be understood through certain performance indicators. Considering the performance indicators as depicted in Table 9.2, it is seen that Dhalai has consistently created higher average person-days per household than the state average except in 2009–10. In terms of provision of 100 days of work to the households also the district's performance is better than the state average and it has increased from 10.37% in 2008–09 to 43.22% in 2014–15.

Table 9.1 Employment scenario of MGNREGS in Dhalai district of Tripura

Indicators	2008–09	2009–10	2010–11	2011–12	2012–13	2013–14	2014–15
Job cards (HHs)	78,134 [13.00]	73,982 [11.89]	68,447 [10.96]	71,824 [11.92]	76,810 [11.98]	79,152 [12.22]	78,426 [12.50]
Employment demand (HHs)	76,875 [14.00]	72,156 [12.81]	68,178 [12.23]	69,499 [12.25]	74,130 [12.41]	75,756 [12.52]	76,272 [12.87]
Person-days (Nos. in lakhs)	75.77 [21.58]	49.69 [10.80]	58.59 [15.64]	62.72 [12.80]	68.61 [13.26]	67.08 [12.76]	68.11 [15.21]

Note Figures in the parentheses indicate share of Dhalai in Tripura
Source Computed from www.nrega.nic.in

Table 9.2 Performance indicators of MGNREGS in Dhalai district

	Indicators	2008–09	2009–10	2010–11	2011–12	2012–13	2013–14	2014–15
1	Average person-days (Nos./HH)	98.56 [63.95]	67.18 [79.83]	86.05 [67.23]	90.25 [86.00]	92.96 [87.00]	89.15 [87.69]	90.17 [77.08]
2	HHs with 100 days (%)	59.85 [10.37]	17.35 [37.09]	47.31 [14.61]	45.86 [35.72]	58.87 [37.93]	47.23 [47.14]	62.03 [43.22]
3	Women person-days (%)	54.80 [41.09]	35.20 [38.45]	34.11 [38.21]	32.49 [33.42]	40.84 [37.93]	50.01 [47.11]	48.74 [49.60]
4	Work completion rate (%)	76.16 [91.92]	85.63 [98.41]	96.56 [97.98]	68.40 [87.75]	79.08 [96.09]	97.24 [94.19]	84.78 [71.86]
5	Utilisation of funds (%)	97.24 [94.48]	104.38 [75.82]	98.55 [99.04]	83.74 [93.78]	99.84 [92.92]	95.55 [91.17]	100.72 [103.30]

Note Figures in the parentheses indicate the corresponding figures of Tripura
Source Computed from www.nrega.nic.in

Table 9.3 Allotment ratio of SCs and STs in Dhalai district

	2008–09	2009–10	2010–11	2011–12	2012–13	2013–14	2014–15
Schedule Caste (SC)	1.07	0.90	0.94	0.95	0.94	0.95	0.94
Scheduled Tribes(ST)	0.99	1.07	1.06	1.03	0.99	0.98	1.04

Source Computed from www.nrega.nic.in

In terms of female participation, the district has not always been ahead of the state average though the percentage of women person-days have improved slightly between 2008–09 and 2014–15. In terms of the work completion rate, the district has been lagging behind the state average for the entire reference period until 2013–14.

Wherein the improvement continues in the subsequent year also, actually, the work completion rate in the district has been most impressive in 2013–14 only. The fund utilisation in the district has been impressive and has been higher than the state average for most of the years except for 2014–15. The fund utilisation has been more than 100% for both Dhalai and the state owing to the usage of earlier leftover funds.

From the point of equity and inclusion of the socially excluded classes, Table 9.3 depicts that allotment ratio for SCs was 1.07 in 2008–09 and has consistently been less than 1 (one) for the rest of the reference period. In case of the STs, the allotment ratio has been above 1 (one) in 2009–10, 2010–11 and 2011–12, but declined in subsequent years and again reached 1.04 in 2014–15.

It should be noted that the allotment ratio for STs shows a decreasing trend since 2009–10 till 2013–14. The lower score for the SCs is similar to other parts of the

Table 9.4 Average person-days, HH with 100 days and WCR among the RD Blocks of Dhalai (2012–13, 2013–14 and 2014–15)

Blocks	Average person-days (Nos./HH)			HH with 100 days (%)			Work completion rate (%)		
	2012–13	2013–14	2014–15	2012–13	2013–14	2014–15	2012–13	2013–14	2014–15
Ambassa	94.86	90.22	93.37	49	17	55	98.05	99.23	88.46
Chawmanu	98.19	91.61	99.00	75	10	56	99.55	98.83	71.93
Dumburnagar	95.45	92.96	115.10	62	22	85	99.82	100.00	89.76
Durga Chowmuhani	85.73	86.02	93.47	32	15	54	95.51	97.29	94.32
Manu	93.17	85.55	94.70	63	20	54	99.82	96.73	64.76
Salema	91.72	91.83	99.56	53	16	65	100	99.82	94.41

Source Computed from www.nrega.nic.in

state but the lower score for the STs is quite surprising, as for the state as a whole the allotment ratio has been in favour of the community (Bhowmik 2013). The below 1 (one) score in allotment ratio for the socially marginal class indicates that the 'others' (unreserved) category has a favourable allotment ratio. In this context, it may be noted that the unreserved category in Dhalai is a minority unlike other parts of the state (Table 9.4).

The intra-district performances at the RD Blocks level for the 3 years (2012–13, 2013–14 and 2014–15) show that Chawmanu (98.19) lead in terms of the average person-days per household for 2012–13, while Dumburnagar is at the top for the two other years with an average of 92.96 and 115.10 person-days for 2013–14 and 2014–15, respectively.

These two RD Blocks are at the top again in terms of provision of 100 days of work to the households for the corresponding years. It is important to note here that the performance of the blocks in providing 100 days of work has shown a sharp decline in 2013–14 as compared to 2012–13 and has increased again in 2014–15.

On the other hand, the Salema RD Block had the best work completion rate for 2012–13 and 2014–15, while Dumburnagar achieved a 100% work completion rate in 2013–14. Though the average person-days generated per household has been similar among the RD Blocks, there has been significant variation in the mean average person-days among the 3 years of reference with 2013–14 being different at 5% level of significance.[4]

In terms of the proportion of households getting 100 days' work, the yearly variations are of strong statistical significance.[5] In terms of the Work Completion rate, there are wide variations among the years, owing to lower rates in 2014–15, which, however, is likely to increase in latter period following completion of leftover works in the next year. However, it may be noted that the differences in the

[4] $F = 7.37$, $p = 0.010$.

[5] $F = 33.34$, $p = 0.00003$.

Table 9.5 Average person-days, HH with 100 days and WCR in the study area (2012–13, 2013–14 and 2014–15)

Blocks	Average person-days (Nos./HH)			HH with 100 days (%)			Work completion rate (%)		
	2012–13	2013–14	2014–15	2012–13	2013–14	2014–15	2012–13	2013–14	2014–15
DC Para	91	84	92	45	64	61	97	100	98
Kalachari	87	78	88	18	41	70	99	100	99

Source Computed from www.nrega.nic.in

rates of average person-days, households with 100 days and work completion rate among the RD Blocks are not different statistically.

In this context, we may note from Table 9.5 that among the two study villages, DC Para has had higher average person-days for all the 3 years, while Kalachari has been a better performer in terms of work completion rate. The proportion of households with 100 days of work has been higher in DC Para in the first 2 years while in 2014–15, Kalachari was ahead. Interestingly, the performances of both the GPs are better than the average of the Durga Chowmuhuni RD Block of which they are component in terms of the performance indicators save for the average person-days in 2013–14 and 2014–15.

9.3 Impact on Households

As stated in Sect. 9.1, the objective of the study was to understand how the MGNREGS affect the life and livelihood of the rural poor. The present section, therefore, attempts to examine the impacts of the scheme particularly on income generation and livelihood strategies. Moreover, the attempt was to examine the awareness level of the participants about the scheme as well as explore their assets in possession.

9.3.1 Profile of Sample Workers

The sample respondents were truly representatives of the heterogeneous demographic and socio-economic mix that Tripura exhibits (Table 9.6). Most of the respondents in Kalachari panchayat were SCs (70%), while OBC and general households were also found albeit in lesser numbers. On the other hand, the sample respondents from DC Para were predominantly from the tribal communities, though almost 15% came from the SC communities. In all, the sample consisted of 43 ST households and 42 SC households. The ST respondents of DC Para were primarily followers of Christianity, while the five unreserved households in Kalachari practiced Islam, the remaining being Hindus.

Table 9.6 Basic profile of sample MGNREGS workers

	Kalachari (*n* = 50)	DC Para (*n* = 50)	Total (*n* = 100)
1. Community			
(a) ST	–	43 (86)	43
(b) SC	35 (70)	7 (14)	42
(c) OBC	10 (20)	–	10
(d) Others	5 (10)	–	5
2. Religion			
(a) Hinduism	45 (90)	11 (22)	56
(b) Islam	5 (10)	–	5
(c) Christianity		39 (78)	39
3. Family size			
(a) Mean	4.98	5.54	5.26
(b) Max	7	7	7
(c) Min	3	4	3
4. Age (years)			
(a) Max	59	66	66
(b) Min	41	36	36
(c) Mean	45.5	51.34	48.42
5. Ration Card			
(a) APL	0	0	–
(b) BPL	43 (86)	28 (56)	71
(c) Antyodaya	7 (14)	22 (44)	29
6. Occupation			
(a) Cultivators	1 (2)	10 (20)	11
(b) Day labourers	46 (92)	39 (78)	85
(c) Traders	3 (6)	–	3
(d) Unemployed	–	1 (2)	1

Notes Figures in the parentheses indicate percentage
Source Computed from Field Survey, 2015

The average family size, 5.54, is higher in DC Para as compared to that of Kalachari, 4.98. Interestingly, the average household size in Dhalai as per Census 2011, 4.48, is lower than that of both the sample villages. Respondents from DC Para belonged to a wider age group as compared to that of Kalachari with both the oldest and the youngest, aged 66 and 36 years, respectively, belonging to the former. The mean age of the respondents of DC Para is also higher than that in Kalachari.

Interestingly, all the respondents across the two GPs possessed BPL (Below Poverty Line) ration cards and 44% of the households from DC Para possessed Antyodaya card. In all, 29% of the respondents possessed Antyodaya cards. The occupational patterns of the respondents show a clear dominance of daily labourers in both the villages, while a few cultivators were also part of the sample in DC Para.

Interestingly, three persons from Kalachari were petty businessman, who did not miss the opportunity of supplementary income through MGNREGA. A respondent from DC Para claimed to be unemployed for he had no other alternative except for the MGNREGS assignments.

9.3.2 *Experience of the Scheme*

The respondents (86%) were well informed about the provision of unemployment allowances in the scheme but none of them have ever received any such allowance. Quite contrary to this, the provision of compensation for being assigned work at a distance more than 5 km was hardly known to the respondents. Only eight respondents from DC Para were aware of such facilities.

Again, 53 respondents were aware of the provision of payments within 15 days of completion of work. On the other hand, the system of holding meetings in advance to fix/decide the work was not known to any respondent. Table 9.7 also shows that the most important source to obtain information about MGNREGS has been the Ward Member in Kalachari while in DC Para, the officials in the GP are the most prominent sources. Neighbours, relatives and villagers have been the

Table 9.7 Awareness and Information about MGNREGS (Nos.)

Category	Indicators	Kalachari (n = 50)	DC Para (n = 50)	Total (n = 100)
Knowledge about MGNREGS	Provision of unemployment allowance	44 (88)	42 (84)	86
	Compensation for travelling far off	0	8 (16)	8
	15 days time limit for payment	29 (58)	24 (48)	53
	Meetings in advance	0	0	0
Sources of information	Neighbours, relatives and villagers	17 (34)	19 (38)	36
	Ward members	33 (66)	8 (16)	41
	GP Officials	0	23 (46)	23
TGBRAIJC	Less than 7 days	41 (82)	38 (76)	79
	Between 7 to 14 days	9 (18)	12 (24)	21
WPBAAOW	Less than 7 days	38 (76)	32 (64)	70
	Between 7 to 14 days	12 (24)	18 (36)	30
Custody of job card	Self	36 (72)	12 (24)	48
	Head of family	14 (28)	38 (76)	52

Notes TGBRAIOJC—Time gap between registration and issue of job card; WPBAAOW—Waiting period between application and allotment of works; Figures in the parentheses indicate percentage

Source Computed from Field Survey, 2015

source of information for more than 35% of the total respondents. Most of the respondents (79%) had received their job cards within 7 days of application. Similarly, the time gap between the application and allotment of works has been less than 7 days for most of the respondents (70%), whereas the work was assigned within 14 days for the rest.

It may be noted that though MGNREGS is a demand-driven scheme, the participants hardly know it. To them the scheme is similar to previous programmes where they got assignments whenever any such work was undertaken by the authorities. The Job cards are generally in possession of the respondents themselves; however, in DC Para, for 38% of the respondents, the job cards were in possession of the head of the household. It may be noted here that there have been instances of job cards being in possession of the ward members in earlier times (Bhowmik and Bose 2015).

9.3.3 Impact on Income

The sample respondents, as seen earlier, are mostly from labourer households and seek to avail any income opportunities that come their way. The annual household income earned by the sample workers from two villages varied from a low of ₹ 32,400 to a high of ₹ 96,000.

From Table 9.8, it is seen that the average annual household income of the respondents from Kalachari, ₹ 53,376, has been higher than that obtained in DC Para, ₹ 38,400 per annum. The income slab from ₹ 48,001 to ₹ 54,000 have had the highest frequency in Kalachari, 46%, while in the other villages, 52% of the sample respondents survive with less than ₹ 3000 per month for the household. In all 94% of the respondents in DC Para earns less than ₹ 42,000 per annum. Nevertheless, it may be noted that the average annual household income of the sample respondents is ₹ 45,888 per annum.

Table 9.8 Household income of the sample respondents (in Rs./annum)

Rs./Annum	Kalachari	DC Para	Total
Less than 36,000	0	26 (52)	26
36,001–42,000	1 (2)	21 (42)	21
42,001–480,000	11 (22)	2 (4)	13
48,001–54,000	23 (46)	0	23
54,001–60,000	9 (18)	0	9
Above 60,001	6 (12)	1 (2)	7
Mean	53,376	38,400	45,888
Max.	69,600	96,000	96,000
Min.	42,000	32,400	32,400

Notes Figures in parentheses indicate percentage
Source Computed from Field Survey, 2015

The comparative economic prosperity in the non-tribal dominant Kalachari and the relative lower levels of income in the tribal majority areas of Dhan Chandra Para are evident from the pattern of income distribution itself, with the median of the former being much higher than that of the latter. However, we may note that the income spread in DC Para is much wider than that in Kalachari because of a respondent quoting of a much higher annual income which is visible as an outlier in the adjoining Fig. 9.1. The maximum household income in Kalachari GP is ₹ 69, 600 per annum, which is also an outlier though not as big as that of DC Para.

Table 9.9 shows that the annual income of the households from MGNREGS is approximately ₹ 12, 000 per annum in the district. The average household income from the scheme is higher in DC Para, ₹ 12, 420 per annum, which accounts for more than 32% of the annual income of these households. The contribution of the scheme is somewhat lesser in Kalachari, ₹ 11, 800 per annum.

One cannot deny the fact that the intervention of MGNREGS has had a stimulus on the livelihood of the rural workforce by augmenting their income levels. The responses of the sample respondents also confirm this point. The income earned through MGNREGS activities has certainly uplifted the economic status of the respondents, as is evident from Table 9.10. The differential in income level is highly significant across the study regions.

The increase in absolute terms has been higher in Kalachari as compared to DC Para, even though the contribution of MGNREGS income is higher in the latter.

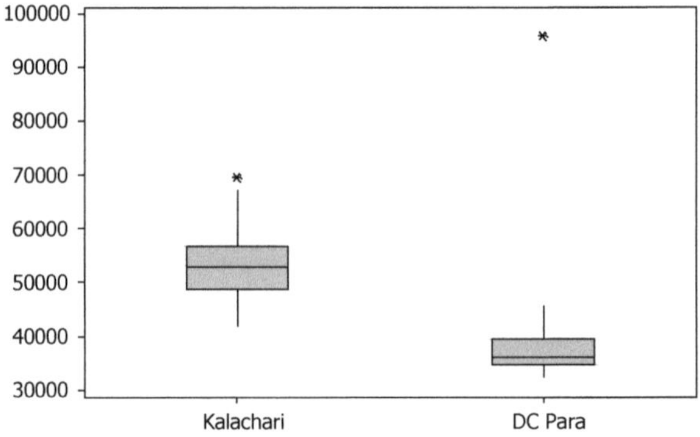

Fig. 9.1 Income spread among the MGNREGS workers in Dhalai (Rs./Annum). *Source* Computed from Field Survey, 2015

Table 9.9 MGNREGS intervention to sample households

MGNREGS contribution	Kalachari	DC Para
Average household income from MGNREGS (in Rs. per annum)	11,800.00	12,420.00
Average share of MGNREGS income in aggregate income of participating households (%)	22.1	32.34

Source Computed from Field Survey, 2015

Table 9.10 Results of paired sample *t* test for pre- and post-MGNREGS programme of the respondents ($N = 60$)

GPs	Average monthly income(Rs. in 2015 prices)		% Change	*t* test
	Pre-NREGS	Post-NREGS		
Kalachari	3432	4448	29.6	16.71***
DC Para	2431	3200	31.63	11.44***

***Significant at 1% level
Source Computed by the authors

The relative importance of MGNREGS in DC Para and on the tribal households is due to the lack of alternative sources of income for these people. Kalachari is situated near the subdivisional headquarter Kamalpur and most of the respondents often find casual employment in the town and thus their dependence on the scheme is much lower.

On the contrary, the residents of DC Para were traditionally jhum[6] cultivators and hardly had any access to wetland rice cultivation or any other rural non-farm activities and informal sector wage job. With declining jhum cultivation, these tribal people depend a lot on government welfare programmes and hardly have any alternative sources of income. The contribution of the scheme to these tribal households has certainly been phenomenal. The average monthly income during the pre-NREGS period has been statistically different than that of the post-NREGS period (2014–15) in both the GPs.

9.3.4 *Impact on Quality of Life*

As noted, there is no doubt about the positive impact of the scheme on the participating households. Increased household earnings arising from the higher employment opportunities have been the most prominent outcome of the scheme. All the households from Kalachari and DC Para have vouched for their increased employment opportunities, which is evident in the increased income among the households. Better healthcare facilities, fall in school dropouts and reduced out-migration have been the other positive outcomes from the scheme (Bhowmik and Bose 2015).

The status of asset possession among the sample households is reflected in Table 9.11. Considering the scenario of possession of 'production assets',[7] it is found that 16 and 20% of the respondents in Kalachari and DC Para have land ownership and the number has remained unchanged in the post-MGNREGA period also. Interestingly, the usage of bicycle has decreased in recent years in both the

[6]Also known as Shifting Cultivation; Jhum is the local name.

[7]Items which help in income generation.

Table 9.11 Assets possessed by sample households (%)

Assets	Kalachari		DC Para	
	Pre-NREGS	Post-NREGS	Pre-NREGS	Post-NREGS
Production assets				
Land	16	16	20	20
Bicycle	68	52	62	58
Consumption assets				
Mobile	72	88	24	74
DVD/CD players	52	64	64	80
Television	44	66	30	72
Fan	70	82	72	88

Source Computed from Field Survey, 2015

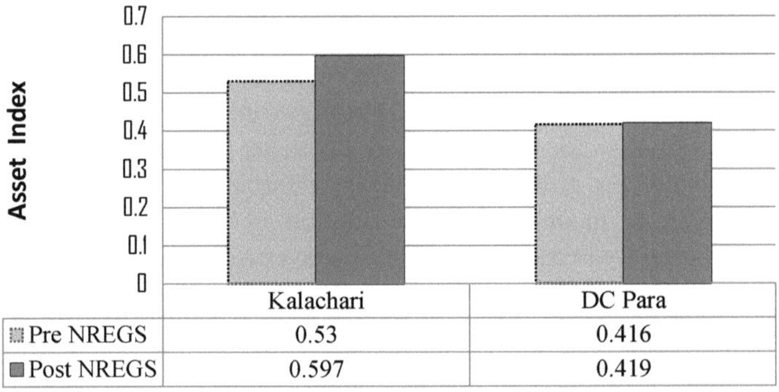

Fig. 9.2 Asset index of the sample respondents. *Source* Computed from field survey, 2015

GPs with the intensity being more in Kalachari. On the other hand, within the ambit of 'consumption assets',[8] it is found that the possession of mobile phones increased by large proportions particularly in DC Para. Other consumer durable assets like television (mostly Black and White), DVD/CD players (cable TV network is limited), and fan have also increased among the respondent households.

Figure 9.2 shows that the households of Kalachari GP are better endowed in terms of asset possession than the representative households of DC Para, as expected. The aggregate asset index increased from 0.416 to 0.419 for DC Para, while that for Kalachari, it increased from 0.530 to 0.597. It is important to note here that the index for Kalachari indicates greater changes as compared to DC Para owing to the fact that increased income at the latter following MGNREGS has been spent more on meeting basic necessities while in the former, for many households, the fund flow from the scheme has been a supplementary income and thus enabling purchase of assets.

[8]Items which do not directly help in income generation.

9.4 Recent Changes and Its Impact

That quality of life of the participating households has improved owing to MGNREGA in the Dhalai district of Tripura which is evident from the above section, whereby distinct increases in income and asset base of the households are visible. However, the issue which pertains at this juncture is whether the activities undertaken in the scheme over the years led to creation of sustainable assets. It has often been argued that the benefits accrued in the form of income generation for the masses have had a trade-off with creation of sustainable productive assets and livelihood opportunities (Aggarwal et al. 2012). One has no doubts that from the point of equity the scheme has had immense success in Tripura (Talukdar 2008; Bhowmik 2013) and Dhalai district (Roy 2012) has also not been an exception.

However, the new Central government appears to be focussing more on efficiency aspects as is evident in its proposed changes in the programme and its modalities. Linking the scheme to the agricultural sector and ensuring creation of productive agricultural assets by earmarking 60% of the works and funds at the district level for the development of land, water and trees is expected to augment the agrarian economy.

In this context, it may be noted that water conservation and harvesting, drought proofing, micro-irrigation and rural connectivity has been the most prominent form of work in DC Para as well as in Kalachari GP. Land development is also an important activity; however, the sample participants have themselves opined that non-permanent earth works have been of very limited utility.

The revised modalities also call for deeper focus on convergence with other departments for greater technical guidance, greater professionalism and higher resource availability for works. However, the issue of convergence is still at infancy in Tripura though proposals worth ₹ 567.34 crores, with 40% contribution from 10 line departments, have been received by the MoRD from the state in 2014–15.[9] In all, 249 works have been undertaken under convergence in the state across the eight districts of which North Tripura district has the maximum number, 82, followed by Unakoti district with 60 works. Only 10 works have been assigned to the Dhalai district.

In this context, it may be noted that the priority of works set up by the state government under the convergence road map[10] includes rural sanitation, construction of all-weather roads, construction of animal shelter, creation of water bodies, flood protection works, horticulture/forest plantation, vermicompost preparation and rural water supply, and assigns 28.5% of the Labour Budget of MGNREGA.

However, in the study area, none of the respondents were aware of any activities under the convergence scheme. One respondent, however, expressed that he had heard that convergence would be occurring in future and that is likely to benefit

[9]http://nrega.nic.in/netnrega/convergence/conindex.aspx, dated 28/11/2015.

[10]http://nrega.nic.in/netnrega/writereaddata/Circulars/Roadmap_Convergence_tripura.pdf.

them further. On the other hand, the GP functionaries are well aware of the convergence initiatives and though there are no such schemes operational present in their functional area, they are hoping to have such programmes in near future and are extremely optimistic about linkages to agricultural activities. Works undertaken for creation of water bodies show signs sustainability as fishery/aquaculture has been initiated in Kalachari.

Another area of concern regarding the scheme across the country has been regarding the leakages during the implementation owing to inadequate supervision and vigilance which the central government proposed to solve through strengthening of the social audit mechanism by involving the rural youth in a bigger way for overseeing purposes for greater transparency.[11] Issues of corruption and fund embezzlement have also cropped up in Tripura and some government officials have been arrested for their involvement in scams relating to the scheme in recent years.

The sample respondents, however, opined that they have not witnessed and are not aware of much corrupt practices or fund leakages in their area though issues of favouritism often exist while assigning work to the job seekers. The central government has also highlighted the delays in wage payment as a hindrance to the smooth functioning of the scheme, however, in the study area; all the respondents were unanimous in expressing that they generally received their wages within 15 days of work. The usage of the Business Correspondent model by State Bank of India has facilitated easier payments to the participating households in time. The active interest taken by the state government has enabled the smooth functioning of MGNREGS in the state, though planning for works is also a major concern in many of the states.

However, there are problems regarding the preference of non-permanent earth works in certain areas of the state including our sample GPs. Inadequate supervisory staff and limited technical staffs are the major challenges in the state as is observed from the state. The support of the state machinery for the scheme is well known and it is without doubt that the large number of person-days generated through MGNREGS has been instrumental in consolidating the power of the ruling government over successive elections at various levels. The introduction of the output-based payment system in 2014–15 is also considered as a challenge by many participants for obvious reasons.

Nevertheless, one cannot deny the fact that MGNREGS has had significant impact on the life and livelihood of the participating households in the state, as a whole, and in the interior tribal dominant parts of the state, in particular. The scheme has led to greater financial inclusion, ensured better education for the children, improved the health standards, reduced out-migration and lead to the empowerment of women in the state (Talukdar 2008; Bhowmik and Bose 2015).

In this context, it may also be noted that MGNREGS cannot be considered as the sole factor for these improvements in the quality of life because implementations of various other governmental schemes have been in practice and the outcome is

---

[11]http://nrega.nic.in/netnrega/writereaddata/Circulars/Note_on_changes_in_MGNREGA.pdf.

certainly due to a combination of all these factors. The building of all-weather roads through PMGSY has led to easier transportation access for tribal hamlets like DC Para as a result; there is a decline in the number of bicycles among the households who prefer using the newly available public transport system/network. However, one cannot avoid providing a caveat. The increasing monetary inflow has led to the stupendous growth of gambling culture in the sample regions and lots of the workers are hooked to the online single digit lottery which has spelled doom for many in region already.

9.5 Conclusion and Implications

On the basis of the above discussion, one has no doubt that MGNREGS has had an impact on the life and livelihood of the participating households in the Dhalai district of Tripura. Most of the participants in the scheme are from households that survive on selling labour on a daily basis. As they do not have any regular source of income, they look for odd jobs. The scheme assures them of a certain level of annual income, which is certainly an important component of their livelihood strategy. Provision of work and the additional income has helped their living conditions as is evident from the increased asset base.

The tribal households owing to their limited access to land ownership are more dependent on state initiatives and MGNREGS has certainly been a boon for them. The support of the state government to the scheme is because of their likeness for greater state role in the economy which enables in gaining political support as is evident in the electoral results at various levels in Tripura. The Left Front holds an absolute majority at the Panchayat, TTAADC and Legislative Assembly levels which was certainly possible due to the support of the tribal people, who have benefitted due to the monetary support through the MGNREGS.

However, the most interesting observation regarding the scheme in the district is the decreasing trend in the allotment ratios for the STs suggesting that others and unreserved categories are also not being neglected in terms of work allocation.

References

Aggarwal, A., A. Guptaand, and A. Kumar. 2012. Evaluation of NREGA wells. *Economic & Political Weekly* 47 (35): 24–27.

Bhowmik, Indraneel, and Pritam, Bose. 2015. Efficiency and Impact of MGNREGS in Tripura. *Social Change and Development* 12 (1): 1–19.

Bhowmik, Indraneel. 2013. MGNREGS in Tripura: A Study on Efficiency and Equity. *NLI Research Studies Series*, No. 102/2013.

Dreze, Jean, and Christian Oldiges. 2007. *How is NREGA Doing?* Available at www.knowledge.nrega.net, last accessed on 27 Jan 2012.

Dreze, Jean, and Reetika Khera. 2009. The Battle for Employment Guarantee. *Frontline 26* (01).

Editorial. 2014. Why This Attack on MGNREGA? *Economic and Political Weekly* XLIX (43 & 44).

http://nrega.nic.in/Netnrega/WriteReaddata/Circulars/Convergence_Guidelines_MGNREGA_Schemes_Rubber_Board.pdf, last accessed on 03 Dec 2015.

http://nrega.nic.in/netnrega/writereaddata/Circulars/Note_on_changes_in_MGNREGA.pdf, last accessed on 03 Dec 2015.

http://nrega.nic.in/netnrega/writereaddata/Circulars/Roadmap_Convergence_tripura.pdf, last accessed on 03 Dec 2015.

http://www.tripurainfoway.com/news-details/TN/14478/centre-s-mgnrega-fund-curtailment-in-tripura-rampant-corruption-shadows-mr-clean.html, last accessed on 03 Dec 2015.

Jha, Raghabendra, and Raghav Gaiha. 2012. NREGS: Interpreting the Official Statistics. *Economic and Political Weekly* 47 (40): 18–22.

Ray, Sanjay. 2010. Implementation of NREGS in Tripura: An Evaluation. *The NEHU Journal* VIII (1).

Roy, Jayanta. 2012. *Impact Analysis of Mahatma Gandhi National Rural Employment Guarantee Act Programme in Tripura*. Unpublished Ph. D. Thesis awarded at University of Agricultural Sciences, GKVK, Bengaluru.

Sen Roy, Deepjoy, and Debabrata Samanta. 2009. *Good Governance and Employment Generation through NREGA: A case Study of Gram Panchayat in West Bengal*. Available at www.researchgate.net, last accessed on 04 Aug 2013.

Talukdar, R. B. 2008. 'NREGA Shines for Tripura Women', *India Together*, June 30. Available at www.thehindu.com, last accessed on 04 Dec 2013.

Thapa, Namrata. 2012. *Employment status and human development of tea plantation workers in West Bengal*. Available at www.cds.edu, accessed on 12 Nov 2013.

The Shillong Times. 2012. *Tripura Tops in NREGA Implementation*. Available at www.theshillongtimes.com, last accessed on 23 Aug 2013.

Usami, Yoshifumi, and Vikas Rawal. 2012. Some Aspects of the Implementation of India's Employment Guarantee. *Review of Agrarian Studies* 2 (2).

Part III
MGNREGA: Micro Level Case Studies

Chapter 10
Inter-sectoral Linkages and Multipliers of MGNREGA in a Rainfed Village in Karnataka: Applications of Social Accounting Matrix (SAM)

Gourav Kumar Vani, P.S. Srikantha Murthy and Madhusudan Bhattarai

10.1 Introduction

Overall economy of India has been growing over 7–8% over the last one decade, however, unemployment and poverty situation are also rampant across the country. Over 50% of its population in India cannot make two dollars a day for living, and are living under acute situation of poverty. Even after 70 years of Independence, almost 1/3rd of the world's poor populations are concentrated in India alone. Thus, providing employment to swallowing pool of growing population and uplifting the mass population out of the poverty are now the two gravest concerns in India, one of the fastest growing economies in the world recently.

Since the initiation of first five year planning period in India since 1951 reduction of unemployment through creation of jobs and poverty alleviation are the major objectives of the strategy and planning process in India. Both unemployment and poverty are also in fact interlinked. Poverty reduction can be achieved only by increasing purchasing power of the poor which depends on providing them employment. Hence, most of the poverty alleviation programmes attempted in India

G.K. Vani (✉)
College of Agriculture, Powarkheda, Madhya Pradesh, India
e-mail: kumaragri.vani1@gmail.com

P.S. Srikantha Murthy
Department of Agricultural Economics, University of Agricultural Sciences, GKVK, Bengaluru, Karnataka, India
e-mail: pssrikanthamurthy@gmail.com

M. Bhattarai
Jalsrot Vikas Sanstha (JVS), 20694, Kathmandu, Nepal
e-mail: madhu.bhattarai2010@gmail.com

M. Bhattarai
ICRISAT, Hyderabad, India

M. Bhattarai et al. (eds.), *Employment Guarantee Programme and Dynamics of Rural Transformation in India*, India Studies in Business and Economics,
https://doi.org/10.1007/978-981-10-6262-9_10

since independence till to-date are somehow linked at employment generation, particularly for employment generation in rural sector (Yadav and Panda 2013). However, only limited success has been achieved in terms of reduction of rural poverty in India, and it is still an unfinished development agenda in India. Since, the work force[1] growth in India has always outpaced the growth of job creation and provision of public and private sector employment.

During 1983–94, unemployment rate decline from 8.3 in 1983 to 5.9% in 1994. However, after adopting liberalization policies in several sectors including agricultural, the unemployment in India rose to a decade high levels of 7.32 and 8.28% during 1999–2000 and 2004–05, respectively (Yadav and Panda 2013). The increased on unemployment in early 2000s was not all due to high population growth but was also partly due to structural changes in economy, and with rapid pace of growth of share of service sector in the economy. Interestingly, the overall economy grew at very rapid pace during the period of 1990s and early 2000s, but unemployment did not decline rather it further grew, creating a further rift in farm and non-farm sectors of the economy, and social tensions across the regions. Hence, it was felt necessary to provide jobs to swelling rural population specially in periods of agriculture to address the rapidly growing problems of unemployment and underemployment in rural areas in early 2000s. As a remedial measure to the growing unemployment and distress in the rural areas in early 2000s, the Government of India, then led by UPA government, enacted the National Rural Employment Guarantee Act (NREGA) 2005 to address rising unemployment and chronic level poverty in the country, by providing a minimum survival level of 100 days of constitutionally guaranteed wage employment in a year to every household in rural India. The employment to be delivered by the local authority across the rural India. This programme was renamed as MGNREGA and was also made as a nationwide programme in 2009.

With this background, this chapter quantified village economy wide inter-sectoral linkages of MGNREGA. More specially, taking a dryland village of a northern Karnataka state, in the following section, we provide various inter-sectoral linkages of the economic activities and transfers of goods and services across the sectors (agents) within the village economy. This is done by taking framework of social accounting matrix (SAM) (details on SAM are in Bellu 2012; Thorbecke 2000). Then, we present the detailed results on direct, indirect, and total effects of the MGNREGA interventions in a village wide context. Then, at the end of the chapter, we provide conclusions and implications out of the empirical analysis for improving implementation of MGNREGS programme.

[1]All the persons who are actually engaged in economically productive activities constitute work force and those who are either part of work force or are willing to be part of it are said to constitute labour force. Thus labour force connotes a larger meaning than work force.

10.2 Inter-sectoral Linkages of MGNREGA in an Economy

An economy consists of three broad sectors, namely agriculture, industry and service sector. Each sector has several different sub-sectors (Bellu 2012). Agriculture is considered to be the primary sector and a pre-cursor for development of all other sectors of the economy (Mellor 1976). This is also to ensure adequate employment and food security to all, including to industrials and service sectors of the economy (see, Mellor 1999). Agriculture is in fact a low productivity sector with surplus labour that should generate surplus labour and food for the growth of other sectors of the economy (Mellor 1999; Lewis 1954).

As agriculture productivity and farm income grows, it would generate additional demand for manufacturing goods and services, ultimately also helping to expansion of manufacturing goods and services in the economy. This type of backward and forward linkage of agriculture with the manufacturing and other sectors of the economy would also generate multiplier effects in the local economy (Mellor 1976, 1999), when there is an additional investment in terms of expanding demand of the primary sectors. An economy with strong linkages of backward and forward would also ensure for higher multiplier effects and higher growth in the economy as such via increased demand for input and production of additional outputs and feedback effect in the economy (Thorbecke 2000; Bellu 2012).

10.2.1 Impact of MGNREGS on the Village Economy

When MGNREGA was enacted in 2005, it was envisaged to strengthening employment and livelihood security of rural poor by ensuring minimum level of 100 days of employment to the households, at the same time also benefiting other sectors of the economy—and the village economy as such—by creating assets and public goods in the rural areas. In this process, it is expected that not only the households who participate in the MGNREGA work activities but other better-off households in the rural areas would also be benefited from MGNREGA due to transfer and inter-sectoral linkage effects across the sectors, and through the multiplier effects in the local economy (see Hirway et al. 2008).

A large number of empirical studies on MGNREGS available so far have focused largely on the efficacy of the scheme in achieving targets set under the 2005 Act. As a result, these studies have considered only direct employment creation through this programme, but neglecting the indirect and intersectoral linkages and village economy wide impacts produced by the MGNREGS investment done in the village economy (Hirway et al. 2008; Vani et al. 2015). In this context, this chapter assesses the economic impact of MGNREGS in a Markabbinahalli village in Bijapur district located in northern Karnataka state.

10.2.2 Socioeconomic Profile of Markabbinahalli Village

Markabbinahalli is a typical dryland village in Karnataka, and located in a vast track of semi-arid tropical region of India. There is neither a dug well, nor a canal or river to provide irrigation water for growing crops, hence farmers have to totally depend upon rainfall for farming purpose. Though this village is located nearby a seasonal river, by the name '*Doni*', its water is very saline and is unfit for irrigation. Because of the salinity of river water, groundwater in the village has also become saline, and not useful for irrigation as well as for drinking purpose. In this respect, farmers' in the village practice purely rainfed agriculture, a unique feature of farming in the village, and is also the reason for selecting to study[2] the inter-linkages effects of MGNREGA interventions. Other features and farming characteristics of the village are described in Vani (2015).

There are about 400 households in the village with a population of 2,545 persons. This is a predominantly agrarian village with majority of the households depending on agricultural wage employment (41%) for their livelihood, followed by farming (39%), caste-based occupations (7%), non-agricultural labour (8%) and others (5%) (Desai et al. 2012).

Out of about 1,000 ha of geographical area of Markabbinahalli village, 935 ha is under agricultural use (rainfed farming). About 90% of land is deep to medium black cotton soil and the remaining 10% of area comprises of medium black sandy loam soil. This village receives a rainfall of about 625 mm per annum within just 40 rainy days in a year (Details in Vani 2015; Desai et al. 2012).

10.3 Social Accounting Matrix (SAM)

Social accounting matrix (SAM) framework is used to study the inter-sectoral linkages within the village economy, and to analyze village economy wide impact of MGNREGA interventions. A SAM is an organized matrix representation of the accounts and transactions of different activities, actual or imputed, within an economy and with respect to the rest of the world (Adelman et al. 1988). In other words, SAM is a square matrix and an extension of Leontief input output matrix and is a useful tool to summarize an economy and its financial as well as non-financial (barter) transactions, occurring in a year, in a meaningful way with flexibility to add social dimensions (Subramanyan 2007; Adelman et al. 1988).

SAM works on double accounting principle of formal accountancy which states that every debit must be accompanied by corresponding credit in the books of accounts. Every row in SAM records a receipt for respective account and every

---

[2]This village is also part of Village Dynamics in South Asia (VDSA) Study conducted by ICRISAT, and so large set of households and other basic features of data about the village, even historical changes, are.

column in SAM records a payment from the same account (details are in Subramanian and Sadoulet 1990). Row and column total should match for each account in SAM. For the present study, a SAM of 82 × 82 size was constructed. Schematic representation of SAM constructed for the present study is given in Table 10.1. A brief discussion on major account is done in the following sections below.

10.3.1 Assumptions of the Village SAM

We have constructed village SAM for Markabbinahalli village with assumptions and restrictions on certain activities of SAM, as listed below. Details on these assumptions for construction of village SAM can be found in Bellu (2012) and Thorbecke (2000).

- The village economy is an open economy, i.e. there is free movement of goods and services between the village and the rest of the world.
- The village economy has the price elasticity of supply equal to infinity, i.e. the village economy does not suffer from supply side constraints.
- The economy is demand constrained, so that any increase in demand or monetary injection from exogenous account is met by the necessary production.
- All households are the owners of the factors of production. Therefore, all the factor incomes shall accrue to the household account in the SAM directly or indirectly.
- All the adjustments are quantity adjustments and prices do not vary. Input prices do not change either in response to changes in input demand and the production technology stays unaltered.
- Economic agents take prices as given and value of all income elasticity is unitary.
- The relationship between endogenous and exogenous variables are linear (i.e. hypothesis of lack of substitution between different inputs and factors for all productive sectors and between different final goods for all institutions).
- All the elements of coefficient matrix are assumed to be fixed, i.e. a_{ij} or average expenditure propensities must be calculated from SAM as parameters and marginal expenditure propensities are equal to average expenditure propensities.
- Expenditure equals income in endogenous accounts.
  Due to above assumptions SAM is a static analysis.

Table 10.1 Schematic representation of SAM constructed for the present study

	Expenditure							
		Activities	Commodities	Factors	Household	Institutions	Savings and investment	ROW
Receipts	Activities	–	Domestic production	–	–	–	–	–
	Commodities	Intermediate inputs	–	–	Household consumption	Consumption	Stocks	Exports
	Factors	Value added	–	–	Value added	Factor payments	–	Factor earnings
	Household	Profit	–	Factor payments	Inter-household transaction	Financial transfers	Imputed value of own inputs	Remittances
	Institutions	–	–	–	Taxes and donations	Financial transfers	–	Receipts
	Savings and investment	Imputed value of own inputs	Drawings from stocks	–	Savings	Savings	–	Deficit BOP
	ROW	Imports	–	Factor payments	Payments	Payments	Surplus BOP	–

Note: *ROW* Rest of the world, *BOP* Balance of payment

10.3.2 Different Accounts and Components of Village SAM

Major activities and components of the village SAM constructed are summarized in this section. Detailed information pertaining to these activities in the studied village can be found in Vani et al. (2015). Likewise, theoretical aspects of these elements are discussed in Bellu (2012) and Thorbecke (2000).

Activities The activity account represents here production activities in the village economy. Activity account in column makes payment for all services and goods procured as input in the process of production. Whereas, in the row, activity account can receive money payment from only commodity account for domestic supplies of goods and services (Thorbecke 2000; Subramanian and Sadoulet 1990).

Agriculture production and Charcoal making were considered as the production activity. Likewise, service sectors-related activities included the following: agricultural inputs trade, agricultural commodity trade, charcoal trade, machinery services, tailor, barber, grinding mill, repair and maintenance, private school, government school, government Ayurvedic hospital and SHGs. Within agriculture, production of jowar, wheat, pigeon pea, cotton and chickpea crops were considered as individual production activity, while minor crops such as sunflower, safflower and onion along with livestock were clubbed together and were considered as other agricultural enterprises.[3]

Commodities In this study, commodity accounts consider the same items as those under activity account. Commodity account supplies the goods and services to the village economy and rest of the world, and in turn receives the money from respective accounts. In the column, commodity account makes payment to activity account, and to savings and investment accounts for domestic supplies and for previous year's saved/remained goods, respectively (see, Bellu 2012).

Factors The factor account in this study consists of two components, namely labour services and capital services. Labour services component can be classified either into hired and family labour services or into male and female labour services as per the need. We grouped labour as hired and family labour uses. Labour receives capital services from different activities, receives contribution made by capital, and similarly it receives remuneration for providing labour to the different activities. Since factors of production are owned by households, these two sub-accounts of factor account transfer the money received to household account (details in Subramanian and Sadoulet 1990).

Institutions In this case, the institution account represents households (by land holding size sub-category), the village local government (in the present study *Gram Panchayat*), and religious institutions (here it is the Temple). The household is shown to be separated from the Institution column in SAM. The village local government collects funds from state government and also tax from residents of the

[3]Other agricultural enterprises are referred to as "Others" in original 82 $\times$ 82 SAM.

village. Tax collected is transferred to the state government through rest of the world. Gram Panchayat also spends funds received from the state government on developmental and non-developmental activities. Subsidies, pension, grants and aids are shown as financial transfers. Likewise, temple institution receives donations from the villagers and spends it on various religious activities. If donations exceed expenditure then it is a savings of temple institutions.

Households Households account makes payment for purchases made by households within and outside the village economy. It receives the income earned by households from different occupations both within and outside the village economy (Bellu 2012). Remittances sent and received are also channelled through this account. In this study, households were divided into five VDSA[4] categories, namely landless, marginal, small, medium and large as presented in Table 10.2. These households in each category were selected for survey with proportionate and purposive sampling framework as noted earlier.

Savings and Investment Accounts The saving and investment account receives the savings of the households (including cash in hand and stock of goods remaining at the end of the year including crop and livestock outputs). Savings were derived as the residual at the end of the year after deducting the consumption from opening stock at the start of the year and quantity supplied during the year (Bellu 2012). In this study, Gram Panchayat is assumed to invest in MGNREGP, first, Panchayat transfers money to savings and investment accounts and from there, it is channelled to MGNREGP commodity account, which is considered here as an investment.

Rest of the World (ROW) This ROW account represents the economy outside the village selected for SAM analysis (Bellu 2012). If any agent of economy (activity, institutions) spends on goods and services from outside the village, then it is channelled through the rest of the world account. Rest of the world account also channels in remittances, receipts and income from outside the village economy. In this study, to balance the account within SAM framework, balance of payment (BOP) is also assumed in the village economy, like every country has BOP account.

10.3.3 Calculation of Multiplier

Using the standard framework of SAM analysis, the empirical estimated SAM model is written as

$$y_j = \sum_i w_{ij} + \sum_i x_{ij},$$

[4]VDSA: Village Dynamics studies in South Asia, A Project undertaken by ICRISAT, Hyderabad.

Table 10.2 Households classification by landholding size and sampling framework used in Markabbinahalli, Karnataka, 2013

Category	Land classification[a] (ha)	No. of households in the village[b]	Sample size
Landless	<0.1	110	6
Marginal	0.1 to <1	43	3
Small	1 to <2	89	4
Medium	2 to <4	86	4
Large	>4	72	3
Total		400	20

Source [a]Markabbinahalli village at a glance produced by ICRISAT (Desai et al. 2012)
[b]Markabbinahalli Gram Panchayat records

where y_j is the *j*th column total and a vector of y_j would constitute *Y* vector. *W* is a matrix of endogenous accounts with elements w_{ij} and *X* is a matrix of exogenous accounts with elements x_{ij} (Details in Bellu 2012).

In the SAM model, the activity, commodity, factor and household accounts were assumed to be endogenous, as a standard practice of SAM analysis (Thorbecke 2000). Exogenous accounts were considered as public administration (Village Panchayat), savings and investment account and rest of the world account. These exogenous accounts were aggregated because expenditure from these accounts was all exogenous types (Bellu 2012).

Upon dividing each cell of SAM by its respective column total we get coefficient matrix *A* whose elements are a_{ij}. Mathematically, it can be represented as

$$a_{ij} = \frac{w_{ij}}{y_j}.$$

The above equation can be written as

$$Y = AY + X.$$

After some rearrangements the above equation can be written as

$$(I - A)Y = X.$$

And further, the above equation can be written as

$$Y = (I - A)^{-1}X = MX,$$

where *M* is a SAM multiplier matrix, consisting of coefficients m_{ij}. Coefficient m_{ij} is the total impact on account *i* because of a unit shock in account *j*.

In our case, we estimated three types of multipliers, namely, output, household income and employment multipliers. This was done selecting activity column for which multipliers were to be calculated and then all row values for commodity accounts, labour accounts and household accounts were summed up, respectively.

Percentage change in output of a particular sector can be referred to as percentage impact.

This was calculated as

$$\text{Percentage\_impact\_on\_}i\text{th\_account} = \frac{m_{ij} * x_{ij} * 100}{B_i},$$

where, m_{ij} is multiplier value for ith account due to a unit shock in jth account, x_j is amount of shock in jth account, B_i is the base value of ith account.

Note: A multiplier value of 2 is interpreted as 200% increase on that account only if $B_i = x_j$. That is, one unit of exogenous shock produces two unit of total output in the economy.

10.3.4 Sampling Framework and Data Collection

For the study, both primary and secondary data were collected for the full cycle of agricultural year 2012–13 (From 1 June 2012 to 31 May 2013). Purposive sampling was done for collection of data from the households. Following ICRISAT–VDSA study criteria and Government of India census survey criteria, households were classified into five strata, namely, landless households and marginal, small, medium and large land holding households as indicated in Table 10.2. From each household stratum only 5% of households were chosen as representative samples. They were chosen in such a way as to represent all occupations practiced in the target village, so that the sample truly reflected the village economic conditions.

Primary data regarding details of employment provided, receipts and expenditure were collected from different economic agents including shops (Agricultural input shop, canteen[5], provision store) and service providers (tailor, barber, drivers, labourers, and so on). Structured questionnaire were used to collect data from villagers. In the questionnaire information on the transaction both within and outside the village were recorded separately and sourcewise.

Secondary data were collected from Government institutions (Gram Panchayat, anganwadi centre, school, post office, healthcare centre, financial institutions located in Devarhippargi and Satihal towns, and ICRISAT VDSA database) and official websites http://nrega.nic.in/netnrega and http://panchamitra.kar.nic.in.

[5]Canteen is a service providing entity including tea shop. Canteen and tea shop differs only in respect of no. of different services provided to customers.

10.4 Inter-sectoral Linkages of MGNREGS Expenditure

Table 10.3 provides SAM of 82 × 82 dimension coerced to 16 × 16 dimensions. From SAM, multipliers were estimated, as noted earlier. Table 10.4 provides a matrix of aggregate multipliers (aggregate of output, employment and income multipliers). From this table it is evident that highest inter-sectoral linkages were through other commodity trade[6] based on highest multiplier value of 3.74, among all endogenous accounts. Other commodity trade was followed by charcoal making (3.63), cotton trade (3.53) and jowar (sorghum) trade (3.51).

On the whole, trade leads in inter-sectoral linkages and therefore a rupee of additional expenditure in trade brings more prosperity to village than any other activity. Agriculture is second in the list of activities having high inter-sectoral linkages followed by charcoal. MGNREGS was ranked at much lower level among all activities based on multiplier value (Table 10.3). In fact Government services like anganwadi, school and ayurvedic hospital had better multiplier values than MGNREGS. Trade alone provides employment equal to that provided by MGNGREGS and charcoal making, which employs workers throughout the year, and provides more employment than that by trade.

MGNREGS had very low multiplier value due to both low inter-sectoral linkages and high proportion of spending going to rest of the world. Out of total spending of ₹ 1.5 million (or 15 lakhs), only 28% was spent on labour and rest of the expenditure was incurred on materials which were purchased from outside the village. From MGNREGS accounts, within the village economy, its expenditure was only on labour component; hence the multiplier value for MGNREGS will be always less than the multiplier value for hired labour services (3.05).

10.4.1 Analysis of Impact of MGNREGS

Tables 10.5 and 10.6 provide the multiplier effect of MNGREGS. From the results presented in Table 10.5 it is evident that multiplier effect of MNGREGS on the whole village economy of Markabbinahalli was very weak as indicated by a multiplier value of the magnitude 1.86 (total of output, employment and income multiplier values). Of the 44 endogenous accounts, multiplier value was highest for hired labour services (0.288) followed by landless family households (0.107), small family households (0.095), marginal family households (0.069) and large family households (0.059).

A multiplier value of 0.288 implies that if the final demand for MGNREGS in the economy increases by 1 Rupee the demand for hired labour services in the

[6]Other commodity trade includes trade of sunflower, safflower, onion, milk, egg and any other agricultural/animal products or by-products which are not included in other category of agricultural products.

Table 10.3 Aggregated social accounting matrix for Markabbinahalli village (values in Rs. 000')

	Activity					Commodity					Factor services		HOUSE	INST	S&I	ROW
	AGRI	CHAR	NREGA	TRD	OTH	AGRI	CHAR	NREGA	TRD	OTH	L	C				
AGRI	0	0	0	0	0	34,237	0	0	0	0	0	0	0	0	0	0
CHAR	0	0	0	0	0	0	1,830	0	0	0	0	0	0	0	0	0
NREGA	0	0	0	0	0	0	0	1,503	0	0	0	0	0	0	0	0
TRD	0	0	0	0	0	0	0	0	17,420	0	0	0	0	0	0	0
OTH	0	0	0	0	0	0	0	0	0	26,539	0	0	0	0	0	0
AGRI	1,096	0	0	7,234	0	0	0	0	0	0	0	0	3,403	0	0	23,600
CHAR	0	0	0	820	0	0	0	0	0	0	0	0	1,010	0	0	0
NREGA	0	0	0	0	0	0	0	0	0	0	0	0	0	0	1,503	0
TRD	2,014	0	0	500	12	0	0	0	0	0	0	0	1,454	0	500	12,940
OTH	2,919	0	0	216	73	0	0	0	0	0	0	3,420	10,165	0	35	9,711
L	8,675	915	422	416	241	0	0	0	0	0	0	0	1,035	364	0	5,208
C	3,634	0	0	0	0	0	0	0	0	0	0	0	4,751	0	0	0
HOUSE	8,185	915	0	4,226	13,572	0	0	0	0	0	16,777	0	4,798	4,688	6,044	2,703
INSTI	0	0	0	1	46	0	0	0	0	0	0	0	7	0	0	6,510
S&I	5,845	0	0	0	262	1,096	0	0	0	0	0	214	11,695	1,505	0	0
ROW	1,869	0	1,081	4,006	12,333	0	0	0	0	0	500	4,751	23,591	7	12,534	0
Total	34,237	1,830	1,503	17,420	26,539	35,333	1,830	1,503	17,420	26,539	17,277	8,385	61,907	6,563	20,616	60,672

Where *Agri* Agriculture, *Char* Charcoal, *TRD* Trade (includes both Agro-input and commodity), *OTH* Other service providers, *L* Labour services (including family labour), *C* Capital services, *HOUSE* Households, *INSTI* Institutions (Panchayat and temple), *S&I* Savings and investment, *ROW* Rest of the world

Table 10.4 Aggregate multipliers[a] for selected accounts in SAM of Markabbinahalli village (2012–13)

Rank	Particulars	Aggregate multiplier
1	Others commodity trade	3.74
2	Charcoal making	3.63
3	Cotton trade	3.53
4	Jowar trade	3.51
5	Wheat trade	3.46
6	Anganwadi centre	3.37
7	Pigeon pea trade	3.35
8	Chickpea trade	3.20
9	Repair and maintenance shop	3.12
10	Family labour services	3.09
11	MGNREGS	1.86
12	Machinery hired out	1.41
13	Agri-inputs trade	1.40
14	PDS shop	1.05
15	SHG	1.00

Note Multiplier value of selected accounts are presented here, details results can be found in the authors' another publication, Vani (2015)

[a]It is inclusive of all the three multipliers, namely employment, income and output multiplier

economy increases by 28 paise. Of these 44 accounts 11 accounts had zero or negligible multiplier values. But since the size of each account and multiplier value for each account differed due to expenditure under MGNREGS was different, increase in value of these accounts when the final demand for MGNREGS in Markabbinahalli increases by ₹ 1 million (or ₹ 10 lakhs (hypothetical) are presented in Table 10.5.

Maximum impact can be observed in hired labour services (2.92%), the area where MGNREGS had been expected to have the highest impact. But this increase is likely to be very small due to low intensity of MGNREGS works and very large size of agricultural labour services (₹ 8.68 million, 50.23% of total labour receipts in the village) and very weak linkages of MGNREGS with rest of the accounts. This 2.92% impact on labour account is equal to 961[7] labour days or providing full-time employment to three households in a year at the rate of 320 days of employment in a year or 100 days of employment for nine households under MGNREGS.

Second largest impact was observed on small family households (1.02%) followed by landless households (0.95%). From simulations, on the whole, impact of

[7]Rs. 288,438/Rs. 300 per day = 961.46 labour days, Rs. 288,438 will be the increase in labour account due to Rs. 1 million (or Rs. 10 lakh) of additional investment from Table 5 and Rs. 300 was the prevailing wage rate for agriculture in the studied village.

Table 10.5 Impact of additional investment by MGNREGS activity in a village economy of Markabbinahalli, Karnataka, 2013 (a policy simulation)

Particulars	Aggregate multiplier for MGNREGS	Additional impact by injection of another Rs. 1 million (in Rs.) in MGNREGA	Base value for agriculture year 2012–13 (in Rs.)	Percentage change (impact)
Hired labour services	0.2884	288,438	9,875,531	2.92
Small family households	0.0950	95,019	9,288,363	1.02
Landless households	0.1071	107,097	11,282,571	0.95
Provision store	0.0370	37,015	5,031,080	0.74
Marginal households	0.0696	69,632	10,440,276	0.67
Medium households	0.0568	56,790	10,652,084	0.53
Charcoal making	0.0078	7,781	1,829,654	0.43
Capital services	0.0292	29,178	8,384,979	0.35
Other commodity	0.0116	11,622	3,831,617	0.30
Large family households	0.0597	59,690	20,244,151	0.29
Family labour services	0.0099	9,938	7,400,994	0.13
Wheat commodity	0.0027	2,646	2,522,986	0.10
Transport services	0.0055	5,490	8,891,502	0.06
Pigeon pea commodity	0.0026	2,555	8,880,075	0.03
Total	1.8555	1,855,486	169,099,228[a]	1.10[b]

Note Results for selected accounts are presented here, details results can be found in the authors' another publication, Vani (2015)
[a]This is not exactly column total since it also includes the value of other accounts, which had zero multiplier value, not shown in table
[b]1.10 is not the column total, instead 1.10 = (Rs. 1,855,486/Rs.169,099,228) × 100

Table 10.6 Summary of impact additional investment of Rs. 10 lakhs in MGNREGS in village economy of Markabbinahalli (from a policy simulation)

Particulars	Base value for agriculture year 2012–13 (Rs.)	Multiplier value	Impact of additional investment in MGNREGS	
			Rs.	% change
Output multiplier[a]	81,528,134	1.14	1,139,000	1.40
Employment multiplier[b]	61,907,445	0.30	298,000	0.48
Household income multiplier[c]	17,276,525	0.39	388,000	2.25

[a]Output multiplier includes jowar, pigeon pea, chickpea, wheat, cotton, charcoal and other commodities produced within village and all services provided in the village, i.e. trader, tailor, barber, PDS shop, anganwadi centre, government hospital, etc.
[b]Employment multiplier includes hired and family labour
[c]Household income multiplier includes landless, marginal, small, medium and large family households

additional investment of ₹ 1 million (or 10 lakhs) in MGNREGP was only 1.1% increase in total volume of transaction in aggregate or ₹ 1,855,486 (Table 10.5), but in labour equivalents it implies 6,184 labour days or full time employment to 18[8] households at the rate of 340 days of employment per year per household. That is, the indirect impact on labour employment was 84.46%[9] of total impact of 1.1%. The impact was very weak keeping in view the primary objective of livelihood security embedded in the framework of MGNREGA activities.

In Table 10.6, simulation results for multiplier effects of an additional investment of ₹ 1 million (₹ 10 lakhs) investment in MGNREGS are presented as output, employment and household income multipliers in a summarized form. Of all the three multiplier effects, output had highest value of 1.14 followed by household income (0.39) and employment (0.30), but the highest impact was on household income (2.25%) followed by output (1.40%) and the least impact was on employment (0.48%).

Output multiplier value of 1.14 for MGNREGP activity implies that for an additional rupee of investment made in the programme, there will be 1.14 times increase in the demand for output in the economy over existing demand for output. Similarly, an employment multiplier value of 0.3 for MGNREGP activity means that for an additional rupee of investment made in MGNREGP there will be 0.3 times increase in demand for labour in the economy. A household income

[8]Here, all calculations are done at prevailing agricultural wage rate of Rs. 300 per day. Rs. 1,855,486/Rs. 300 per day $\approx$6,184 labour days. This means 6,184 labour days/340 days per household $\cong$18 households (person) would be given a full year of employment of 340 days of employment per year.

[9]$100 - (961/6{,}184) * 100 \approx 84.46$.

multiplier value of 0.39 for MGNREGP activity implies that due to additional investment made in MGNREGP activity, income of households increase by 0.39 times over the existing income level in the economy.

10.4.2 Possible Reasons for Low Impact of MGNREGP on the Village Economy Could be as Follows

1. Scale of MGNREGP operation: MGNREGP in the village was carried out on a very small scale. Total outlay in MGNREGP in year 2012–13 was to the tune of ₹ 1 million (15 lakhs). This sum is too low compared to the size of the village economy, i.e. only 0.89%[10] of the total of all endogenous accounts of SAM.
2. Poor Linkages: Linkages of MGNREGP with other accounts were very weak, due to less proportionate expenditure on hired labour services in the village. All material components used by the MGNREGS for construction of building were procured from outside the village which amounted to ₹ 10.81 lakhs, about 72% of total expenditure incurred under MGNREGS. Most of the fund out of material expenditure was incurred on purchase of cement, bricks and steel for construction of Rajiv Gandhi Seva Kendra in Markabbinahalli village. This reflects the fact that projects with high capital needs and long gestation periods have lower multiplier effects at least in short[11]-run period. Thus, there was weak linkage between MGNREGP and rest of the economy. Hence, MGNREGP could not make any perceptible impact on village economy.
3. Material to Labour Ratio: The proportion of labour services among overall outlay was only 28% as against 60% mandated. This sum was ₹ 4.2 lakh, only a meagre 4.25%[12] of total labour income in the village.
4. Wages under MGNREGS: Agricultural wage rate (₹ 300 per day) and non-farm wage rate (₹ 350 per day) in the study area were higher than the MGNREGP wage rate of ₹ 174 per day. On an average, in a year, a family worked for 27 days under MGNREGP, 80 days in non-farm activities and 253 days in agriculture sector. With the prevailing wage rates for different activities, the total family income was Rs. 10,859,814.[13] Income from MGNREGP (₹ 4,698) formed only 4.32% of total annual family income. Hence, workers were also not attracted to MGNREGP works (Details in Vani et al. 2015).

---

[10](1,500,000/169,099,228) * 100 = 0.89%, as shown in last row–fourth column in Table 5.

[11]In this study, we have only estimated multiplier value in a year period, these infrastructures remains in village for long period and would have other indirect benefits which have not been captured in this study. This is a limitation of a SAM based analysis in static framework, as well.

[12]Rs. (420,000/Rs. 9,875,531) * 100 = 4.25%, as shown in first row–fourth column in Table 5.

[13]Rs. 300 per day * 253 days + 27 days * Rs. 174 per day + 80 days * Rs. 350 per day = Rs. 108,598.

5. Demand-Driven Programme: Instead of being a demand-driven programme, MGNREGP had become programme prepared and executed by office bearers as per their wishes. Hence local people did not show much interest in making the programme a success.
6. Migration: Since the village is nearer to Karnataka-Maharashtra state border and employment opportunities are better in nearby Solapur and district headquarter Bijapur, people tend to migrate to these places during drought year and Rabi and Summer seasons. Migrant workers earned wage income of ₹ 400–500 per day per person at the destination market, which was substantially higher compared to MGNREGS wage rate @₹ 174 per day per person. As a result, MGNREGA could not stop migration of workers to far away, but women and older persons who cannot travel far distance for higher wage employments (Details are in Vani 2015).
7. Awareness about MGNREGS: During survey work it was found that many of the villagers were unaware of the provisions of MGNREGS. This is also a reason for lower participation of workers for the programme—even among the pool of workers remained in the village and who were looking for the employment during slack period of farming. All of these also led to a weak supply driven programme in this particular village, unlike the case in other villages or other parts of Karnataka.

10.4.3 Limitations of the Study

This study has its own limitations in terms of methodology followed and the degree of generalization done based on the results obtained. These limitations can be summed up as follows:

(a) Status of MGNREGP in the village: Since MGNREGP was not implemented with vigour in the village, low value of multipliers was obtained. Hence, the result can neither be interpreted as failure of MGNREGP to generate employment and income nor its inherent capacity to generate employment and income.
(b) Characteristics of the selected Village: Since the village selected for the study follows a complete dry land agriculture, number of activities, volume and value of each activity are less than that would be possible in a typical wet land village.
(c) Institutional Setup: Since SAM is an analysis that takes into account institutions prevailing in the economy and MGNREGP is thought to be demand-driven programme, results obtained cannot be generalized to other areas with different institutional setup and different degree of demand for MGNREGP.
(d) Choice of study area: In this study, the sample village chosen did not represent the village with adequate MGNREGP expenditure. The choice of VDSA village of ICRISAT was mandated.

(e) Limited time availability for survey: Due to less time available for data collection work, instead of conducting census survey for entire households, we have adopted sample survey method for data collection work. This might have resulted in lower accuracy of estimates and also some errors in balancing the SAM, than the data that could have been gathered following the census method for the construction of the village SAM.

10.5 Conclusion and Implications

Inter-sectoral linkages and multipliers are the key concepts behind implementation of MGNREGA like rural development and employment schemes so that besides the direct benefit transfer to the programme benefited households in the rural areas, it can also benefit in terms of infrastructure development and asset creation in the village economy. Besides, by directly injecting over a million Rupees in a couple of months in a year in a rural village, and transferring this amount to rural poor, the MGNREGS also help in creation of additional demand for services in the rural economy, such as benefiting the local retail shop owners, allied services activities, transportation, production of food grains and vegetables within the local economy resulting in an increase in the purchasing power of large number of rural poor households. This in turn creates multipliers or inter-sectoral linkages in the village economy and its surrounding geographies. MGNREGS was thus envisaged in 2005 to provide employment during the lean periods of the year, and to offer benefits to large segment of the village economy.

However, it was found that in the studied village in Karnataka state, the programme had limited success in terms of generating higher employment and income multipliers. The reasons for lower value of multipliers in this particular village are discussed in details in earlier section. The key learning's from the outcomes can be stated in the form of necessary and sufficient conditions while implementing MGNREGS in other villages in dryland regions of India.

This includes creating awareness among all the stakeholders, including the workers, village leaders and Panchayat officials, about the programme and its provisions, well ahead of implementation of MGNREGS work in the village. This would also help workers to plan ahead of time, whether to stay in a village and work for MGNREGA activities or to migrate to other places in lean season of farming operations. The sufficient condition is efficient and enthusiastic leadership, well informed and responsible administration which will ensure that MGNREGS works would be taken in consultation with all stakeholders well in advance. Then, to develop strong inter-sectoral linkages in the village economy and to get better multiplier effects, the village administration needs to contain the leakages of MGNREGA amount for activity on machinery uses or skilled work or on materials and goods that would benefit more to the sectors outside the workers in the village and welfare of local village community. Of course, the distributional implication of the programme appears to be significant, and the local Panchayat and MGNREGA agency have greater stake in the selection of proper work/activities, which determine what scales of income and employment multipliers are generated in the village economy, as discussed in the Chapter.

References

Adelman, I., J.E. Taylor, and S. Vogel. 1988. Life in a Mexican Village: A SAM Perspective. *The Journal of Development Studies* 25 (1): 5–24.

Bellu, L.G. 2012. *Social Accounting Matrix (SAM) for Analysing Agricultural and Rural Development Policies: Conceptual Aspects and Examples*. Rome: FAO.

Datt, G., and A. Mahajan. 2013. *Indian Economy*, 436–472. New Delhi: S. Chand & Company.

Desai, T.S., G.D.N. Rao, V.R. Kiresur, and M.C.S. Bantilan. 2012. *Markabbinahalli Village at a Glance*. Patancheru, Andhra Pradesh: International Crops Research Institute for the Semi-Arid Tropics.

Hirway, I., M.R. Saluja, and B. Yadav. 2008. *The Impact of Public Employment Guarantee Strategies on Gender Equality and Pro-poor Economic Development*. UNDP Research Project No 34.

Lewis, W.A. 1954. *Economic Development with Unlimited Supplies of Labor*, 139–191. Manchester School.

Mann, N., and V. Panda. 2012. *MGNMREGA Sameeksha: An Anthology of Research Studies on Mahatma Gandhi National Rural Employment Guarantee Act 2005, 2006–12*. Ministry of Rural Development, Government of India, and Orient Black Swan Publisher.

Mellor, John W. 1976. *The New Economics of Growth*. Ithaca, NY: Cornell University Press.

Mellor, J.W. 1999. *Faster More Equitable Growth—The Relation Between Growth in Agriculture and Poverty Reduction*. Agricultural Policy Development Project Research Report No. 4. Abt Associates Inc. Washington, DC: Prepared for USAID Bureau for Global Programs Center for Economic Growth and Agricultural Development.

Subramanian, S., and E. Sadoulet. 1990. The Transmission of Production Fluctuations and Technical Change in a Village Economy: A Social Accounting Matrix Approach. *Economic Development and Cultural Change* 131–173.

Subramanyan, A. 2007. *Distributional Effects of Agricultural Biotechnology in a Village Economy: The Case of Cotton in India*. Ph.D. thesis, University of Hohenheim, Germany.

Tanvi, V., and L. Schuknecht. 2000. *Public Spending in the 20th Century: A Global Perspective*. Cambridge: Cambridge University Press.

Thorbecke, E. 2000. The Use of Social Accounting Matrices in Modelling. In *26th General Conference of the International Association for Research in Income and Wealth, Cracow, Poland*, vol. 27, August.

Vani, G.K. 2015. *Impact of MGNREGA on Livelihood Security in Bijapur Districts of Karnataka: A SAM Analysis*. Unpublished MS thesis, UAS, Bangalore.

Vani, G.K., P.S. Murthy, M.G. Chandrakanth, G.M. Gaddi, H. Chandrashekar, N. Nagaraj, and M. Bhattaraid. 2015. Employment Generation, Labour Migration and MGNREGP Intervention: Evidences from a Village Level Study. *Agricultural Economics Research Review* 28 (Conference): 267–274.

Yadav, N., and M. Panda. 2013. *Indian Economy*, 220–221. Meerut: Arihant Publication (India) Limited.

Chapter 11
Economic Impacts of MGNREGA in Dryland Region of India: A Meso and Micro Study in Selected States

N. Nagaraj, P.S. Srikantha Murthy, M.G. Chandrakanth, Madhusudan Bhattarai and Namrata Singha Roy

11.1 Introduction

Besides wage income and guaranteeing employment for at least 100 days per household in a financial year, in practice, the activities of MGNREGS have also provided other benefits like generating productive assets, protecting the environment, empowering rural women and reducing rural-urban migration. In this perspective, the MGNRWEGA scheme in fact also aims to achieve sustainable development in rural India through improved natural resource management. In India, poverty is still rampant, though Poverty Head Count Ratio declined from 45.3 in 1993/94 to 22.9 in

N. Nagaraj (✉)
GPS Institute of Agricultural Management, Bengaluru, Karnataka, India
e-mail: nagaraj.nareppa@gmail.com

P.S. Srikantha Murthy
Department of Agricultural Economics, University of Agricultural Sciences, GKVK, Bengaluru 560065, Karnataka, India
e-mail: pssrikanthamurthy@gmail.com

M.G. Chandrakanth
Institute for Social and Economic Change (ISEC), VKRV Rao Road, Nagarbhavi, Bengaluru 560072, Karnataka, India
e-mail: mgchandrakanth@gmail.com

M. Bhattarai
Jalsrot Vikas Sanstha (JVS), 20694, Kathmandu, Nepal
e-mail: madhu.bhattarai2010@gmail.com

M. Bhattarai
ICRISAT, Hyderabad, India

N.S. Roy
Department of Economics, School of Economics and Commerce, Adamas University, Kolkata, West Bengal, India
e-mail: nsingharoy@gmail.com

M. Bhattarai et al. (eds.), *Employment Guarantee Programme and Dynamics of Rural Transformation in India*, India Studies in Business and Economics,
https://doi.org/10.1007/978-981-10-6262-9_11

2011/12 (GoI 2015). When we consider the overall efficacy of the programme, several issues rose affecting the performance of MGNREGA on the ground, and misappropriation of fund at the local level, etc. In this context, this chapter discusses to what extent MGNREGA has been successful in achieving the MDG of 'Eradicating Extreme Hunger and Poverty'. Likewise, has MGNREGA programme been successful in providing 100 days of employment per annum and social protection to rural families demanding employment?

In this context, the overarching objective of this study is to evaluate the performance of MGNREGA in the reduction of poverty and distress in selected dryland states of India. The specific objectives are: (a) to analyze whether MGNREGA programme has been successful in providing 100 days of employment per annum to rural families demanding employment, (b) to what extent the MNREGA has offered social protection to the rural poor, and (c) how far this programme guarantees sustainable development through improved natural resource management conditions. The study combines employment generation aspect, social aspect, as well as environmental, and community scale of benefits through natural resource management in rainfed tropical region of India, which is a most vulnerable zone to climate change issues in the country.

With this background, this chapter is organized as follows: The Sect. 11.2 describes the context and the salient features of the MGNREGS. Section 11.3 discusses briefly the objectives of the study, then illustrates study methodology, source of data, sampling methods and empirical tools used in this study, Sect. 11.4 provides an inter-state comparative perspective of the implementation of MGNREGA across the six states selected. This is done in terms of provision of employment, gender and social inclusion and wages earned. Then, Sect. 11.5 analyzes micro-level evidence on the role of MGNREGA in selected sites in Karnataka state. This involves natural resource management and water conservation, village development, and community development. The last Section provides the conclusion and policy implications of the study.

11.1.1 Features of the MGNREG Act and Sustainable Development

The MGNREGA scheme marks a paradigm shift in implementing rural development programme in India by way of ensuring the right of employment to the rural people, especially women. Thomas (2010) argued that 'NREGA is unique in the sense that, it gives primary importance to women participation and empowerment as well as a corruption less implementation of the wage employment programme through social auditing by Gram Sabhas'. By ensuring regular work at minimum wages, the thrust was to be on 'employment first, with growth as an outcome', rather than vice versa (Bhaduri 2005).

The striking feature of the MGNREGA is that it not only provides employment to combat chronic poverty, to grow resilience against drought, deforestation, soil erosion, etc. but also aims at generating productive assets, protecting the environment, empowering rural women, and arresting rural-urban migrations. The impact of climate change falls differentially on people, and the poor are the most vulnerable to its adverse impact. NREGA, by encouraging works on water harvesting, flood protection, afforestation and plantation helps to insulate local communities from adverse effects of climate change (Sharma 2011). In this sense, the objectives and overall criteria adopted for implementing MGNREGA in 2011/12 were, in fact, consistent with the nation's overall goal and objectives (targets) set in meeting the Sustainable Development Goals by 2030 and its targets and milestones on several fronts.

MGNREG act is the most prominent act in the history of Independent India in terms of ensuring grass-root level participation of every citizen and beneficiary in local development process, through democratic process, multi-layered social audit and transparency mechanism by involvement of the civil society, comprehensive planning at village level towards sustainable and equitable development, etc. (Reddy et al. 2014; Pankaj and Tankha 2010). Some of the important features of the Act are to improve the quality of life of rural households who are vulnerable to out-migration in search of daily wage employment by channelizing the wage workforce towards developmental activities at the village level itself.

In this context, a study by Esteves et al. (2013) quantifies the environmental and socio-economic benefits generated by the works implemented under the Mahatma Gandhi National Rural Employment Guarantee Act. The same study has also assessed the potential of these benefits to reduce vulnerability of agricultural production and livelihoods of the beneficiaries, post-implementation (2011–12) as compared to pre-MGNREGA (2006–07), to current climate variability and showed reduction in agricultural and livelihood vulnerability due to implementation of works under the Act and resulting environmental benefits.

11.2 Methodology and Data

This study attempts to address implications of MGNREGA at both macro and micro scale of analysis. For macro-scale of analysis, we have analyzed implications of MGNREGA across six states of India, which are predominantly dryland states with higher percentage of crop acreage under a rainfed system of production than the irrigated production system. Then, the meso-level analysis is supplemented by doing a micro-level assessment on implications of MGNREGS on selected indicators of rural development at stratified randomly selected block, and then randomly selecting households in these blocks in the state of Karnataka.

11.2.1 Across States Level Analysis

The comparison across states on the impacts of MGNREGS on selected indicators of rural development and sustainable developments were carried out using the data and statistics largely from the official sources of data on MGNRGA implementation across the states provided by MGNREGA authority, Ministry of Rural Development (http://www.nrega.nic.in/). The national level data are too generic to make any meaningful assessment on any specific performance indicators of MGNREGS. Whereas, disaggregated data at the state level would discern the factors that make a difference in these performance indicators. Six states which broadly represent the dry regions of agro-climatic sub-regions of semi-arid tropics of India are taken for the analysis. Therefore, we have taken following six states for across states comparative analysis, and they are: Karnataka, Rajasthan, undivided Andhra Pradesh, Gujarat, Madhya Pradesh and Maharashtra. The comparative assessment of performance of MGNREGA on selected indicators across the six states of India was done taking data from MGNREGA report (2012–13) as well as MGNREGA reports for 2008–09 and 2010–11 fiscal years.

11.2.2 District and Taluka Selection in Karnataka State for Micro-Level Studies

The micro study was done by selecting few schemes based on stratified random sampling method in dryland regions of Karnataka. In particular, a modest attempt has been made to analyze the economic impact of MGNREGA on income and employment in the most disadvantaged districts of Karnataka to provide micro-level evidences along with meso (macro) level analysis across the states, as noted earlier.

Following criteria were adopted to select districts to undertake a study with regard to various issues related to the implementation of NREGA in Karnataka state.

In the first stage, selected districts of Karnataka were identified for a survey to cover all the three phases through which NREGA has been implemented in Karnataka state. In the second stage, based on the financial performance and number of person-days of employment generated, Ministry of Rural Development, GOI, has classified districts in each of the state into two categories: good performing districts and poor performing districts. Out of these lists, we decided to select four districts for field site observations and micro-assessment, covering two from good performance districts and two from poor performance districts. In particular, we selected Chitradurga and Davanagere as good performing districts, and Shimoga and Hassan were selected as poor performing districts, based on the MGNREGA performances indicators provided at the government reports (website). The same criterion was adopted to select two taluks\blocks within the selected districts. In the third stage of sample selection, within the selected blocks, four Gram Panchayats were selected randomly and one work was selected in each Gram Panchayat in such a way that out of four works three are ongoing and one is a completed work. In the fourth stage of sampling, 40 NREGA beneficiaries were selected per taluk to collect detailed information by using structured schedule on performance and implications of MGNREGA to individuals and at community scales. In addition, interaction meetings and series of Focus Group Discussions

(FGDs) were conducted with state, district and taluk/block level stakeholders of MGNREGS work activities.

MGNREGA work activities in Karnataka have been implemented since 2006, and by 2008, the annual budget of MGNREGA in the state was about Rs. 3,580 million generating 9 million days of employment across the 27 districts in a year. Focus Group Discussions and Participatory Impact Assessment (PIA) were used for in-depth understanding of the impacts and wider implications of the MGNREGA activities on the targeted communities at different scales, such as communities, households, and at individual members identified from the selected villages of Karnataka. The micro-data compiled from these schedules were analyzed using simple statistical tools like averages, ratios, percentages and graphical presentations.

11.3 Implementation of MGNREGA: A Comparative Overview Across Six States

The comparative assessment across the states on implementation of MGNREGA was done taking selected performance indicators of the MGNREGS, such as the extent of fulfilment of the basic entitlements in terms of days of employment, duration of employment, age-wise employment, season-wise work demand pattern and the extent of involvement of women for MGNREGA work. The results are summarized below by each performance indicator.

11.3.1 Trends in Employment Sought and Offered by MGNREGA

Table 11.1 presents the results of the comparative overview across the selected states on average person-days of employment per household and households with 100 days of employment. The results also provide a gleam of demand for and supply of MGNREGA related employment across states selected for comparative analysis. The performances of MGNREGA widely varied across the states of India, as clearly illustrated by the huge variation on these performance indicators across the states (Table 11.1).

For example, in 2008–09, the households registered under MGNREGA demanded employment varied from 20% in Maharashtra to 75% in Rajasthan. The demand for employment in 2011/12 also varied across the states. It declined at huge scale in Rajasthan, Gujarat and Maharashtra. This reduction in demand for employment under MGNREGA in these states may be due to more attractive labour market wage outside of MGNREGA, and outside of agriculture. We accept the fact that it is difficult to isolate the real impact of MGNREGA on employment only based on simple average related data as shown in Table 11.1. The employments are also affected by other economic factors like spillover effects from economic growth,

Table 11.1 Level of employment sought and offered by MGNREGA across the 6 states between 2008–09 & 2012–13

State/period	Households registered for employment (millions)	Proportion of households seeking/demanding employment	Proportion of households offered employment	Employment provided in no. of person-days per household	Proportion of women provided employment	Proportion of households availing 100 days of work
1. *Karnataka*						
2008–09	3.4	26.5	98.9	32.1	50.4	3.0
2012–13	5.7	33.0	68.0	49.0	47.0	7.7
% of change	68.0	25.0	-31.0	53.0	−7.0	157.0
2. *Rajasthan*						
2008–09	8.5	75.3	100.0	75.8	67.1	41.3
2012–13	9.9	39.3	86.3	46.0	68.0	8.6
% of change	16.0	−48.0	−14.0	−39.0	1.0	−79.0
3. *Andhra Pradesh (undivided)*						
2008–09	11.3	50.2	100.0	48.0	58.2	8.5
2012–13	12.6	53.7	84.5	45.0	59.0	8.5
% of change	12.0	7.0	−16.0	-6.0	1.0	0.0
4. *Gujarat*						
2008–09	2.9	29.6	100.0	25.0	42.8	5.8
2012–13	3.8	19.6	90.8	41.4	42.9	7.7
% of change	31.0	−34.0	-9.0	66.0	0.0	33.0
5. *Madhya Pradesh*						
2008–09	11.2	46.4	100.0	56.6	43.3	18.8
2012–13	12.1	29.3	99.4	39.8	42.4	5.6
% of change	8.0	−37.0	−1.0	−30.0	−2.0	−70.0

(continued)

Table 11.1 (continued)

State/period	Households registered for employment (millions)	Proportion of households seeking/demanding employment	Proportion of households offered employment	Employment provided in no. of person-days per household	Proportion of women provided employment	Proportion of households availing 100 days of work
6. *Maharashtra*						
2008–09	4.8	18.9	99.8	46.3	46.2	3.6
2012–13	7.1	23.2	98.8	53.7	44.5	14.2
% of change	48.0	23.0	−1.0	16.0	−4.0	294.0

Source www.nrega.nic.in (18.4.2014)

urbanization, non-farm rural growth, rural non-farm employment, increased literacy, introduction of minimum wages act, and so on. All of these factors also often coincide with the impact of MGNREGA.

Table 11.1 also shows that almost 100% of households who demanded employment got offer to work under MGNREGA in the initial periods of its implementation (2008–09), and the situation was same across all of the six states. This trend continued in Madhya Pradesh and Maharashtra, however, this was not the case in Karnataka, Rajasthan, Andhra Pradesh (undivided) and Gujarat. In Karnataka, unmet demand was as high as 30%. These states are with extremely varying socio-economic, cultural and political conditions. The reduction in the proportion of households for MGNREGA may be because of higher rural infrastructure development work, higher wage levels and an overall situation of labour shortage. These alternate factors may attract less number of labour force opting for physical work under MGNREGA with wage rate less than the statutory minimum wage in the state.

Over the same period, in Karnataka, Gujarat and Maharashtra, the number of person-days per household increased by 53, 66 and 16%, respectively, while it experienced a decline of 39, 6 and 30% in Rajasthan, undivided Andhra Pradesh and Madhya Pradesh, respectively. The sharp reduction in demand for MGNREGA work in Rajasthan could also be the reason for highest reduction in person-days in this state. This indicates that MGNREGA work could become un remunerative for them, given the lower wage of MGNREGS than alternate options in rural areas.

In sum, the set indicators in Table 11.1 provide us a mixed performance of MGNREGA across the selected six states. In some states, MGNREGA was able to generate sufficient manual work for unskilled labour, but not for all. It is therefore also important to know whether these jobs are sustainable or not, and how the situation would change in the coming years.

11.3.2 Share of Women in Workforce Under MGNREGA

The MGNREGA Act has given priority to women. Accordingly, in implementation also it has mandated a minimum of one-third of the work funded by MGNREGA should be reserved for women. As such, the women participation varied from 40 to 70% across sample states: in Rajasthan, undivided Andhra Pradesh and Gujarat, the proportion of women force continued to be almost the same in 2012–13 compared to 2008–09. But, the proportion of women participation slightly declined in Karnataka (7%), Madhya Pradesh (2%) and Maharashtra (4%). It means that the proportion of women participation has not changed over the years. It is a noticeable fact that, though in Rajasthan MGNREGA was not functioning well, the proportion of women employed was maximum (68%) among all the six states.

11.3.3 Duration of Employment Under MGNREGA

Duration-wise employment patterns across the states are presented in Table 11.2. Almost 50% of the households in all six states got only about one month of work annually under MGNREGA programme. Only about 30% of the households got about 60 days work per annum, and 20% got 61 to 99 days work per annum in the period studied. Only 9% of the households each in Rajasthan and undivided Andhra Pradesh, 8% in Karnataka, Gujarat, Maharashtra, and 6% in Madhya Pradesh got employment for 100 days per annum. The data suggest that MGNREGA activities were not providing 100 days of wage employment uniformly across states (Table 11.2).

Table 11.2 Duration-wise employment provided under MGNREGA in SAT states

State/period	Number of days work undertaken by families per year				Total no. of HHs. attending MGNREGA work (in million)
	1–30 days	31–60 days	61–99 days	100 & more days	
	Proportion of households attending to work (%)				
Karnataka					
2011–12	40.4	30.0	26.6	3.0	15.7
2012–13	40.4	26.0	25.9	7.7	7.0
% change	–	–	–	157.0	–
Rajasthan					
2011–12	34.6	30.8	26.9	7.7	17.6
2012–13	41.2	31.4	18.8	8.6	12.0
% change	–	–	–	12.0	–
Andhra Pradesh (undivided)					
2011–12	–	–	–	–	4.0
2012–13	42.8	28.2	20.5	8.5	14.0
% change	–	–	–	–	–
Gujarat					
2011–12	50.9	26.4	17.4	5.3	5.4
2012–13	48.1	27.0	17.3	7.7	6.2
% change	–	–	–	45.0	–
Madhya Pradesh					
2011–12	45.0	27.0	20.0	7.8	10.0
2012–13	50.3	26.8	17.3	5.6	7.1
% change	–	–	–	−28.0	–
Maharashtra					
2011–12	50.9	23.4	12.6	13.1	8.1
2012–13	31.0	37.0	24.0	7.7	4.3
% change	–	–	–	−41.0	–

Source Same as Table 11.1

11.3.4 Pattern of Age Profile of Employed Persons Under MGNREGA

An age-wise disaggregated analysis of the workers participating in MGNREGA gives better insights of the performance of MGNREGA across the states. The results of the disaggregated analysis for 2011–12 are illustrated in Fig. 11.1. Around 40–56% of the persons employed under MGNREGA were below 40 years of age. It shows MGNREGA has also attracted young and able-bodied persons, contradictory to the findings from several other studies on the topic.

In undivided Andhra Pradesh, around 50% MGNREGA workers were of 40–60 years, whereas, 41% were from the youth category. In Karnataka, the situation was opposite, compared to the middle age, 17% more youngsters were engaged in MGNREGA work in 2012–13. In the period, the total number of employed persons in Karnataka was almost half than that of the undivided Andhra Pradesh. But people working below 40 years were almost 20% higher than in undivided Andhra Pradesh. Major proportion of workers employed, i.e. more than 40% belonged to the age group of below 40 years across states. Thus, MGNREGA also increased employment opportunities for youth across the states, along with women and others.

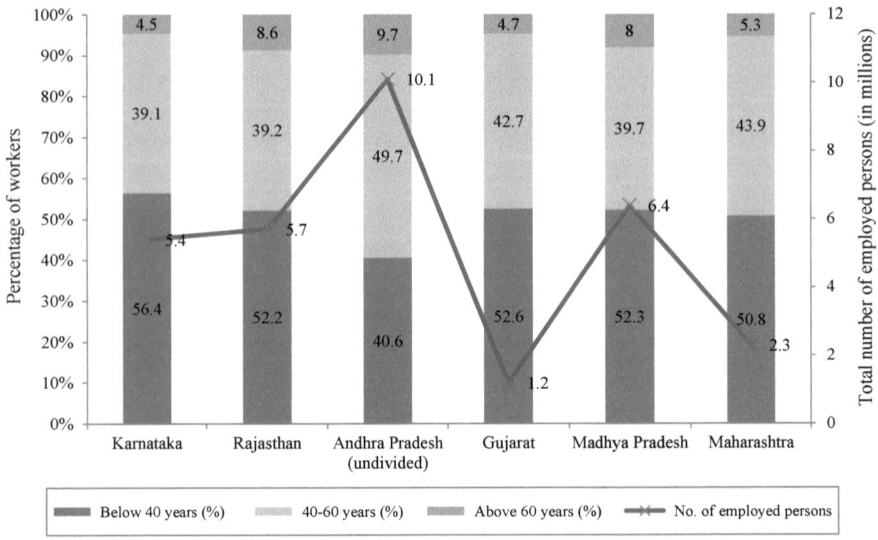

Fig. 11.1 Age-wise details of employed persons under MGNREGA in selected states

11.3.5 *Effective Targeting of Disadvantaged Group: Social Dimension of NREGA*

We also evaluated differentiating the impact of MGNREGA on the extent of coverage of socially disadvantaged groups like SC, ST and women? To test whether a social protection scheme like MGNREGA is reaching the right social group or not.

An attempt has been done to assess the extent of inclusion of the social groups (and women members) in relation to their share in work participation[1] under MGNREGA across the six states. The results are summarized in Table 11.3. The SC household participation in the MGNREGA also depends upon relative share of SC population in each of the state. The proportion of SC population in the state total varies from as low as 6.87% in Gujarat to as high as 18.45% in Andhra Pradesh. For the country as a whole, there was a decline in the share of SC households in the total person-days of employment under MGNREGS from 26.71% in 2008–09 to 22.02% in 2011–12, only with a marginal increase in Andhra Pradesh, Madhya Pradesh and Rajasthan. In Maharashtra, there was a sharp decline in participation of SC in NREGA work over the years.

The share of ST households in the total employment created in 2008–09 was disproportionately very high level—more than double their population share in the selected states, then it declined over the years, but still their participation is relatively at a high level. Earlier, Reddy et al. (2014) reported that the population share of ST in the first phase of MGNREGA implemented districts was significantly higher and most of the ST households suffer from extreme poverty, for whom, MGNREGA work is of great relief (and social safety nets) and an option to protect their livelihoods in lean season of farming. The higher share is a positive inclusion, and the decline of their in share in later years may suggest not decline in their actual employment to the programme, but increasing trend of participation of other social groups under MGNREGA activities.

MGNREGA is designed to encourage women to participate in wage payment under MGNREAG within the vicinity of their villages. On an average, the participation rate of the women's workforce surpassed the statutory level of a minimum of 33% set across the states. However, there are several factors like sociocultural, economic and locational factors which affect women's participation in physical work under MGNREGA. Earlier, Pankaj and Tankha (2010) reported that the MGNREGS works have broadened women's choices by opening them a new avenue of paid employment under a government programme rather than working for a privately operated farm or non-farm works, and by reducing economic dependence of women members in rural poor households.

The results in Table 11.3 also show that regardless of cultural differences, in all of the six states selected, women's share in MGNREGA employment was higher

[1]Earlier, Reddy et al. (2014) have also suggested to check share of SCs and STs in the total number of employment created.

Table 11.3 Share of SCs, STs and women in total person-days of MGNREGA employment (%)

State	% of SC population to total population[a]	% share of SCs in MGNREGA employment		% of ST population to total population[a]	Percentage ST share in MGNREGA employment		Rural female participation rate[b]	% Women person-days to total person-days	
		2008–09	2011–12		2008–09	2011–12		2008–09	2011–12
Andhra Pradesh	18.45	25.85	26.99	8.39	14.05	18.36	34.1	59.83	57.79
Gujarat	6.87	10.64	7.85	21.63	60.52	40.26	42.7	46.83	45.23
Karnataka	18.39	31.14	15.7	8.41	15.97	8.3	45.9	57.76	45.93
Madhya Pradesh	15.7	14.79	21.16	25.35	51.85	27.42	36.6	45.23	42.65
Maharashtra	10.93	18.46	5.8	13.42	36.62	17.11	47.4	47.78	45.98
Rajasthan	17.88	12.78	16.76	15.52	64.05	24.54	40.7	68.92	69.17
All states	17.82	26.71	22.02	10.63	31.94	18.25	32.7	46.52	48.15

[a]Census 2001 and http://www.nrega.nic.in
[b]FWPR based on NSS 61st Round (2004–05) Usual Principal and Subsidiary Status and http://www.nrega.nic.in
Source Reddy et al. (2014)

than average of women work participation rates in these respective states. It appears that MGNREGA opened up a new window for the ease of livelihood specially for rural women and successfully mainstreaming them into the contemporary process of economic development.

11.3.6 MGNREGA and Wage

The MGNREGA work related guidelines from Ministry of Rural Development clearly mentioned that the wages for MGNREGS funded works have to be paid according to the minimum wages as prescribed under the Minimum Wages Act 1948 for agricultural labourers. Likewise, equal wage rate is to be paid to male and female workers. When the Scheme was launched in 2006, an indicative wage rate of ₹ 80 per person-day was proposed. This meant that workers engaged under MGNREGA would be assigned physically measurable work equivalent to ₹ 80, as a Standard Schedule of Rate. Later, in 2009 the indicative wage was raised to ₹ 100 per person-day. Further, it was agreed to revise the base indicative wage rate of ₹ 100 indexed on the basis of inflation rate (Reddy et al. 2014).

Figure 11.2 presents the average nominal and real wage[2] rate per person-day across the six states selected from 2006–7 to 2011–12. Though nominal money wage rates have been rising over the years, the real wage rates have been virtually stagnant for Gujarat, Rajasthan and Madhya Pradesh. In contrast, Karnataka experienced a steep increase in wage rate in both nominal and real terms, especially after 2009–10. Whereas, in Andhra Pradesh, real wage declined over the years from 2006 to 2012. In Maharashtra, trends in wage rate behaved in ‘U’ shape, it started with higher value, then reached a minimum level of 80 ₹ in 2008–09, and again showed a tendency of acceleration from 2010 onwards.

11.3.7 Season-Wise Trends in Employment Generation Under MGNREGA

Table 11.4 shows the season-wise work demand pattern under MGNREGA across the six states. In Karnataka, the demand for labour to do MGNREGA work in the peak season of farming (Kharif and Rabi season together) has increased from 38 to 72% within a year, indicating scarcity of labour for farm work. Whereas, the reduced demand in summer season further creates seasonal unemployment, as farm work would also be very less in summer season.

[2]Real wage rate was derived by deflating the money wages by Consumer Price Index for Rural Labour at 2009–10 base year.

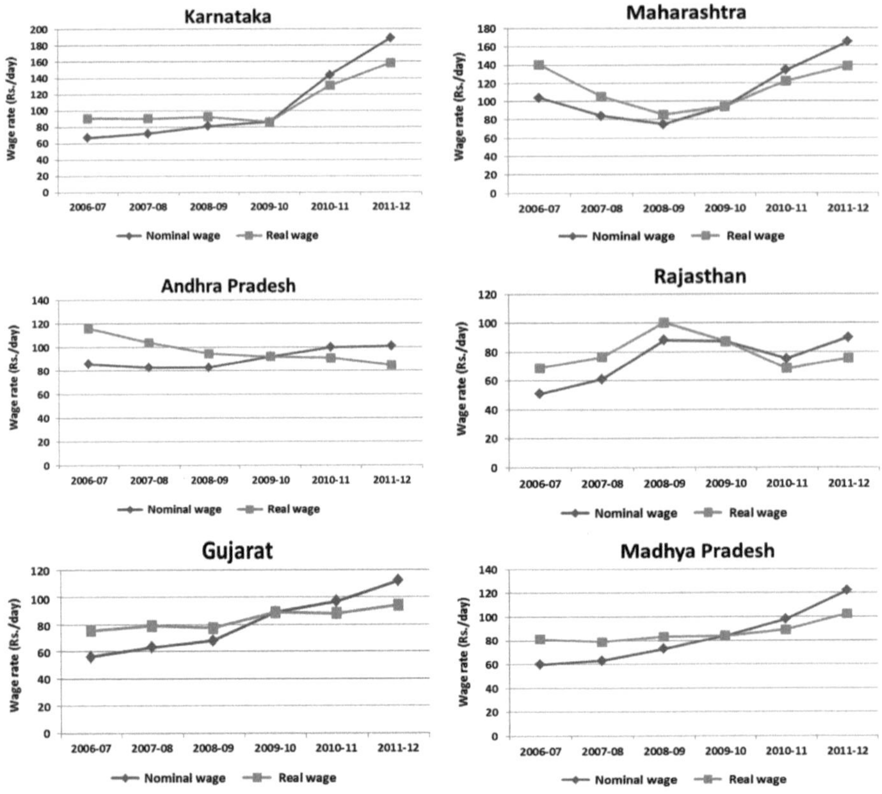

Fig. 11.2 Trends of MGNREGA nominal average money wage and real wage per person-day in selected states. *Source* www.nrega.nic.in; Real wages are 2009–10 base

Apart from that, total annual demand for employment in 2011–12 was highest in undivided Andhra Pradesh (47 million), and lowest in Gujarat in recent years. The low share of work for MGNREGA compared to annual demand suggest that MGNREGA is not the sole reason for the problem of labour scarcity in rural India. Several other factors are also responsible for this observed phenomenon on shortage of labour in agricultural activities in rural India in recent days.

11.4 Natural Resource Management and Sustainability Under MGNREGA: A Micro Study in Karnataka

In addition to 100 days guaranteed employment in a financial year to a poor rural household, MGNREGA also aims at regenerating the environment by enhancing productivity of land and forest by execution of works such as construction/renovation of irrigation tanks, ponds, water harvesting trenches and check dams. These

Table 11.4 Season-wise work demand pattern under MGNREGA in selected states

Season	Proportion of persons employed in MGNREGA as % of annual demand										
	Karnataka		Rajasthan		Andhra Pradesh[a]	Madhya Pradesh		Gujarat		Maharashtra	
	2010–11	2012–13	2010–11	2012–13	2012–13	2010–11	2012–13	2010–11	2012–13	2010–11	2012–13
Kharif (June–Sept)	9.1	14.8	37.5	32.6	30.7	31.9	32.0	22	33.2	19.4	33.3
Rabi (Oct–Jan)	28.8	57.3	14.3	25.9	16.1	22.9	18.8	24.1	25.3	13.4	16.9
Kharif + Rabi season (June–Jan)	37.9	72.1	51.8	58.5	46.8	54.8	50.8	46.1	58.5	32.8	50.2
Summer (Feb–May)	62.1	27.9	48.2	41.5	53.1	45.2	49.2	53.9	41.5	67.2	49.8
Total annual demand for employment (in million)	11	10	20.4	16	47	19.8	15	5	3.5	1.5	7

Note [a]For Andhra Pradesh, data for 2010–11 is not computed
Source As per Table 11.1

physical assets will persist for a longer time, if well managed by the local communities, and thereby MGNREGA has a potential to foster a regional economic growth. In this context, MGNREGA works are not only employment and livelihood generating (CSE 2006a), but also with the potential to produce sustainable rural development outcomes. In the following sections, we present the role of MGNREGA in water conservation activities, based on the detailed micro-level studies in Karnataka.

11.4.1 Water Conservation Activities Under MGNREGA

MGNREGA operational guidelines stipulate that priority of work shall be given to community assets and water conservation structures. In all the four districts that we visited in Karnataka, water conservation and renovation of traditional water bodies accounted for more than 50% of the fund utilized under MGNREGS (Fig. 11.3). In a relatively better-endowed district, such as Shimoga, which had excellent surface water resources, 60% of the MGNREGA expenditure was on water conservation through water harvesting, renovation of irrigation tanks, cleaning of irrigation channels, provision of irrigation to tail end areas and flood control. This reflects the important role of MGNREGA in water conservation activities. In Chitradurga district, 74% of the MGNREGA expenditure in a year was devoted to water conservation activities, by harvesting water and offering protective irrigation to farms

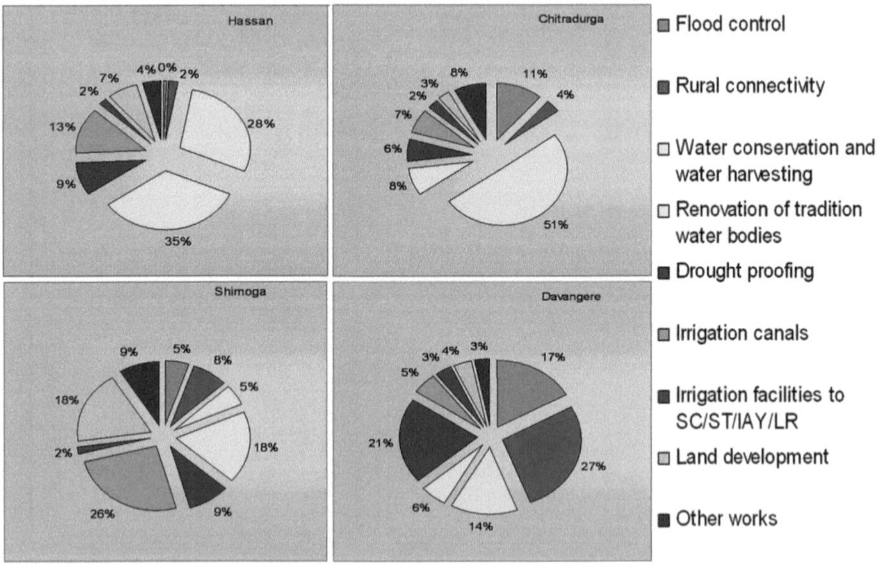

Fig. 11.3 Utilization of funds under MGNREGA (2009–10). *Source* The lead authors' project report, Nagaraj et al. (2009)

and drought proofing. This enabled Chitradurga to provide water to farmers during the critical periods and seasons.

Davanagere is a most disadvantaged district, where around 50% of the MGNREGA expenditure was incurred on water conservation. Thus, the micro-level results in Karnataka state also suggest that natural resource management has received greater emphasis in MGNREGA programme, as noted earlier.

11.4.2 Impact of MGNREGA on Village Development

In the studied villages in Karnataka, we also documented the type of benefit that accrued to the villagers by the community works like rehabilitation/desiltation of tanks, construction of water bodies, laying out of canals/roads. It was observed that rejuvenation of water bodies and water conservation activities considerably benefited the village—communities by augmenting additional area under irrigation and improving ground water recharge for all in the community. Consequently, in the studied villages, there was an increase in area under irrigation both under tank and well commands that enabled improved income of the farmers. The general benefits accrued to the beneficiaries by the types of rural development and NRM work activities undertaken by MGNREGA are presented in Table 11.5. Likewise, some of the selected village development works taken up under MGNREGA are shown in Fig. 11.4.

Table 11.5 Impact of MGNREGA on village development in selected districts

	Work executed	Impacts	District/Taluk
1	Desiltation of tanks	Improvement in water impounding Facilitating ground water recharge Double cropping Increased irrigated area Improved water bodies	All districts
2	Water conservation practices like construction of check dams	Improvement in water table was discernible Water table improved by 50–100 feet	All districts
3	Regeneration of water bodies	Drinking water available for livestock even during summer months	Davanagere (Harappanahalli) and Hassan
4	Clearing of drainages and diversion of flood water flow	Drainage related problems like flooding of roads and houses in the low lying areas during rainy days, blocking vehicular traffic and stagnant water creating health hazards solved	Shimoga (Bhadravati), Chitradurga (Hiriyur), Davanagere
5	Bunding and land development activities	Reduced soil erosion and improved land productivity	Shimoga (Bhadravati), Hassan (Arasikere)
6	Road works	Improvement in rural connectivity	Shimoga (Bhadravati)

Source PIN-NREGA-UASB, (2009)

Fig. 11.4 Village development works taken up under MGNREGA

11.4.3 MGNREGA: Community-Level Benefits

In addition to individual level benefits, community works like rehabilitation of tanks, construction of water bodies, repairs and laying out of canals have resulted in improving ground water recharge and augmenting area under irrigation. These outcomes benefit the community at large, and do not benefit only the work participating households. Here two unique case studies in the villages surveyed in Karnataka are presented to illustrate the kind, nature and scale of community-level benefits acquired under NGREGA programme (Table 11.6).

Nagenahalli village in Hassan district has a village tank spread over 23 acres, which was heavily silted and the tank bund of which was in a dilapidated state. Usually, the tank had supported only one paddy crop a year. Table 11.7 gives the benefits accrued because of MGNREGA work programme implemented in Nagenahalli in those years.

Rejuvenation of this village tank was planned under MGNREGS with a total budget of ₹ 10.3 lakhs (or ₹ 1.3 million). The work executed in 11 month period benefited 146 households in the village by providing them additional irrigation to 80 acres of land for growing crops. The tank now supports for growing two crops of paddy in a year, which is generating an additional income of ₹ 20 lakhs per annum. In addition to the employment of 7,102 person-days generated while implementing the programme, this MGNREGS work has also ensured drinking water to animals in all the seasons and has recharged 5 bore wells: these benefits have not been accounted here.

The second study was conducted in Kodakani village of Soraba Taluka, located in Shimoga district. Soraba Taluka falls in a flat terrain, which possesses about 1600 tanks. Unfortunately, earlier, most of these tanks were neglected resulting in heavy siltation of these tanks, with reduced live storage capacity of the tanks. Feeder channels of most of the tanks were clogged and hence water inflow into the tanks gradually declined. All of these factors also led to a reduction in irrigation water availability, reduced cropping intensity, productivity and employment opportunities, but paradoxically also with unexpected flooding during a heavy downpour. As a result, the agricultural workers migrated to coffee growing areas in the neighbouring districts for stable employment and income.

Table 11.6 Case studies

	Case study 1	Case study 2
Location	Nagenahalli in Merkuli Gram Panchayat; Hassan District	Kodakani Village, SorabaTaluk, Shimoga District
Year	2007–08	2007–08
Type of work executed	Disiltation of Tank and strengthening of tank	Desilting of tank and repair of feeder channel
Total budget	Rs. 10.3 Lakhs. (Material: 4.48 Lakhs, Labour: 5.82 Lakhs)	Rs. 6.5 Lakhs

Table 11.7 Benefit accrued by MGNREGA activity in Nagenahalli

Particulars of benefit accrued	Status before MGNREGA	Status after MGNREGA
Area irrigated by the tank (Acres)	80	160 (in two seasons)
Cropping intensity (percent)	100	200
Paddy production in a year in the tank command area (quintals)	2000	4000
Additional returns (Rupees)	–	20 lakhs
Number of families benefited by additional irrigated water availability	–	146
Employment generated by MGNREGA (person-days)	–	7102
Number of bore wells recharged	–	5
Water availability for animals	–	In all seasons

Source Field Survey by authors in 2010 and in 2011

Haluru tank under the Kodakani Gram Panchayat, under Soraba Taluk in Shimoga district, has a command area of over 300 acres. Due to heavy siltation, the tank was not supporting more than one crop in a year until 2008. Under NREGS, with a budget allocation of ₹ 6.5 lakhs, a feeder channel with a length of 0.5 km was repaired and the tank was desilted after 2008. As a result, second paddy crop could be cultivated in 100 acres and more than 42 bore wells were recharged. The production of Paddy then increased by 20–22 quintals per acre for all. This is a community scale benefit of work implemented under the MGNREGA, which was also actively supported by the villagers, especially the wage earners. The work force that undertook the work, women folk who often faced the severity of the water shortage in a local community outnumber the male workers by 2.5 times. This development is in the right direction of women empowerment, as well.

11.5 Conclusions and Implications

The results from comparative analysis across the states and micro-level analysis presented in this Chapter clearly suggest that at meso- or macro-scale of analysis, the performance of MGNREGA is uneven across the six states selected for the study. Even after 6–7 years of its implementation, the performance of MGNREGA in terms of person-days generated varied widely across the six states studied. The potentiality of MGNREGA work to provide 100 days of wage employment is far away from its realized evidences across the states. Only 7–12% of the households out of total participants availed 100 days of employment per annum under the MGNREGA work.

Likewise, the trend of MGNREGA work of absorbing higher proportion of youth population poses some serious implication in terms of youth employment in other sectors of rural economy. This increased demand for labour to do MGNREGA work in Kharif and Rabi seasons in Karnataka, whereas the reduced demand for work in summer season creates a seasonal imbalance on employment in the rural economy. Given the huge variations in real wages of agricultural and employments under MGNREGA across the states, problem of increased labour scarcity, which is more prominent in the peak season of farming in India, cannot be attributed only to MGNREGA, but it is due to a range of complex socio-economic and structural factors prevailing in the country. The spillover effects of economic growth, urbanization, non-farm rural growth, rural non-farm employment, increased literacy, the introduction of minimum wage act, etc. all of these factors also affect rural labour market and level of labour scarcity in a place at any moment of time, as discussed in the Chapter.

To have a maximum outcome and livelihood impacts upon rural poor, the time frame of MGNREGA work needs to be adjusted such a way it would ensure employment security in the villages in slack season of farming. It must create more jobs and more employment in slack season of farming so that the agriculture sector would not be adversely affected at the same time livelihood of the rural poor will also get secured. In Karnataka, only 50% of the households, who registered under MGNREGA, actually demanded employment under MGNREGA, which is due to attractive labour market opportunity outside of MGNREGA and outside of agriculture in Karnataka state. Over 60% of households in Karnataka were provided employment for less than 60 days under the MGNREGA.

Moreover, besides employment benefits, community-level benefits of MGNRGS, through asset creation, are also substantial. They include desilting irrigation tanks and construction of check dams benefiting bore wells through groundwater recharge, ensured source of drinking water for livestock even during summer months, improved rural connectivity due to more rural access roads in villages, construction of school building for children, and reduction in drudgery of travelling to far away schools, and so on. These indirect benefits of MGNREGS were also substantial level.

The overall sub-optimal performance of MGNREGA in the six states selected here may be due to the fact that MGNREGA wage rates are not as remunerative as market prevailing wages rate for un-skill labour work for non-farm activities. Hence workers usually prefer for non-farm labour, especially sand mining and other rural non-farm work, which provides as high as around Rs. 600 per person per truck load (in couple of hours), compared to ₹ 350 per person-days under MGNREGA work scheme in Karnataka. Also, women cannot do drudgery work as done by men and in the event of non-availability of men labour, the only alternative left is to use the machinery to meet the compulsory need to execute MGNREGS works in rural areas. Thus, the use of machinery in MGNREGS in many cases is by default needed.

Though MGNREGA works were able to assure sustainable development through improved Natural Resource Management (NRM) in some regions, but it also failed in most of the cases in providing social protection where the leadership of implementing agencies of MGNREGS was weak and the leaders lacked dynamism in terms of selection of work and making participation of the whole village while selecting work activities and in bringing more funds to the village from high-level authority. Stringent rules and regulations of MGNREGS also resulted in an inordinate delay in executing works and making timely payment to workers, which deter the labour force who need daily payments of their wages to purchase the daily food needs.

Acknowledgements We wish to thank immensely the Ministry of Rural Development, GOI, New Delhi for having funded this research project, through the University of Agricultural Science, Bangalore, and Dr. Rita Sharma, Secretary Rural Development, Ms. Amita Sharma, Joint Secretary, NREGA, MoRD, Ms. Neelakshi Mann and other staff of MoRD for their guidance and support. Our special thanks to Dr. P. C. Jaffer, IAS, Director MGNREGS, Government of Karnataka, Bengaluru, for his support and encouragement. We would like to thank our respondents and key resource persons for sparing their valuable time during our interactive meetings and survey work across the districts/talukas in Karnataka state.

References

Bhaduri, Amit. 2005. *Development with Dignity*, 107. New Delhi: National Book Trust.

CSE. 2006a. An Ecological Act: A Backgrounder to the National Rural Employment Guarantee Act. Draft report of a public hearing, 17 August 06, New Delhi: Centre for Science and Environment.

Esteves, Tashina, K.V. Rao, Bhaskar Sinha, S.S. Roy, Bhaskar Rao, Shashidharkumar Jha, Ajay Bhan Singh et al. 2013. Agricultural and Livelihood Vulnerability Reduction through the MGNREGA. *Economic and Political Weekly* 48 (52).

GOI. 2010. Mahatma Gandhi National Rural Employment Guarantee Act 2005: Report to the People. 2 February 2006 to 2 February 2010, MoRD, GoI.

GOI. 2015. *India Country Report: Statistical Appraisal*. GOI, New Delhi: Ministry of Statistical and Planning.

MDG. 2009. The Millennium Development Goals Report 2009, New York, United Nations. Available at: http://www.un.org/millenniumgoals/pdf/MDG_Report_2009_ENG.pdf.

MIS Report. 2014. http://164.100.129.6/netnrega/MISreport3.aspx?fin_year=2013–2014.

MIS Report. 2013. http://164.100.129.6/netnrega/MISreport3.aspx?fin_year=2012–2013.

MIS Report. 2011. http://164.100.129.6/netnrega/MISreport3.aspx?fin_year=2010–2011.

MIS Report. 2009. http://nrega.nic.in/netnrega/MISreport1.aspx?archive=Y&fin_year=2008–2009.

Nagaraj, N., P.S. Srikantha Murthy, H. Chandrashekar, G.S. Mahadevaiah, and M.G. Honnaiahand Chandrakanth. 2009. *Professional Institutional Network: National Rural Employment Guarantee Act (NREGA)*. Bengaluru: University of Agricultural Science.

Pankaj, A., and R. Tankha. 2010. Empowerment Effects of the NREGS on Women Workers: A Study in Four States. *Economic and Political Weekly* 40 (30): 45–55.

Narasimha, Reddy D., A. Reddy, N. Amarender, Nagaraj, and Bantilan Cynthia. 2014. *Impact of Mahatma Gandhi National Rural Employment Guarantee Act (MGNREGA) on Rural Labour Markets*. Working paper series no. 58. Patancheru-502324, Andhra Pradesh, India: International Crops Research Institute for the Semi-Arid tropics. 40 pp.

Sharma, A. 2011. The Mahatma Gandhi National Rural Employment Guarantee Act, in Sharing Innovative Experiences-Successful Social Protection Floor Experiences, New York, USA: UNDP.

Sudarshan, R.M., R. Bhattacharya, and G. Fernandez. 2010. Women's Participation in the NREGA: Some Observations from Fieldwork in Himachal Pradesh. *Kerala and Rajasthan. IDS Bulletin* 41 (4): 77–83.

Thomas, E. M. 2010. The Relevance of NREGA in Ensuring a Corruption Less Wage Employment Programme and Women Empowerment A Case Study. http://www.napsipag.org/pdf/EM_ THOMAS. Pdf.

Part IV
MGNREGA: Governance Challenges and It's Future Perspectives

Chapter 12
Can Employment Guarantee Scheme (EGS) Ensure Inclusive and Resilient Growth in Rainfed Areas: Convergence Lessons Learned and Way Forward

Ravindra Adusumilli and Ashima Chaudhary

12.1 Introduction

MGNREGS emphasises on drought proofing, soil conservation, land productivity and water security as the principle areas for taking up works under the sub-head of natural resources development. Creation of 'durable assets' is a central tenet of investment decisions in the scheme; it protects MGNREGS investments from being used as 'labour subsidies' in production which can potentially influence crop choices and production relations.

Converging MGNREGS with other regular programmes of government to contribute to agriculture growth has been a major policy concern recently. Several efforts were made across the country and by the Department of Rural Development (DoRD) to evolve convergence guidelines (Ministry of Rural Development 2009-10). The expanded list of permissible activities defined in the revised guidelines of the scheme also emanates from this concern.[1]

This paper presents a case to make MGNREGS more effective in strengthening agriculture, livestock and fisheries in rainfed areas. It builds on the field experiences

---

[1]GO No. 11017/17/2008-NREGA (UN) (Part-II) approved works as per the revised Schedule I (Para 4 (1) 1. (ii)) of the MGNREGA and GO No. 11017/17/2008-NREGA (UN) (Part-II) Comprehensive treatment of watersheds—Works based on watershed management under MGNREGA as per the revised schedule I, MGNREGA.

R. Adusumilli (✉) · A. Chaudhary
Watershed Support Services and Activities Network (WASSAN), Hyderabad, India
e-mail: raviwn@gmail.com

A. Chaudhary
e-mail: caashima@gmail.com
URL: http://www.wassan.org

M. Bhattarai et al. (eds.), *Employment Guarantee Programme and Dynamics of Rural Transformation in India*, India Studies in Business and Economics,
https://doi.org/10.1007/978-981-10-6262-9_12

of WASSAN and Revitalising Rainfed Agriculture Network in engaging with MGNREGS and agriculture in rainfed areas across several states.[2]

A brief overview of impacts of the programme across the country is first attempted. This is followed by an analysis of the convergence efforts by DoRD and some state governments as can be observed from the Government Orders/Department Circulars. Gaps in the convergence framework are brought out based on the field experiences. Against this backdrop, a framework is presented to use MGNREGS investments for strengthening rainfed agriculture systems. The discourse, as explained later, is around having more interpretative flexibility in defining 'durable assets' and taking a broader perspective on what constitutes 'natural resources development'. In this effort, it appears that the primacy of MGNREGS is better reflected as a means of securing employment guarantee, and not to subsume it under asset creation, enhancing efficiencies, or any other social or economic objective.

12.2 MGNREGS and Its Impacts on Agriculture

Much of the impacts of MGNREGS were mainly through improvements in land development, water harvesting and bringing more land into productive use. This is expected as around 51% of the overall investments in MGNREGS were on soil and water conservation and related works (Table 12.1).

A comprehensive review of studies on the impressive impacts of MGNREGS was presented in 'MGNREGA Sameeksha' (Shah 2012).The review presents the multifarious impacts of MGNREGS across the country. Impacts are observed on aspects of increased area under irrigation, land brought into cultivation, changes in crop pattern, increased productivity of crops. Based on a multidisciplinary rapid survey of the works taken up in Chitradurga district of Karnataka, Tiwari et al. (2011) conclude on the multiple gains of the investments on providing environmental services and reduced vulnerability to climate change.

The varied impacts of MGNREGS mostly emanate from the derivatives of works related to soil and water conservation, land development, silt application and plantation. As the 'MGNREGA Sameeksha' observes, 'literature on the impact of MGNREGA on agricultural productivity is neither uniform nor conclusive'. There will also be problems of attributing impacts to the works alone. The impact of MGNREGS on wage markets, farm labour scarcity and related impact on agriculture is much contested. The present paper stays away from this debate and focuses on the Scheme's direct relation with agriculture development.

[2]Rainfed areas are considered as those with less than 40% irrigation. Revitalising Rainfed Agriculture Network (www.rainfedindia.org) is a national network engaged in evolving relevant policy framework for the development of rainfed areas.

Table 12.1 Category-wise expenditure of MGNREGS in financial year 2013–14 and 2015–16

Category of work	Expenditure in FY 2013–14 (in %)	Expenditure in FY 2014–15 (in %)	Expenditure in FY 20015–16 (in %)
Rural connectivity	35.13	32.61	26.97
Water conservation and water harvesting	13.64	13.83	14.32
Renovation of traditional water bodies	12.09	12.23	14.01
Category IV work	7.83	10.75	11.89
Land development	8.93	8.63	9.9
Drought proofing	5.95	5.33	6.72
Micro irrigation works	5.26	4.77	6.41
Flood control and protection	5.09	4.07	4.16
Other works	1.9	1.69	1.95
Rural sanitation	2.46	3.21	1.25
Fisheries	0.14	0.23	0.22
Rural drinking water	0.08	0.10	0.1
Total	100	100	100

Source MGNREGS Reports
http://164.100.129.6/netnrega/MISreport4.aspx?fin_year=2013-2014&rpt=RP and http://164.100.129.6/GRAPH/graphnewxml.aspx?source=national

12.3 Practices on Convergence

MGNREGA clearly mandates convergence of investments. MGNREGA with its inter-sectoral approach opens up opportunities for convergence with different programmes. A broader view on convergence is taken in the 'MGNREGA Sameekhsa', 'The aim of convergence is to optimise public investments made under existing schemes through suggested ways of linking and steering them towards a common/shared recipient end, both physical (area, infrastructure, natural resource) and human (person, group, agency)'. 'Area' and 'Agency' are the two bases for convergence in this approach.

The following three types of convergence mechanisms are generally observed in practice:

1. Agency-based convergence: Budgets are made available to an Agency for implementation of works in its mandate; an example is MGNREGS budgets given to Forest Department to take up conservation works in forest areas.
2. Geography-based convergence: converging investment in a given Panchayat or location by different agencies.
3. Plan-based convergence: A convergence window is opened up during the planning process.

These are not mutually exclusive categories. Plan-based convergence may involve the same agency or a different one in its implementation.

In practice, much of the discussion related to convergence is around sharing labour costs from MGNREGS. One of the circulars on convergence with IWMP typifies this view; 'It must be ensured that the material-intensive shall be taken up under IWMP and all the other labour-oriented works shall be done only under MGNREGS' (Government of India 2008). Such convergence does not change the scope of the intervention but only expands the scale of operation of physical asset creation, mostly related to soil and water conservation.

While appreciable impacts are seen in natural resources related asset creation, as different studies point out, it is argued that this approach does not harness the real potential of MGNREGS in strengthening rainfed agriculture. In all these efforts at convergence, the scope of MGNREGS is limited to soil and water conservation, land development and plantation.

In the subsequent sections, first, the unique features of the programme are identified, elaborate on the requirements of rainfed agriculture and explore the scope of MGNREGS to make a larger impact on rainfed agriculture.

12.3.1 Unique Features of MGNREGS

Several features of MGNREGS make it more attractive as a driver of growth in production and livelihoods in rainfed areas:

1. Universality of its presence and larger coverage of rainfed geography
2. Demand-based investments
3. Focus on labour
4. location-specific works with Gram Sabha/Panchayat vested with the authority of deciding on the works
5. Social audit
6. Human resource base with skills established on ground to implement the programme.

There is no other programme in the rural landscape at present that has such versatility in spread, budget allocation, human resources base and amenable for decentralised decision-making and above all, a wider outreach to rainfed areas. These unique features of MGNREGS potentially make it possible to develop decentralised, participatory, location-specific and labour-oriented support systems for rainfed agriculture. This is in contrast with the present external input centred agriculture extension system driven by subsidised inputs and highly centralised programmes with 'limited' outreach holds greater promise in making an impact on rainfed agriculture.

Low budget allocations for facilitation support, mandate of compliance with employment generation demands, administrative over load and lack of robust back-end technical support, however, limit the scope of MGNREGS making a larger impact on agriculture on its own.

12.4 Distressed Rained Agriculture

Rainfed agriculture is facing multiple problems. Climate uncertainties and variability are increasing. Farmers' disinterest in rainfed agriculture is resulting in the neglect of private investments and lack of attention in aspects like maintaining soil productivity, crop systems and their management. These factors compound the risks and low profitability of rainfed agriculture.

Rainfed systems survive on the amount of rain harvested and retained in the soil profile. Soil organic matter plays a critical role in the process. Organic matter in soils is maintained in the soil systems through a process of integration of livestock, recycling of crop and animal residues and a mix of crop systems. Diversity in production systems, multiple livelihood options and flow of services and inputs across agriculture and livestock systems are traditional risk management strategies followed in rainfed areas.

These integrated systems are breaking down as farmers are increasingly relying on chemical fertilisers and other external inputs. Bare soils with poor organic matter increase climate vulnerability of rainfed agriculture systems manifold. Increase in real wages, problems of labour availability, family labour in particular, are altering farmers' choices towards more external input dependent, unsustainable and risky practices. Groundwater depletion is at an alarming rate making much of the private, high cost of investments in dysfunctional bore well. Farmers' distress spreading across rainfed areas in the country is a symptom of a deeper malaise of rainfed agriculture.

12.4.1 Revitalising Rainfed Agriculture

Several consultations in the Revitalising Rainfed Agriculture Network over the last 8 years brought out the need for critical policy corrections that impinge on the productivity and farmers' income in rainfed agriculture.

The most relevant for the current discussion are the following:

1. A move towards provision of irrigation to fill in soil moisture deficits arising out of increasing drought spells in extensive rainfed areas as a concept of irrigation.
2. Increasing public support to improve soils, particularly on promotion of farmers' practices to improve soil organic matter.
3. Revival of the millet crop systems at scale into the household consumption, state nutrition programmes and in farming.
4. Establishing a seed system that can provide seeds of diverse, locally adapted crops and varieties in time and at affordable prices managed by communities.
5. A transition to agro-ecology—crop systems and agronomic practices that improve local agro-ecology, such as system of rice intensification, NPM—managing pests without using chemical pesticides, LEISA—low external input sustainable agriculture, etc.

6. Mechanisation for agriculture labour, to improve their productivity and skills.
7. Focus on strengthening pastoral and agriculture-integrated extensive livestock systems (that are grazing/foraging based).
8. Bringing numerous seasonal and perennial water bodies into quality fish production.

The RRA Network suggests a landscape approach for strengthening the rainfed production systems integrally. The 12th Plan document and the NRM and Rainfed Farming Sub-Group recommendations also reiterate these propositions.[3] Watershed programmes constitute a sound system-based approach aimed at addressing problems of natural resource management. Various programmes aimed at improving crop productivity and the present support systems, however, are not in sync with sustainable natural resource management with resource degradation problems continuing unabated. Resource conservation and sustainable use, and management for enhanced productivity need to be seen in unison. The Working Group makes a strong case for integration of productivity enhancement with NRM as the core strategy of rainfed areas development. Given the inherent diversity of natural resources in rainfed areas, the health and dynamic inter-relations of the natural resource base (land, water and biomass) are direct determinants of the productivity and incomes from economic activities using these resources.

Apart from physical investments in the above process, the transition to a more secure, productive and remunerative rainfed agriculture requires a wider engagement with farmers, tenants and agriculture labour on effecting a transition to agro-ecology-centred approaches that reduce costs and enhance productivity.

12.4.2 Agriculture Extension and Rainfed Agriculture

Designed for delivering 'Green Revolution', the current agriculture extension system is modelled on a 'transfer of technology' paradigm. The Green Revolution technology is mostly embedded in external physical inputs—new seeds, fertilisers and pesticides. Extension involves promotion of these external inputs through subsidies and disseminating the research station evolved 'package of practices' tailored mostly to usage of these external inputs. Highly centralised and compartmentalised in their knowledge, these extension systems are fast losing their relevance in the context of rainfed systems where the problems are complex and highly location specific.

Some of the key challenges in the re-design of appropriate agriculture extension for revitalising rainfed agriculture (see Table 12.2).

Unlike in irrigated agriculture, productivity of rainfed agriculture systems is integrated with natural resources management. For example, productivity of sheep

[3]http://planningcommission.gov.in/aboutus/committee/wrkgrp12/agri/wg_NRM_Farming.pdf page 1.

Table 12.2 Agriculture extension for revitalising rainfed agriculture

Sl. No.	Present focus	Needed shift in focus
1	Few crops – Major cereals and pulses and commercial crops Few animals – Intensive dairy Few water bodies – Fisheries in large, perennial water bodies	Multiple crops – Millets, minor pulses and oil seeds, trees All animals – Draft animals, small ruminants, backyard poultry, pigs, etc. All water bodies – Seasonal and perennial; private and commons
2	Input-centric extension (technology is embedded into external inputs)	Knowledge- and skill-centric extension as much of the technology is around management, i.e. soils, crop systems, pests, weeds, etc.
3	Subsidy (for inputs) led	Facilitation/knowledge-centric and skill-based transition of labour
4	Isolated, i.e. mostly focus is within crop inputs	Integrated with natural resources, i.e. much of the actions in increasing productivity lie in natural resources base and how it is managed within the crop systems. For, e.g. soil organic matter is important to hold moisture in the soil; and it comes from crop residues and better soil conservation and tillage practices

and goats in extensive system is a function of fodder base in the grazing tracts and effective public (livestock) healthcare service delivery systems. The movement of animals, in turn, fertilises the commons and even the private lands. Investments in these areas are in the nature of 'public goods'; the benefits of such investments are difficult to contain within the private farm boundaries. Farmers' would be reluctant to invest on these for the same reason.

How to restore the agro-ecology and environmental flow across integrated crop-livestock-commons systems? What constitutes the role of farmer and what is the role of state? And therefore, what is the scope of public investments in the revival of agro-ecology? These questions still remain. The mainstream agriculture, livestock and fisheries programmes are couched in a different paradigm that is not much relevant for rainfed areas. Even for subsidised fertilisers applied, for example, needs moisture and organic matter in the soil to be more productive to give higher yields.

The need is for developing an appropriate public investment programme that can effectively enable farmers to shift towards sustainable agro-ecological approach to farming. Can MGNREGS play any effective role in this process without compromising its own objectives?

As several evaluation studies suggest, MGNREGS investment on soil and water conservation infrastructure itself has substantial impacts. As findings of the Chitradurga study (Tiwary 2011) illustrates, MGNREGS has provided multiple environmental services and reduced vulnerability, apart from providing employment and income to rural communities. The environmental services include groundwater recharge, water percolation and increased water storage in tanks, increased soil fertility, reclamation of degraded lands and carbon sequestration. These services contributed to and had positive implications for, increased crop and livestock production. The scheme activities also contributed to reduce vulnerability of agricultural production to uncertain and low rainfall. The implications measured in this study are only for about 1–3 years of implementation of the scheme; a much longer period of observations are needed to understand the full extent of environmental services and the potential for vulnerability reduction given the gestation period in ecological, hydrological and soil processes. Such efforts also contribute to meeting challenges of climate change. However, the scope of MGNREGS can be much larger given its unique strengths mentioned earlier.

12.5 Boundary Conditions for Expanding the Scope of MGNREGS

At the outset, it is important to lay down some boundary conditions for expanding the scope of MGNREGS so that its constitutional mandate is not compromised and that it would not inadvertently influence the existing production relations or labour markets. Four such principles can be thought of:

1. MGNREGS investment should crowd-in private investments and should not compete with or substitute for private investments.
2. Works should not get subsumed into agriculture as regular labour subsidies without adding '*asset value*' to natural resources—as it will have substantial impact on production relations. Having a finite period for specific 'MGNREGS—projects' will help in avoiding creation of perpetual dependency.
3. Scheme investments must result in improving productivity of the natural resources and drought proofing. The scope of asset creation can be new assets, renovation of old assets or making the existing assets functional or improving the quality of assets/natural resources.
4. Must potentially result in more wage employment generation or higher aggregate wage incomes in the production system to enhance employment opportunities.

12.5.1 Expanding the Scope of MGNREGS for Rainfed Agriculture

Within the above boundary conditions, to explore ways in which MGNREGS investments can be effective in addressing sustainability and growth of rainfed agriculture we first, outline these and provide the argument subsequently.

1. *Enabling Sustainable Agriculture Transitions*: Support in agriculture labour to attain new skill sets to aid in sustainable agro-ecological transitions
2. *Extend centralised services to make sustainable agriculture practices viable* at farm level, i.e. agriculture practices that improve the quality of natural resources
3. *Incubation of labour intensive local enterprises* that can potentially replace external industrial inputs with local labour intensive inputs in agriculture to aid in more employment intensive agriculture growth
4. *Creation of 'public good-services'* (beyond manual earth/labour work) that help in reducing private costs for farmers

These propositions are further illustrated in the following section.

12.5.2 Enabling to Sustainable Agriculture Transitions

Subsidised external inputs played a key role in transitions like Green Revolution. Unlike these input-embedded technologies, agro-ecological transitions are often labour and management intensive requiring labour with new skills. Who will bear the costs of labour getting trained and available in the market with new set of skills? This falls on the initial innovators or on the extension programmes. System of Rice Intensification (SRI) is a classic case.

Transition to SRI requires availability of labour pool that can transplant early seedlings in square-grid and labour who can weed with a mechanical weeder as against the conventional manual weeding. Experience suggests that mere farmers' awareness or interest is not sufficient for transiting to the new systems; availability of labour with these new skills in the market is a crucial determinant of the spread of SRI. These are typical public goods and farmers will have higher transaction costs in training labour in SRI skills and giving them adequate opportunity to practice and shift to new skills. Once the skill-transformation takes place, studies suggest that there will be savings for farmers on input costs and gain through increased productivity (Adusumilli and Bhagya 2011; Ranganathan et al. 2013). This can potentially increase wages for labour with the new skills creating a win-win situation.

Improvement on sets of skill of agricultural labour is not any part of Agriculture Department's mandate, of either centre or state government agencies. Agriculture Department, with the present structure across states, do not have the ability to operationalize such a programme on skill improvement of un-skill labour in rural India. SRI promotion in programmes like National Food Security Mission (NFSM) gets limited to demonstrations and distribution of implements to farmers. MGNREGS is well placed to work with labour in acquiring the new skills as it has the apparatus to manage such work. A detailed operational process for enabling such transition to SRI is developed by WASSAN for National Consortium on SRI (NCS 2012).

12.5.3 Provision of 'Public Good' Services

Availability of certain key-services will help in reducing input costs for farmers. To illustrate, a transition to non-pesticide management of insect pests (NPM) approach requires regular pest surveillance. Identifying and marking the threshold levels of pest incidence at an early stage helps farmers to take much cheaper and easier preventive measures at right time-saving in high costs of pesticide sprays later on. Getting farmers' regularly visit fields for pest monitoring is one of the biggest challenges in the promotion of NPM. Local pest surveillance is also a 'public good'. If collectively done, it saves large private expenditure. One way to support NPM transition is to establish such pest surveillance mechanism at Gram Panchayat/ habitation level.

Livestock disease surveillance, local weather monitoring and dissemination of weather forecasts and agro-advisories are also of the same nature in terms of work-types and nature of execution. Providing such services under MGNREGS should only be transitory, i.e. for a defined period; once the services are used and systems operational, additional investments may be made to use MGNREGS institutional systems for continued support for such functions.

12.5.4 'Agro-Ecological Restoration' as Durable Asset Creation

Soil and water conservation works are taken up largely under MGNREGS and even in the watershed development programmes. Production in the rainfed systems largely depends on the amount of rainfall harvested (with in the few rainy days) and retained in the soil profile; soil profile is the largest store house for rainfall. Encrustation of the surface, poor permeability and lack of organic matter constrain soils in rainfed areas from harvesting and retaining rainfall. If properly done, the incremental rainfall harvested in soil profile may far exceed the rainfall harvested through water harvesting.

The works taken up in MGNREGS are limited to soil conservation (prevention of runoff) and of late, construction of composting structures like NADEP after the revised guidelines. Both these interventions are inadequate for substantially increasing soil organic matter. A composting structure (a pit or a brick-enclosure) built under MGNREGS is inadequate for motivating rainfed farmers to practice composting or adding organic matter to soils. The operations involved in transporting biomass, filling-in the pits, watering, overturning, harvesting and transporting of the compost requires considerable attention and labour. For lack of such labour available, farmers' find it easier to shift to chemical fertilisers to meet the crop-nutrition requirements. But, use efficiency of fertilisers, water harvesting and retention in soil profile depends on organic matter in the soil.

Organic farming usually considers a period of 3 years to recuperate soil health and the local agro-ecology to offset productivity losses in transition.

In similar lines, MGNREGS can provide common pool-services in few of the components required for compost making at homesteads and farms such as digging, planting of biomass trees, watering, overturning or harvesting. This will reduce the total labour costs for individual farmers to make addition of organic matter viable for farmers. This part support to composting must be seen as a way of improving soil health and restoring soil biology adding substantially to the asset value of the land and does similar function as water harvesting.

Even 10% of the annual fertiliser subsidies invested on this, may result in substantial benefits in (a) improving fertiliser use efficiency, (b) improving soil health and reducing fertiliser use, and (c) move towards low external input agriculture (d) improved soil moisture to sustain short drought spells. Moreover, if farmers shift to local compost making it creates demand for wage employment.

Either this can be made part of MGNREGS or an allocation from Agriculture Department can be made (to the equivalent of 10% of fertiliser subsidies) separately, to be implemented by MGNREGS machinery.

Unfortunately, the perception of 'durable assets' in MGNREGS at present is limited to physically measurable constructions (digging, filling of earth and brick and mortar). If comprehensive measures are taken up in addition to soil conservation, the same soil with improvement in its quality in say, a block of 10 ha of rainfed agriculture can potentially reduce the costs to the farmer, provide better resilience to climate variability, improve productivity and may even reduce the subsidy burden by substituting local material for subsidised inputs. Soil is after all, a public good (irrespective of the private property regimes) that the present generation has to protect and improve for future generations. When the markets fail to generate required surplus for farmers to be able to invest on soils, the responsibility falls on the state to invest and protect this national asset.

The same analogy can be extended to other qualitative aspects of public goods that can potentially provide environmental services. Insect ecology if restored, for example, can improve the predator complex to reduce pesticide costs of individual farmer. Agro-ecological restoration needs to be considered as a 'durable asset', even if it does not involve brick, mortar or earth work.

12.5.5 Incubation of Labour Intensive Enterprises in Sustainable Agriculture Transitions

With the fast spread of NPM and organic agriculture, the scope for local inputs to substitute for external chemical inputs which are often subsidised has increased; such demand is also universal across the rainfed areas. Conversion of this potential demand into local enterprises needs considerable skilling, innovations and effective demand generation; MGNREGS can be an effective platform in incubating such local labour intensive enterprises. Provision of labour subsidy for such enterprises for a defined incubation period can be an effective instrument for their promotion.

These enterprises are the key to ecological restoration, reducing the costs of production, reducing the chemical load in products and can potentially generate employment. One such option is also to promote 'labour guilds' equipped with knowledge, material and required implements/machinery to take up service contracts in agriculture. This will address the twin problems of employment generation at higher wage rates and addressing the issue of farm labour scarcity for key operations. The experiments like the one in Kerala on 'food security army'[4] merit such consideration; this involves a shift from daily wage labour to 'labour-service guilds' taking contract of operations; MGNREGS is well equipped to promote such guilds.

12.5.6 Enabling Services for Natural Resources Management

Natural resources related assets will have short lifespan if they are not managed. Management of commons, land degradation, groundwater, management of water bodies, protection of biomass and such other principle requisites for community led agro-ecological regeneration often get crippled by lack of participation due to high transaction costs for individuals. Traditional systems of water management also collapsed in several places as state did not take over such management functions. The '*neerati*' or water distributor system in tank irrigation system is dysfunctional in several cases for lack of willingness of farmers' to pay for the services of *neerati.* The collective grasing systems, especially in kharif season, that are prevalent across India are slowly collapsing.

MGNREGS can effectively play a role in restoring these community-based natural resources management systems and even modernise the services. Viability gap-provisioning for the people involved in these systems help in revival of the traditional systems or in the formation of new natural resources management systems.

[4]http://www.indiawaterportal.org/news/keralas-paddy-war-food-security-army-swings-actiontransplanting-rice-300-acres-land-five-days.

12.6 Operationalisation of 'Expanded Scope of MGNREGS'

In all the above, MGNREGS with its unique positioning across the country and institutional capacity to work with rural labour can play a substantive role. However, the non-negotiable boundary conditions (mentioned earlier) for expanding the scope of MGNREGS must be complied with. The instrumentalities of expanding the scope could be the following.

12.6.1 Finite Time Period

MGNREGS must only support transitions with a defined time period, which substantially involves labour and their skills.

(a) **Not to Compete or Substitute Farmers' Investments**: Support only the additionally or the viability gaps on which farmers' are not forthcoming with investments or effort.
(b) **Have a technical programme**: It is important to recognise that MGNREGS is not a technical establishment. Unless there is a technical programme associated with the 'work', the assets created will not sustain nor get integrated with the production. Water body created without a programme on establishing support services and knowledge transfer on fisheries, for example, is most unlikely to result in increased fish production. To be effective, MGNREGS works must be embedded in a technical programme. Such technical programme must have technical capacities in planning and execution and have complementary investments to fulfil the programme requirements.
(c) **Community Resource Persons**: An approach that is widely accepted across several programmes is building capacities in the community and experienced farmer-led extension. The requirement for low-end technical services on a wide scale can be met effectively with this approach. This can be a potential 'Skill-Indian Agriculture Mission' spearheaded through MGNREGS platform.
(d) **Using MGNREGS as a Platform**: Though MGNREGS investments in labour are much coveted for convergence, a much greater strength lies in its ability to reach out to labour and labour payment systems that are well established in several states. For initiatives like skilling labour, incubation of enterprises, etc. special allocations may be made within MGNREGS within defined 'programme areas' which can be integrated with the programmes of agriculture, animal husbandry or other departments. Such provisions also enable the services to flow smoothly even when the demand for employment is low.

12.7 Summary

In summary, MGNREGS is uniquely positioned to make a substantial contribution to drive sustainability, resilience and growth in rainfed agriculture, livestock and fish production systems. Its strength lies in its universal presence, focus on labour, well laid out systems of payments, social audit and intensive coverage of rainfed geography. All that is needed is providing interpretative flexibility on the concept of 'creation of durable assets' in natural resources development and drought proofing.

Expanding the scope of 'durable assets' to include environmental services, quality of natural resources that can potentially crowd-in private investments in employment-intensive production will enable the Scheme to build a larger support system for rainfed agriculture. Such expanded scope of MGNREGS may include (a) enabling sustainable agriculture transition, provision of critical public goods; (b) provision of labour intensive services that are 'public goods' in nature; (c) seeing agro-ecological restoration as a 'durable asset'; (d) incubation of labour intensive enterprises that aid sustainable agriculture transitions; and (e) enabling services for natural resources 'management' (as against merely considering their development). The paper also lays out some boundary conditions for not compromising the constitutional mandate of MGNREGA. Such expansion of scope of the Scheme without compromising its own objectives can potentially have a multiplier effect of its investments in achieving resilience and growth of rainfed agriculture.

References

Adusumilli Ravindra, and Laxmi Bhagya. 2011. Potential of the system of rice intensification for systemic improvement in rice production and water use: The case of Andhra Pradesh, India. *Paddy Water Environ* 9: 89–97.http://link.springer.com/article/10.1007/s10333-010-0230-6#/page-1.

Government of India, 2008. GO No. 11017/17/2008-NREGA (UN) (Part-II) approved works as per the revised Schedule I (Para 4 (1) 1. (ii)) of the MGNREGA and GO No. 11017/17/2008-NREGA (UN) (Part-II) Comprehensive treatment of watersheds—Works based on watershed management under MGNREGA as per the revised schedule I, MGNREGA.

Ministry of Rural Development (MoRD), 'Guidelines for Convergence: Leveraging NREGA for Sustainable Development through Inter-sectoral Convergence', Ministry of Rural Development, 2009–10.

NCS. 2012. Enhancing Employment and Sustaining Production: Framework for Integration of SRI with MGNREGS. (http://www.wassan.org/sri/documents/SRI_MGNREGS_2012.pdf).

Ranganathan, C.R., K. Palanisami, K.R. Karunakaran, and Upali Amarasinghe. 2013. Doing different things or doing things differently. *Economic and Political Weekly* XLVIII(8).

Shah, Mihir. 2012. MGNREGA Sameeksha An Anthology of Research Studies on the Mahatma Gandhi National Rural Employment Guarantee Act, 2005 2006–2012. Ministry of Rural Development, Government of India.

Tiwari Rakesh, H.I Somashekhar, V.R. Ramakrishna Parama, Indu K. Murthy, M.S. Mohan Kumar, B.K. Mohan Kumar, Harshad Parate, Murari Varma, Sumedha Malaviya, Ananya S. Rao, Asmita Sengupta, Ruth Kattumuri, and N.H. Ravindranath. 2011. MGNREGA for environmental service enhancement and vulnerability reduction: Rapid appraisal in Chitradurga District, Karnataka. *Economic and Political Weekly* 66 (20): 9.

Chapter 13
The Journey of MGNREGA: Changing Approaches and Challenges

Amita Shah, Aasha Kapur Mehta, P.K. Viswanathan and Nicky Johnson

13.1 The Context

Casual agricultural labourers are the largest group among the chronically poor in India. Most poor rural households are either landless or near-landless, bear a higher dependency burden, are illiterate and depend on wages (Mehta and Shah 2001; Bhide and Mehta 2004). Access to work and wage rates vary across regions, occupations and gender. Special interventions are needed to ensure productive employment for the poor who are able-bodied and can earn through work and thereby escape from poverty.

The Mahatma Gandhi National Rural Employment Guarantee Scheme (MGNREGS) was seen as a major milestone in the anti-poverty policies in Independent India. MGNREGS has its roots in the Maharashtra Employment Guarantee Scheme (MEGS)—a flagship initiative of the Government of Maharashtra that was the first state to recognise the right to work and made a commitment to provide unskilled work on demand to all adults in rural areas.

A. Shah
Gujarat Institute of Development Research, Ahmedabad, Gujarat, India
e-mail: amitagidr@gmail.com

A.K. Mehta (✉)
Department of Economics, Indian Institute of Public Administration, New Delhi, India
e-mail: aashakapurmehta@gmail.com

P.K. Viswanathan
Amrita School of Business, Amrita Vishwa Vidyapeetham
(Deemed to be University), Kochi, Kerala, India
e-mail: pkviswam@gmail.com

N. Johnson
Centre for Management in Agriculture (CMA), Indian Institute of Management, Ahmedabad, Gujarat, India
e-mail: nickyjohnson00@gmail.com

M. Bhattarai et al. (eds.), *Employment Guarantee Programme and Dynamics of Rural Transformation in India*, India Studies in Business and Economics,
https://doi.org/10.1007/978-981-10-6262-9_13

Ever since the early phase of the MEGS, a large number of scholars, NGOs, policy makers and government agencies extensively studied the MEGS to understand the process and its impact on employment and poverty reduction in rural areas. Encouraged by the performance of the MEGS, in 2005, the Government of India launched the nationwide scheme to provide employment guarantee to the rural masses under the Mahatma Gandhi Rural Employment Guarantee Act (MGNREGA). It is now a decade since the programme was launched. How has implementation of MGNREGA progressed from its initial phase to the present phase? Does this vary across states and social categories? How have rural households benefited from it? What has been gained?

The nature and content of the MGNREGA itself has undergone significant changes over the past decade from being a mere employment guarantee scheme to a core flagship programme being scaled up in convergence with many other development programmes by the national and state governments. Has convergence been implemented in practice? If so, how has this been implemented? These are some of the questions that this paper seeks to answer.

At the same time, a large number of studies based on detailed analysis of the status of implementation and the outcomes of MGNREGA point out that the programme had lost its initial vigour. There are concerns about lack of fulfilment of the basic premises on which the programme was founded. The dismay in the overall performance[1] of the programme stems from the fact that a vast segment of the rural populace (especially, the youth) continues to be dissociated with the programme either due to the low wages paid or due to the lack of adequate number of days of gainful employment available or even due to the sheer absence of opportunities to improve skills and thus improve the socio-economic status. This raises several issues and challenges in the current context of high economic growth with increasing inequalities, regional disparities,[2] widening rural–urban divide and the increasing rural distress in the country (Kundu and Varghese 2010; Suryanarayana and Das 2014; Kohli 2015; Chand et al. 2007). While realising this, the Twelfth Five-Year Plan (2012–17) emphasised the need for inclusive growth in terms of poverty reduction, regional balance, inequality reduction, empowerment and employment generation (GoI 2013, as cited in Suryanarayana and Das 2014).

---

[1]Performance of MGNREGA has been far from satisfactory in recent years in terms of the average number of days of employment generated per household, percentage of actual expenditure made against total funds available and the percentage of works completed (Jha and Gaiha 2012). Instances are many where the works undertaken for asset creation remained incomplete along with poor quality of such assets created (GoI 2014; ILO 2014; Drèze and Khera 2009).

[2]At the all-India level, it was found that the relatively deprived social groups, STs and SCs, have been left out of the growth process and the other social groups (OSGs) perform the best. The finding on increasing disparity between the poorest and richest states was corroborated by the estimates of: (i) coefficient of variation, which increased from 17.59 to 30.78% for mean [per capita consumption expenditure]; and (ii) index of dispersion, which increased from 17.63 to 32.98% for rural mean per capita consumption across major states between 1993–94 and 2011–12 (Suryanarayana and Das).

Is there a need to go beyond the present approach while moving forward with MGNREGA? The basic questions, therefore, are to get an understanding of what worked and did not work and why and determine whether it should continue as a dole-based employment guarantee programme or be scaled up as a development programme with long-term strategies and action plans?

In fact, these questions are yet to receive adequate attention in the policy and academic discourse across the country. Far from being an academic analytical exercise, the search for answers to these questions might provide some useful insights towards redesigning the future course of MGNREGA and the related development policies that address the needs specifically of the youth, women, disadvantaged groups and regions that are still in distress despite the decade long existence of the programme.

While MGNREGA remains the most important strategy for creating rural employment, a closer understanding of the same in the emerging context may help in attaining the basic goals of poverty alleviation and equity. Unfortunately, lack of a nuanced analysis of the interrelationships between employment, poverty alleviation and equity amongst the varied social groups, over time and space, has made it difficult to understand the developmental dynamics of MGNREGA. This paper is an effort to address some of these gaps and the questions raised above.

The analysis is based on data from the official MGNREGA sources (MGNREGA website and the Ministry of Rural Development) from 2006–07 to 2014–15. While the MGNREGA is a significant modification over the MEGS, we also try to draw on some parallels between the MEGS and the MGNREGA while discussing the impacts and outcomes in a comparative perspective. Though these comparisons have been already made by some scholars, the effort here is to approach the MGNREGA from a comparative framework of time, space and activities vis-a-vis the MEGS.

The chapter is organised into four sections, including this introduction. Section 13.2 provides a snapshot of employment generation programmes from the 1970s through the MEGS to MGNREGA as well as their role and relevance for achieving growth and poverty reduction in India. Section 13.3 provides a detailed analysis of the statewise extent of participation in MGNREGA in the context of poverty levels, drought conditions as well as the socio-economic status of the rural households over time. Section 13.4 is the concluding section of the paper and highlights some of the critical challenges undermining the potential of MGNREGA. It also argues the case for a paradigm shift in approaches and design of the programme as a strategic development intervention with long-term impacts on the economy and society.

13.2 The Transition from MEGS to MGNREGA

Historically, employment generation programmes in India have a chequered history of over four decades (Shah et al. 1998) and were an integral aspect of the public works programmes introduced as part of poverty reduction strategies under the planned development regime. As these programmes were primarily intended at providing employment to a vast segment of the illiterate and unskilled workers in the rural areas, they were rarely considered as 'economically productive' and remained a major point of contention between academics and policy makers. The earlier debates on employment programmes centred on the effectiveness of the self-employment versus wage employment programmes in reducing poverty in India, with a clear divide between scholars. For instance, some scholars, such as Dandekar and Rath (1971), Rath (1985), Dreze (1990) and Dev (1996) favoured wage employment programmes and advocated for employment guarantee schemes (EGS) in view of their self-targeting nature and the associated benefits. On the contrary, while Krishna (1973) advocated for direct poverty reduction programmes (rather than employment generation programmes), Dantwala (1978) argued that self-employment programmes (like the IRDP) needed to be promoted, as they were thought to help improve the skills of the workers. The underlying argument was that more emphasis on wage employment programmes would create a genre of workers who would always tend to depend upon either the state or other agencies to provide such employment opportunities. On the other hand, self-employment programmes make the workers independent and skilled over time.

The MEGS was seen as the largest employment guarantee experiment in India and was initially launched as a drought relief programme in the 1970s. It was continued as an anti-poverty programme that could be replicated in other parts of the country. Rajasthan was the first state that adopted the EGS as a drought relief programme, following the drought in the state in the year 2000. A strong people's movement led to the demand for jobs to provide drought relief. The Supreme Court of India also supported such schemes that link the right to food with the right to work. Eventually, this resulted in the enunciation of the total rural employment scheme, called the Sampoorna Gramin Rozgar Yojana (SGRY), which was the precursor of MGNREGA (Desai et al. 2015).

MGNREGA was modelled on the MEGS that had evolved as one of the most important programmes aimed at reducing rural poverty and distress. In many respects, MGNREGS adopted the basic features of the MEGS with significant changes in coverage of the rural households and content as is evident from Table 13.1.

This table presents a brief comparative overview of the basic approaches followed by the two employment guarantee programmes. It is important to note that as they progressed, both the programmes were recast with the goal of reaching out to the poor, landless and socially discriminated households. The approach followed was to support these social groups within the existing socio-economic structure, rather than creating a new one.

In what follows, we try to discuss some of the important aspects of the MEGS and the MGNREGS in a comparative perspective. This would help us to reflect on the gaps in the basic approach in planning and design for employment generation while moving from the MEGS to MGNREGS, which would further help in setting new pathways for future interventions.

The MEGS required that the employment be 'gainful to the individual and productive to the economy' i.e., that 'on completion of the works undertaken, some

Table 13.1 MEGS and MGNREGS: Comparing the basic design features and changes

Design features	MEGS	MGNREGS	Changes
1. Objectives	To provide gainful and productive employment to those who needed work and were prepared to do unskilled manual labour, but could not find work on their own	Enhancement of livelihood security of households and strengthening of the livelihood resource base of the rural poor through unskilled manual work	Shifted from the original idea of providing employment to those in need of work for the enhancement of livelihood security
	To create durable community assets for longer term development	Provision of social safetynet to reduce migration of rural poor households in the lean period; creation of productive assets to ensure development of rural areas; protecting the environment; empowering rural women; fostering social equity, etc.	
	The jobseekers be provided with work within 8 km of their residence	Right to obtain work within a radius of 5 km	More localisation of the employment opportunities
2. Coverage	Thirty-three out of 35 districts of Maharashtra (excluding Mumbai City District and Mumbai Suburban District)	**Phase I**—From 2 February 2006: 200 districts. **Phase II**—Extended to an additional 130 districts, of which, 113 were notified on 1 April 2007 **Phase III**—Extended to the entire country from April 2008	MEGS—12 districts in 1970 and then 33 districts in 1972 MGNREGA—Phase 1—200 districts in 2006 and Phase 3—295 districts in 2008
3. Days of work	Round-the-year guarantee with the understanding that works will not be initiated during the peak agricultural season	100 days per household—additional 50 days in drought-prone areas	From round-the-year guarantee for each adult to a limit of 100 days for all adults in a household in 1 year—additional 50 days in case of drought

(continued)

Table 13.1 (continued)

Design features	MEGS	MGNREGS	Changes
4. Women	All adult women equally entitled to demand work as are all adult men	Since right to work is at the level of all adults in the Household, women's right to work is subsumed within the household. The Act requires that one-third of beneficiaries must be women	MEGS—Women were given equal rights in employment. MGNREGA—mandatory share of one-third of all potential households
5. Target group	Open to all adult individuals regardless of caste, gender, income group. Self-targeting or target based on low wages and unskilled arduous work	Open to all adults at the household level regardless of caste, gender, income group. Self-targeting or target based on low wages and unskilled arduous work	From individual adults to all adults (able-bodied) at the household level

Source Based on Shah and Mehta (2008)

durable community assets should be generated'. The priority areas for works included labour intensive components of irrigation projects, percolation and storage tanks and underground bandharas; soil conservation and land development works; afforestation and social forestry; roads including internal village roads; and a few years ago individual beneficiary schemes such as Jawahar wells, horticulture, etc. (Shah and Mehta 2008).

Initially, the impact of the MEGS was quite impressive. For instance, in the three decades after the scheme formally commenced in 1972, it financed 3597 million person days of work on irrigation, soil and water conservation, reforestation and local roads (Krishnaraj et al. 2004). An average of 120 million days a year were provided, spread across hundreds of thousands of separate work sites (Moore and Jadhav 2006). Nevertheless, Shah and Mehta (2008) noted that the employment generated had varied significantly over time. While the number of person days generated through the MEGS increased rapidly from 48.1 million in 1974–75 to a peak of 205.4 million in 1979–80, it declined thereafter to 13.33 million in 1987–88 and further to an all-time low of 7.80 million in 1989–90. However, by the period 2004–05, the employment generation under MEGS rose from 110 million in 2000–01 to 222 million person days in 2004–05 (Shah and Mehta 2008), followed by a decline to 169 million in 2005–06 (Government of Maharashtra, Department of Economics and Statistics). One of the important features of the employment generation activities under MEGS was that women workers constituted more than half of the beneficiaries. Person days of employment generated for women during the period 1996–97 to 1999–2000 were around 58% on average (Shah and Mehta 2008).

The MEGS had disintegrated much before it was converged with the MGNREGS. As indicated by some scholars, the decline had started in the late 1980s and its subsequent impact remained relatively low. Once it was passed into law with guaranteed funding independent of the annual budget process, it was felt that the EGS no longer needed active proponents. The beneficiaries were also too dispersed, and their dependence on EGS was quite irregular, irrespective of the drought or distress conditions that prevailed in the villages. Eventually, the level of political and bureaucratic zeal attached to the Scheme also faded away. The changing development priorities diverted attention to other programmes (Moore and Jadhav 2006).

Shah and Mehta (2008) attributed three main factors as responsible for the decline of the MEGS, notwithstanding the unspent money earmarked for the same. The first reason was the growing economic diversification and increasing opportunities in non-farm activities, especially in urban areas. Second, the scope for undertaking productive work benefiting the landed households had by then reached near saturation, especially in the heartland of western Maharashtra, thereby resulting in reduced demand from the dominant agrarian class. Third, was the dilution of the grassroots movements, which had played a crucial role in generating demand for work at earlier stages of the programme. Since the scheme had emerged out of social mobilisation, and also allowed multiple manifestations of movements, dilution of grass root mobilisation during the late 80s and onwards dissipated the momentum for demanding work (Shah and Mehta 2008).

Concerns were also raised about the overall impact of the MEGS on poverty reduction in Maharashtra. While studies show that some people were able to cross the poverty line, the wider impact of the MEGS on enabling the poor to escape from poverty was limited. This was reflected in the high percentage of people below the poverty line in Maharashtra, with estimates of poverty remaining above or close to the all-India average. Further, the impact on asset creation was limited, as the emphasis was more on wage employment rather than sustainable asset creation. Although work was to be provided 'on demand', poverty reduction was constrained by: (a) low wages for given work; (b) limited number of days of work per person actually provided; (c) non upgradation of skills; and (d) the limited ability of the schemes to foster development of the areas where projects were initiated; (e) limited community mobilisation for demanding work, leading to limited coverage of workers, especially outside the few districts in which works were concentrated and during non-drought years and (f) limited administrative systems for monitoring and tracking the implementation of the scheme (Shah and Mehta 2008).

The MEGS was scaled up into NREGA and was implemented in 200 districts at the national level in the first phase (2006), mainly based on the larger potential of employment generation for the vast segment of the rural households. The distinction of 'right to work' has made it an unparalleled development intervention in the history of the country. As noted by Dreze (2011), MGNREGA has played a very important role in bringing the 'right-based' approach of development, especially in rural India. Started initially as a 'right to work', it has now emerged as the single most important instrument that supposedly guarantees an array of associated rights or entitlements of a worker. These entitlements include the: (a) right to a job card; (b) right to demand and receive work within 15 days; (c) right to unemployment allowance; (d) right to plan and prepare a shelf of projects; (e) right to obtain work within a radius of 5 km; (f) right to worksite facilities; (g) right to notified wage rate; (h) right to receive wages within 15 days; (i) right to compensation for delay in payment of wages and (j) right to time-bound redressal of grievances and (k) right to conduct concurrent social audits and social audit of all MGNREGA expenditure.

A quick review of the broader content and guidelines of the MGNREGA shows that a number of important aspects were taken into consideration while designing it with a hope that it will be a major step ahead of MEGS in terms of the larger economy-wide impacts and social welfare.

A vast literature on the status of implementation and impacts of MGNREGA is already available in the form of books, journal articles, reports by the national as well as international agencies and government departments. Though a detailed review of the literature on the MGNREGA is outside the purview of this chapter, a brief review of the major impact of the programme is presented. It may be noted that the majority of studies examined the performance of MGNREGA in various states in both micro- and macro-settings and highlighted the issues that emerged across these study sites related to its implementation and functioning. Most of these studies were undertaken using appropriate methodology and many of them also used interdisciplinary research methods relying on both quantitative and qualitative techniques.

By and large, the literature on MGNREGA falls into three broad categories as highlighted in a study by Kannan and Jain (2013). Accordingly, the three categories of literature included: (a) studies reflecting on the design and implementation related issues; (b) those examining the outreach and impact of MGNREGA and (c) those attempting to build a national level comprehensive profile of MGNREGA implementation.

Several analysts examined the changing profile of the rural labour markets in the post-MGNREGA context and reported that the programme had significant impacts in terms of employment creation, wages and other associated benefits across states, though with notable variations. However, the overall trends in the number of man days generated under the MGNREGA had shown a declining trend especially since 2010–11. This has been a major cause for concern regarding the effectiveness of the programme. The total number of person days generated had increased more than threefold from 0.91 crore during 2006–07 to 2.84 crore during 2010–11, followed by a decline thereafter to 2.3 crore in 2012–13 and 1.67 crore in 2014–15 (MoRD 2015). While this decline in the number of person days may also reflect the declining popularity of the programme, the evidence based on secondary data as well as primary field studies suggests that the entire decline in person days generated cannot be attributed to the increasing prosperity in rural areas (Himanshu et al. 2015).

At the same time, a large number of studies highlight the instrumental role played by the MGNREGA in creating multiple socio-economic, environmental and ecosystem impacts (David 2008; IISC 2013) as well as rural asset creation (Kannan and Jain 2013; Tiwari et al. 2011; Shah 2012). The instrumental role played by the MGNREGA has been identified in terms of: (a) women's economic empowerment stimulating increased labour market participation (Pankaj and Tankha 2010; Narayanan and Das 2014; Viswanathan and Mandal 2012); (b) social inclusion and financial inclusion[3]; (c) sustainable asset creation in rural areas[4] (Desai et al. 2015; Verma 2011; Verma and Shah, this volume); support to the disabled; (d) protection against distress migration and (e) rise in money and real wages and an increase in reserve price of labour and reduction in gender wage gap (Usami 2011; Chandrasekhar and Ghosh 2011; Dutta et al. 2012; Ghose 2012; Kannan and Jain 2013; Jose 2013). Another major impact has been the enhanced participation of the poor and the socially vulnerable households and workers (agricultural wage labourers, Adivasis, Dalits and other backward classes and landless, marginal and small farmers) and thus, MGNREGA was instrumental in reducing poverty among these groups (Desai et al. 2015) to a greater extent.

---

[3]Under MGNREGA, employment was provided to 5.62 Crore Households and it also resulted in an average increase in household income by around Rs. 6,000 per year. As part of financial inclusion, 9.29 crore bank/postal accounts are opened and the scheme also resulted in the increase of purchasing power in rural areas (Niti Aayog 2015).

[4]Based on a study in a Gujarat village (Nana Kotda) in South Gujarat, Hirway et al. (2010) reported that the expenditure on various NREG works had generated multiplier impact on the rural economy, even though the impact was low due to the various leakages in implementation.

A report by the Planning Commission (GOI 2013) also highlighted some of the notable achievements under the MGNREGA. Among the important observations are that: (a) the MGNREGA has led to a significant increase in monthly per capita consumption expenditure of rural households; (b) MGNREGA works have been described as 'Green' and 'Decent' i.e., the scheme creates decent working conditions by ensuring workers' rights and legal entitlements, providing social protection and employment and environmentally sustainable works that regenerate the ecosystem and protect biodiversity; (c) MGNREGA has had a more direct and positive impact on reducing distress migration as compared to migration for economic growth and other reasons.

Apparently, it seems that the interface between MGNREGA and the major segments of the rural households, especially the vulnerable social categories, has not received the due attention it warrants in the emerging context. We consider that such an effort may help us answer 'whether and how the MGNREGA has impacted the rural economy in terms of the perceived goals of the programme'. Hence, in the next section, we present a detailed analysis of the causality or the nexus between the major sources of vulnerability and the extent of participation in MGNREGA across the major states. We define the major sources of vulnerability of the states in terms of: (a) incidence of poverty; (b) occurrence of drought and (c) the preponderance of the social groups, viz. SC, ST and women.

For the purpose of analysis, we classify the states into four categories in terms of work participation of the rural households in MGNREGA, viz. (a) Very low (0–14%); (b) medium (15–30%); (c) high (>30 to 45%) and (d) very high (above 45%). We have estimated the level of participation of rural households in MGNREGA in 20 major states over the 9-year period from 2006–07 to 2014–15. Based on the long-term trends in household participation in MGNREGS works, 4 of the 20 states (Punjab, Haryana, Maharashtra and Gujarat) were classified as states with low level of participation; 8 states (Bihar, Odisha, Uttar Pradesh, Karnataka, Kerala, Jammu & Kashmir, Assam and Uttarakhand) reflected medium level of participation; 5 states, (Andhra Pradesh, Jharkhand, Himachal Pradesh, West Bengal and Madhya Pradesh) had high level of participation; while 3 states, (Rajasthan, Tamil Nadu and Chhattisgarh) had very high level of participation.

13.3 MGNREGA and Its Interface with Poverty, Drought and Vulnerable Social Groups

While examining the one-to-one correspondence between the major vulnerability conditions and participation in MGNREGA over the decade, we posit a question: has participation in MGNREGA been positively influenced by the extent of poverty, the occurrence of drought or the socio-economic characteristics of the household? In other words, we expect higher incidence of poverty to be associated with higher participation of rural households in MGNREGA.

13.3.1 Overall Trends in Rural Household Participation in MGNREGA

At the outset, we examine the overall trends in rural household participation in MGNREGA across states. The analysis compares the statewise work participation during the entire period 2006–07 to 2014–15 as well as compares the changes in participation during the first 5-year period and the last 4-year period. The results are presented in Table 13.2. We follow the classification of states based on the four levels of rural participation in the programme as noted above.

Table 13.2 Trends in rural households' participation in MGNREGA, major states—2006–07 to 2014–15

No	States based on extent of participation	Changes in participation of rural households in MGNREGA (%)		
		2006–07 to 2014–15	2006–07 to 2010–11	2011–12 to 2014–15
A. Very Low participation (0–14%)				
1	Punjab	6.6	4.9	8.6
2	Maharashtra	6.7	3.8	10.0
3	Haryana	6.7	4.7	9.0
4	Gujarat	11.1	12.5	9.4
B. Medium participation (15–29%)				
5	Bihar	16.7	23.0	9.9
6	Odisha	18.4	18.3	18.5
7	Uttar Pradesh	19.5	19.1	20.0
8	Karnataka	19.5	21.7	17.0
9	Kerala	23.5	14.2	36.2
10	Jammu & Kashmir	24.5	17.8	32.0
11	Assam	26.9	31.9	21.4
12	Uttarakhand	27.4	25.0	30.1
C. High participation (30–44%)				
13	Andhra Pradesh	30.0	36.5	22.4
14	Jharkhand	32.4	37.4	26.9
15	Himachal Pradesh	32.6	28.6	37.3
16	West Bengal	33.6	28.4	39.7
17	Madhya Pradesh	35.8	42.8	28.3
D. Very high participation (45% above)				
18	Rajasthan	45.8	50.8	40.5
19	Tamil Nadu	47.2	32.0	65.1
20	Chhattisgarh	52.4	52.1	53.0

Note The figures are simple averages for the respective periods

Source Total employment provided from MGNREGA Public Portal accessed in February, 2016 www.nrega.nic.in and Rural Households from Census India, 2011

Three of the four states with low level of participation in MGNREGS reflect participation rates that are just below 7% during the entire period under consideration. However, comparing the level of participation between the two time periods (2006–07 to 2010–11 and 2011–12 to 2014–15) shows that there was a notable increase in rural participation during the latter period (2011–12 to 2014–15) in these three states. The highest increase in participation was in Maharashtra (from 3.8 to 10%), followed by Haryana (from 4.7 to 9%) and Punjab (from 4.9 to 8.6%). Gujarat is an exception to this trend, as there was a decline in the participation of rural households (from 12.5 to 9.4%) during the last 4 years.

In the case of eight states reporting medium level of participation during the entire period of analysis, some interesting trends emerge. Some states, which were classified as medium rural participation states improved their status by moving to the next category of high participation states over time. These states are Kerala, Jammu and Kashmir and Uttarakhand. On the contrary, states, such as Bihar, Assam and Karnataka reported a decline in participation, while Odisha and Uttar Pradesh reported a consistent level of rural participation during the two periods.

States with higher levels of participation such as Andhra Pradesh, Jharkhand and Madhya Pradesh, reported a decline in their participation rates during 2011–12 to 2014–15, while Himachal Pradesh and West Bengal reported an increase compared to the first 5-year period.

Amongst the three states reporting very high participation, estimates for Tamil Nadu doubled from 32 to 65% between the two time periods, while Rajasthan reported a decline by about 10% and Chhattisgarh reported a marginal increase from 52 to 53%.

13.3.2 MGNREGA—Poverty Nexus Across States

Is there a correspondence between the level of poverty and extent of participation in MGNREGA? The results are presented in Table 13.3 and are quite revealing. We note that MGNREGA, which has an ultimate objective of reducing poverty by providing employment especially to the very poor rural households, does not seem to have resulted in improving the situation in terms of high participation in case of the states with high incidence of poverty.

Of the four states with very high levels of poverty (above 45%), Chhattisgarh is the only state that has correspondingly very high participation of rural households in MGNREGA. In comparison, Jharkhand and Madhya Pradesh have high (but not very high) levels of participation and Odisha medium level of participation in MGNREGA.

Interestingly, the state of Gujarat with high levels of poverty has very low level of participation in the programme. The proportion of households depending upon MGNREGA is also disproportionately low in states like Assam, Bihar and Uttar Pradesh despite high levels of poverty. West Bengal shows a close correspondence between high levels of poverty and high participation in the programme.

Table 13.3 Correspondence between poverty and level of participation in MGNREGS across states, 2006–07 to 2014–15

Poverty level	State level participation of rural households in MGNREGA (%)			
	Very low (0–14%	Medium (15–29%)	High (30–44%)	Very high (>45%)
Very high (45% or more)	–	Odisha	Jharkhand, Madhya Pradesh	Chhattisgarh
High (30–45%)	Gujarat	Bihar, Uttar Pradesh, Assam	West Bengal	
Medium (15–30%)	Maharashtra	Karnataka	–	Rajasthan, Tamil Nadu
Low (15% below)	Haryana, Punjab	Jammu & Kashmir, Kerala, Uttarakhand	Andhra Pradesh, Himachal Pradesh	–

Source Authors' compilation based on data accessed from the MGNREGA portal, www.nrega.nic.in

Maharashtra with medium poverty incidence reports very low participation in the programme while Rajasthan and Tamil Nadu that are clubbed in the same poverty category have very high participation in the programme.

At the other end of the spectrum, of the seven states with low levels of poverty (below 15%) two states, Haryana and Punjab are also quite distinct in that there is correspondingly low level of participation in the programme. However, despite low incidence of poverty, Andhra Pradesh and Himachal Pradesh show high participation rates in MGNREGS while Jammu & Kashmir, Kerala and Uttarakhand report medium levels of participation.

Overall, the data contradicts the postulated relationship and raises questions of whether supply side issues of State capacity and willingness to support MGNREGA works persist or whether there are demand-side issues such as delayed payments that lead to such contradictory relationships.

We further discuss the lack of correspondence between level of poverty and MGNREGA participation by examining the trends in expenditure in MGNREGA and the relative share of the states in the cumulative expenditure and poverty over time. The results of the analysis are presented in Table 13.4.

It may be seen from Table 13.4 that the share of low participation states was the lowest in the cumulative expenditure on MGNREGA in both the periods, i.e. 3.32% during 2006–07 to 2010–11 and 7.12% during 2011–12 to 2015–16. On the other hand, these groups of states accounted for almost 12% of the total BPL population at the national level. The other categories of states with medium to very high levels of MGNREGA participation had reported a notable increase in the expenditure on MGNREGA activities over time. Though the low participation states reported almost a 30-fold increase in the cumulative expenditure on MGNREGA, the average amount of cumulative expenditure incurred by these states was much lower than in the categories of states with medium to very high levels of participation in the programme. For instance, during the period 2011–12 to 2015/16, the cumulative average MGNREGS expenditure of low participation states was Rs. 63.29 crore, as

Table 13.4 Share of states in expenditure on MGNREGA and population below poverty line

Level of participation	Cumulative expenditure (Rs. Crore)		Share in poverty (% of rural population—BPL)	
	2006/07 to 2010/11	2011/12 to 2015/16	2004/05	2011/12
Low	10.71 (3.32)	316.46 (7.12)	12.27	11.94
Medium	53.87 (33.39)	638.49 (28.74)	52.26	52.86
High	91.34 (35.38)	1232.48 (34.67)	23.67	23.23
Very high	98.38 (22.86)	1388.31 (23.44)	10.66	10.72

Note The figures in brackets indicate the relative share of the respective groups of states. The figures covers only 20 states as listed in Table 13.2
Source Authors' estimates based on MGNREGA data and rural poverty estimated by the Rangarajan Committee

compared to Rs. 277.66 crore in case of very high participation states, Rs. 246.5 crore in respect of high participation states and Rs. 127.7 crore in case of medium participation states. Thus, it seems that the states had shown distinct variations in terms of implementing the programmes under MGNREGS with thin distribution of resources in the case of the low participation states.

13.3.3 Drought and MGNREGA Participation

We now turn to another important question, 'whether the incidence of drought conditions would have a bearing on MGNREGA participation across states?' One may anticipate that a decline in rainfall or the sudden occurrence or continued prevalence of drought conditions may increase the level of participation in MGNREGA. In this regard, we have examined the trends in fluctuations in rainfall (normal and drought year) and participation in MGNREGA in the corresponding year across the 20 states over the 9-year period (Table 13.5).

States responded differently to the changing rainfall situations (see Table 13.5). The deviation from normal rainfall ranged from 11 to 100% during the drought year. Data pertaining to the severity of drought conditions that prevailed in the states is presented in column 5 of the Table. The year in which drought was experienced varied across states. However, there are no clear patterns across states with regard to participation in MGNREGA and occurrence of drought.

In many states, the normal rainfall years have reported significant participation in the programme especially in the case of states with medium, high and very high participation rates. On the other hand, the response to ameliorating distress during the drought period through participation in MGNREGA varied significantly across states. For instance, the work participation levels have been notably weaker in case of low participation states (as low as 5.7% in Haryana), while it doubled to over 70% among very high participation states such as Rajasthan and Tamil Nadu. However, even in this category, participation in MGNREGA declined from 54.3%

Table 13.5 Drought and level of participation in MGNREGA across states over time

Rank [1]	Level of MGNREGA participation [2]	Rainfall (normal year) (% deviation from normal) [3]	% of MGNREGA participation (normal year) [4]	Rainfall (drought year) (% deviation from normal) [5]	% of MGNREGA Drought Year [6]
A. Low participation (0–14%)					
1	Punjab [2008–09; 2012–13]	7.6	4.7	−20.6	7.0
2	Maharashtra [2010–11; 2012–13]	21.9	3.5	−11.4	12.1
3	Haryana [2012–13; 2008–09]	9.8	9.7	−100.1	5.7
4	Gujarat [2010–11; 2012–13]	44.8	16.4	−40.2	9.9
B. Medium participation (15–29%)					
5	Bihar [2007–08; 2012–13]	18.8	25.9	9.8	12.0
6	Odisha [2006–07; 2011–12]	20.7	19.1	−33.4	17.0
7	Uttar Pradesh [2013–14; 2014–15]	6.8	18.6	−25.6	14.2
8	Karnataka [2009–10; 2012–13]	16.1	46.0	−11.3	16.5
9	Kerala [2007–08; 2012–13]	17.2	4.1	−25.2	37.5
10	Jammu & Kashmir [2013–14; 2009–10]	20.0	40.0	−34.2	21.9
11	Assam [2012–13; 2014–15]	−12.6	22.2	−24.6	16.5

(continued)

Table 13.5 (continued)

Rank [1]	Level of MGNREGA participation [2]	Rainfall (normal year) (% deviation from normal) [3]	% of MGNREGA participation (normal year) [4]	Rainfall (drought year) (% deviation from normal) [5]	% of MGNREGA Drought Year [6]
12	Uttarakhand [2010–11; 2009–10]	19.4	38.8	−37.7	38.0
C. High participation (30–44%)					
13	Andhra Pradesh [2010–11; 2006–07]	43.6	44.1	−39.9	16.1
14	Jharkhand [2007–08; 2010–11]	5.9	39.0	−39.2	43.0
15	Himachal Pradesh [2013–14; 2009–10]	16.4	39.5	−35.5	39.4
16	West Bengal [2013–14; 2014–15]	15.7	42.6	−16.3	34.9
17	Madhya Pradesh [2013–14; 2007–08]	36.3	24.6	−50.1	44.7
D. Very high participation (45% above)					
18	Rajasthan [2013–14; 2009–10]	35.9	35.9	−83.4	72.9
19	Tamil Nadu [2008–09; 2012–13]	30.0	36.6	−27.4	73.1
20	Chhattisgarh [2013–14; 2009–10]	10.7	54.3	−36.3	49.2

Note Figures in parentheses indicate the (%) deviation from normal rainfall. Years in square brackets indicate the reference years for columns 3 and 4 and 5 and 6, respectively. The first year in the bracket refers to cols. 3 and 4 and second year to cols. 5 and 6
Source see Annexes 1 and 4

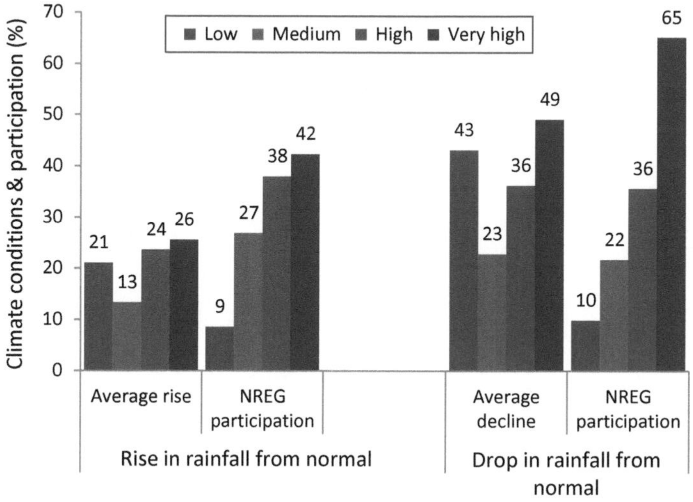

Fig. 13.1 MGNREGA participation of states during extreme climate conditions. *Source* Table 13.5

to 49.2% in Chhattisgarh. Several other states have reported reasonably high levels of work participation during the drought years as well (Fig. 13.1).

Thus, while the extent of participation in MGNREGA during normal rainfall years has been quite significant across the medium, high and very high participation states, the participation during drought years does not seem to be quite significant across states with very few exceptions of Maharashtra (in low participation category), Kerala and Uttarakhand (medium participation states). The levels of MGNREGA participation have been notably high in respect of states with high and very high participation rates (Figs. 13.2 and 13.3).

The lack of correspondence between drought and MGNREGA participation as evident from many states, especially in states with low and medium participation needs to be corroborated in terms of two major factors. First, there could be a time lag in identifying the drought-hit areas, planning and implementing the programme supported with allocation of the necessary financial resources. Since the financial allocations are to be made by the central government (MoRD) and the state governments or the implementing agencies often do not have the necessary resources, the delays in implementation are quite natural as commonly observed in several studies on MGNREGA in particular. Second, the choice of activities undertaken also may have a bearing on participation.

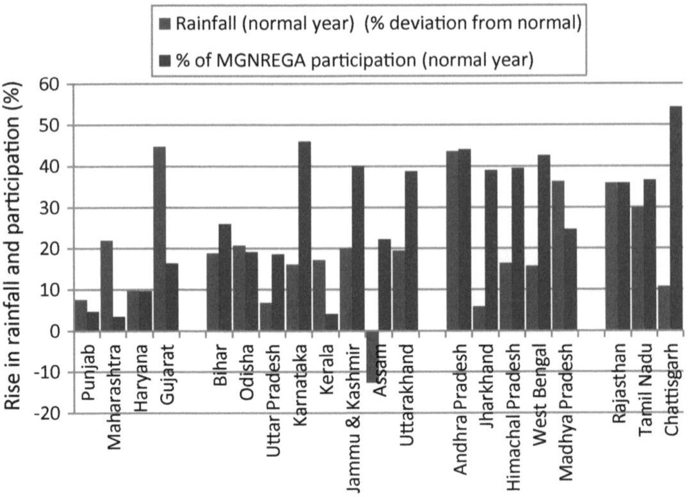

Fig. 13.2 Rise in rainfall and participation in MGNREGA, major states. *Source* Table 13.5

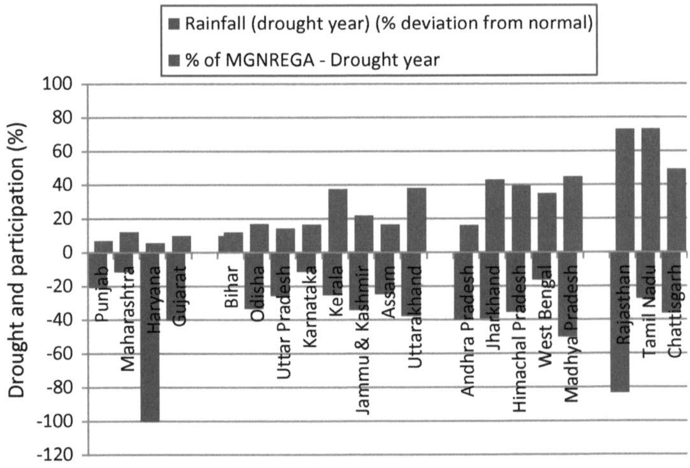

Fig. 13.3 Drought years and participation in MGNREGA, major states. *Source* Table 13.5

13.3.4 MGNREGA and the Marginalised Groups

One of the important observations emerging from a large number of studies on MGNREGA (including the chapters in this volume) is that the programme has led to increased participation by the vulnerable social groups, i.e. SCs, STs households and women. Hence, this subsection examines the status and trends in participation of the marginalised social groups in MGNREGA.

The statewise scenario of participation of marginalised groups, viz. SC, ST and women in MGNREGA is presented in Table 13.6. Participation of women in MGNREGA was high in several States with the highest levels being report as 91.4% in Kerala and 80% in Tamil Nadu. However, participation was very low at 20% in Uttar Pradesh, 29% in Bihar and 16% in Jammu and Kashmir—lower than the nationally stipulated norm of 33%. The share of SCs was highest at 58.6% in Punjab, 42.1% in Haryana and 43.5% in Uttar Pradesh. Person days among STs were highest in Madhya Pradesh (40.4%) and Jharkhand (38.6%).

Among states with low household participation, the presence of SC and ST households (as expressed by their combined share) was very high in Punjab (77%) and Gujarat (54%), followed by Haryana (42%) and Maharashtra (36%). Participation of women was also high in these states, with the highest percentage reported from Gujarat (45%), followed by Maharashtra (44%), Punjab (41%) and Haryana (37%).

In the case of states with medium levels of participation by rural households in MGNREGA, the extent of participation was highest for SCs/STs in Odisha (59%), followed by Uttar Pradesh (48%), Bihar (42%) and Assam (40%), etc. It was also noticed that within the SC/ST categories, the relative share of the ST households was the highest in Odisha (36%) and Assam (30%). Similarly, the states that had higher participation of SC households in MGNREGA were Uttar Pradesh (43.5%), followed by Bihar (37%) and Odisha (22%). The percentage of women's participation in MGNREGA in case of medium participation states was extremely high in Kerala (91%), followed by Karnataka (44%), Uttarakhand (43%), and Odisha (36%).

In the case of states with high levels of rural participation in MGNREGA, the combined share of SC and ST was notably high for Madhya Pradesh (59.5%), closely followed by Jharkhand (57%) and West Bengal (46%) while it was 39% in Andhra Pradesh and Himachal Pradesh. More than half of those who participated in MGNREGA work were women in Andhra Pradesh (57.5%) and Himachal Pradesh (51.6%).

In the three states with very high levels of rural participation in MGNREGA, the combined share of SC/ST was only half (51–52%). The relative share of ST households benefiting from the programme was high in Chhattisgarh (35%) and Rajasthan (27%), while the share of SC households was the highest in Tamil Nadu (35%). The extent of women's participation was the highest in Tamil Nadu (80%), followed by Rajasthan (68%) and Chhattisgarh (46.36%).

Thus, from the above analysis of the status of participation by the major social groups in MGNREGA, it may be concluded that the combined share of SC/ST households was the highest in states with low, high and very high participation of households in MGNREGA, while the extent of women's participation was extremely high in states with very high levels of participation (Fig. 13.4). Three states reported extremely high levels of women's participation, viz. Kerala (91%), followed by Tamil Nadu (80%) and Rajasthan (68%). The states with low level of MGNREGA participation also indicated a greater share of SC and ST households in the MGNREGA compared to other states.

Table 13.6 Status of participation of SC, ST and women in MGNREGA, 2006–07 to 2014–15

No.	Level of MGNREGA participation % of total rural HH	Total person days (in Crore)	SC person days (%)	ST person days (%)	SC/ST person days (%)	Women person days (%)	Others person days (%)
A. Low participation 0–14%							
1	Punjab	5.58	58.63	18.58	77.2	41.04	22.78
2	Maharashtra	38.54	13.47	22.41	35.9	44.06	64.12
3	Haryana	6.90	42.06	NA	42.1	36.97	49.65
4	Gujarat	24.87	14.21	39.84	54.1	44.95	45.95
B. Medium participation 15–29%							
5	Bihar	79.46	36.84	5.13	42.0	28.90	58.03
6	Odisha	53.75	22.36	36.30	58.7	35.98	41.34
7	Uttar Pradesh	185.19	43.52	4.82	48.3	19.76	51.65
8	Karnataka	64.67	17.40	10.87	28.3	43.78	71.73
9	Kerala	39.81	13.54	6.69	20.2	91.38	79.78
10	Jammu & Kashmir	15.23	8.79	17.03	25.8	16.44	74.17
11	Assam	41.92	9.67	30.24	39.9	27.64	60.09
12	Uttarakhand	13.41	20.17	5.31	25.5	42.70	74.51
C. High participation 30–44%							
13	Andhra Pradesh	200.16	23.95	14.80	38.8	57.54	61.26
14	Jharkhand	57.39	17.91	38.64	56.6	31.80	43.45
15	Himachal Pradesh	18.66	27.39	11.44	38.8	51.63	61.16
16	West Bengal	128.10	30.27	15.86	46.1	32.56	53.87
17	Madhya Pradesh	179.93	19.08	40.38	59.5	42.99	40.51
D. Very high participation 45% above							
18	Rajasthan	228.82	23.82	26.78	50.6	67.85	49.40
19	Tamil Nadu	205.61	34.74	6.68	41.4	80.08	58.58
20	Chhattisgarh	96.68	16.68	35.08	51.8	46.36	48.24

Note Share of person days for each social category is in parenthesis. Figures are averages for the reporting period
Source MGNREGA Public Portal accessed in February, 2016 www.nrega.nic.in

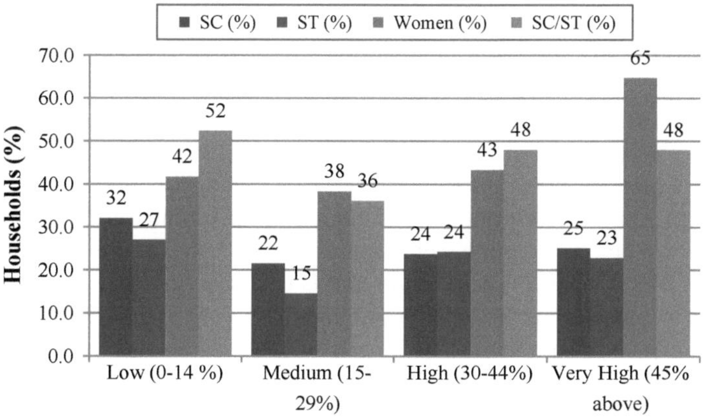

Fig. 13.4 Share of social groups in MGNREGA across states with different levels of rural participation. *Source* Based on Table 13.6

Based on the above analysis, it may be noted that a larger proportion of social groups, such as SC and ST were able to benefit in states such as Punjab, Haryana and Gujarat, where the overall household participation was lower. The proportion of SC/ST households benefiting from the MGNREGA was also seen to be highest across states with medium and high levels of MGNREGA participation, such as Odisha, Uttar Pradesh, Jharkhand, Madhya Pradesh, West Bengal, Chhattisgarh, Rajasthan and Tamil Nadu. Notably, these states also reported higher percentages of ST households being benefited under the programme. It was also observed that a higher proportions of SC households benefited from the programme in Punjab, Haryana, Uttar Pradesh, West Bengal, Bihar and Tamil Nadu. Thus, it may be concluded that the MGNREGA has been significant in reaching out to the marginalised social groups in most states. However, an important question here is whether the state-supported interventions such as MGNREGA would reduce (if not ameliorate) the existing class differences based on the socio-economic categories? Or, do such State-supported programmes lead to further deepening or perpetuating the existing differences? This is a major challenge needing further discussions as to how the state support could be recast to bring about equity across social groups on par with the mainstream groups.

13.4 MGNREGA: Challenges and Way Forward

From the foregoing analysis, it emerges that though MGNREGA has significantly contributed towards improving the status of the rural households, the programme is beset with many challenges. In what follows, we discuss some of the pertinent challenges that MGNREGA needs to address.

In order to overcome some of the major constraints as well as to achieve greater success in implementation of MGNREGA, '*convergence planning*' was introduced in 2009 by the Ministry of Rural Development (MoRD), Government of India. It was anticipated that the efforts towards inter-sectoral convergence of development programmes would lead to not only optimum utilisation of public funds but also maximum returns on the public investments along with rise in employment, wages and earnings. Convergence planning is thought to help bring all the developmental programmes in one single implementation package, as also discussed in chapters by Mishra and Mishra; and by Adusumilli and Chaudhary (in this volume). However, it is not clear 'whether the MGNREG programme has made any dramatic impact on the livelihoods when implemented in convergence with other rural development programmes'.

The Report of the First Common Review Mission (2016a) constituted by the Ministry of Rural Development to review the implementation of rural development programmes in eight States observed 'strong scheme convergence' in some states while others need to plan better for convergence.[5]

In Mayurbhanj district in Odisha, the CRM team found significant efforts to enable sustainable livelihoods through convergence of MGNREGA with schemes and funds from line departments. There is convergence of MGNREGA with horticulture plantation, with Anganwadi centres/ICDS in using MGNREGA labour to construct Anganwadis, with agriculture, through dug wells, ponds, check dams, etc., to enable increased crop yields, with animal husbandry through construction of goat sheds and azola pits and with NRLM in growing and developing sabai grass products. MGNREGS work has been used for setting up bamboo fences for schools in Jashipur block, Mayurbhanj as also to dig stagger trenches between cashew plantations to stop the wastage of rainwater and reduce soil erosion in Jashipur block in Mayurbhanj.[6]

While the convergence initiatives are yet to get a wider adoption across states, it has been found that the states, which have incorporated convergence planning in implementation of programmes, focus more attention on schemes such as rural sanitation, works on individual lands and rural connectivity. The success of convergence initiatives requires active participation of the relevant line departments and other stakeholders in planning, management and execution of the works. More specifically, in the absence of coordinated efforts by the participating agencies and proper integration of works, convergence initiatives may fail to deliver the desired outcomes, particularly in respect of creation of quality public assets and thereby employment generation.

---

[5]Ministry of Rural Development (2016a).

[6]Ministry of Rural Development (2016b).

The next important and perhaps a daunting challenge is to have more inclusive strategies in the employment guarantee programme, specifically targeting the rural youth. As has emerged from several studies, the inclusive nature of the programme currently is largely constrained by the non-participation of a vast segment of the rural youth in MGNREGA, who consider that the programme does not rise to their aspirations. Two points merit attention here. First, though MGNREGA had made significant positive impacts on rural wages (see also chapter by Narayanamoorthy et al., this volume), in many states, especially, Kerala, Punjab, Andhra Pradesh, Haryana, Karnataka, Bihar, Rajasthan, West Bengal, Jharkhand and Uttarakhand, the MGNREGA notified wages are lower than the minimum wages for unskilled agricultural work, which acts as a major obstacle in attracting workers, especially the youth, who often prefer migrating to urban areas in search of high wages. Second, the profile of the existing works is such that they neither warrant using technical skills nor provide avenues for learning new skills or technical expertise.

The results emerging from a recent study by NCAER[7] (Desai et al. 2015) are quite revealing in this regard. Based on data gathered on age groupwise trends in participation of workers (in the age group 15–59 years) in MGNREGA and other agricultural and non-agricultural activities of the rural households, it was found that the extent of participation in MGNREGA among male workers in the age group of 15–29 years was 22.3% and hardly 13% in case of female workers. Whereas, the extent of participation of these age groups in agricultural labour activity was 45% for males and 33% for females. The proportion of male workers reported to be engaged in non-agricultural activities was 62% among males. Quite interestingly, an overwhelming proportion of these age groups prefers to be nonworking (prefer leisure for work) than working in MGNREGA.

This leads to the next important issue of women's economic empowerment due to MGNREGA. Obviously, almost all the studies on MGNREGA highlight its positive impact on significantly increasing the participation of women in the programme. As observed by Desai et al. (2015), about 45% of female MGNREGA workers were either not working or worked only on a family farm during 2004–05, i.e. before MGNREGA was launched. This signifies that the programme has given the first opportunity to almost half of the rural working women to enter the MGNREGA labour market and earn cash income, which had significantly enhanced their self-esteem, power within the household and control over resources (Pankaj and Tankha 2010; Narayanan and Das 2014; Viswanathan and Mandal 2012; Desai et al., 2015).

The gender dynamism in MGNREGA as reported from many states underscores the need for scaling up the programme as an effective instrument for gender mainstreaming in India, though with variations across states. However, there are several challenges that the country may face in order to transform the MGNREGA

[7]The NCAER study was quite unique in terms of its coverage and methodology adopted. It surveyed 26,000 rural households that were interviewed twice, once in 2004–05 before MGNREGA's passage and again in 2011–12, after the programme had been extended nationwide.

as an effective instrument for gender mainstreaming. An important challenge is how to revamp the programme especially in states with lower women's participation so as to create more work and employment opportunities for including women. It also calls for policies and interventions to adequately address the innate structural infirmities/problems of the MGNREGS that restrain women's participation in the scheme in states with low levels of women work participation.

Perhaps, this takes us to the earlier discussion on the importance of skill building as an integral aspect of employment guarantee programme as cautioned by Dantwala (1978), who argued that skill-based workers could command much higher wages. This calls for recasting the MGNREGA activities to attract more rural youth. In this regard, mention may be made of some of the new initiatives of the national government, such as the Pradhan Mantri Kaushal Vikas Yojana[8] as well as the Make in India[9] initiative. Nevertheless, the scope and relevance of these initiatives are yet to be explored in terms of integrating MGNREGA with these initiatives.

Yet another challenge is taking the MGNREGA to the contours of economic and social development rather than approaching it merely from an employment guarantee programme viewpoint. This is all the more important given the fact that the wage gains (earnings) from MGNREGA do not get translated into poverty reduction on a significant scale due to the simultaneous causation of food price inflation as argued by some[10] (Ghose 2012; Kannan and Jain 2013). Moreover, it may also be noted that the wage earnings realised from MGNREGA are also too meagre to make any significant dent on reduction of household vulnerability and poverty. The drastic decline in the number of average person days of employment per household especially since 2010–11 also would have significantly weakened the influence of wage earnings in reducing or even minimising the poverty burden on the household.

In fact, MGNREGA interventions assume greater significance in the heightened context of distress induced by persistent drought in rural areas. This raises an important issue as to 'whether MGNREGA should also continue as a drought relief measure in the drought-hit areas'. By virtue of the notification by the Ministry of Rural Development (MoRD), the drought-hit areas are entitled to get 50 additional days of employment from the existing 100-day mark[11]. But, this is a real challenge

[8]The objective of this skill certification and reward scheme is to enable and mobilise a large number of Indian youth to take up outcome-based skill training and become employable and earn their livelihoods.

[9]The 'Make in India' initiative launched by the Government of India to promote manufacturing in 25 sectors of the economy shall lead to job creation and consequently generate need for skilled manpower.

[10]The surge in inflation during recent years had curtailed considerably the magnitude of real benefits to be gained from the NREG (Kannan and Jain 2013: 51).

[11]The MoRD moved a Cabinet note to expand the scope of MGNREGA by extending the number of annual work entitlement days from 100 to 150 in areas to be declared drought-affected by the respective state governments. This comes in the wake of a prospective monsoon failure for a second consecutive year as forecasted by India Meteorological Department (IMD). Expansion of the work entitlement days by 50 stems from the concern that there would be greater demand for

as currently only 4% of the employed households are able to get 100 days of employment (during 2014–15) due to either rationing of work or lack of availability of work. Even when the programme was at its peak of success, only 14% of the rural households had 100 days of work (during 2008–09), which had declined to 10% and remained at that level until 2013–14. This calls for revisiting the programme and the implementation strategies to make them much more sensitive to the drought-affected regions as a measure of livelihood security and distress mitigation. That said, the challenges are serious, as the vibrancy and sustainability of the programme invariably depends on the financial strength of the implementing agencies (national and state governments).

Last but not least, focussing on the links between right to work (realised through MGNREGA), ecology and health, there is no doubt that these three aspects of overall human development, especially among poor, have to get integrated in the next phase of development. The specific question that needs immediate understanding is to know the macro-micro level interactions in rural India. In the absence of this, it may lead to 'double-discrimination' of the rural poor who are still waiting to become an important part of the development process.

From a future perspective, MGNREGA should take into consideration the multifunctional nature of the impact that the assets, related mainly to natural resources, are expected to generate, especially, if initiated through a developmental mode. The various facets of the impact may thus, include not only income and employment, but also larger developmental objectives such as environmental sustainability, intra-village equity and building of institutional capacities through democratic decentralisation.

(Footnote 11 continued)

wage-related work in drought-affected districts. Further, it will be applicable to only those households which complete 100 days of work.

Annex 1: Total Rural Household, Total Employment/Worked in MGNREGA and MGNREGA HH as a % of Total Rural HH (2006–07 to 2014–15)

State name	Total rural households (2006–07)	Total employment provided (2006–07)	MGNREGA HH in a state as a % of total rural HH (2006–07)	Total rural households (2007–08)	Total employment provided (2007–08)	MGNREGA HH in a state as a % of total rural HH (2007–08)	Total rural households (2008–09)	Total employment provided (2008–09)	MGNREGA HH in a state as a % of total rural HH (2008–09)	Total rural households (2009–10)	Total employment provided (2009–10)	MGNREGA HH in a state as a % of total rural HH (2009–10)
Andhra Pradesh	13,396,092	2,161,395	16.13	13,559,706	4,803,892	35.43	13,725,317	5,699,557	41.53	13,892,951	6,158,493	44.33
Assam	4,773,807	792,270	16.60	4,896,726	1,402,888	28.65	5,022,810	1,877,393	37.38	5,152,140	2,137,270	41.48
Bihar	14,464,464	1,688,899	11.68	14,915,181	3,859,630	25.88	15,379,943	3,318,698	21.58	15,859,187	4,127,330	26.02
Chhattisgarh	3,780,387	1,375,802	36.39	3,890,785	2,284,963	58.73	4,004,406	2,270,415	56.70	4,121,345	2,025,845	49.15
Gujarat	6,344,093	226,269	3.57	6,427,751	290,691	4.52	6,512,511	850,691	13.06	6,598,389	1,596,402	24.19
Haryana	2,781,576	50,765	1.83	2,832,140	70,869	2.50	2,883,623	162,932	5.65	2,936,042	156,406	5.33
Himachal Pradesh	1,190,481	109,417	9.19	1,213,943	271,099	22.33	1,237,868	445,713	36.01	1,262,265	497,336	39.40
Jammu and Kashmir	1,346,486	121,328	9.01	1,385,543	127,368	9.19	1,425,733	197,975	13.89	1,467,088	320,715	21.86
Jharkhand	4,203,737	1,394,108	33.16	4,303,968	1,679,868	39.03	4,406,589	1,474,073	33.45	4,511,657	1,702,599	37.74
Karnataka	7,310,833	1,011,021	13.83	7,433,792	549,994	7.40	7,558,818	896,212	11.86	7,685,948	3,535,281	46.00
Kerala	4,559,690	99,107	2.17	4,474,561	185,392	4.14	4,391,020	692,015	15.76	4,309,039	955,976	22.19
Madhya Pradesh	9,412,822	2,866,349	30.45	9,724,920	4,346,916	44.70	10,047,365	5,207,665	51.83	10,380,502	4,714,591	45.42
Maharashtra	12,151,339	0	0.00	12,356,942	474,695	3.84	12,566,024	905,788	7.21	12,778,644	535,994	4.19
Odisha	7,317,374	1,394,169	19.05	7,465,755	993,360	13.31	7,617,146	1,199,006	15.74	7,771,606	1,398,300	17.99
Punjab	3,064,349	31,648	1.03	3,120,971	49,690	1.59	3,178,638	149,902	4.72	3,237,371	271,941	8.40
Rajasthan	8,184,202	1,175,172	14.36	8,431,002	2,170,460	25.74	8,685,244	6,373,093	73.38	8,947,153	6,522,264	72.90
Tamil Nadu	8,884,689	683,481	7.69	9,009,873	1,234,818	13.71	9,136,820	3,345,648	36.62	9,265,556	4,373,257	47.20
Uttar Pradesh	22,875,790	2,573,245	11.25	23,412,079	4,096,408	17.50	23,960,941	4,336,466	18.10	24,522,669	5,483,434	22.36
Uttarakhand	1,299,914	134,312	10.33	1,324,037	189,263	14.29	1,348,607	298,741	22.15	1,373,632	522,304	38.02
West Bengal	12,477,409	3,083,757	24.71	12,733,804	3,843,335	30.18	12,995,468	3,025,854	23.28	13,262,509	3,479,915	26.24
Total for 20 states:	149,819,536	20,972,514	14.00	152,913,477	32,925,599	21.53	156,084,892	42,727,837	27.37	159,335,695	50,515,653	31.70

(continued)

State name	Total rural households (2010–11)	Total employment provided (2010–11)	MGNREGA HH in a state as a % of total rural HH (2010–11)	Total rural households (2011–12)	Total households worked (2011–12)	MGNREGA HH in a state as a % of Total Rural HH (2011–12)	Total rural household (2012–13)
Andhra Pradesh	14,062,633	6,200,423	44.09	14,234,387	2,914,172	20.47	14,408,239
Assam	5,284,801	1,798,372	34.03	5,420,877	1,349,078	24.89	5,560,457
Bihar	16,353,364	4,738,464	28.98	16,862,940	1,769,469	10.49	17,388,394
Chhattisgarh	4,241,699	2,485,581	58.60	4,365,568	2,725,027	62.42	4,493,054
Gujarat	6,685,400	1,096,223	16.40	6,773,558	822,080	12.14	6,862,879
Haryana	2,989,414	235,281	7.87	3,043,756	277,748	9.13	3,043,756
Himachal Pradesh	1,287,142	444,247	34.51	1,312,510	505,467	38.51	1,338,378
Jammu and Kashmir	1,509,643	499,434	33.08	1,553,433	431,146	27.75	1,598,493
Jharkhand	4,619,231	1,987,360	43.02	4,729,369	1,574,657	33.30	4,842,133
Karnataka	7,815,215	2,224,468	28.46	7,946,657	1,652,116	20.79	8,080,309
Kerala	4,228,589	1,175,816	27.81	4,149,641	1,416,441	34.13	4,072,167
Madhya Pradesh	10,724,684	4,407,643	41.10	11,080,278	3,879,959	35.02	11,447,662
Maharashtra	12,994,862	451,169	3.47	13,214,738	1,504,521	11.39	13,438,334
Odisha	7,929,199	2,004,815	25.28	8,089,987	1,378,597	17.04	8,254,036
Punjab	3,297,189	278,134	8.44	3,358,113	245,453	7.31	3,420,162
Rajasthan	9,216,960	5,859,667	63.57	9,494,903	4,522,234	47.63	9,781,228
Tamil Nadu	9,396,106	4,969,140	52.89	9,528,495	6,343,339	66.57	9,662,750
Uttar Pradesh	25,097,567	6,431,213	25.62	25,685,942	7,327,738	28.53	26,288,111
Uttarakhand	1,399,123	542,391	38.77	1,425,086	469,285	32.93	1,451,531
West Bengal	13,535,037	4,998,239	36.93	13,813,165	5,516,968	39.94	14,097,008
Total for 20 states:	162,667,858	52,828,080	32.48	166,083,403	46,625,495	28.07	169,529,081

(continued)

(continued)

State name	Total households worked (2012–13)	MGNREGA HH in a state as a % of total rural HH (2012–13)	Total rural household (2013–14)	Total households worked (2013–14)	MGNREGA HH in a state as a % of total rural HH (2013–14)	Total rural households (2014–15)	Total households worked (2014–15)	MGNREGA HH in a state as a % of total rural HH (2014–15)
Andhra Pradesh	3,318,164	23.03	14,584,214	3,482,604	23.88	14,762,338	3,299,447	22.35
Assam	1,234,828	22.21	5,703,631	1,261,778	22.12	5,850,491	967,179	16.53
Bihar	2,087,564	12.01	17,930,222	2,059,338	11.49	18,488,934	1,035,562	5.60
Chhattisgarh	2,637,699	58.71	4,624,263	2,512,379	54.33	4,759,304	1,748,290	36.73
Gujarat	681,028	9.92	6,953,377	578,674	8.32	7,045,069	513,190	7.28
Haryana	294,142	9.66	3,099,086	324,919	10.48	3,155,421	217,914	6.91
Himachal Pradesh	514,687	38.46	1,364,755	539,223	39.51	1,391,652	452,659	32.53
Jammu and Kashmir	646,516	40.45	1,644,860	657,588	39.98	1,692,571	332,194	19.63
Jharkhand	1,419,072	29.31	4,957,586	1,138,912	22.97	5,075,792	1,111,175	21.89
Karnataka	1,331,967	16.48	8,216,210	1,450,457	17.65	8,354,396	1,093,906	13.09
Kerala	1,526,283	37.48	3,996,139	1,523,863	38.13	3,921,531	1,380,236	35.20
Madhya Pradesh	3,519,283	30.74	11,827,228	2,908,506	24.59	12,219,379	2,794,169	22.87
Maharashtra	1,624,521	12.09	13,665,714	1,143,837	8.37	13,896,941	1,159,693	8.34
Odisha	1,599,276	19.38	8,421,411	1,710,268	20.31	8,592,180	1,469,320	17.10
Punjab	240,191	7.02	3,483,358	412,104	11.83	3,547,721	288,889	8.14
Rajasthan	4,217,342	43.12	10,076,187	3,615,080	35.88	10,380,040	3,686,831	35.52
Tamil Nadu	7,061,409	73.08	9,798,896	6,267,704	63.96	9,936,960	5,657,572	56.93
Uttar Pradesh	4,947,427	18.82	26,904,396	4,994,721	18.56	27,535,130	3,915,533	14.22
Uttarakhand	439,791	30.30	1,478,467	397,482	26.88	1,505,903	455,294	30.23
West Bengal	5,817,331	41.27	14,386,685	6,132,613	42.63	14,682,313	5,120,407	34.87
Total for 20 states:	45,158,521	26.64	173,116,684	43,112,050	24.90	176,794,067	36,699,460	20.76

Source Total Employment provided from MGNREGA Public Portal accessed in February, 2016 www.nrega.nic.in and Rural Households from Census India, 2011
Note Rural Household for 9 years is calculated by calculating CAGR (Compound Annual Growth Rate)

Annex 2: Statewise Participation of Rural Households in MGNREGA Over Time (2006–07 to 2014–15)

	Categorisation of states based on participation in MGNREGA	Number of states	Rural HH in a state as % of rural HH in 20 states (average for 2006–07 to 2014–15)	HH participating in MGNREGA in a state as a % of total HH participating in MGNREGA in 20 states (2006–07 to 2014–15)	Statewise % Rural HH participating in MGNREGA (average for 2006–07 to 2014–15)	% of persons in poverty in rural areas (2011–12) based on methodology Proposed by Rangarajan Committee
		4			**0–14% (Low)**	
1	Punjab		2.0	0.5	6.6	7.4
2	Maharashtra		8.0	2.1	6.7	22.5
3	Haryana		1.8	0.5	6.7	11.0
4	Gujarat		4.1	1.8	11.1	31.4
	Average				**7.8**	
		8			**15–29% (Medium)**	
5	Bihar		10.1	6.6	16.7	40.1
6	Odisha		4.9	3.5	18.4	47.8
7	Uttar Pradesh		15.4	11.9	19.5	38.1
8	Karnataka		4.8	3.7	19.5	19.8
9	Kerala		2.6	2.4	23.5	7.3
10	Jammu & Kashmir		0.9	0.9	24.5	12.6
11	Assam		3.3	3.5	26.9	42.0
12	Uttarakhand		0.9	0.9	27.4	12.6
	Average				**19.8**	
		5			**30–44% (High)**	
13	Andhra Pradesh		8.6	10.2	30.0	12.7

(continued)

(continued)

	Categorisation of states based on participation in MGNREGA	Number of states	Rural HH in a state as % of rural HH in 20 states (average for 2006–07 to 2014–15)	HH participating in MGNREGA in a state as a % of total HH participating in MGNREGA in 20 states (2006–07 to 2014–15)	Statewise % Rural HH participating in MGNREGA (average for 2006–07 to 2014–15)	% of persons in poverty in rural areas (2011–12) based on methodology Proposed by Rangarajan Committee
14	Jharkhand		2.8	3.6	32.4	45.9
15	Himachal Pradesh		0.8	1.0	32.6	11.1
16	West Bengal		8.3	11.0	33.6	30.1
17	Madhya Pradesh		6.6	9.3	35.8	45.2
	Average				**32.8**	
		3			**45% Above (Very high)**	
18	Rajasthan		5.7	10.3	45.8	21.4
19	Tamil Nadu		5.8	10.7	47.2	24.3
20	Chhattisgarh		2.6	5.4	52.4	49.2
	Average				**47.6**	
	Total	**20**	**100**	**100**		

Source MGNREGA Public Portal accessed in February, 2016 www.nrega.nic.in
Note Poverty Ratio 2011–12 is based on Rangarajan Committee

Annex 3: MGNREGA Households Participation Changes for the Year (2006–07 to 2010–11) and (2011–12 to 2014–15)

Rank	Categorisation of states based on participation in MGNREGA	MGNREGA HH in a state % of total rural HH (average for 2006–07 to 2014–15)	Rank in the first 5 years	Categorisation of states based on participation in MGNREGA	MGNREGA HH in a state % of total rural HH (average for 2006–07 to 2010–11)	Rank in the last 4 years	Categorisation of states based on Participation in MGNREGA	MGNREGA HH in a state % of total rural HH (average for 2011–12 to 2014–15)
	0–14% (Low)			**0–14% (Low)**			**0–14% (Low)**	
1	Punjab	6.6	1	Maharashtra	3.8	1	Punjab	8.6
2	Maharashtra	6.7	2	Haryana	4.7	2	Haryana	9.0
3	Haryana	6.7	3	Punjab	4.9	3	Gujarat	9.4
4	Gujarat	11.1	4	Gujarat	12.5	4	Bihar	9.9
						5	Maharashtra	10.0
	Average	**7.8**		**Average**	**6.3**		**Average**	**9.7**
	15–29% (Medium)			**15–29% (Medium)**			**15–29% (Medium)**	
5	Bihar	16.7	5	Kerala	14.2	6	Karnataka	17.0
6	Odisha	18.4	6	Jammu And Kashmir	17.8	7	Odisha	18.5
7	Uttar Pradesh	19.5	7	Odisha	18.3	8	Uttar Pradesh	20.0
8	Karnataka	19.5	8	Uttar Pradesh	19.1	9	Assam	21.4
9	Kerala	23.5	9	Karnataka	21.7	10	Andhra Pradesh	22.4
10	Jammu & Kashmir	24.5	10	Bihar	23.0	11	Jharkhand	26.9

(continued)

(continued)

Rank	Categorisation of states based on participation in MGNREGA	MGNREGA HH in a state % of total rural HH (average for 2006–07 to 2014–15)	Rank in the first 5 years	Categorisation of states based on participation in MGNREGA	MGNREGA HH in a state % of total rural HH (average for 2006–07 to 2010–11)	Rank in the last 4 years	Categorisation of states based on Participation in MGNREGA	MGNREGA HH in a state % of total rural HH (average for 2011–12 to 2014–15)
11	Assam	26.9	11	Uttarakhand	25.0	12	Madhya Pradesh	28.3
12	Uttarakhand	27.4	12	West Bengal	28.4			
			13	Himachal Pradesh	28.6			
	Average	**19.8**		**Average**	**21.6**		**Average**	**21.2**
	30–44% (High)			**30–44% (High)**			**30–44% (High)**	
13	Andhra Pradesh	30.0	14	Assam	31.9	13	Uttarakhand	30.1
14	Jharkhand	32.4	15	Tamil Nadu	32.0	14	Jammu And Kashmir	32.0
15	Himachal Pradesh	32.6	16	Andhra Pradesh	36.5	15	Kerala	36.2
16	West Bengal	33.6	17	Jharkhand	37.4	16	Himachal Pradesh	37.3
17	Madhya Pradesh	35.8	18	Madhya Pradesh	42.8	17	West Bengal	39.7
						18	Rajasthan	40.5
	Average	**32.8**		**Average**	**36.55**		**Average**	**31.82**
	45% Above (Very High)			**45% Above (Very High)**			**45% Above (Very High)**	
18	Rajasthan	45.8	19	Rajasthan	50.8	19	Chhattisgarh	53.0

(continued)

(continued)

Rank	Categorisation of states based on participation in MGNREGA	MGNREGA HH in a state % of total rural HH (average for 2006–07 to 2014–15)	Rank in the first 5 years	Categorisation of states based on participation in MGNREGA	MGNREGA HH in a state % of total rural HH (average for 2006–07 to 2010–11)	Rank in the last 4 years	Categorisation of states based on Participation in MGNREGA	MGNREGA HH in a state % of total rural HH (average for 2011–12 to 2014–15)
19	Tamil Nadu	47.2	20	Chhattisgarh	52.1	20	Tamil Nadu	65.1
20	Chhattisgarh	52.4						
	Average	**47.6**		**Average**	**51.25**		**Average**	**52.63**
	Total			**Total**			**Total**	

Source MGNREGA Public Portal accessed in February, 2016 www.nrega.nic.in

Annex 4: Normal and Drought Year % Deviation from Normal

State Name	Normal Year	Normal year (rainfall) % Dep	Drought year	Drought Year (rainfall) % Dep
Andhra Pradesh	2010–11	43.6	2006–07	−39.9
Assam	2012–13	−12.6	2014–15	−24.6
Bihar	2007–08	18.8	2012–13	9.8
Chhattisgarh	2013–14	10.7	2009–10	−36.3
Gujarat	2010–11	44.8	2012–13	−40.2
Haryana	2008–09	9.8	2012–13	−100.1
Himachal Pradesh	2013–14	16.4	2009–10	−35.5
Jammu And Kashmir	2013–14	20.0	2009–10	−34.2
Jharkhand	2007–08	5.9	2010–11	−39.2
Karnataka	2009–10	16.1	2012–13	−11.3
Kerala	2007–08	17.2	2012–13	−25.2
Madhya Pradesh	2013–14	36.3	2007–08	−50.1
Maharashtra	2010–11	21.9	2012–13	−11.4
Odisha	2006–07	20.7	2011–12	−33.4
Punjab	2008–09	7.6	2012–13	−20.6
Rajasthan	2013–14	35.9	2009–10	−83.4
Tamil Nadu	2008–09	30.0	2012–13	−27.4
Uttar Pradesh	2013–14	6.8	2014–15	−25.6
Uttarakhand	2010–11	19.4	2009–10	−37.7
West Bengal	2013–14	15.7	2014–15	−16.3

Source India Metrological Department
Note Rainfall of Andhra Pradesh includes Coastal Andhra Pradesh + Telengana + Rayalaseema
Rainfall of Uttar Pradesh includes East Uttar Pradesh + West Uttar Pradesh
Rainfall of Gujarat includes Gujarat Region + Saurashtra & Kutch
Rainfall of West Bengal includes Sub-Himalayan West Bengal + Sikkim + Gangetic West Bengal
Rainfall of Haryana includes Chandigarh + Delhi
Rainfall of Maharashtra includes Madhya Maharashtra + Marathwada + Vidarbha
Rainfall of Madhya Pradesh includes East Madhya Pradesh + West Madhya Pradesh
Rainfall of Rajasthan includes East Rajasthan + West Rajasthan
Rainfall of Karnataka includes Coastal Karnataka + North Interior + South Interior

Bibliography

Bhalla, S. 2009. *National Convention on Making Growth Inclusive: Opportunities, Scope and Challenges at the State Level*. Ahmedabad, Gujarat: Gujarat Institute of Development and Research.

Chand, Ramesh, S.S. Raju, and L.M. Pandey. 2007. Growth Crisis in Agriculture: Severity and Options at National and State Levels. *Economic and Political Weekly*, June 30, 2528–2533.

Chandrasekhar, C.P. and Jayati Ghosh. 2011. Public Works and Wages in Rural India, *Macroscan an Alternative Economics Website*, 11 January.

Dandekar, V.M. and N. Rath. 1971. *Poverty in India*. Indian School of Political Economy, Pune.

Dantwala, M.L. 1978. Some Neglected Issues in Employment Planning. *Economic and Political Weekly* 23 (6&7): 291–294.

David, Rebecca Sharon. 2008. The National Rural Employment Guarantee Act: Towards Governance & Conservation of Natural Resources. *Working Paper No. 37*, June. Anand: The Foundation for Ecological Security.

Desai, Sonalde, Prem Vashishtha, and Omkar Joshi. 2015. *Mahatma Gandhi National Rural Employment Guarantee Act A Catalyst for Rural Transformation*, 210. New Delhi: National Council of Applied Economic Research.

Dev, Mahendra, S. 1996. Employment Guarantee Scheme. *Economic and Political Weekly* 31 (9): 560–563.

Dreze, Jean. 1990. Poverty in India and the IRDP Delusion. *Economic and Political Weekly* 25 (39):A-95–A-104.

Drèze, J. and J. Khera. 2009. The Battle for Employment Guarantee. *Frontline* 26(1).

Dreze, J. 2011. Employment Guarantee and the Right to Work. In *The Battle for Employment Guarantee*, ed. R. Khera, 3–20. New Delhi: Oxford University Press.

Dreze, J., and R. Khera. 2011. Battle for Employment Guarantee. In *The Battle for Employment Guarantee*, ed. R. Khera, 43–80. New Delhi: Oxford University Press.

Dutta, Puja, Rinku Murgai, Ravallion Martin, and Dominique van de Walle. 2012. Does India's Employment Guarantee Scheme Guarantee Employment? *Economic and Political Weekly* 47 (16) (21 April).

Ghose, Ajit K. 2012. 'Addressing the Employment Challenge: India's MGNREGA', Employment Analysis and Research Unit Economic and Labour Market Analysis Department, Employment *Working Paper No. 105*, Geneva: International Labour Organization, 25p.

GOI. 2013. *Twelfth Five-Year Plan (2012–2017): Faster, More Inclusive and Sustainable Growth*, vol. I. New Delhi: Sage Publications.

GoI (Government of India). 2014. *Report of the Expert Group to Review the Methodology for Estimation of Poverty*. New Delhi: Government of India Planning Commission.

Himanshu, Abhiroop Mukhopadhyay, and M.R. Sharan. 2015. NREGS in Rajasthan: Rationed Funds and Their Allocation across Villages. *Economic and Political Weekly* 50 (6): 52–60.

IISC. 2013. Environmental Benefits and Vulnerability Reduction through Mahatma Gandhi National Rural Employment Guarantee Scheme by Indian Institute of Science, Bangalore, Synthesis Report, 51p. http://fes.org.in/studies/report-env-benefits-vulnerability-reduction.pdf.

ILO. 2014. *World Social Protection Report 2014/15: Building economic recovery, inclusive development and social justice* (Geneva, International Labour Office), http://www.ilo.org/wcmsp5/groups/public/—dgreports/—dcomm/documents/publication/wcms_245201.pdf; http://www.social-protection.org/gimi/gess/ShowTheme.action?th.themeld=3985

Jose, A.V. 2013. Changes in Wages and Earnings of Rural Labourers. *Economic and Political Weekly* 48 (26&27): 107–114.

Kannan, K.P., and G. Ravindran. 2011. India's Common People: The Regional Profile. *Economic and Political Weekly* 46 (38) (7 September).

Kannan, K.P., and Varinder Jain. 2013. Historic Initiative, Limited by Design and Implementation: A National Overview of the Implementation of MGNREGA. In *The Long Road to Social Security: Assessing the Implementation of National Social Security Initiatives for the Working Poor in India*, ed. K.P. Kannan, and Jan Breman, 33–80. New Delhi: Oxford University Press.

Kohli, Atul. 2015. Politics of Economic Growth in India, 1980–2005: The 1990s and Beyond. In *Economic Growth and its Distribution in India,* ed. P. Balakrishnan. Orient Blackswan Private Ltd., and *Economic and Political Weekly*, 48–69.

Krishna, Raj. 1973. Unemployment in India. *Economic & Political Weekly* 8 (9): 475–484. (3 March).

Krishnaraj, M., P. Pandey, and A. Kanchi. 2004. Does EGS Require Restructuring for Poverty Alleviation and Gender Equality. *Economic and Political Weekly* 39 (16): 1597–604

Kundu, Amitabh, and K. Varghese. 2010. Regional Inequality and 'Inclusive Growth' in India under Globalization: Identification of Lagging States for Strategic Intervention, *Oxfam India Working Papers Series (OIWPS–VI)*, September.

Ministry of Rural Development, Department of Rural Development (DRD). 2015. *Mahatma Gandhi National Rural Employment Guarantee Act, 2005: Report to the People, 2 February 2015* (New Delhi).

Ministry of Rural Development. 2016a. *Report of the First Common Review Mission: Thematic Report, Volume 1.* New Delhi: Ministry of Rural Development.

Ministry of Rural Development. 2016b. *Report of the First Common Review Mission: State Reports (Odisha Report), Volume 2.* New Delhi: Ministry of Rural Development (forthcoming).

Ministry of Rural Development, Mahatma Gandhi NREGA Sameeksha. 2012. An Anthology of Research Studies on the Mahatma Gandhi National Rural Employment Guarantee Act, 2005 2006–2012. Ministry of Rural Development, New Delhi: Orient Blackswan.

Moore, Mick, and Vishal Jadhav. 2006. The Politics and Bureaucratics of Rural Public Works: Maharashtra's Employment Guaranteed Scheme. *Journal of Development Studies* 42 (8): 1271–1300. (November).

Narayanan, Sudha and Upasak Das. 2014. Women Partiticipation and Rationing in the Employment Guarantee Scheme. *Economic and Political Weekly* 49 (49): 46–53.

Niti Aayog (2015): *Report of the sub-group of Chief Ministers on Rationalisation of Centrally Sponsored Schemes.* New Delhi: National Institution for Transforming India (NITI), 150p. (October)

Pankaj, A., and R. Tankha. 2010. Empowerment Effects of the NREGS on Women Workers: A Study in Four States. *Economic and Political Weekly* 45 (30): 45–55. (July).

Rath, N. 1985. Garibi Hatao: Can IRDP Do It?. *Economic and Political Weekly* 20 (6): 131-40.

Shah, Mihir, D. Banerji, P.S. Vijayshankar and P. Ambasta. 1998. *India's Drylands: Tribal Societies and Development through Environmental Regeneration*. New Delhi: Oxford University Press.

Shah, A., and A.K. Mehta. (2008). Experience of the Maharashtra Employment Guarantee Scheme: Are Could Be There Lessons for NREGS. *Indian Journal of Labour Economics* 51 (2).

Shah, Amita. 2012. Assets Creation and Local Economy Under MGNREGS: Scope and Challenges. In *Right to Work and Rural India*, ed. Ashok Pankaj, 197–225. New Delhi: Sage Publications India.

Shah, Amita., and Aasha Kapur Mehta. 2008. Experience of the Maharashtra Employment Guarantee Scheme: Are There Lessons for NREGS?, *Working Paper No. 118*, Chronic Poverty Research Centre, 37p., https://www.researchgate.net/publication/46476846.

Suryanarayana, M.H., and Mousumi Das. 2014. How Inclusive Is India's Reform(ed) Growth? *Economic and Political Weekly* 49 (6): 44–55. (February 8).

Tiwari, Rakesh, H.I. Somashekhar, V.R. Ramakrishna Parama, Indu K. Murthy, M.S. Mohan Kumar, B.K. Mohan Kumar, Harshad Parate, Murari Varma, Sumedha Malaviya, Ananya S. Rao, Asmita Sengupta, Ruth Kattumuri, N.H. Ravindranath. 2011. MGNREGA for Environmental Service Enhancement and Vulnerability Reduction: Rapid Appraisal in Chitradurga District, Karnataka. *Economic and Political Weekly* 46 (20): 39–44.

Usami, Y. 2011. A Note on Recent Trends in Wage Rates in Rural India. *Review of Agrarian Studies* 1 (1): 149–82.
Verma, Shilp. 2011. *MGNREGA Assets and Rural Water Security: Synthesis of Field Studies in Bihar*. Gujarat, Kerala and Rajasthan, Anand: International Water Management Institute.
Viswanathan, P.K., and Amit Mandal. 2012. NREGS as Instrument of Gender Mainstreaming: An Exploratory Analysis. *Man and Development* 34 (3): 17–36. (September).

Glossary

Local terms specific to India

Angan Wadi Centre (AWC) It is a part of the Indian public healthcare system, providing basic nutrition and healthcare activities in lowest tier of Indian villages. Its basic nutrition and healthcare service includes contraceptive counselling and supply, nutrition education and supplementation, pre-school nutrition and care to children in rural India

Gram Panchyat are at the bottom of the three-tier organisation of Panchayati Raj. Gram Panchayats for a village or group of villages were established earlier

M. Bhattarai et al. (eds.), *Employment Guarantee Programme and Dynamics of Rural Transformation in India*, India Studies in Business and Economics,
https://doi.org/10.1007/978-981-10-6262-9

Index

M. Bhattarai et al. (eds.), *Employment Guarantee Programme and Dynamics of Rural Transformation in India*, India Studies in Business and Economics,
https://doi.org/10.1007/978-981-10-6262-9

MIX
Papier aus verantwortungsvollen Quellen
Paper from responsible sources
FSC® C105338

If you have any concerns about our products,
you can contact us on
ProductSafety@springernature.com

In case Publisher is established outside the EU,
the EU authorized representative is:
Springer Nature Customer Service Center GmbH
Europaplatz 3, 69115 Heidelberg, Germany

Printed by Libri Plureos GmbH
in Hamburg, Germany